Communication at Work

An introduction to business communication and information technology

Desmond W Evans

Pitman

PITMAN PUBLISHING
128 Long Acre, London WC2E 9AN

© Desmond W Evans, 1987

Second edition first published in Great Britain 1987
Reprinted 1988

British Library Cataloguing in Publication Data
Evans, Desmond W.
　Communication at work: an introduction to
　business communication and information
　technology.—2nd ed.
　1. Communication in management
　I. Title
　651.7　　HF5718

ISBN 0-273-02759-X

Typeset by Illustrated Arts Limited, Sutton, Surrey.
Printed and bound in Great Britain

Contents

Acknowledgements

The author and publishers wish to thank the following for permission to reprint the material indicated:

The Department of Education and Science for the extract from their Report on Education No 94 in *Further Education Today* by L M Cantor and I F Roberts, published by Routledge & Kegan Paul

The Oxford University Press for extracts from the *Concise Oxford Dictionary*

Parfums Hermes (Parfums de Paris Ltd) for their brochure 'Making the most of your Perfume'

Pergamon Press Ltd for the extract from their *Dictionary of Perfect Spelling*

Pitman Books Ltd for their memorandum

The Principal of St Albans College of Further Education for the specimen memorandum

Scott Foresman and Co, Illinois, USA, for the extract on word division from *Spelling our Language* Book 8

Sir Isaac Pitman Ltd for their list of Most Commonly Misspelled Words used in Boost your spelling power!

IBM (UK) Ltd and Microsoft Corporation (USA) for their VDU diagram of 'Multiplan' spreadsheet

West Sussex County Council for their permission to use charts from 'County Rate 1986–87'

Introduction

Why learn to communicate?

Simply because it lies at the heart of whatever work people do!

No matter how people earn their living – building houses, selling cars, running offices or providing legal advice – the most important skill they will need in order to work successfully is the ability to communicate with other people.

Though we often take the act of communicating for granted, it involves people in a wide range of activities:

speaking
listening
reading
writing
editing, proofreading, revising
smiling, nodding, frowning etc
studying pictures, diagrams, charts
using numbers instead of words

By using one or more of these communicating skills, messages may be passed from one person to another in order to carry out the business of shop, factory, supermarket or bank.

Working with others

Yet the ability to communicate well requires more than the skills needed to take a telephone message, to write a letter or to sell a television set to a choosy customer. For example, people rarely work entirely on their own – they rub shoulders with typists, clerks, machine operators, directors, with colleagues older or younger, senior or junior. Also in the course of their work, many people are given information which is secret, such as details of a new motor-car design, of plans to cut prices or of personal details of a member of staff.

The good communicator will therefore need to develop not only skills which will enable him or her to work alongside others, but also the personal qualities of tact and discretion, so that confidences are not betrayed or the feelings of others hurt in careless gossip.

Working alone

Though people nowadays tend to work closely with each other behind shop counters, desks or factory machines, they will still be expected to 'get on with the job' alone, without a supervisor constantly 'breathing down their necks'. This means that in every job, people are expected to be able to

COMMUNICATION–AT THE HEART OF ALL WORK!

make decisions – whether to transfer a telephone-call to the boss or deal with it personally, or whether to supply goods on credit to a new customer or to ask for cash. Thus part of the skill of communicating lies in the ability to 'read' a situation and to decide – often quite alone – what action to take.

Using English effectively

At the heart of all communication is the need to use language effectively. Communication uses a range of 'languages', but English in its spoken and written forms are two 'languages' which tend first to spring to mind.

Very often, with friends, we tend to mumble or 'natter' without feeling at all uncomfortable – as long as the message gets through. The task of the sales representative demonstrating a piece of office equipment to important buyers is a very different matter! Similarly, a business letter which gives a quotation for a large order will be very different from the 'jotted' holiday letter sent to a friend. The ability to use English accurately and in a tone and style best suited to a situation is one of the most important communication skills which people at work need to master. Moreover, when the success or failure of a business depends so much on how well its employees communicate with clients and customers, it is no wonder that managers place so much importance on the ability to use English well.

Communication and information technology

Nowadays it is impossible to work effectively in an office or to acquire relevant office work skills without becoming involved in the applications of information technology. Indeed, the initials 'IT' are now used extensively as a kind of shorthand word for the many applications in factories, offices and shops based upon the electronic microprocessor or silicon chip.

During the last 15 years the development of equipment based upon the microprocessor, including computers, facsimile transmitters, electronic cash registers and drawing boards, as well as computer aided design and manufacturing tools, has revolutionised the way in which work is carried out in manufacturing, retailing, distribution and service industries.

It is therefore very important that you make a particular effort to acquire IT related skills, such as using a computer keyboard efficiently and accurately, operating a microcomputer confidently and using a range of software application packages for which the instructions are loaded into a microcomputer, enabling it to carry out certain tasks.

In view of the rapid pace of change in office technology, you will also need to keep abreast of IT developments and to maintain a positive and constructive approach to change. After all, to obtain and to hold down a worthwhile job requires a regular demonstration to employers that the working skills you possess are up-to-date and that you are able to cope confidently with current IT applications.

Where do I come in?

Whether you are studying before taking up a first job, or whether you are already working, by reading this far you have already taken the first and most important step towards becoming a better communicator – you have displayed a desire to learn more about the art of communication! Indeed, the key to your future success is to remember that the ability to communicate is not inborn, it *must* be learnt.

Like anything worthwhile, however, it requires a good deal of determination and hard work, backed up with

regular practice. But, once acquired, such skills are never forgotten, and they will form a keystone to your future success, whatever career you choose to pursue.

Thus your ability as a communicator will stem very much from the efforts which you yourself put into studying the contents of this book. Of course, you will need your teacher's help, and you will benefit from sharing the experiences of others in your group. Basically, however, it is up to you!

Sometimes, at school or college, people tend to switch off. They fail to see the point of what they are doing and long for the day when they are free and can start work. What they fail to realise, however, is that no one possesses any sort of magic ingredient which makes them instantly desirable as employees or which will provide them with a high income and easy time of it for life!

People with a more mature outlook soon realise that life is competitive, and that success usually comes to those who have been prepared to make an extra effort, especially when set-backs occur. Also, it is not always the most naturally gifted who rise to the top – more often, success seems to come to those who simply refuse to be beaten.

In other words, your attitude to your course of study is all-important. This book has been carefully designed to help you to become a better communicator – but it will only succeed if you see the point of it, and really want to become a better communicator. This is where *you* come in!

What help will I be given?

This book is made up of a series of units; each structured to teach you essential communicating techniques. Each one builds upon the last to provide a progressive course aimed at giving you practical and work-related information and skills. In each unit you will cover aspects of oral, written, non-verbal, visual or number communication. In addition, English language sections are included to strengthen your spelling, punctuation, grammar, usage and powers of expression.

At regular intervals the world of work is explored and explained. A number of topics are also included for discussion and analysis, so that you will be able to put forward your own point of view, and at the same time, listen to those of others.

In order to help you test your progress, each unit contains a range of assignments, so that you can check how much you have learned. There are also a number of case studies and situations in which you can measure your own ability to make decisions and to solve problems which commonly occur at work.

Furthermore, the whole bias of the book is on the *practical* – it aims to give you communication skills which will stand you in good stead in your job.

Lastly, while you are using this book, remember always that learning to communicate is not a grim grind; on the contrary, if you enter into the spirit of the thing, you will find it a lot of fun. Learning to deal with people and understanding what makes them tick is, perhaps, the most fascinating study of all!

Unit 1

Breaking the ice!

R.B.JACKSON

Have you ever watched the way people behave in the company of strangers? In a train, some businessmen prefer to bury themselves behind the morning newspaper in order to avoid making any contact with their fellow commuters! At the bus-stop, shoppers may exchange a few remarks such as:

'Lovely weather for the time of year ...'
'Yes, mustn't grumble, must we – anyway, it don't do any good, does it?'

And even if the bus is ten minutes late, the two could carry on, quite happily swapping such obvious, empty and meaningless statements. Even worse, though, is 'the silent one', who sits, say, in a doctor's waiting-room or a secretary's office, waiting with other people for an appointment. He or she utters never a word to a neighbour. Pushed to the extreme, this type of person may manage a grunt or an 'um' or 'er', but really much prefers to sit in total isolation, as if quite alone in the wide world!

Alternatively, have you ever stopped to watch a gang of children playing in the street or park? Or have you ever noticed a team of workmen in a club, or on a day out? What a world of difference there is between the way that strangers behave and the behaviour of playmates, workmates or friends. Firstly the way they talk is different – it's direct, lively, easy and relaxed. Legs are pulled, people interrupt or disagree and everyone tends to take part in the conversation. Secondly, people who know each other well make more eye and body contact – backs may be slapped, or people dug in the ribs, while strangers will tend to avoid making such familiar gestures. Strangers seem very cautious in their behaviour, while friends feel much freer in showing their feelings.

There are many reasons why the same people behave so differently with strangers and friends. When strangers find themselves together, all sorts of attitudes are formed in their minds as a kind of defence to prevent them feeling awkward:

... I don't know this other person, therefore I shall not reveal anything of my *real* self. I'll put on a mask of polite indifference and make only meaningless small talk – if I have to ...

... If I start a conversation with this stranger I might be snubbed or made to feel small. Therefore I'll keep quiet ...

... This stranger cannot possibly have anything to say which would interest me. In any case, I don't much care for the way he/she is dressed. Not someone I would feel comfortable talking to, I'm sure ...

Yet everyone *needs* to communicate with those around – to share experiences, jokes, frustrations, hopes and fears. In fact, members of an office or factory staff will positively look for opportunities to communicate in a real way with workmates or colleagues:

'Charlie, you'll *never* guess what head office have said about our request for a bigger stationery budget!...'

'Here, Linda, who's that new feller just started in Menswear, the one with those big dark eyes?...'

'I'll tell you what, George, they'll never get the failure rate down until they listen to what I've been trying to tell them about the new testing process...'

It is only when people have come to *know* others through work, play or study, that they are prepared to open up, and to trust others with a share of themselves, their inner thoughts, reactions or feelings. And in this way, relationships are formed because one person has felt able to trust another with a part of himself or herself.

With strangers it is different. The sort of contact which occurs in the train, at the bus-stop or in the waiting room tends, through the use of well-tried remarks or statements, to be designed to avoid awkward silences and embarrassment. Next time you are surrounded by strangers, listen to those around you, and check whether this is so.

But for the moment, think about your own class at the start of your course. You may have exchanged a few remarks with one or two fellow students, but the chances are that, for the most part, they are still only a collection of vaguely familiar faces. Yet long before your course is over, you will know a good deal about them, and very probably, you will have formed close friendships with several group members.

Also, if you think back to previous times at school or college, you will almost certainly recall how, after a period of breaking the ice, your group became welded together and you felt part of a team of people who could discuss, argue, criticise and work together in harmony – well most of the time!

Working together is one way of forming a closely knit group of people from a collection of strangers – and so it must be with *your* group. Everyone's attitudes and experiences vary. Each of you will have a unique and valuable contribution to make to the progress of your group during the course. You won't feel able to make it, however, as long as you feel yourself to be among strangers. So the first aim of the course must be for students and teacher to break the ice, to get to know each other. And there's no time like the present!

Ice-breakers

1 Form groups of 3 and spend 10–15 minutes exchanging what you think is the most important information about yourself. You could include topics like family, school, what you do for a living, hobbies and pastimes, likes and dislikes.

At the end of the allotted time, each of the 3 students should spend 2–3 minutes introducing one of the others to the rest of the students.

2 Taking turns in the general group, each student should complete the following sentences according to his or her career ambitions or future plans:

I joined the course because ...
Ideally I would like to be a ...

3 Imagine that you had to give a factual description of yourself to a long-lost relative who had never met you, but who wanted to know what sort of person you were. Write a paragraph of 150–200 words which sets out the main facts about yourself and provides an honest and accurate pen-picture. When all the group have finished, the 'portraits in words' may be pulled out of the hat and read to the group.

Just for fun, try omitting the name from the portrait so that the group can try to guess which member is being described!

4 In a general group discussion, exchange your views on one or more of the following:

My favourite LP; pop-star; film-star; magazine; clothes; TV programme; holiday; pastime.

5 On your way to college or school observe how people behave on the bus or train. Make a mental note and then describe what you saw in a general group discussion.

Mastering the meaning

1 Explain the meaning of 'commuter'. Line A

2 Put into your own words, 'in total isolation'. Line B

3 Explain the meaning of the expression 'legs are pulled'. Line C

4 Write a sentence to explain in your own words the meaning of, 'I'll put on a mask of polite indifference'. Line D

5 Provide another word or expression to replace 'snubbed'. Line E

6 Finish the following statement: If I felt *frustrated*, I would feel ... (See line F)

7 Explain in your own words what a 'stationery budget' is. Line G

8 Find another expression which could replace 'became welded together'. Line H

9 What does it mean if a group works 'in harmony'? Line I

10 Find another word or expression to replace 'vary' in Line J

11 Explain the meaning of 'unique'. Line K

12 Re-read carefully the article 'Breaking the ice!' and then, in your own words, explain why people tend to behave differently among strangers and among friends or colleagues. You should aim to write about 130–150 words.

Discussion topics

1 Why do you think people adopt ways of 'distancing' themselves when they meet and talk to strangers?

2 Is it true that all people are 'stand-offish' when they meet others for the first time? Does such behaviour vary between one race or nation and another? Is such behaviour a peculiarly British way of behaving?

3 Is it true that people tend to want to know those around them well, and to share their experiences frankly? Can you think of any situations when this may not be so? Can you explain the reasons why?

4 How important is it for a class of students to 'mesh' or 'weld' together? Is it likely to make any difference to their success? What may happen if they fail to form a group spirit?

5 Isn't it better that people should 'keep themselves to themselves' and stay reserved when they meet others briefly whom they are unlikely to see again?

Group assignment

Form groups of 4–5 and discuss the following topic for 15–20 minutes. During the discussion, each student should make notes of the views being put forward. At the end of the discussion period, each group should report back to the others in a general group session on what was decided:

Cast your mind back to some recent discos you attended, without a boyfriend or girlfriend. Or if you have been 'going steady' for some time, try to remember how unattached friends behaved. Now, try to decide how a young man or woman sets about getting to know someone he or she would like to dance with or date. Supposing a girl doesn't want to dance with a boy, or wishes to 'call it a day' after one dance – how does she let him know? In the world of the disco is it important that both girls and boys behave politely and with an awareness of the feelings of others in such matters? Is it possible to learn how to handle what may sometimes be an awkward situation when meeting strangers at a disco?

Grammar

The article

The term 'article' is given to the words 'a' and 'the', which are used to introduce naming words, objects or ideas:

the letter   a parcel
a meeting   the effects

When the article 'a' is used, it is said to be indefinite, because the writer is not referring to a particular item:

'There's *a* letter for you.'

But when the word 'the' is used, the item becomes identified as the particular or specific one, and the article 'the' is called 'definite':

'*The* letter you are expecting has arrived.'

Notice also, that 'a' is used to introduce a singular item, while it disappears when the item is referred to in the plural:

'My office has *a* word processor.'
'My office has word processors.'

The indefinite article 'a' becomes 'an' when the word it introduces begins with a vowel:

an open meeting   *an* improvement in sales

Sometimes writers use 'an' to introduce words beginning with 'h':

an hotel   an historical novel

This practice seems to be going out of use, and many words beginning with 'h' are simply preceded by 'a':

'It is a habit I cannot give up.'

The use of the definite or indefinite article does have an effect on the meaning of a sentence. Using 'a' to introduce a naming word conveys a sense that 'no particular one' is being referred to, whereas using 'the' makes the item specific, particular or definite:

'*The* word processor in my office has broken down.'
'*A* word processor in my office has broken down.'

It is also interesting to note that in the second sentence above, the use of 'a' conveys the idea that there are other word processors in the office which have not broken down and are still working.

Sometimes words are used as naming words without any article introducing them:

Damage has been caused to the photocopier.
Beauty is in the eye of the beholder.

Such words are often **abstract** in meaning, that is to say that they describe feelings, emotions or ideas outside the physical world:

Love is needed to make the world go round.
One is more likely to find *happiness* when one stops looking for it.

But such abstract ideas may still be introduced by 'the', if the sense is 'the particular one':

The happiness she sought escaped her.
He was *the* love of her life.

Some words which are formed from verbs to become naming words for ideas or activities may also be used without an article:

I like *typing*. I hate *shopping*.

Leaving is always less agreeable than arriving.

But notice,

The going may be difficult
Going may be difficult

do not mean exactly the same thing!

How to study effectively

Both students and teachers alike tend to take for granted everyone's ability to study a subject or course from start to end effectively and successfully. Yet each year, when national examination results are published, thousands of students – and their teachers – all too often suffer disappointment because lower than expected grades have been awarded or, worse, examinations have been failed altogether.

In many cases the root cause is not that such students were weak or found the course of study too difficult but, quite simply, that they never developed effective and productive study skills in time. Moreover, at certain points in a person's education, the type of course pursued varies and techniques of study that may have worked for one kind of course may prove ineffective for another. It therefore pays to review periodically the kinds of study skills and techniques which may be learned and to discuss in a group of fellow students what approaches are most likely to prove successful.

Clearly a good time for such a review and discussion is now – at the very outset of a new course of study! So read the following tips and guidelines carefully and then discuss in your group the Discussion Topics which follow. Remember that the Golden Rules below have been collected from the experiences of many students over a period of years, but that you must use them to develop a study approach that works for you. For example, some people are able to study totally absorbed with pop music belting out of hi-fi loud-speakers at deafening decibel levels! Others need total quiet and are irritated if someone so much as clears their throat or sneezes. Whatever approach suits you, the best advice is to stick to it – always provided that you never pretend to yourself that you are studying intently when really you are day-dreaming, listening to music or really wasting time chatting with friends round a library study table.

Golden Rules

1 Get organised today!

Being organised in a studying sense means:

(a) Managing efficiently that precious resource of time available for study – each day, each week, each month.

(b) Having to hand the necessary and time-saving study accessories – dictionary, thesaurus, pens, pencils, ring-binders, stationery and, increasingly these days, access to a personal computer.

(c) Having a settled and comfortable study base at college or school, at home and perhaps in the local public reference library. Such a base needs to be free from distractions and have a welcoming atmosphere, since the successful student inevitably spends a significant amount of time either in a favourite corner of a library or 'den' at home.

(d) Having ready access to effective and economic study materials – effective in that they provide up-to-date and easily digested information and economic in that they impart their data quickly and straightforwardly. A wide range of such materials exists today:

textbooks, newspaper and magazine articles, lecture notes and teacher hand-outs, videotapes, audio-cassettes, computer software, viewdata pages of information, photographs, diagrams, etc.

2 Getting organised – making the best use of time available

As we all know, time has a way of dribbling away from us, like water running through our cupped hands, unless we make a special effort to capture it and to use it carefully.

This being so, the best way to catch and hold on to available study time is to make out a weekly time-table from, say, 7 a.m. each morning until 8.30 p.m. each evening (nobody studies effectively in the late evening or at night) and to enter on it for each hour those activities like eating, travelling, classroom or workshop lessons and lectures and times for socialising. What you have left should be a number of hourly slots made up either of private study periods while at school or college and a series of early morning or evening hours when you could get down to some productive work.

Next you should compare these times with the opening hours of your school, college or public libraries and mark in a coloured underscoring those of your study hours you could spend in a library surrounded by reference books and magazines and those you will need to spend in your home study area. In consultation with your teachers and fellow students it is helpful then to arrive at a generally agreed number of hours each week which are designated personal or private study periods.

The final task in allocating time effectively to your studies is to decide what proportion of available private study periods should be devoted to each unit of study making up your course each week, bearing in mind that this may vary from week to week depending on assignments set.

In all such arrangements, the Golden Rule is: having constructed a weekly study timetable, above all, stick to it! Don't allow relatives or friends to break into your study times, try to stick to a routine. We are all creatures of habit and having a routine helps enormously in covering the study ground steadily and enjoyably.

3 Getting organised – study accessories

Some students make a fetish of having beautifully kept files and lovely pencil bags or boxes. They write in all sorts of coloured inks and to the inexperienced eye look to be highly organised. Yet sometimes this organisation is only 'cosmetic'. Only the outward show is impressive, the quality of the actual study notes and materials is either sketchy or superficial. So don't be misled into believing that study accessories are important in themselves. What is important is that you develop habits of always having notepaper and writing implements (and reserves) to hand, that you have settled locations in ring-binders for the notes and handouts of each subject and that, having filed study materials, you know how to locate them again quickly!

Above all, do not fall into the trap of carrying all your study materials as you collect them backwards and forwards to school or college each day. Instead, transfer them daily into secure files at home where they will not be lost. Otherwise you may suffer the awful fate of losing all your study aids shortly before revision – and you would not be the first!

A further helpful tip is to get into the habit of labelling your notes in sufficient detail with such essential information as:

- Date taken
- Source
- Dewey Decimal reference number
- Author's or teacher's name (as appropriate)
- Title of topic

For example:

17 September 198X
Text: Communication At Work
    D W Evans Pitman 651.7

How to study effectively

or:

15 October 198X
Lecture: The business letter
Mrs Hamilton

Letter formats

In this way you will always be able to relocate your sources of information or to ask the appropriate teacher to enlarge on a topic at some future point in time, if you need to check a particular item.

If you are using a personal computer to store data and study information, always be sure to 'save to file' at frequent intervals so as not to lose entered data by inadvertent erasing and so on and always keep security copies of all your study disks. Losing pages of data after hours of keyboarding is a bitter experience best avoided!

4 Getting organised – your study locations

For many people the school, college or public library remains, sadly, a 'no-go area' in that they never go into it! In actual fact, it is a treasure house of short cuts to the wise student who takes the trouble to learn the following:

- How to use the Dewey Decimal cataloguing system to locate books.

- What sort of reference books are held and where.

- What help can be gained from short articles in the stock of journals, newspapers and magazines taken on regular subscription.

- What new books have just been added to the library stock.

Make sure you make effective use of your local library resources and make friends with the librarians who will save you a great deal of time!

Always avoid wasting library study time through engaging in 'nattering' or gossiping with fellow-students. Not only is it really irritating to others trying to work, it also will quickly get you into the librarian's bad books and most of all, it represents valuable time lost to yourself which you can never retrieve.

5 Studying at home

A vital part of an effective study pattern is to have somewhere at home where you really can study in peace and quiet and which you can turn into a kind of office for filing your study materials and for producing notes, assignments and other study products.

Basic but absolutely essential to your making proper use of such a room or area is that it must be properly lit – don't try to study in your own shadow – sufficiently warm, and with a desk or table-top area and chair which provide you with proper support and encourage a good posture. Arm-ache and back-ache are the enemies of regular studying.

Develop the habit of returning your files and textbooks to the same place on your study's bookshelves. It is irritating and time-wasting having constantly to spend time searching through untidy heaps of books and papers for a particular hand-out or photocopy. So have 'a place for everything and everything in its place'.

Lastly, the dining-room table next to the television loudly broadcasting the latest soap opera episode may be an inviting location at which to study on a winter's evening in the company of family or friends. What it certainly won't be is either productive or effective, so don't fall into the trap of using for your studies a location which is really only good for socialising and entertaining!

How to study effectively

Discussion topics

1 Can studying ever take place effectively with pairs or groups working together, or is it only effectively done on one's own?

2 How important is it to take lecture notes?

3 You don't learn much out of books – doing a job's the only effective way to study!
To what extent do you agree with this assertion?

4 The secret of successful studying is knowing how to find precisely what you want in as condensed a form as possible!

5 There are basically only two kinds of information – that you need to keep in your head and that you know where to locate if you need it.

How to study assignments

1 Construct a weekly 'study slot' time-table based on your current activities, including your lessons, part-time job, regular socialising times, etc.

Discuss it with your teacher and then use it as a basis for your programme of studies.

2 In small groups, discuss effective techniques of note-taking and then draw up a helpful ten point guide for your group to adopt.

3 Design an ideal home study area and label each component part. Compare your sketch-plan with those drawn up by fellow students.

4 Write an account in about 250 words on one of the following when you have carried out your research:

    a The Dewey Decimal reference system
    b The ISBN cataloguing reference system for books
    c How a library microfiche reader works
    d What Roget's Thesaurus of English Language does

5 Write a short article for your college or school magazine entitled 'The Do's and Don'ts of Effective Studying'.

How to use a dictionary 1

dĭc'tionarў (-sho-) n

dictionary n. Book explaining, usu. in alphabetical order, the words of a language or words and topics of some special subject, author, etc., wordbook, lexicon, (French–English etc. ~, list of French etc. words with English etc. translation or explanation; dictionary of Americanisms, of architecture, of the Bible, of proverbs, Dictionary of National Biography, Shakespeare dictionary, etc.) [f. med. L dictionarium (manuale manual) & dictionarius (liber book) f. L dictio (see prec., -ARY)]

Ask most people to define the word, 'dictionary', and the chances are they will provide a passable explanation, though probably not in as much detail as the one above, taken from the *Concise Oxford Dictionary*.

Ask the same people whether they possess a dictionary – either at home, in the office, or in a briefcase or book-bag – and the answer would most probably be 'yes'.

Again, ask the same people how often they refer to it and whether they fully understand the abbreviations which accompany each word's explanation, and the answer might be very different!

Why do people so often fail to check the meaning or spelling of a word? The answer lies in the Vocabulary Range diagram. As you see, everyone's vocabulary may be divided into two sections – firstly, the words which a person knows well, and uses regularly, and secondly, the words which a person tends not to use, but which he is able to recognise when he meets them in a book or magazine.

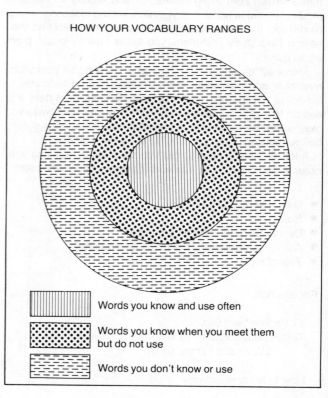

HOW YOUR VOCABULARY RANGES

Words you know and use often

Words you know when you meet them but do not use

Words you don't know or use

The first section may be termed our **active vocabulary**, and the second, our **passive vocabulary**. In addition, there is a third section of words, which a person does not know or use, or recognise. In between the second and third sections lie those words which we recognise when we see them in print – we remember that we have seen them before – but which we have been too lazy to look up! And this is why people tend to use only the words they know well while avoiding unfamiliar ones.

As you can imagine, the number of words a person knows and uses – his *active* vocabulary – varies a great deal between one person and another. A journalist or reporter, for example, might be expected to have a wider vocabulary range than, say, a forester or watchmaker, whose work is more solitary and specialised.

Every student of English and communication, however, needs to widen his or her range of vocabulary, since this will help both oral and written English to be more accurate and interesting. And this is why the ability to use a dictionary effectively and the determination to consult it regularly are so important!

As you will have noticed from the definition of the word 'dictionary' at the head of this section, there are a number of references and abbreviations which may at present seem strange and unfamiliar. Once you have mastered the techniques of consulting a good dictionary, however, you will find that your vocabulary range, spelling and awareness of the force of language will improve greatly. Check the following points carefully and then browse through your own dictionary to see how much more information you are able to gain from it.

Alphabetical entry

Entries in dictionaries are usually made in alphabetical order; that is to say, a comes before b, and b before c and so on. Similarly, if one examines all the words entered in the 'a' section of the dictionary, they will be found to follow the same method. For instance, a word beginning with double 'a' would come before a word beginning with the letters 'ab'. Also, when a word, say, beginning with ab is followed by an 'a', it will come before a word whose third letter is a 'b':

aasvogel
A A U
ab
A B
aba abaya
abaca
aback

This process continues as far along the number of letters in a word as is necessary to establish the alphabetical order:

aba*se*
aba*sh*
aba*sk*

Thus the alphabetical placing of words in a dictionary is decided, not only by the letter with which a word begins, but by moving further into the word until the first difference in letters is discovered.

Alphabet assignments

1 Use your dictionary to write down the word which comes before and the word which comes after each of the following dictionary entries:

abbot buoy convulse drama
indigestion receipt pudding
supermarket unique yoke

2 Put the following list of words into alphabetical order, as if they came in a dictionary list:

digit	reality
great	discourteous
abandon	product
realise	gracious
friend	ecstasy
producer	diet
abbreviate	indifference
greatness	discount
extra	field
difference	straight
foreword	digger
profession	grate
graceful	forward
indifferent	strait

3 Check the meanings in your dictionary of any of the above words which you have not met before.

You *can* spell!

Forming the plural

Fortunately, the plural of most English words is formed by simply adding s to the singular:

pen pens   desk desks
typewriter typewriters

Words ending in y

If y is immediately preceded by a vowel there is no problem, s is added to form the plural:

valley valleys   toy toys

However, there are a number of words where this is not the case because the final y is preceded by a consonant – r, d or b etc. Here, the y is dropped and ies added to form the plural:

secretary secretaries
lady ladies   lullaby lullabies

Words stemming from Old English or Saxon

Words stemming from the Saxon languages form plurals by adding en to the singular or by changing an to en. The following are the most frequently encountered words whose plurals end in en:

man men   woman women
child children
ox oxen
brother brethren (archaic plural)

In such cases the plurals have to be learnt!
   A similar group of words includes those ending in f in the singular. The plural may be formed by either adding s or dropping the f and adding ves. Learn the following by heart:

dwarf	- fs	-ves
handkerchief	- fs	-ves
hoof	- fs	-ves
oaf	- fs	-ves
scarf	- fs	-ves
wharf	- fs	-ves

But note

knife knives   leaf leaves
loaf loaves   sheaf sheaves
shelf shelves   wolf wolves

and

reef reefs
waif waifs

Foreign words brought into English

There are a large number of foreign words, mainly Latin or French in origin, which possess unusual plural forms:

basis	bases
formula	formulae
stadium	stadia
bureau	bureaux
radius	radii

Remember, however, that a number of such words may also take an English plural form:

formulas   stadiums

Words ending in: s x z sh ch ss

Words ending with any one of the above letters or pairs add es to form the plurals:

fox foxes   miss misses   rush rushes
fuzz fuzzes   match matches

Exceptions to the rules

By now, you have probably become reconciled to the idea that the English language generally refuses to meet a 100% rule, so make a note of the following exceptions (and learn them by heart!):

tomato tomatoes   potato potatoes
corps (singular)   corps (plural)
money monies

Boost your spelling power!

Learn these key words by heart

Over recent years, the Pitman Examinations Institute has amassed a checklist of about 200 key words – and those words formed from them – which students of English commonly misspell.

   In each unit, ten of these words will be given for you to study carefully. Try to 'photograph' each of them in your mind's eye, then write down each word in your vocabulary notebook. Notice particularly where the vowels – a, e, i, o, u, – come and whether the common consonants – c, d, f, g, l, m, n, p, r, t, are present singly or in pairs – cc, dd, ff, gg, mm, etc. An asterisk after a word indicates that it is *very commonly misspelled*. Words formed from the base words are shown in brackets and an abbreviation shows each word's part of speech. Finally, the parts of each word which tend to be misspelled are underlined:

absence* n
beginning* n
ceiling n
deceive v (deception n)
efficient adj
familiar* adj (familiarity n)
gauge v, n
harassed v (harassment n)
immediately adv
knowledge n (knowledgeable adj)

Spelling assignment

1 Write down the plural form of the following words, given in the singular:

country   scratch   tableau   knife
German   pony   waif   kindness
soprano   cereal

2 Write down the singular form of the following words, given in the plural:

injuries   dialogues
wharves   heroes
phenomena   curricula
committees   queues
countries   pastes

Be sure to look up in your dictionary any of the above words you have not met before. Find out why some of the words in assignment 2 have a plural which does not end in s.

A microchip memory

Introducing information technology

Nowadays anyone can be forgiven for thinking that information technology needs no introduction at all! Indeed, we can scarcely make a move in the kitchen, in the living room, in the High Street, in the office or factory without encountering the impact of IT in some form or other. Most people, when asked what they most readily associate IT with would say 'computers'. And indeed, the computer is at the heart of IT. Yet the technology of the electronic microprocessor, which enables computers to work at such lightning speeds, is being built almost daily into newly invented devices to perform a multitude of tasks – to help assemble motorcars, guide aeroplanes, route telephone-calls, detect faulty manufacturing or to 'interview' a patient in a doctor's surgery as a means of diagnosing his or her illness!

Whatever the application of IT, its basis lies in the ability of electrical pulses or currents to travel around complicated circuits near the speed of light. This characteristic of electrical energy makes possible the computation or reckoning of a host of calculations in a second, or even a millionth of a second! Thus a computer built around the microprocessor is able to perform in a trice calculations which would take a human brain hours or months to carry out. And yet, computer experts love to tell their students that computers are 'basically stupid pieces of hardware' that only know the difference between 'on' and 'off'! What they mean is that the whole complex network of electrical 'messages' being sent around the computer ending as words on its screen or text on its print-out depend quite simply on the computer's ability to recognise an electrical current as being 'on' or 'off'! This capacity can be transformed into a code which consists of 0s and 1s arranged in sequences. For instance, 101 stands for the number 5 and 1000001 for the letter A. Such a code is called 'binary' since it is made up of only two numbers, 0 and 1.

Such a short and simple explanation of the basic technology of IT serves to open up the subject but, as you well know, computers did not suddenly appear overnight like mushrooms on every manager's or secretary's desk. As in all technological and scientific developments, IT resulted from the patient researches of gifted inventors over the past 200 years. In fact, it is no exaggeration to say that IT represents the outcome of civilised man's enquiring mind and practical accomplishments over the past 10 – 20 000 years, when he first started to look beyond satisfying his survival needs.

For example, though IT specialists in the early days predicted the paperless office, IT still uses a great deal of paper – developed as papyrus by the ancient Egyptians. The numbering system which Western computers employ, whether the binary 01 or the decimal 0123456789, are the invention of ancient Arabic cultures. In hardware terms, the plastics which abound in the manufacture of computing equipment were developed from oil, recovered as a result of mining techniques acquired over centuries. Ancient Greeks pondered upon the power of electricity as manifested in the lightning of thunder storms and it took several centuries, from the 17th century onwards, for methodical and often daring scientists across the world to learn how to tame and employ this amazing source of energy.

The time chart on pages 10 and 11 display some of the principal developments which preceded the invention of the microprocessor or 'silicon chip' in the 1950s and 1960s.

Development of information technology timechart

pre-3500 BC	Signs and speech
c 3500 BC	Earliest known writing (cuneiform), Mesopotamia
63 BC	Tiro, Rome invents a shorthand which is taught and used to record speeches
100 AD	Paper invented in China
c 300	First parchment book
c 1450	Paper mills in England. Invention of moveable type in Europe
1476	W Caxton, book printed in English
c 1590	Invention of lead pencil
1714	Henry Mill, patent for a typewriter
1837	Samuel Morse (USA) produces his first telegraph
1839	First British commercial use of electricity: Cooke and Wheatstone's telegraph lines open in London
1843	Principles of facsimile transmission patented by A Bain
1852	B Dancer, invention of microfilm
1867	James Maxwell proves the existence of radio waves
1868	Scholes develops his typewriter, forerunner of modern typewriter
1874	Remington Corporation (USA) markets the developed Scholes typewriter
1876	First words transmitted on a telephone by Alexander Bell
1878	Bell predicts the current telephone network
1882	Vertical filing systems introduced
1897	First Cathode Ray Tube (CRT) invented by K F Braun
1901	Guglielmo Marconi sends radio signals from Cornwall to Newfoundland
1913	Vacuum tube amplifier (the valve) produced by H D Arnold. First long-distance telephone cable laid
1920	First electric typewriter in commercial use
1925	John Logie Baird produces first real television
1928	Baird demonstrates first colour television pictures
1931	Page-printing teleprinter introduced by Creed
1936	British Broadcasting Corporation (BBC) starts the first public television service in the world
1946	ENIAC – Electronic Numerical Indicator And Calculator – the first modern electrically powered computer demonstrated, Pennsylvania, USA

1947	The transistor is invented by Brattain and Barden
1949	First computer (EDSAC) with stored memory is demonstrated in Cambridge, England
1950s	Start of long-distance direct dialling of telephone calls
	Photocopying devices on general sale
1956	IBM Corporation develops computer disc drive
1958	First satellite radio message
1960	Laser light beam developed by T H Maiman (initials stand for: Light Amplification by Stimulated Emission of Radiation)
1964	IBM Corporation markets its Selectric Typewriter with memory function – forerunner of word processing equipment
1966	ITT Corporation (USA) develops fibre-optics technology
1967	British Post Office introduces its Data Processing Service
1971	Intel Corporation (USA) produces first commercially applicable microprocessor Floppy disc drive introduced for computer programming
1970s	Rapid development of microcomputer-based equipment and systems – microcomputer, stand-alone word processor, optical scanner, etc
1974	Xerox Corporation introduces the 'daisy' print wheel
1979	British Post Office transmits its Prestel viewdata service
1980	British Post Office begins to introduce its 'System X' computerised telephone network
1981	British Telecommunications Act: establishes British Telecom as public corporation separated from the Post Office. Also permits the introduction of private enterprise into telecommunications
1980s	Developments in information technology proceed apace – more powerful microprocessors, area net working for electronic mail, etc, experimental work on voice input into computers, 'wristwatch TV', improved 'bubble' memory for microcomputers, fibreoptic transmission of messages, work with electronics at 'faster than light speeds', widening of information technology education in Great Britain from primary schools upwards IT introduced extensively into factory production techniques: CADCAM – Computer Aided Design, Computer Aided Manufacture and, CIM – Computer Integrated Manufacture

How IT came about

In the world of science and technology advances are generally made through a mixture of brilliant insights which lead to sudden developments and a steady pace of enquiry over decades and centuries eventually leading to a new field of technology being established. Such a mixture of 'hundred metre sprints and marathons' characterises the invention and development of our present-day computer technology.

Though it is possible to drive a computer successfully without knowing either how it works or how it came about, the conscientious student naturally wants to have a straightforward idea of 'what is under the bonnet' and how it got there!

Essentially, today's computer is the product of an extensive series of inventions and discoveries which occurred in the tremendous flowering of physical science in the 18th and 19th centuries. Some of the principal elements of these discoveries and inventions were:

- The ability to harness and control electrical currents.

- The development in the 19th century by Charles Babbage of a mechanical 'Analytical Engine' for proces-

sing number calculations – perhaps the true forerunner of today's electronic computer.

- The introduction by George Boole in the mid 19th century of a system of logic in which ideas or propositions were basically true or false. This system lent itself to the process in modern computers where electrical currents are passed through a series of gates or switches which are either 'on' or 'off'. Similarly, the development of binary counting enabled these pulses of electricity to be represented as sets of 0's or 1's.

- The evolution of a system of printing known as engraving where pictures or drawings were produced on sheets of metal as a result of acids eating away those parts of the picture not required. The lines and blocks which were left raised up on the metal sheet thus formed the picture from which paper prints could be taken. This process was known as etching and was widely used in newspaper production in the 19th century before the advent of the photograph.

- Also in the 19th century, the textile industry's output and versatility was revolutionised by the introduction of a series of cards which were used in conjunction with

Babbage's Analytical Engine
Courtesy of The Science Museum

the loom to provide a set of programmes which drove the loom automatically and thus produced particular patterns in the woven materials. They worked very much like the punched cards which were used to programme computers in the 1960s and early 1970s.

Inventors like Charles Babbage were very much ahead of their time, however, and it was not until significant advances were made in the 20th century in the field of electronics that the electrically driven computer could be brought into being.

- The success of Guglielmo Marconi in sending radio signals from Cornwall to Newfoundland in 1901 led to the development of the wireless or radio and thus to the thermionic valve. These looked rather like transparent light bulbs. They contained two plates in a vacuum across which electricity could be passed and a signal amplified. Thus they enabled the radios to be heard from a distance and did away with the ear-phones of early crystal sets.

Moreover, from a computing point of view, they could be used as a kind of switch to control the movement of electrical pulses around complicated circuits. And it was from such vacuum tubes or valves that the forerunner of today's electronic computer was built in the USA in 1946. Gene Bylinsky writing about the Electronic Numerical Indicator and Calculator (ENIAC) as it came to be known called it 'a fickle monster' – it apparently weighed some 30 tons and contained 18 000 valves! And it only needed the filaments of a single valve to burn out for the whole machine to come to a halt.

Between 1946 and 1971 a whole range of electronic inventions were marketed as the peoples of the world became hungry for domestic and leisure goods after the deprivations of the Second World War.

- Important in this respect was the development of the transistor which did the job of the valve but was only the size of a cold capsule. Moreover, it had no moving parts and was thus extremely reliable. Like the valve it could be used as a switch and amplifier and it brought in the 'Tranny Age' of the 1950s, enabling teenagers – to the outrage of some – to take their music with them wherever they went by means of compact and light-weight portable radios.

This by-product of the transistor or semi-conductor to enable goods to be made smaller and lighter proved to be very significant in the evolution of the electronic computer. In the 1960s much research was carried out in 'solid state electronics' and circuit boards were created which could carry out extremely sophisticated electronic tasks within a very small space. At this time in the United States, research work was proceeding to reduce the size of ponderous 'mainframe computers', to lessen the power needed to run them and to increase their capacity to process more information more quickly.

- This ability was brought about by the invention of the microprocessor or 'silicon chip'. Its development was a masterpiece of ingenuity allied to several technologies. Basically the silicon chip is a set or series of miniaturised electronic circuits built upon each other in three dimensions like a kind of layer-cake. Each circuit is etched on to a wafer chip of silicon by means of a process called photolithography.

Simply, it works like this. A team of expert electronic engineers produce large drawings of the electronic circuitry they want on metre square drawing boards. These drawings are in two dimensions but will eventually be placed on top of each other to produce a three dimensional effect. Each drawing is miniaturised to the size of a postage stamp through a process of specialised photography. Then the pattern of the circuits is etched on to its silicon base by a system of lithography, not dissimilar to that used by engravers in the 19th century.

Almost miraculously a series of 'gates' or switches – like the transistors of the 1950s – is built into each chip so that the routes and stops and starts of electrical currents are controlled and intercepted without any moving parts being needed.

The microprocessor interprets these electronic signals as 'ons' or 'offs' and working in conjunction with the other components of the computer converts them into the 0s and 1s of binary code. Ultimately, these sets of binary digits (bits) are transformed into the text, pictures or numbers displayed on the computer's screen.

Make your mind up time ...

A case study

Jenny Richards sighed as she lay on her studio bed, idly flicking through her tapes, looking for something to play. The trouble was, she couldn't find anything that seemed right for someone who couldn't make up her mind!

She thought how funny it was that life always seemed to turn out differently from the way she had imagined it. At 14 she had yearned to be 16, to have a chance to mould her life the way she wanted it to be. Perhaps to start work, or go to college, or maybe to enjoy some of the privileges which went with being a sixth-former. But, now her 16th birthday was fast approaching and GCSEs were more than just a dark cloud on the horizon, life seemed far too complicated. More than that, trying to decide what sort of career to aim for seemed like some sort of refined mental torture!

It simply wasn't fair! Her friends had all found it so easy. Linda already had the promise of a job in the gift department of the local department store. Sue had

R.B.JACKSON

always wanted to study A level History and English Literature anyway, while Tanya had just received confirmation of a place at the college to study beauty therapy, subject to her exam results.

Jenny absent-mindedly put a tape of her favourite singer into her hi-fi and stared at the ceiling. A succession of career girls seemed to float past her. Air hostess, silk scarf flying in the breeze, stepping off Concorde in New York. Sipping tea in a kimono in Tokyo. Surf-riding in Hawaii. Trouble was, you had to be 18. Hotel receptionist, booking in all those film stars and famous visitors. Maybe. But how would you cope with a double-booking? Or someone who only spoke Japanese? The image of brisk efficiency faded. Perhaps a private secretary. There would be important meetings to attend and distinguished clients to deal with. Later, of course, there would be drinks in some plush bar, followed by an expensive dinner with her boss – a small thank-you for staying on late to type some letters ... the prospect seemed quite exciting.

Yes, maybe that was it. Private secretary. Of course, it would only be for a few years. Jenny had already decided on marriage and a family. And if she had her way, her future husband would already have made his way in the world. He might be a doctor, in which case secretarial training could prove useful. She could help reorganise his surgery. Or he might be an up-and-coming manager. Then she would know what to say when she entertained his business clients.

But all that was still *years* ahead. Abruptly she became aware of the hum of the tape-deck, the first side already having played through during her day-dreaming.

'Jenny! How many more invitations do you want for tea? Your egg's getting cold! And what about all that homework afterwards? I *really* don't know what to make of you at all, sometimes!'

Wearily, Jenny rolled off her bed and made her way downstairs. No, being nearly 16 was not nearly as much fun as it was made out to be!

Assignments

1 Discuss the following in your class:

(*a*) What attitude is Jenny taking to deciding on her career?
(*b*) What action do you think Jenny should take?
(*c*) What factors in general should teenagers take into account when choosing a career path?
(*d*) How can parents and teachers best help?

2 Write an article in about 300 words offering teenagers of 15–16 years of age advice on choosing a career.

3 Make a case, in a written account of about 300 words, for following a further education or sixth form course as preparation for a career.

Syntax: what is a sentence?

One of the most important differences between speech and writing is the way in which ideas are put into words. When people talk to others, they often express themselves in a kind of shorthand:

No go! Too right!
Where'd you get it? Down the town.
If you like. OK!

A great deal of spoken English takes the form of slang, colloquial or familiar words and expressions which would not be appropriate in written English. The reason for this is that ideas are often clearest when expressed in grammatical sentence form; and arguments and ideas are usually best understood when written in carefully structured, continuous prose. Also, it happens that this form of writing is generally accepted, save in informal jottings or notes.

In developing syntax skills, therefore, it is extremely important that you build up complete confidence in your own ability to construct sentences which are grammatically correct.

Specialist word: syntax

Though **syntax** sounds a rather technical word, all it means is the way in which we put together groups of words to make messages.

To begin with, then, a rule is needed against which to measure any piece of writing to see whether it satisfies all the requirements which a sentence has to meet.

Definition of a sentence

A sentence is an idea, expressed in a connected set of words which is complete in itself, can stand alone and convey a meaning fully and completely:

The morning post arrived.
Jean finished the word processing.
The typist was late for work.

Now compare the three above examples with the following:

after the midday lunch-break
going into the office hurriedly
in reply to your letter of 3 May

In each of the first three examples, the reader is satisfied that the idea is fully stated – nothing needs to be added. In the second three, however, the reader is left 'in the air', waiting to know what happened after the midday lunch-break or who was going into the office hurriedly and what for, and what is to be stated in reply to the 3 May letter.

Furthermore, it does not help to disguise such non-sentences with opening capital letters and closing full-stops:

Going into the office hurriedly.
In reply to your letter of 3 May.

Though it must be admitted that such 'camouflage' makes them look more respectable, but they are *still* frauds!

The doer word

What makes a sentence genuine and properly respectable, then? Firstly, it needs a **doer** – somebody or something who is 'doing' the action of the sentence. In the first three examples, the **doer** words are:

The morning post
Jean
The typist

Sometimes doer words are the names of people or things:

Bob drove to London.
Concorde is a famous airliner.
The clerk added up the list of figures.

Doer words sometimes extend to several words, taken as a single whole:

Each of the envelopes contains a cheque.
The eager salesman talked endlessly.

As a guide, **doer words** occur very often in English sentences at the start (but be careful – not always!).

> **Rule 1**
> To qualify as a sentence, a group of words must have a **doer word(s)** which controls or governs the action of the sentence. Such a word or words is called **the subject of the sentence.**

In special sentences, those which give orders, the doer word or subject is sometimes left out – it is understood:

Stop! (You) stop!
Leave it alone! (You) leave it alone!

Apart from such special constructions, sentences need doer words/subjects to be present – no subject, no sentence!

The action word

As well as needing a subject, sentences also need a word or group of words which will describe the **action:**

The morning post *arrived.*
Jean *finished* the word processing.
None of the typists *was* late for work.

In some **action words**, the very action being described make them easy to recognise:

The clerk *cut* the string on the parcel.
The manager *opened* the box-file.
The receptionist *picked up* the telephone.

In such situations it is easy to create a mental picture of what is happening and to identify the action word. Sometimes, however, the action word conveys an ongoing, continuous state:

The window *is* open.
The accountant *considered* the matter.
Jack *studied* the report at length.

Also, action words may take the form of a connected group of words:

The floppy disks *have been formatted.*
She *may have spoken* too soon.
The leaflets *should be printed* by tomorrow.

Whether such action words come singly or in groups, whether they clearly show an action taking place or express a state of mind, *whenever they carry out the action of the subject*, they are called **verbs.**

Rule 2
To qualify as a sentence, a group of words must include an action word (or group of words) known as the **verb** which expresses the action of the subject – no verb performing this job – no sentence!

Sentence assignments

1 Identify the subject word (or group of words) in each of the following sentences:

(a) The office juniors were chatting noisily.
(b) Quickly and easily, Jenny despatched the fax document.
(c) All the letters had to be finished before five o'clock.
(d) The sales manager and his assistant decided to make one more call.
(e) Envelopes, parcels and packages lay on the desk unopened.
(f) 'Don't go yet!'

2 Identify the word (or group of words) acting as the verb in the following sentences:

(a) The clerk was amending the spreadsheet.
(b) 'You will need a larger envelope.'
(c) Two electronic typewriters had been ordered.
(d) 'Put a new ribbon in the printer, please.'
(e) After lunch he caught the train to Manchester.
(f) 'The unimportant mail will have to wait.'
(g) The factory inspector is coming next week.

3 Study the following groups of words carefully. Identify which of them are true sentences. If you find any which are not, write down what they lack:

(a) Going down the road slowly.
(b) She was very busy.
(c) In connection with your enquiry.
(d) 'Have you finished the report?'
(e) Filed alphabetically in the cabinet.
(f) As a result of poor maintenance and neglect.
(g) Simon left hurriedly.
(h) 'Over there!'
(i) According to the age and experience of the applicant.
(j) Further to our recent telephone conversation.
(k) 'Heave!'
(l) The two girls missed the bus.
(m) Checking carefully for the error in the print-out.

Punctuation

Capital letters and full-stops

Starts and stops

As we have just learned, writing proper sentences means knowing when and how to start and stop. The opening and closing ends of a sentence are clearly marked for the reader: a capital letter at the beginning of the word which starts a sentence; and a full-stop after the word which ends it. The next sentence is introduced by another capital letter and so on:

Bob called into Jenny's office to collect the outgoing mail. She asked him to wait while she finished an important letter. Once all the letters were ready, Bob hurried back to the mailroom.

Exceptions to the rule

Though the most frequent use of the full-stop is to show the end of a sentence which contains a subject word and verb governed by it, full-stops are sometimes used to indicate the end of groups of words which are *not* sentences in the strictest sense:

Try Fizz! *Bubbly and tangy*!
Delicious taste. Fantastic!

Advertising writers deliberately construct such short 'sentences' which have no subject word or verb to provide a punch to the images they create. Script-writers often use the same technique to increase a sense of suspense in dialogue:

Bank robber: Move over there. *Against the wall*. Move it, I said! *OK. Now, the key*! C'mon! Right, everybody keeps still and nobody gets hurt.

In the above examples the exclamation mark has been used to end sentences, replacing the full-stop. It indicates excitement or anger or emotion.

Remember: never use a full-stop and an exclamation mark together. The point at the bottom of the exclamation mark replaces the full-stop.

A word of caution, however: advertisers and script-writers are experts and are striving quite deliberately for special effects. Also, what may be quite acceptable in the form of the *spoken* word may not be right for the letter or report. So, at this stage, you should concentrate on writing grammatically correct sentences. Also, even in creative writing, the exclamation mark is best used sparingly.

Abbreviations

Another common use of the full-stop is to show that a word has been contracted or abbreviated:

e.g.   for example (Latin *exempli gratia*)
etc.   and so on
P.S.   Post Script – after writing
enc.   enclosure

Sometimes, however, words are abbreviated simply by putting the initials together:

OBE   BBC   RSVP   ref   Cres

Increasingly, such abbreviations are typed without full-stops.

There are also further rules governing the use of full-stops in letter layouts which will be dealt with later in the unit dealing with letter format.

Omissions

Lastly, full-stops are sometimes used to show that a piece of text has been omitted from a quotation:

'The costs are likely to prove too high ... It has therefore been decided to cancel the project.'

Activities and assignments

1 Write an account of what points you think should be taken into consideration when someone is trying to decide upon a career.

2 (*a*) 'Have you seen the stapler?'
(*b*) 'Do you happen to have a stapler I could borrow?'

Explain the difference in meaning in examples *a* and *b* which stems from using 'the' and 'a' in front of the word stapler.

3 The following sentences contain a word you have met in this unit. You are given its first letter. Write it out in full, being careful to spell it correctly!

(*a*) Someone who travels daily to work by bus or train is a c – – – – –.
(*b*) Letters, notepaper and envelopes are called s – – – – – –.
(*c*) A feeling of awkwardness or shyness is called e – – – – – – – –.
(*d*) A shortened version of a word is an a – – – – – – – – –.
(*e*) Someone who enjoys special favours is said to have p – – – – – – – – –.

(*f*) Words which are used only in familiar dialogue are said to be c – – – –.
(*g*) If you don't do something on purpose, you do it a – – – – – –.
(*h*) Words listed in the order a, b, c, etc are said to be listed a – – – – – – – –.
(*i*) To break into someone's conversation is to i – – – – – – – –.
(*j*) If two objects are not identical, they must be d – – – – – –.
(*k*) F – – is a 'shortened' expression for a system which sends messages across the world in minutes.

4 Look up the following words in your dictionary and write down their meanings in your vocabulary notebook:

encounter   profession   executive
audio   transcription   phonetic   laser
administer   foyer   suite   dictation

Make a careful note how each is spelled!

5 Write an account of your first impressions on joining the course of study you are now following. Exchange and compare your impressions by reading your account to the group.

6 Re-write the following in sentences:

(*a*) jenny arrived in the office at half-past nine she was out of breath and flustered normally she was very punctual however this morning the alarm-clock had rung as usual at seven o'clock it was not like jenny to sleep through it quietly she made her way to the manager's office to apologise for arriving late she was readily excused by Mr Jones who knew of her usual good time-keeping and valued her work

(*b*) don't stop i just wanted to borrow some disks if you don't mind i hope i'm not disturbing you i know how easy it is to lose the place when people interrupt since you have stopped i might as well ask for some letterhead paper as well as you probably know we're overdue for some stationery in the department i can't understand why there's been a delay thanks very much i'll return it later

7 Identify which of the following are grammatically correct sentences:

(*a*) After the ball was over.
(*b*) The letter was typed hastily.
(*c*) It is lost.
(*d*) Following your recent request.
(*e*) She asked for an increase in salary.
(*f*) Don't stop!
(*g*) In connection with your enquiry of 2nd May 19—.
(*h*) They have not arrived yet.
(*i*) Because of a shortage of continuous stationery.
(*j*) Late in the afternoon Jenny finished the report.
(*k*) At about six o'clock in the morning last Tuesday.
(*l*) As a result of your letter of 21st April about the non-delivery of five reams of typing paper.
(*m*) Having passed the examination with distinction at the third attempt.
(*n*) 'Quickly!'
(*o*) After a long search the clerk found the report in the wrong file.

8 Find out what the following abbreviations stand for:

AA   a/c   BA   C   caps   c/o   col
do   ed   et seq   fob   hon sec
ie   lc   ll   Mme   np   pp   RAM   SEN
uc   viz   VDU

9 Find out the major achievements of Charles Babbage in the 19th century and write a short biography of his life (about 250 words) for display on your group noticeboard.

10 Carry out your research and, with the help of cut-out photos, drawings and diagrams, outline the important features of designing and producing a microprocessor or silicon chip.

11 Again, first do your research in your college or school library and then write in about 150 words an account explaining how one of the following works:

(*a*)   a valve in a 1940s – 1950s wireless.

(*b*)   a transistor

(*c*)   a cathode ray tube (the 'screen' of a tv).

12 In groups of 3–4 make a checklist of as many uses of the computer in present-day society as you can think of in ten minutes.

When you have finished, compare your list with those drawn up by other groups in your class.

Unit 2

Sending and receiving communications

Doing what comes naturally?

By the time we reach our teens, we probably take the ability to communicate for granted – as merely 'doing what comes naturally'. After all, each of us has been around for quite some time and managed well enough at home, school, college or work. Yet whether we realise it or not, each of us has learned an immense amount about language and communication by the time we become teenagers. In early childhood we soon learned how to recognise pleasure or annoyance in our parents' faces or words. We then learned how to read, to write and to interpret numbers and diagrams. We even came to understand the silent language of communication expressed in faces, gestures and body movements – the body language of non-verbal communication. Moreover, we have used this array of skills to become an active member of the family, school
(A)

or working group, whether in social or work activities.

To be successful in a future career, however, requires further effort. The process of communicating will become more complex. There will be traps and pitfalls to be avoided in making our way successfully through the maze of adult human relationships. For example, the receptionist or secretary will almost certainly find it necessary to possess the skills needed to calm down an angry customer or visitor; the salesman will need a fund of persuasive skills if he is to sell consistently; the accountant will need to be able to compose a letter effectively which manages to secure the payment of an overdue account without losing a tardy customer's goodwill.
(B)
(C)

The ability to communicate successfully in such situations does not stem from a 'hit or miss' approach, relying on instinct or intuition, but from expert use of the range of techniques which are available and which can and must be learned! It is therefore essential to have an understanding of the process through which people communicate, whether one-to-one, or in groups, whether across a room, or over long distances. It is also necessary to be expert in
(D)

What happens when a message is sent and received

sender

1 Idea
forms the idea of the message

deciding what to convey to receiver

2 Encoding
puts it into a communication language

choosing the most effective 'language'

3 Route
sends it via a chosen route

selecting the most suitable route e.g. post or telephone

receiver

informing sender message interpreted correctly

checking all aspects of message are understood

understanding the 'language' used by the sender

confirms it has been received and understood

checks it is fully understood

'decodes' the language of the message

6 Feedback　　　**5 Interpreting**　　　**4 Decoding**

<u>All</u> six stages must be carefully completed if the message is to be sent, received and <u>acted upon</u> successfully!

the various communication 'languages' which may be employed, to know the advantages and disadvantages of the different routes by which messages are conveyed, and to know why the communication process sometimes breaks down and what to do if it does. The diagram on page 19 illustrates the communication process, between a 'sender' and a 'receiver' of a message, broken down into six main stages:

1 Idea

Before a sender can communicate an idea, he must first think clearly along these lines:

What, exactly, do I want to 'say'?
What am I trying to achieve?
What kind of person am I 'saying' it to?

Failure to pose such questions at the idea stage often results in thoughts being uttered which may cause embarrassment to both sender and receiver alike:

'Oh, I'm *so* sorry! I didn't mean it to sound like that!'

Also, when ideas are not carefully formed, the message often becomes vague or ambiguous, so that the receiver is unable to understand it or to act upon it.

2 Encoding

Having decided upon what message to send and why, the next stage is to select a communication language best suited to the nature of the message and the situation in which it is to be sent.

The languages of communication
the spoken word
the written and printed word
non-verbal communication:
   expression
   gesture
   body positioning
number
visual and pictorial communication:
   charts, graphs,
   films, photographs, etc

The electronic revolution has provided us with a wide range of equipment for relaying messages in any of the following 'media' languages:

loudspeakers, telephones, intercoms, film cameras, videotaping equipment, printing presses, word processors, closed circuit television, computers, electronic accounting machines, over-head projectors, etc

There are, however, many pitfalls for the unwary communicator – some messages are best written, so that a record may be kept. Often a quiet spoken word will have the best results; a picture or graph convey instantly what minutes of talk fail to impart. Moreover, whatever language is chosen, it is absolutely essential that it is one which the receiver fully understands – otherwise the process of sending a message is bound to break down.

3 Route

Once the language of the message has been selected, it is necessary to choose the best route for sending it to the receiver. The spoken word may be routed via:

face-to-face contact,
telephone, intercom, loudspeaker, etc

The written word may be sent through:

the postal service, telex, electronic message switching, magazine, journal, circular, etc

Similarly, graphs, charts, diagrams or tables may be used to convey number communications.
Care is needed when choosing the route – the postal system may not work fast enough for an urgent message, and so a telephone-call, electronic mail or faxed message may prove more suitable. Similarly, the need to obtain immediate responses to suggestions may require a meeting using the spoken word rather than a series of memoranda to staff. Thus effectiveness is always the main yard-stick in choosing a route, followed closely by cost and time.

4 Decoding

At this stage, responsibility for the message passes to the receiver. He must ensure that he understands the language used by the sender – it must be common to both of them. This may involve consulting a dictionary, checking on past records or confirming sets of figures. It may also involve the sharing of specialist knowledge or work experiences.

5 Interpreting

Not only must the receiver understand the language of the sender, he must also be sure that he uncovers any hidden meanings or underlying feelings or attitudes which the sender also conveys in the message – a disappointed customer may convey, for example, annoyance and irritation about a faulty product. Such feelings have to be coped with in addition to supplying, say, a replacement electric iron.

6 Feedback

Lastly, the receiver must ensure that the sender is made aware of the success of his passing on of the message. With the spoken word a nod or word of agreement may be all that is needed, but with the written word, an answering letter may need to be sent, or a telex message immediately despatched. From the sender's point of view, it is vital that confirming feedback is received, otherwise he will not know whether to proceed with the next part of the message, or whether the receiver is acting upon, for example, the instructions which have been sent to him.

Mastering the meaning

1 What does the term 'non-verbal communication' mean? Line A

2 What do you understand by the expression 'make our way successfully through the maze of adult human relationships'? Line B
Re-write the idea more simply in your own words.

3 Why does a salesman need 'a fund of persuasive skills'? Line C

4 Explain what is meant by the word 'intuition'. Line D

5 Explain in a paragraph of *your own words* (only using specialist vocabulary when you have to) what happens when a message is sent and received.

6 Why is it important for the sender to have formed a clear idea of the nature and purpose of his message before routing it?

7 Why is it so important for the receiver of a message to share the sender's communication language?

8 Can you think of a situation in which it would be better to make a telephone-call than to write a letter – and vice versa? Write down brief descriptions of the two situations.

9 Why is it so important for the sender to receive feedback from the receiver concerning the receipt and understanding of the message?

10 What happens when the sender does not receive any feedback?

The following checklist supplies a list of questions which you should ask yourself whenever acting as a sender or receiver of messages. They will help you to ensure that you are carrying out your role effectively.

Any questions?

Sender questions

What do I wish to convey?

Why do I wish to send the message?

Who, exactly, should receive my message?

What action or response am I hoping for from the receiver?

What would be the best communication language to use?

Are there any pitfalls in my choice of route for the message?

Will the receiver understand my choice of language and want to act on my requests?

What can I do to positively help the process?

Receiver questions

Do I clearly understand the language of the message?

Do I need to check up on any aspect of it?

Am I doing enough to ensure that I shall understand the sort of languages I am likely to receive messages in?

Am I giving the message all my attention and concentration?

Have I fully understood all the implications of the message or have I missed any underlying meanings?

Do I need to ask the sender for further explanations or enlargements?

Have I ensured that the sender has received feedback that I have received and understood the message?

Discussion topics

1 'If you've something to say – simply say it!' Is this good advice for a would-be communicator?

2 Is *how* you say something as important as *what* you have to say?

3 'Being a good communicator is a natural gift. You either have it or you don't. Simple as that!'

Group assignment

Form groups of 5–7 students. The first member of each group should compose in writing a message of some 30 words, including some names, dates, times, etc ... He or she then *speaks* the message to the next team member (out of earshot of the others). The message is passed on until it reaches the last member, who writes it down.

Compare in each group the first and second written versions and see if they differ. Also, consider why directors of large organisations try to limit the number of grades or layers of staff between the bottom and the top.

Grammar

The noun

So far, we have referred to 'doer' (or naming) words to describe certain parts of speech. In actual fact, we have been referring to **nouns. Noun** is the technical word for that part of speech which acts as label or identity tag for all the objects, articles or things which surround us.

From the moment man began to speak, he needed to invent words to act as identifying names for all that he saw around him and used:

wood, rock, cave, axe, bone,
stick, skin, river, meat

The term noun, then, is used to identify that part of speech which acts as a name for either an article, person or idea.

Common nouns

The nouns which identify all the components of the world in which we live are called **common nouns**. Modern man might refer to:

television, ice-cream, helicopter, strikes, management, city, crowd

Common nouns may be divided into two groups, those which are used to describe the parts of the physical world in which we live, which are called **concrete nouns**:

motorway, park, chair, apple, subway

and those which are employed to label thoughts, feelings, emotions or concepts, which are called **abstract nouns**:

love, efficiency, tact, laziness, ability

Proper nouns

As well as common nouns, names or identities are needed for all the single or individual creations in the world. No two human beings are ever the same; there will only be one King Lear or Mona Lisa. Such unique creations, whether people, places, works of art or architecture are called **proper nouns**. They are easy to recognise since they all begin with capital letters. When they are titles of books or plays they may also be enclosed in quotation marks:

William Shakespeare   Birmingham   Thames
'Macbeth'   'Gone With the Wind'   The Tower of London

Collective nouns

Sometimes, for convenience, we refer to a collection of identical or similar objects, animals or people by putting them into a single category – 'a something of ...' That 'something' referred to is called a collective noun:

a herd of cows, a pack of cards, a team of footballers, a troupe of dancers, a bevy of beauties

Mostly, such collective nouns take a singular verb:

The troupe of dancers *arrives* tonight.
The stock of typewriter ribbons *is* running short.

Occasionally, we may refer to such collective nouns in the plural, if we are really thinking of the separate parts they stand for:

The team are arguing among themselves.
The panel of adjudicators are discussing the merits of the finalists.

It is important that you learn to recognise nouns easily, whether as single words or word groups, because nouns form the subjects of sentences. As you already know, all sentences must possess at the very least a subject and a verb. And you know that sooner or later, someone you work for will be expecting you to be able to write grammatically correct sentences, or to correct draft letters which may not be grammatically correct. So, it pays to *know*. Check how much you now know by working through the following assignments.

Assignments on nouns

1 Give each of the following nouns its correct 'label' – common, proper or collective:

smoke, jury, conductor, gaggle, king, Elvis Presley, eskimo, copse, photograph, Tower of London, Muhammed Ali, batch, secretary, British Airways.

2 Say which of the following nouns are concrete or abstract:

track, jealousy, care, sky, tower, notebook, happiness, jumper, pin, age, annoyance, pedestrian, skill, speed, star, loyalty, kindness, nut.

3 Identify the nouns in the following sentences:

'Poor old Jack, he's missed the train again!'
My dog likes going for walks.
'Have you read "Kes"?'
The report was ready, so Jenny took it into Mr Jones' office, and put it on his desk.
'Hard work will produce the results the company needs!'

The verb

The verb is the part of speech which conveys action. If we think of the subject of a sentence as a doer word, then the verb is the word (or group of words) which expresses the doing:

SUBJECT	VERB	
(proper noun)		
Jane	cut	her hand.
(common noun)		
The clerk	was checking	the invoices.

Sometimes you can see the action that the verb is expressing:

to glide, to slip, to explode, to shatter, to drill, etc

Sometimes verbs are used to indicate thought processes, moods or feelings:

to dream, to ponder, to consider, to hate, to mock, to wonder, to reflect, to regret, to hope, etc

while still others are used to express behaviour:

They *argued* furiously.
They *cooperated* fully.
She *disagrees* with him.

Parts of the verb

Different parts of the verb are given names for identification. The root or base of the verb, from which all parts are formed, is introduced by the word 'to' and is called the **infinitive**:

to go   to instruct   to repeat

When tenses of the verb are formed, then sometimes a part of the verb ends in 'ing', when it is used with other verb parts to form a tense:

I am *coming*   I shall be *going*

Such a word is called a **present participle**.
In addition, there is a past part of the verb (which often ends in -ed) which is also used to form a tense:

The parcel has *arrived*.
The door had been *broken* some time.

Such a part of the verb is called the **past participle**.

The tenses of the verb

When verbs are used to carry out the action of the doer or subject of the sentences, they can appear in a number of tenses. Tenses of the verb are used to show whether the action is taking place in the present, past or future. There is also a tense called the conditional which indicates an *intention* to do something not yet carried out.

Active or passive?

Each tense (of certain verbs which take objects – see page 24) may be expressed either in the active or the passive. To check the difference, consider the following two sentences:

1   The secretary *opened* the letter.
2   The letter *was opened* by the secretary.

Clearly they are two ways of saying the same thing, but in **1**, the subject, 'the secretary' is performing the action of 'opening'. Whenever this happens, the finite verb is said to be **active**. In **2**, however, although 'The letter' is the grammatical subject of the sentence, it obviously did not open itself, so the real 'doer' has to be identified: 'by the secretary'. Such constructions are said to be **passive**, because the real doer is not the subject of the sentence.

It is important to be able to recognise the difference between active and passive, since the use of the passive could save you from a great deal of trouble:

'Mum! I have just broken the iron!'

The probable result is a good telling off, but what if you say, instead:

'Mum! The iron has just been broken!'

Then, it sounds as if it happened quite anonymously, because 'by me' has been left out.

The passive is used a great deal by people who don't wish to appear involved in bad news:

'Your contract has been terminated.'

is very different from saying:

'I am dismissing you!'

Remember that verbs used in the passive need to be helped by the verbs 'to be' or 'to have':

'has been terminated'   'was opened'

Also, the past participle of the verb is always used.

Table of tenses

Infinitive:	**to type**	
Present participle:	typing	
Past participle:	typed	

Present	*Active*	*Passive*
simple	(he) types	is typed
continuous	is typing	is being typed

Past		
simple	typed	was typed
continuous	was typing	was being typed

Past perfect		
simple	has typed	has been typed
continuous	has been typing	

Pluperfect		
simple	had typed	had been typed
continuous	had been typing	

Future		
simple	will type	will be typed
continuous	will be typing	

Future perfect		
simple	will have typed	will have been typed
continuous	will have been typing	

Conditional present		
simple	would type	would be typed
continuous	would be typing	

Conditional perfect		
simple	would have typed	would have been typed
continuous	would have been typing	

Note: Most English verbs take the -ed ending in the past. Some, however, about 200 in number, have changed forms in the past which have to be learnt:

to tell:	told
to be:	was
to sing:	sang

These verbs are called irregular. When in doubt check your dictionary.

Agreement

Remember that the subject and its verb *must* agree at all times. A singular subject must have a singular verb:

She types the letter.

A plural subject takes a plural verb:

They sort the post.

In some colloquial speech the agreement is disregarded – we was there – such freedom is not permitted in the written word!

Assignments on verbs

1 Pick out the subjects and finite verbs in the following sentences:

(a) The good news spread quickly.

(b) The clerks will be informed if necessary by the office manager.

(c) The parcel was posted before 5 pm.

(d) Just before noon the factory whistle is sounded.

(e) 'In spite of competition the sales target has been reached.'

(f) 'The spare parts will arrive by tomorrow afternoon.'

2 Say whether the verbs you have identified in the above sentences are active or passive.

3 To check your mastery of irregular verbs, write out the tenses of the following:

to arise:	1st person singular past simple active
to bear;	(= to carry) 3rd person singular feminine future perfect simple active
to flee:	3rd person plural perfect simple active
to grind:	(= make into powder) 3rd person singular past perfect simple passive
to lend:	2nd person plural past perfect continuous active
to mow:	1st person singular conditional present simple active
to pay:	3rd person feminine singular past continuous active
to ride:	3rd person plural future continuous active
to shear:	3rd person singular impersonal (it) past perfect simple passive

What is a sentence?
Golden rule checklist

The following golden rules will enable you to check if the sentence is grammatically correct:

1 Subject

All sentences must have a subject.

(But remember, sometimes it may be acceptably left out as understood: (You) Duck! (You) Leave!

2 Verb

All sentences must contain a verb which satisfies the following three requirements:

Number:

It must be either singular or plural

Person:

It must be first, second or third:

Singular			Plural		
1st	2nd	3rd	1st	2nd	3rd
I	you	he	we	you	they
		she			
		it			

Tense

It must be in a tense – present, past, future etc.

Subjects must agree in number and person with their verbs.

Grammatically correct sentences *may* include additional word groups, but they *must* have a subject and verb.

Specialist word: finite

When a verb in a sentence meets the above three requirements of number, person and tense, it is said to be a **finite** verb. All grammatically correct sentences must possess a finite verb.

He only arrived yesterday!

A case study

Harry, Jim, Sue and Nicky all work as junior clerks in the office administration department in the head office of Electrix Motors Ltd. The company manufactures a wide range of electrically powered motors for use in industry. At present, all four are sitting round a table in the staff restaurant having their mid-morning coffee break.

Harry: What do you make of the new feller then?

Sue: What new fellow do you mean?

Harry: You know, the stuck-up blond-haired feller who's just joined us in the office!

Nicky: Oh, him! *I* think he's rather dishy, actually! Wears his hair short, well-dressed, blue eyes…

Harry: Yeah, that's the one! Right stuck up, if you ask me!

Jim: Well, what's he done to you, Harry? He only arrived yesterday!

Harry: Fancies himself, that one! There I was, doing some collating for Mr Jenkins – a batch of sales instructions for the reps – I had all the sets of pages set out in numerical order. Anyway, he just walked by me and said he knew of an easier way to do it! I mean, I don't suppose he knows where the main entrance is yet! Telling me how to do my job!

Sue: I'm sure he wasn't, Harry. Perhaps he *did* know a better way, though. And even if he did, perhaps he was, you know, just trying to be friendly, to get to know you…

Harry: Well, he's going a funny way about it.

Nicky: Who has he been assigned to?

Harry: Miss Fox, I think. She'll soon sort him out, mark my words!

Jim: Well, I had a brief word with him yesterday afternoon – just after he had come out of Miss Fox's office. Didn't seem a bad sort to me. Bit sure of himself, perhaps. Still, it's bound to take him a while to fit in – find his way about.

Nicky: Does he play badminton by any chance? Perhaps I should see if he wants to join the Sports Club?

Sue: Well, I know someone he's made a hit with. And I reckon that someone will soon be having a spot of trouble with some collating, if I know that someone!

Nicky: Oh, be quiet, Sue. I'm only, well, just thinking he might be glad to join the badminton group, just to make a few friends here.

Harry: Well, if that doesn't beat all! She'll probably be offering him my place in the team by next week.

Jim: Well, Nicky, here's your chance to ask him. He's just coming this way with a cup of coffee in his hand.

Sue: Go on, Jim, ask him to join us. I'm sure Harry's *dying* to get better acquainted.

Jim: No sooner asked than done... Hello, Peter, isn't it? Come and join us. This is Sue French, Nicky Wilson, Harry Jackson, and I'm Jim Thomas – we met briefly yesterday afternoon...

Assignments

Discussion topics

1 Do you think Harry's initial response to Peter is justified?

2 How would you describe Nicky's attitude to Peter? Is she likely to make a sound judgment about Peter?

3 What would you say to Peter if you were Miss Fox, telling him about starting to work in the office administration department?

Written assignments

1 Carry on writing the dialogue of the meeting of Peter with his new colleagues, until they go back to the office. Assume that Peter is anxious to start off on the right foot with the junior clerks.

2 Write an essay outlining the sort of problems someone is likely to encounter when joining a new group of fellow-students or work-mates. Suggest how such problems might best be overcome.

You *can* spell!

Prefixes

The good news about prefixes is that they do not affect the spelling of the base word!

necessary: un/necessary   act: inter/act
appear: dis/appear   form: trans/form

Prefixes are used in English to change or modify the base word. Most prefixes come originally from Greek or Latin, though some stem from the Germanic languages and are easier to recognise:

al(l) = all: altogether   mis = not: misunderstand

The following prefixes are some of the most commonly occurring in English. Learn carefully what they mean (but remember that the explanations below are only indications of meaning) and check the way they are spelled. In this way you will find it much easier to guess the meanings of unfamiliar words and also increase your spelling power! Where alternatives are given, this is due to the changes which occur when the root prefix is used with different base words:

<u>im</u>possible   <u>in</u>digestible   <u>ir</u>regular

a, ac, ad:	to, towards, in addition
ab:	off, away from
ambi:	of both kinds
ante:	before, in front of
anti:	against
arch:	chief, foremost
bi, bin:	of two
com, con, cor:	with, together
contra:	against
dis:	away from, not
dis, duo:	of two
e, ex:	out of, away from
geo:	of the earth
im, in, ir:	not, into
inter:	among
intra:	within
intro:	towards, in, into
mal:	bad

mis:	not, wrongly, badly
mono:	one, single
non, not:	not
ob, oc:	in the way of
per:	through
phil:	lover of
photo:	of light
poly:	many
post:	after
pro:	for, on behalf of
psycho:	of the mind, soul, spirit
se:	apart, without
semi:	half
sub:	under, below
super:	above, over
theo:	of gods
trans:	across, through
tri:	of three
un:	not
uni:	of one

Examples

The following examples show how prefixes combine with base words to change or provide meanings:

adhesion, adjudicate, amphibious, antenatal, antiseptic, bicycle, binary, contradict, disagree, duologue, exit, geography, geometry, intravenous, interdependent, introduce, misinform, maladjusted, monorail, nonentity, obliterate, perambulate, philosopher, philatelist, photograph, polygamy, protect, postdate, postnatal, psychology, semi-circle, superintendent, submarine, theology, transcribe, tricycle, unmindful, university.

Now check the meanings of all the above words you have not met before. Consult your dictionary for their origins and meanings and enter them in your vocabulary notebook.

Prefix spelling trap

Take special care to learn the pronunciation and spelling of: phil, photo and psycho, so you do not fall into the trap!

How to use a dictionary 2

The following explains how the entry for a word may be made up in *The Concise Oxford Dictionary*. Many other dictionaries adopt similar procedures:

Accepted spelling(s)

Against each entry is given the accepted spelling (or spellings) of the word:

centre   center
show (arch) shew (arch = archaic = no longer used)

Note that some words may be spelled in alternative but equally acceptable ways.

Pronunciation

The accepted way in which the word is pronounced is also supplied. To help with pronunciation, the word is shown in a phonetic spelling. (Phonetic means 'as the word sounds'.)

co'lour, co'lor (ku ler)
sĕ'cateurs (-erz)

Note that the symbol ˘ stands for a short vowel and – for a long vowel. The symbol ' after a part of the word (the syllable) means that the part immediately before it is given the stress when pronouncing the word:

sĕ'condlў rever'se artĭfi'cial

Parts of speech

Immediately after the entry of a word, an abbreviation is given to show what part of speech it may be used as:

desk, n (n noun)
young, a & n (a adjective)

Note that some words may act as different parts of speech depending how they are used.
Other abbreviations include:

vt   verb transitive
adv   adverb
pron   pronoun   etc

The different parts of speech will be explained and illustrated in various units throughout the book. You have already met and mastered the basics of the noun and verb. You will discover how helpful it can be to be able to recognise a part of speech at work in a sentence. It will enable you, for example, to distinguish easily between stationary and stationery, principle and principal etc, and therefore to know for sure how to spell the one you want!

Colloquial words

If a word is used informally – colloquially – then the abbreviation colloq is used after its entry:

bike n & vi (colloq)

If you are not sure, especially in a piece of formal writing, whether a word you wish to use is colloquial, then check your dictionary!

Forming the plural

Most plurals in English are formed by adding s to the singular form, but where the plural is formed in a markedly different way, it is shown in the entry:

appendix n (pl ~ices or ~ixes)

Note that here either form is acceptable.

aquarium (pl ~ums or ~a)
cherub (pl ~s or ~im)

More than one meaning

Sometimes a word may be capable of possessing more than one meaning, depending on the sense in which it is used:

dictator 1 Absolute ruler...2 One who dictates for transcription

In such instances, many dictionaries will supply the various meanings which the word may possess and provide examples for their use.

Specially coined words

Some words have found – and are still finding – their way into the English language as a result of popular use. Many words, now respectable, began their lives as slang. Others record the names of inventors or popularisers:

wellingtons mackintosh cardigan hoover (and perhaps, soon, kleenex)

Sometimes a famous doctor or inventor's name may be given to a new discovery:

Addison's disease: T Addison discoverer d 1860

Compound words

Some words may be used when linked to others by a hyphen to form a new word. Such new words are called 'compound words' and are often included in check-lists in word entries:

prairie-chicken   end-product

Such compound forms may be indicated after the symbol ~ which indicates the basic entry word:

master   ~ -at-arms
hand   ~-me-down

In this way, the dictionary helps you to increase your word power by providing examples of how compound words may be formed or how the base entry word may be used in popular expressions or sayings.

Helpful extras

In addition to providing a very extensive list of words in alphabetical order, many dictionaries include further tables of useful information, such as abbreviations commonly in use:

RSPCA   BSc   OHMS   AA

Many also provide conversion tables for imperial and metric measures and may have additional 'late entries' of words new to English. Make sure you explore your dictionary and discover *all* the help it has to offer you.

Word origins

Etymology is a word which means 'the original root language of the word'. For example, the word photograph is made up of two Greek words, 'photo' which means light, and 'graph' which means writing. Thus a photograph is, at its simplest, writing with light. The original language of a word from which the English word derives is indicated by an abbreviation. For example:

OS   Old Saxon
ME   Middle English
L   Latin
Gk   Greek
F   French

A list of such abbreviations is usually given in a dictionary for reference.

Spelling dictionaries

One of the most frequent reasons for using a dictionary is to check on the accepted spelling of a word. Now this is not difficult, *if* you already have a shrewd idea of how the word should be spelt and particularly how it begins. Consider, however, the plight of the would-be speller who has not an inkling that the word 'psychologist' begins with a silent p. He would waste a lot of time checking through the s entries beginning 'si-'.

In such instances, the normal dictionary may not be much help. Nowadays, however, help is available in the form of spellers' dictionaries. Such dictionaries have entries, not in an alphabetical order, but in a simple phonetic spelling order, as the example below shows. As you will see, after the phonetic entry (or entry variations) the correct English spelling of the word is given.

diskwiet	disquiet
diskwolification	disqualification
diskwolify	disqualify

If you know spelling to be one of *your* weak points, such a spellers' dictionary would prove an extremely wise investment.

It's up to you!

Having mastered the meaning of the various explanations which follow each dictionary entry, the key to increased powers of expression is now yours! All you need is the will to use your dictionary – whenever in doubt. So now, it really is up to you.

Dictionary assignments

1 Find out what the following dictionary abbreviations stand for:

arch c cl colloq dial E etym f fig ON phr
pl pp pref pron ref sing sl sp suf t unkn wd

2 Find out how the following place-names are pronounced. You will find a Dictionary of Pronunciation in the reference section of your library:

Amiens Arkansas Bayeux Cherbourg Hertford
Munich Rouen Teignmouth

3 Find out how the following proper names are pronounced:

Aphrodite Botticelli Chopin Pepys Van Gogh
Goethe Nobel

4 Look up the following words in your dictionary and write down what they mean and the language they come from:

algebra kayak piano piccanniny whisky syrup
assassin nitwit

5 Find out what the following words and expressions mean and where they come from:

carpet-bagger bunkum fellah marathon snooker
no room to swing a cat

6 Find out what the following prefixes stand for:

hyper per tele pre an

7 Find out the imperial or metric equivalents of the following:

1 mile (in kilometres)
1 gallon (in litres)
1 kilogram (in pounds)
1 hectare (in acres)
1 stone (in kilograms)

Punctuation

The comma

No substitute for full-stops

The first point to make about using the comma in written English is that many writers use it much too frequently. Certainly it is no substitute for the full-stop and care should always be taken to ensure that commas have not crept in and ousted full-stops from their rightful place:

'I shall be ready at four o'clock.

When would you like to collect me?'

Commas can be vital to meaning

There are times when the absence of a comma completely changes the meaning of a statement:

'Are you feeling any better?'
'No worse!'
'Are you feeling any better?'
'No, worse!'

Breathing and sense pauses

One of the chief uses of the comma is to provide the reader or writer of English with a breathing space or an opportunity to absorb what he has just read:

The report which Jim was writing was proving hard work, and he envied his office colleagues, already on their way home in the evening sun.

The comma before 'and he envied...' could be left out, but including it helps the reader to pause and to contrast John's hard work with his envy for his more fortunate colleagues.

It is also worth pointing out that, though the word 'and' is not usually preceded by a comma, sometimes it may be – especially when it helps to make the sentence easier to understand.

Dividing items in a list

Another important use of the comma is to divide single words or word groups which are being listed in a sentence:

The dictating machine was new, shiny, elegant and just what he wanted!
Jenny checked the list of office supplies she had been asked to order. She needed a printer ribbon, envelopes, stamps and sticky labels.

Note that in both the above sentences no comma is needed before the 'and' which introduces the last item in the list.

Sometimes the word groups making up the list may each include quite a number of individual words:

Typing several letters, taking dictation from Mr Harris, attending meetings to take minutes, answering the telephone and looking after visitors were all part of Jenny's busy day.

Again, no comma precedes the 'and' introducing the last item in the list.

Separating insertions from main ideas

Another use of the comma is to separate the main idea of a sentence and a secondary idea which has been inserted between, for example, a subject and its verb:

The salesman, who was anxious to make a sale, greeted the chief buyer eagerly.

Here, the main idea is,

The salesman greeted the chief buyer eagerly.

'who was anxious to make a sale' has been put in after the subject to tell us more about his state of mind.

Conclusion: pause providers and dividers

Commas may be regarded basically as pause providers and dividers; but remember this golden rule:

If the idea following the comma is complete in itself and can stand by itself, the comma should almost certainly be a full-stop!

Punctuation assignments

Insert commas correctly in the following sentences:

1 In his pocket the junior clerk had a penknife two postage stamps a piece of string four brown rubber bands and a keyring.

2 'Excuse me could you tell me if Mr Brown has left for Dover or if he is still in the office?'

3 'Ask Mr Jones the chief buyer and he will explain the procedure to you.'

4 The secretary who had left a confidential memorandum on her desk for all to read was reprimanded by her principal.

5 Collecting the mail opening it sorting it into piles for each section and delivering each pile were Jane's first task each morning.

6 'Anyway if he does come I shall make every effort to see him although I can't promise as I have a very busy morning in front of me.'

Boost your word bank!

Each one of us has an existing bank or stock of words – our active vocabulary – with which we feel at home and comfortable. For a lucky few, this range of words and expressions may already be very large, in which case they will have an edge over others by being able to select the word which is precisely right, technically accurate or particularly appropriate. Many more people, however, have a limited vocabulary. Such people settle too frequently for a dull and tired range of over-used and under-communicating words:

'Go to the disco last night?'
'Yeah.'
'Wha'dyou think of it?'
'Great, wasn't it!'
'Yeah, great!'
'Your Tony there?'
'No, I chucked 'im last week, didn't I!'

Although a conversation of sorts is taking place and 'messages' are being conveyed, neither speaker has really communicated very much at all to the other – beyond the fact that both liked the disco and one has stopped going out with her boyfriend. Moreover, such an empty conversation is unlikely to hold the interest of either speaker for very long, and neither is likely to be very successful in communicating to the other how she really feels – about the disco or the boyfriend. Both simply lack the vocabulary or word power to make what they are saying colourful, interesting or stimulating!

Golden Rules

Fortunately, it *is* possible for every student of communication to improve his or her vocabulary both widely and rapidly! All that is needed is a method and some willpower! If you set out to follow the golden rules below, you, your teacher and those around you will soon notice a striking improvement in your ability to express yourself more accurately and more vividly:

1 Obtain a good pocket dictionary.

2 Invest in a small but stout vocabulary pocket notebook. Make sure you always have it by you to jot down *every word or expression* you meet which is unfamiliar.

3 Check the spelling of printed words carefully. If you meet a strange word in print, make sure you copy it correctly into your vocabulary book.

4 Make a 'best attempt' at spelling words you meet as 'the spoken word'.
Then when you come to check them in the dictionary, make sure you have them spelled correctly.

5 In your next spare moment, check your new words in your dictionary.
Either between classes or at home, make a point of copying out the meanings of your fresh 'catch' of new words into your vocabulary book.
It is often very helpful when meeting strange words in print to write down the sentences in which they occur, so that you have models.

6 At regular intervals, check through the recent 'finds' in your vocabulary book.
In this way you will soon come to remember firmly the meaning of each new word.

7 At the earliest opportunity *use* the new words you have acquired.
Whenever you can, try to introduce one of your new words into your conversation or into a piece of writing. Don't feel nervous about such practice – especially not in the classroom.

8 Enlarge your range of reading material.
Every large bookseller and newsagent today holds a stock of general interest and specialised hobby magazines and newspapers. Similarly, your college and local public library will carry a wide range of magazines and periodicals as well as books.

Make it a habit to read something of interest and pleasure *every day*! Most of us broaden our vocabulary range simply by reading and by meeting new words a number of times until we 'absorb' their meaning.

9 When you speak or write, never settle for the lazy man's word.
Rather, seek to use an expressive word and avoid flat, empty words like: get, got, nice, great, kind of, really, a lot, ever so, etc.

10 Most important, take a pride in how you speak or write. After all, this is the way in which you will convey to others 'the real you', so why let yourself down by settling for less than the best!

The impact of IT upon the business world

While the development of the microprocessor can be traced back over the past 200 years, the pace of its research and development quickened in the 25 years between 1945 and 1970. As we have already seen, the pressure upon electronics designers to evolve a compact computer stemmed largely from the size and expense of mainframe computers – only the larger national and multinational companies could afford them.

During the same period, consumer mass-markets were re-established, clamouring after such goods as washing-machines, hi-fi equipment, micro-ovens, central heating, colour television sets and a host of what salesmen call 'consumer durables' – those articles which make life easier, less 'hassle', more enjoyable and labour-saving. When the Intel Corporation of the United States introduced the first commercially available microprocessor or silicon chip in 1971, they started an industrial and commercial revolution which quickly swept around the globe and soon embraced every sector of industry, commerce and public service.

The revolutionary design features of the microprocessor which so attracted equipment and machine manufacturers, as well as the ultimate end-users of the electronics, were:

- miniscule dimensions – about as thick as a ring-binder's cover and the size of a postage stamp.

- reliability – as it possessed no moving parts there was virtually nothing to break down or go wrong in its make-up.

- cost – what had previously cost thousands of pounds or US dollars to purchase in terms of computing capacity could be acquired for the price of pub-lunch!

As a result, manufacturers could well afford to introduce its sophisticated calculating and decision-making features into a host of goods without increasing manufacturing costs significantly. For example, pocket calculators soon became wafer-thin and able to perform the most complex calculations while holding data in a memory bank. Similarly, such calculators were also given features like holding a range of formulae and mathematical information which the expert user could draw upon simply by reaching into his inside jacket pocket or into her handbag!

During the 1970s, manufacturers rushed to bring to the market a wide range of appliances and equipment, which were the result of the introduction of the microprocessor, as the table opposite illustrates.

Note that the impact of the microprocessor was not restricted to the retail or consumer market. It found its way just as speedily into the aeronautics industry, agriculture, mining and general manufacturing.

So far, in examining the impact of IT upon the business world, we have tended to concentrate upon the hardware – the boxes of electronics, the keyboards and VDUs (Visual Display Units) which go to make up a computer.

Yet without the equally important 'software', the hardware would be about as useful as a broken-down washing machine on a rubbish tip! Indeed it is the software – the comprehensive set of instructions recorded either permanently into the computer's memory, or on to 'floppy' or 'hard' disks which the computer can access, which enables it to perform the host of jobs that engineers and software designers have created for it. The information which, for example, converts the computer into a word processor for displaying text on its screen for one assignment, or a spreadsheet calculations table for another, illustrates how versatile a computer can be, depending on the kind of software package which is being used to activate it.

We shall be examining software in more detail in a later Unit. For the moment, however, it is important to concentrate upon an overview of how and why IT affected industry and commerce.

The advent of the computer during the past 20–30 years brought about one thing in particular – change! Sometimes the pace of this change was so rapid that managers and workforces scarcely had time to digest one aspect of technological change before another arrived to be adopted. Some of the principal changes brought about by the arrival of IT upon the business scene are listed opposite.

Industrial and commercial applications of IT chart

Primary sector Industry	IT applications
Mining	control of underground coal cutting, grading and transportation equipment.
Agriculture	control of animal feeding equipment – frequencies and amounts
	record-keeping – cropspraying, milk yields, calving, etc.
Fisheries	deep sea trawler navigation equipment, shoal finding equipment
Power	systems control in monitoring complex, power demand forecasting, nuclear reactor inspection via remote control

Secondary sector Industry	
Motor vehicle manufacturing	robotics in building and paint-spraying processes
	use of computers in designing parts and products
General assembly manufacturing	use of computer-driven lathes, milling machines to manufacture in pre-set patterns and processes
	electronic testing of finished products to improve quality control and to minimise loss of profits via excessive waste, etc.
	development of most economic and cost-effective working processes via work-study analyses

Tertiary sector Industry	
General distribution	use of computers to structure most cost effective itinerary for delivering goods to customers
Retailing	installation of point-of-sale computerised cash-out tills which automatically total goods sold by product and re-order direct from company warehouse
	communication from head office to chainstore branches of changes in individual product prices
Banking	introduction of 'cashpoint' dispensers which check a customer's credit-worthiness instantly before issuing cash required
	home banking – making adjustments to one's bank account via home tv screen and computer attachment.
Information services	introduction of viewdata services which provide directories of data pages and the opportunity to, for example, send for a holiday brochure and booking form after having scanned a tv screen page of information broadcast for a travel agency
Solicitors, doctors' practices, accountants' offices	use of databases to store and access information about clients or patients and to keep accounts of fees due or patients seen for NHS payments, etc

Changes that came in the wake of IT

- Experienced as well as junior staff had to learn a whole new set of skills and specialisms – for example, word processing or computerised accounts procedures.

- Some people's jobs disappeared as a result of IT being introduced into factories and offices; other people were able to secure some of the new jobs which IT created, such as computer programmer or systems analyst.

- The structures of organisations changed and patterns of work altered radically as IT became more widely employed. For instance, the way in which an entire accounts department functioned changed with the introduction of computers, since the recording of a sales transaction could automatically add an invoiced sum to an account customer's monthly statement without a series of tasks having to be carried out manually and laboriously. Computers can save duplication of work and tedious attention to detail.

- Whole production processes in factories can be carried out by computers which control manufacturing equipment.

- The function of offices as information processing centres was transformed by the introduction of electronic equipment which excelled at information processing. The work of clerks, secretaries and office managers became less preoccupied with dull tasks like typing the third draft of a complex report (the word-processing package took the drudgery out of such jobs) and more involved in providing better support with the aid of more accurate information which could be supplied far quicker.

Westbrook Stores and gift shop go computer!

A case study

Harry and Rita Johnson had been 'open all hours' ever since they bought their first general stores shop in Westbrook some 20 years ago. Westbrook had always been a busy village which had gradually been joined on to the much larger neighbouring town of Northwood as a result of a string of expensive housing developments, constructed since the war.

About ten years ago, as a result of the increasing population of Westbrook, a commercial property developer built a precinct of six shops with flats over the top of each to serve the thriving community. Harry and Rita saw this development as a 'once and for all' opportunity to expand their business and to protect all their hard-won custom from competition. So they obtained a large mortgage and moved into one of the shops in the middle of the precinct. Within a week, a bold and eye-catching fascia was erected over the shop announcing that 'Westbrook Stores' had arrived!

In the years that followed, Harry and Rita worked really hard to develop the range of stock they held and to meet the changing needs of the local populace, by ploughing most of their profit back into the business.

Harry had started out principally as a general grocer and had expanded into frozen foods with the advent of freezers, and into the more exotic packed shellfish and smoked fish which the affluent wives of local professionals bought for suppers and dinner parties. By the same token, of recent years his tins of processed peas had to vie for shelf space with tinned mangoes and beansprouts.

About two years ago Harry seized upon an opportunity to take over a newsagent's rounds and so started to sell newspapers and magazines. Naturally his need for assistance became urgent and he appointed two young assistants to help out and reorganised his shop's display and serving areas.

Also, Westbrook Stores began to serve customers farther afield when Harry took on a third assistant, Ben Drayton, who drove the shop's Ford Transit and spent his time delivering made up orders of groceries to account customers who lived in the adjacent rural villages and who found it more convenient to have groceries delivered – especially where both husband and wife worked. Many such deliveries included weekly standing orders for items such as eggs, butter, flour, sugar, cereals and so on.

A different type of clientèle were the housewives and pensioners who lived nearer to Westbrook Stores and came in regularly for a social chat as much as for purchases. Being a shrewd small business man, Harry had set up some years ago a Christmas Club for such customers to help them to save up for the luxuries and special groceries and confectioneries which otherwise they might not have afforded. Each week, therefore, some 85 customers came in to make a payment into their Christmas Club accounts which Harry managed, not entirely out of an annual sense of goodwill but because he hoped that at least some of the money given out at Yuletide might be spent on his Christmas fare!

Eighteen months ago a shop next to Westbrook Stores was put up for sale and this time it was Rita who saw a good business opportunity to be had. She pestered Harry unmercifully until at last he gave in and ordered a longer fascia board to span the two shops – Westbrook Stores and Gift Shop! Rita 'went to town' and had soon built up a handsome stock of ornaments, scarves and belts, jewellery, toys and fancy goods. Inevitably, Harry needed to appoint a fourth assistant to help Rita, who had a knack of selling to ladies in particular who only came in to her shop to look round.

While to Harry and Rita's many customers they seemed to be a model of successful retailers, behind the scenes problems were growing weekly. The expanded stock had filled every conceivable corner of the Stores shop and precious time was wasted hunting for goods which Harry vaguely remembered had been put into stock some time ago.

Harry and Rita's social life was virtually non-existent since they had to spend so many evenings updating and pricing account customers' monthly statements and relating invoices to Ben's delivery notes. Harry found himself throwing away damaged and old stock that really could have and should have been sold months earlier.

Increasingly, Harry found himself locked away in his office doing the paperwork side of the business which he had never really liked – accounts, payroll, reconciling his own purchases with the invoices and accounts he received, keeping an eye on the newspaper delivery records and so on.

Harry and Rita's only child, Frances, had spent many of her formative years playing with soap boxes, cartons and the various forms of packaging beloved of retail distributors and, as she had not long been enrolled on a business course at the College of Technology in Northwood she felt she was in a good position to offer Harry and Rita some well-meant advice. After supper one evening she dropped casually into the conversation the following:

'Dad – Mum, you know, I've been thinking. You really ought to look into what these microcomputers can do nowadays to help people running small businesses like yours. We had a lesson today which showed us how an integrated accounts package works and a spread sheet – they're really great for taking all the hard work out of keeping financial and number records! You could also keep all sorts of records on file and find them in a trice!'

'Hm, that's as may be,' grunted Harry, who was a man rather set in his ways, for all his retailing success. 'But what happens if you lose the lot in the computer, if it won't cough it up when you want the information? Seems a bit risky to me, having all that data locked up in the innards of some piece of electronic gadgetry! Anyway, I'll tell you what, all the family business will come your way some day, so it's time you made a contribution to it. You do some proper finding out – costs of a computer set-up, what in actual, factual detail a computer could do to help our two shops, and if I think it's worth while, I just might get one! And if they're as time-saving as you say they are, then it won't take up too much of your spare time to help me get the hang of it!'

Frances beamed, partly because she felt she had at last made a real contribution to the future of the family business, and partly because she was already envisaging the microcomputer helping her with her College homework!

Assignment

As Frances Johnson (her role could be undertaken by individual students or small student groups) carry out the careful research which Harry asked for and find out in what ways a microcomputer with appropriate software packages could help to make the administration of Westbrook Stores and Gift shop quicker and easier to undertake.

As part of this assignment, find out what computers are currently on the market which would meet Harry and Rita's needs (including the costs of appropriate software) and include these details and the description of the most suitable computer – in your view – in a written report for Harry and Rita.

You should include any helpful brochures or leaflets you acquire during your research.

When you have completed your report, compare it with others produced by your group's students and see what are the most useful features discovered.

Activities and assignments

1 List the six stages in the Sender–Receiver communication process.

2 Write down the various 'languages' in which people communicate.

3 Outline the points which a the Sender and b the Receiver should bear in mind when they are exchanging a message. You should write about 130 words on each.

4 What differences and additions has IT brought about in the third 'Routes' Stage of the communication process?

5 Explain what meaning is present in each of the following prefixes:

monorail	transport
tricycle	superstructure
subway	antenatal
contradict	exit
geography	theology

6 Explain briefly what is meant by:

a common noun
a proper noun
a collective noun

Provide three examples of each.

7 Explain what is meant by the term 'finite verb'.
Compose two sentences and then underline the finite verb in each.

8 Compose a sentence with an active verb and another sentence with a passive verb. Underline the verb in each case.

9 Compose a sentence for each of the following verb tenses:

    a conditional simple active
    b future continuous active
    c past perfect simple passive
    d present continuous passive

10 Give three instances when a comma should be used in sentences.

11 Spell the following words by completing the letters which have been left out. To help you, each dash stands for an omitted letter:

c − − ling   (top of a room)
de − − − ve   (to mislead)
− − owl − − − e   (wisdom)
bur − − −   (office)
a − − o − − − dation   (housing)
emb − − − − − − ed   (shy, awkward)
i − − − − − − te   (move in to a country)
− − − − − t − list   (one who collects stamps)
t − − − l − gy   (study of religion)
int − − − − pt   (break into a conversation)

12 Write a short story about the experiences of a teenage boy or girl starting a new job.
Before you start your story, find out about the kind of job you will be using in your story. It will make the details true to life.

13 Make your notes first, and then describe to your group your experiences in any part-time job you have had. Try to include any unusual, unexpected or humorous occurrences.

14 Form a number of small groups. Imagine you work in the personnel department of a large company. As the company regularly takes on school-leavers, it has been decided to produce a booklet for each new employee. It will provide information about the firm and offer advice. As a group, compose the page of the booklet which offers hints on how to be a good communicator. When each group has composed its version, exchange them and decide which one is most effective and why.

15 (*a*) In groups of 3–4 students review the 'industrial and commercial applications of IT' chart on page 33 and see how many additional uses of microprocessors and computers you can add to the list in about ten to fifteen minutes. Then write down what you consider the main changes in work, leisure and social habits and practices which have resulted from the introduction of IT applications in general.

(*b*) First carry out your research and then write an article of about 350 words which explains how the introduction of IT into both the sales and administration procedures of supermarkets has changed the ways in which they operate. Include in your article some examples of the benefits which customers now enjoy as a result.

(*c*) In groups of 2–3 students discuss the impact of the changes which the introduction of IT has brought about in our daily lives and make a checklist of what problems and difficulties you consider may justifiably be put down to IT developments.
For example, is there a danger of a massive computer controlling people's lives, like a Big Brother?
Have employees ever lost their jobs because of the introduction of computers?
Will a computer-based society in the near future lead to people having less direct, face-to-face personal contact with each other?

Boost your spelling power!

Learn these key words by heart

Remember, an asterisk after a word indicates that it is very commonly misspelled:

accommodate* v	
believed* v	(belief n)
certain* adj	(certainty n)
decision* n	(decide v)
embarrassed v	(embarrassment n)
foreign adj	(foreigner n)
guard* n v	(guardian n)
height* n	(high adj)
immigrate v	(immigration n)
liaison n	(liaise v)

Check, in your dictionary, the meaning of any word you do not know and enter it in your vocabulary book.

Unit 3

Business organisations

Organisations come in many shapes and sizes, from the one-man street trader selling fresh fruit or novelty goods to the vast multi-national companies spread throughout many parts of the world.

(A)

The shape of an organisation depends of course on what it does, and so it is necessary to become familiar with the three basic sectors of business activity.

The primary sector

(B) The primary sector, or first sector, *obtains* the raw materials which man turns into the millions of products and articles used in daily life.

Examples of such industrial undertakings include:

mining   fishing   quarrying
oil extraction   forestry   agriculture

The secondary sector

Once the raw materials have been mined or harvested, they are taken to factories, where they are made into the items the public demands. Thus the secondary sector *makes* goods.

Some manufacturing industries are called 'heavy' and others 'light'. Heavy industries build the large products or machines needed by our society. Shipbuilders, for example, construct the huge tankers needed to transport oil around the world, and heavy engineering companies build the generators used in power-stations or the bulky furnaces at the heart of a steelworks.

(C) At the other end of the scale are the light industries which work with fine components, such as the quartz watch industry, or the electronic microprocessor industry.

In some manufacturing processes, articles are made under one roof, from raw material to finished product. Other manufacturers make 'semi-finished' goods such as sheets of steel, ready to be made into cutlery or car bodies.

Yet other processes concentrate on the complicated assembly of pre-constructed parts. The motor-car industry, for example, usually buys in finished products – batteries, wheels, tyres, headlamps, etc. – which are assembled into motorcars.

The tertiary sector

The third, or tertiary sector *provides services* to the general public.

Finished products need to be transported to shops and stores – distribution. Then the process of retailing – displaying goods in shop-windows and on counters – takes place. Some shops specialise in selling certain goods – office equipment, electrical appliances or shoes – while others, departmental stores and hypermarkets, stock an extremely wide range of goods. Indeed, the shopping trend now seems to be away from the small shop to the spacious store, with adjacent car-park and a wide choice of brands and products.

In addition to the distribution and retailing operations, the tertiary sector also includes the range of specialist services which offer help, advice or information to the consumer. Such organisations include:

banks, insurance companies, word processing bureaux
employment agencies, solicitors,
estate agents, doctors, plumbers

In the public service field, such services include:

Education   Consumer protection
Welfare services   Public libraries

Inter-dependence

All for one and one for all!

The complex structure of our modern society has resulted in each of the three sectors becoming dependent on the other two. Without the manufacturing and service industries, there would be no outlet for the collected raw materials. The retailer cannot sell what the manufacturer has not made. Neither retailer nor manufacturer can manage without someone to transport produced goods throughout the country. All three sectors rely on banks to secure, transfer and lend money.

Indeed, inter-dependence is the foundation of modern industrial economies – just think for one moment of all the cooperation needed to bring you your morning pint of milk or newspaper, or to produce the smart new shirt or party-dress.

Mastering the meaning

1 Explain in your own words, 'vast multi-national companies'. Line A

2 What type of activity does an organisation in the primary sector pursue? Line B

3 Explain the difference between 'light' and 'heavy' industries.

4 What is a 'component'? Line C

5 Explain the difference between 'semi-finished goods' and 'pre-constructed parts'.

6 What activities are carried on in the 'tertiary' or 'third' sector?

7 Explain why each sector is 'inter-dependent' – relying upon the other two.

Written assignments

1 Select an industry in either the primary, secondary or tertiary sector and find out what it does and how it is run. When you have collected enough information, write an account explaining its activities.

2 Compose an account of your reasons for preferring a career in *one* of the three industrial sectors.

Research and oral assignments

1 In groups, research the business activities of one of the following:

a supermarket; a factory; a bank;
a county hall department; a primary sector enterprise

Make notes of your discoveries and then, as a group, present your findings orally to your general group.

2 Prepare your material and then give a three minute talk to your general group on:

(a) Why communication may break down
(b) Inter-dependence in today's society
(c) How to communicate successfully

What happens when we talk?

Man, alone, has developed the ability to communicate extensively by talking – by transforming the ideas in his mind into a spoken language which can be heard and understood by others. Without human speech, there would have been no evolution of man as we know him today. Yet even now, millions of years after it all began, many problems, misunderstandings and even conflicts stem from people's inability to speak their thoughts clearly or to listen properly.

Human speech results from a complex series of movements of the diaphragm (a kind of bellows under the lungs), vocal chords, soft palate, tongue, teeth, lips and facial muscles. The muscles of the diaphragm cause air to be expelled past the vocal chords, which vibrate. The 'noise' which comes out of the mouth and nose is varied according to the shape of the mouth and throat, and the position of tongue, teeth and lips.

In order to check this process, say the following words, and notice what is happening at the underlined points:

bee tea guard heart open awful yes three
trough jelly catch phew! prime underline

Also, notice what happens in very similar words which are pronounced differently:

nuts nets nits gnats knots newts notes nights

In each of the above words, the sounds are distinguishable because of the different positions of our speech apparatus.

Vowels

Basically, vowel sounds are the 'open' sounds of speech:

happy bomb get pip hut hate boom cheep
pipe note

As you can see, some vowels are long and some are short.

Diphthongs

Diphthongs are rather like vowels, except that they join two vowel-like sounds together:

f<u>ea</u>r   v<u>oi</u>ce   h<u>ou</u>r

Consonants

Some consonants take the form of 'hard' sounds:

<u>g</u>un   <u>k</u>een   <u>t</u>au<u>t</u>   <u>b</u>ang   <u>p</u>ound

while others have a softer sound:

<u>j</u>elly   <u>sh</u>iver   <u>ch</u>ive<u>s</u>

Occasionally in English, we construct words where the sound is intended to imitate the idea:

POW!   SPLAT!   MIOUW!   CLANG!

The effect of the spoken word

Certainly much of the effect which words have upon the listener or reader stems from their sounds, and the impact of the group of sounds which an idea expressed in words may make:

What passing-bells for these who die as cattle?
Only the monstrous anger of the guns.
Only the stuttering rifles' rapid rattle...

These are the opening lines of a very moving poem by a poet of the First World War, Wilfred Owen, called *Anthem for Doomed Youth*. In the second and third lines, Owen brings to our ears the booming sounds of big guns and the staccato effect of many rifles firing at will.

If we contrast the impact of the poetry with the drab emptiness and, indeed, meaninglessness of some utterances,

'Had a good day, dear?'
'Oh, not too bad. Quite nice really. Anyway, no good grumbling!'

we soon realise that two aspects of the spoken word matter very much:

● choosing vivid and interesting words and phrases

● saying the words in a lively and arresting way

If our vocabulary is poor and dull, if the way in which we speak our thoughts is monotonous and flat, then we shall soon begin to bore our listener, who will 'switch off' and let his attention wander to someone or something else more interesting.

Accent and pronunciation

English is almost certainly the richest language in the world in terms of the range of accents and pronunciations used. Yet this very richness is sometimes the source of emotional reactions. Though it is virtually impossible to decide on which accent is 'right' or which 'wrong', some people scorn the accents of those who 'talk posh' or who are 'all lah-di-dah'. Equally, other people may look down on those whose speech they consider 'common' or 'unrefined'. In this way, prejudice where accent is concerned may divide people quite unnecessarily.

However, in the world of business, it *is* important to develop clear, pleasant and attractive habits of speech. Correct grammar is very important too. You are unlikely to make a sale to a customer, for example, if your speech is lazy and ugly:

'Ang on a sec, arl seefi gotta anuvver one in me van.'

This does not mean, however, that you put on an artificial accent – which is immediately detected and which sounds horribly false:

'Aouw, quaite modom, aill just enquiuh if waive any in stock. Whot saize was it?'

Consider the likely effect that the following examples of slurred, distorted and compressed speech are likely to have on the listener:

'Sawright, didnurt – itmeyand!'
'Ai saiy! Lucinda's come a croppah! Haws reahed – gel's fawlen awf!'
'Sreelyokay!'
'Canelpyew?'
'Yorwannitonafone!'
'Sbuddyeretseeyah.'

Delivery and intonation

We naturally employ rhythms in our speech, saying some words or syllables quickly and others more slowly. In this way we are able to emphasise key words. What do you think, for example, would be the likely emphasised words in the following:

'I'm not interested in any excuses, if it happens again, you're fired!'
'Sorry to butt in on you like this, could you possibly lend me your cassette player?'

'If you want my opinion, the whole thing's a complete waste of time!'

Also, the way we make our voice rise and fall helps the words we say to get attention and to stress the most important ones:

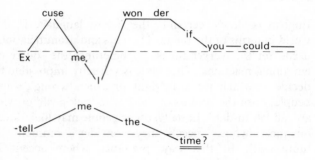

Imagine what a dull and dismal world it would be, if everyone went around, like robots, saying every word at an even pitch and emphasis:

Ex – cuse – me – I – won – der – if – you – could – tell – me – the – time?

It is very important when speaking to use the techniques of delivery and intonation to help your listener(s) to follow the important parts of your speech. To make what you say more lively and interesting, use changes of pace and pitch and pauses.

Speech mannerisms

Whether we realise it or not, we all possess a number of favourite expressions which we over-use in conversation. These mannerisms, which some people use with irritating frequency, include:

you know
you see
er
um
andah
I mean to say
if you see what I mean

Very often the speaker is quite unaware that such irritating speech mannerisms are occurring after almost every phrase. Be careful. Think what you are saying!

Don't become a cliché collector!

The other type of mannerism which creeps into speech is the over-use of stale, tired and quite colourless expressions – clichés as they are called. The following words and phrases belong to this washed-out, worn-out category:

really great; at this moment in time; very nice; not too bad; fair; thing; get/got; fantastic; rough; grotty; it's all happening!; all right; a lot; situation; don't mind if I do; if you like.

How much would the following conversation tell you, for example, about the business studies course?

A   How are you getting on in typing?

B   All right.

A   So am I.

B   Do you still have to look at the keys?

A   Yeah!

B   Yeah, so do I! Miss Jones don't like it though.

A   No, she don't half go on if she catches you.

B   Yeah! Here, what do you make of the new accounts teacher?

A   Yeah! he doesn't half talk funny.

It is unlikely that the two young ladies who might have had such a conversation learned anything beyond: they are both progressing quite well at typewriting but are still experiencing some difficulty with touch typing; the accounts teacher has, apparently, a peculiar accent.

It is only too easy to fall into the trap of becoming a 'cliché collector'. But the effect of trotting out endless, empty clichés is that you appear to have nothing really worth saying – and of course that isn't the case!

Assignments

1   Tape record one of your group doing one of the following spoken activities:

(a)   describing a recent play or film seen on TV or at the cinema
(b)   outlining the process of communication in the six stages between sender and receiver
(c)   persuading the general group of the need to: avoid the smoking habit; or look after one's appearance; or be considerate towards others

Then, in small groups, play back one of the recordings and, as a group, discuss the presentation of the talk and make a checklist of how the 'influencers' (see page 31) were being used and how they help to make the talk effective.

Ten golden rules of speaking

Remember the following Golden Rules of Speaking and you will capture and keep your listeners' attention:
1 *Think* before you speak!
2 Speak clearly and attractively
3 Choose the *best* words — not just the first words that spring to mind
4 Avoid ugly and lazy pronunciation
5 Don't slur or distort words
6 Use variations in pitch and rhythm to achieve emphasis and interest
7 Avoid irritating speech mannerisms
8 Don't rely on clichés
9 Make sure your listener(s) are following what you say
10 Know when to stop to allow others to have *their* say!

2 In groups of three, carry out the following assignment:
Each member takes on, in turn, the role of A or B or C.
A tells B what he enjoys about the various subjects of the course, and also outlines those parts he finds difficult to master. B listens to A, while C observes A and B. After about three minutes, change roles, so that each student acts as speaker, listener and observer.
At the end of the activity, compare notes on how the influencers were at work (see page 31).

3 Individual students should spend some 10–15 minutes preparing notes on one of the following:

What I do in my spare time
My favourite pop group
My kind of book
What I would do with £500
My long-term ambition
Where I would like to live

Students should then pair off. In turns, each student should give his account to the other for about 3–5 minutes. Then the listener should tell the speaker what parts of the account he thought most interesting and most effectively told. After both accounts have been given, each pair should jointly draw up a checklist of the ways which each had found to make the account effective.

4 In small groups spend 5–10 minutes discussing one of the following topics:

How is life at work likely to change in the next 10–20 years?
How far have women really become liberated during the past 10 years? Is there still some way to go?
Has the role of the man in work and at home changed significantly in recent years?
To what extent is education after the age of 11 an adequate preparation for finding a satisfactory career? What changes could you suggest to make the process more effective?
What qualities are important in an efficient office worker?

Each student should make notes of the main points of the discussion as it proceeds.

Either one spokesman reports the main points of the group's discussion to the general student group,
or each student writes a short account of the main points of the discussion, and these are exchanged around the groups of other students for comparison.

Using the spoken word effectively

Using the spoken word effectively requires just as much practice and effort as the techniques of good writing. Though the skills of speaking take time to learn, it should be borne in mind that millions of workers in shops, offices and factories spend as much as three-quarters of the working day using only the spoken word as the medium of communication; while some people scarcely ever use the written word at all. Yet many people for whom accurate, precise or persuasive speaking is an essential tool of the job spend little or no time in trying to develop their speaking skills. The diagram on page 42 shows those aspects of the spoken word which will influence its effectiveness. Consider each 'influencer' in detail and, in discussion, try to decide what bearing each has on speaking effectively and listening successfully. The notes which follow will help you to focus your attention on some of the main factors:

Accent Nowadays, the fact that someone has a regional accent matters much less than it did thirty years ago. The impact of television in our homes has meant we listen to a wider range of regional and international English accents. Also, many more people move away from home to find work. But is there a problem if people use dialect words frequently?

Pronunciation How much does clear pronunciation matter? What is the effect of someone using lazy habits of speech or talking artificially 'posh'?

Pitch Have you ever come across someone who talks in a flat, deliberate monotone? If speech is to be interesting, there must be higher and lower 'pitches'. For example, how do people convey that they have come to the end of an utterance?

Emphasis How are key words emphasised?

Intonation Similarly, what would be the effect of speaking at a set pace, where every word was spoken at the same speed? Try it and see!

Vocabulary Not only is it important to select words which are appropriate in a given situation (when, for instance, would it be wrong to use slang or colloquial expressions?) but it is also important to

Tone, style decide when to speak firmly or gently, with determination or soothingly.

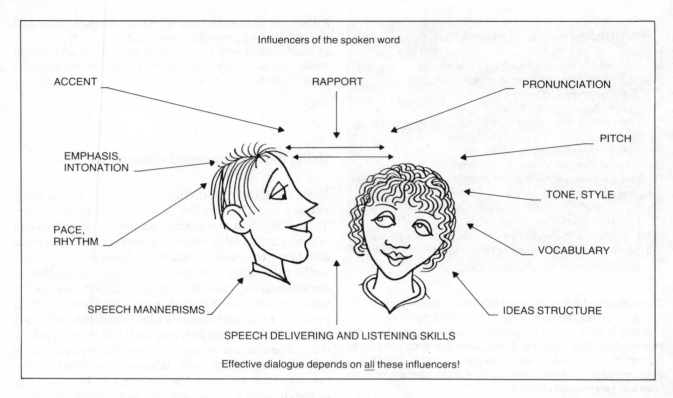

Influencers of the spoken word

ACCENT   RAPPORT   PRONUNCIATION

EMPHASIS, INTONATION   PITCH

PACE, RHYTHM   TONE, STYLE

VOCABULARY

SPEECH MANNERISMS   IDEAS STRUCTURE

SPEECH DELIVERING AND LISTENING SKILLS

Effective dialogue depends on <u>all</u> these influencers!

Structure	It is also essential to speak fluently, so that ideas are seen to be clearly structured, and not blurred
Mannerisms	by 'ums' or 'ers' or 'you knows'.
Rapport	How important is it to establish friendly relations with one's opposite number?

All these factors affect the spoken word

How to find out

A wise man once said:

'There are basically two kinds of knowledge – the kind you have to carry around in your head, and the kind you can easily find out – if you know where to look!'

Everyone likes to watch quiz programmes or 'mastermind' competitions, where contestants display their often amazing ability to recall names, places, facts and figures. And yet, if one really thinks about it, it is obvious that no single person can hope to amass and hold in his head the now staggering sum of human knowledge.

Indeed, only an eccentric would try! Yet not so long ago, education consisted largely of learning chunks of poetry or prose off by heart and memorising long tables such as the

dates of the kings and queens of England. Much of the information which reluctant pupils struggled to learn proved useless to them in later life – the British colonies of the 1950s no longer exist; even the English counties of the 1960s are very different now.

Today, man's attitude to storing and using knowledge and information is much more realistic and enlightened. In education more emphasis is placed on acquiring skills in logical thinking, decision-making, developing reasonable attitudes and learning *how* to find out from the mass of libraries, data banks and information storage resources.

Indeed, the importance of the enormous amount of factual data, often assembled over a lifetime of painstaking care by experts, must not be underestimated. For example, the ship's captain and pilot would be unable to leave harbour without making reference to a table of tides. Secretaries would be reduced to making wild guesses at spellings or pronunciations unless they had dictionaries to help them. Similarly, sales assistants would be constantly on the telephone to suppliers, if they did not have catalogues and price-lists to refer to.

Knowing how to find out, and where to look for specialist information, is therefore an essential skill for anyone preparing for a career in commerce or public service.

Managers, secretaries and clerks make constant reference to all sorts of dictionaries, reference books, yearbooks, guides, tables, and a host of specialist journals and magazines. At present, much of the information used in business is still stored in book or journal form. Increasingly, however, computer-based information storage systems called databases are becoming much more widely used, displaying on terminal computer screens information relayed from a mainframe computer's memory bank.

The role of the library

Nevertheless, the library still provides the main source of general knowledge and information. All that is needed to make the most of this vast body of knowledge is the ability to use the systems the library employs to store and catalogue its wealth of 'know-how'.

Libraries have existed for thousands of years – ancient Egyptians, Greeks and Romans prized learning and, once they had mastered the techniques of writing and the production of paper-like materials, they recorded all sorts of scientific, religious, historical and literary works which were stored in their libraries.

Such 'one-off' works in manuscript were very precious and kept with loving care for the very few people who could read them. In the Dark Ages in Europe, monks spent life-times copying and illustrating religious manuscripts. It was not until the invention of the printing press and moveable type that books were produced in numbers and became available to many more people. However, it was not until the latter half of the nineteenth century, when the Victorians introduced compulsory schooling, that everyone learnt to read. The national network of municipal libraries was also developed at this time. Thus, at last, everyone had the chance to learn to read and write, and to have free access to books, newspapers and journals. Since then, man has never looked back. He is hungry for knowledge and uses it in a host of applications – research papers, legal cases, plans and maps, directories and dictionaries – in the course of running a business or administering a local government department.

Today, all organisations rely a great deal upon the services which libraries supply. Most executives or their secretaries need occasionally to seek a librarian's help to use the store of reference books at a local reference library. Many large companies have their own specialist libraries.

The Dewey Decimal System

Once people in the 19th century began to amass their knowledge in university or town libraries, it became necessary to devise a system for storing the books in a way that was both logical and, at the same time, capable of accepting additions and extensions.

The father of the modern library indexing system was Melvil Dewey (1851–1931). He was an American and invented a 'Dewey Decimal System' while working at a training library in Albany in 1876.

Book classification outline

000	**General Works**
030	Encyclopaedias
070	Journalism
100	**Philosophy**
150	Psychology
200	**Religion**
220-280	Christianity
290	Non-Christian Religions
300	**Social Sciences**
310	Statistics
320	Political Science
330	Economics
340	Law
350	Public Administration
355-359	Armed Forces
360	Social Services
370	Education
380	Commerce
385	Railways
390	Customs, Folklore
391	Costume
400	**Language**
420	English Language
430	Germanic Languages
440	French
450	Italian
460	Spanish
470	Latin
480	Greek
490	Other Languages
500	**Science**
510	Mathematics
520	Astronomy
530	Physics
540	Chemistry
550	Earth Sciences
551.5	Meteorology
560	Palaeontology
570	Life Sciences
580	Botanical Sciences
590	Zoological Sciences
600	**Technology**
610	Medicine
620	Engineering
630	Agriculture
635	Gardening
640	Household Management
641.5	Cookery
650	Business Practices

658	Management
660	Chemical Technology
670-680	Manufacturing
690	Building
700	**The Arts**
710	The Landscape, Town Planning
720	Architecture
730	Sculpture, Metalwork
740	Drawing
745	Decorative Arts
745.5	Handicrafts
746.44	Embroidery
750	Painting
760	Graphic Arts
770	Photography
780	Music
790	Recreations
792	The Theatre
793-799	Sports and Games
800	**Literature**
810	American Literature
820	English Literature
830-890	Other Literatures
See 400-490	Languages
900	**Geography, History**
910	Geography, Travel
913	Ancient World, Archaeology
914	European Geography and Travel
915-919	Other Continents
See 930-990	History
929	Genealogy
930	Ancient History
940	History, Europe
950	Asia
960	Africa
970	North America
980	South America
990	Australasia
998	The Polar Regions
B	**Biography and Autobiography**

Dewey's system is based on dividing all human knowledge into ten broad categories. Each category is identified by a three-digit code number coming before a decimal point:

000.	general books	600.	technology
100.	philosophy	700.	the arts
200.	religion	800.	literature
300.	social sciences	900.	geography, history
400.	language	B	biography,
500.	science		autobiography

Within each section of one hundred points, the broad area of, say, languages is sub-divided into a series of specialist areas. Thus books on the English language are to be found in the 420s. Alternatively, in the applied science section, books on business English applications are in the 651 section. Further degrees of specialisation are indicated by the use of numbers *behind* the decimal point:

651.74 English for commercial students
651.77 committees
651.78 report writing

while a further area of specialisation is introduced at a slightly later point: 653.424 Pitman 2000 Shorthand Dictation Practice.

In this way, the Dewey Decimal System is able to expand to include modern technologies like micro-electronics or newly-devised shorthand systems.

Libraries using the Dewey system display their books in consecutive order, starting with the 000s and ending with the 900s. In most libraries, books which are not lent out, but retained for reference are kept in a separate area, but indexed in the same way.

It should be noted that the Dewey system is not international. The Americans have now replaced it with their Library of Congress system which uses a series of numbers and letters to break down knowledge in a similar way. In Great Britain, however, the Dewey Decimal System is widely used, save in some universities.

Once you have mastered the logic behind Dewey's system, it will now take you only a minute or two to locate the section you need. The table on pages 43–44 will show you how the ten categories are further broken down.

The catalogue system

It is difficult to generalise about library cataloguing systems, since many libraries employ different variations on the Dewey or Library of Congress theme.

Most libraries now employ a form of computer-based cataloguing, and organise the records of the books they stock under the main headings of:

author or **subject**

Under the author section, the authors are listed alphabetically and each book is listed below its author. Under the subject section, books are indexed according to where they come in the Dewey or Library of Congress coding.

Some libraries record this information on cards filed in labelled boxes, others hold the information in large ring-binders of modified computer print-out.

Golden rule ▄▄▄▄▄▄▄▄▄▄

If, at any time, you are unable to find what you want quickly – ask the librarian! No one knows his or her library better, and he or she will prove a helpful information source.

It is important, when one's work relies upon sources of information, to build up a checklist of useful reference books. Of course the nature and scope of such a checklist will depend on the type of job – the solicitor will need to know where to find information relating to law in all its aspects, the production manager will need to know where to check on established rules for manufacturing different types of machine. The office worker will need to know about postal charges, directories of organisations and companies, specialist dictionaries and business reference books.

The following list is intended for such an office worker. It is by no means exhaustive, but will provide a basis from which to build:

Dictionaries
Oxford Shorter English Dictionary
English Pronouncing Dictionary
The Pergamon Dictionary of Perfect Spelling
Cassell's New Spelling Dictionary
Dictionary of Acronyms and Abbreviations
A Dictionary of Modern English Usage
Fontana Dictionary of Modern Thought
Oxford Dictionary of Quotations
Pitman Dictionary of Shorthand

Use of English
The Complete Plain Words
Roget's Thesaurus
ABC of English Usage
Usage and Abusage
The King's English

Directories
Kelly's Directories of Streets
Kelly's Directory of Manufacturers and Merchants
Current British Directories Yearbook
Guide to Current British Periodicals
British Telecom Telephone and Telex Directories

Yearbooks
British Standards Yearbook
The Post Office Guide
Whitaker's Almanac
The Municipal Yearbook
Social Sciences Yearbook
BBC, ITV Handbooks
Various Trades' Handbooks e.g. Engineering

Business Reference Books
ABC Railway Guide
Who's Who
Who Owns Whom
Kompass

Titles and Forms of Address
How to Find Out About Secretarial Practice
Basic Medical Vocabulary
Businessman's Guide
The Secretary's Yearbook
Business Terms, Phrases and Abbreviations

Encyclopaedias
Encyclopaedia Britannica
Larousse Illustrated International Encyclopaedia

Hotels and restaurants
Egon Ronay's Lucas Guide Yearbook
AA Guide to Hotels and Restaurants in Great Britain and Ireland
The Good Food Guide

Newspapers
The Independent
The Times
The Financial Times
The Guardian
The Daily Telegraph
The International Herald Tribune

Periodicals
2000
Memo
Business Education Today
Business Equipment Digest
Business Systems and Equipment
Commerce International
Computer News
New Society
Economist
New Statesman
Journal of the Institute of Bankers
Caterer and Hotelkeeper

Boost your spelling power!

Learn these key words by heart

Remember, an asterisk after a word indicates that it is very commonly misspelled:

maintenance* n	(maintain v)
necessary* adj	(necessity n)
parallel adj	
permissible adj	(permit v n)
sentence* n,v	
sincerely adv	(sincere adj)
transferred v,pp.	(transfer n v)
unconscious adj	(unconsciousness n)

valuable* adj   (value n v)
woollen adj   (wool n)

Check, in your dictionary, the meaning of any word you do not know and enter it in your vocabulary book.

Punctuation

The apostrophe

Considering its shape – like a comma above the line – and considering its size – about as large as a pin-head – the apostrophe manages to cause many writers a lot of trouble! This trouble is basically of three kinds.

Apostrophe trouble

- It does a vanishing trick when it should be present and hard at work!
- It appears in the wrong place!
- It does a high-wire act, balancing right over an s, not sure whether to perch in front or behind it!

Curing the trouble

'Taming' the rogue apostrophe into obedience is simple and straightforward provided that the roles it performs are fully understood.

The apostrophe s

When the apostrophe is used in conjunction with a final s at the end of a word, it is being used to mean:

of him; of her; of it; of them

Thus instead of writing:

The desk of the secretary
The office of the manager
The book of David

we may write:

The secretary's desk

The manager's office
David's book

The rule for showing ownership is simple: **add an apostrophe then an s.**

The pay of the secretary *becomes* The secretary's pay

The cloakroom of the women *becomes* The women's cloakroom

If the word already ends in s (as often happens in plurals), the final s is usually omitted:

The room of the typists *becomes* The typists' room

The desks of the managers *becomes* The managers' desks

Note: Sometimes if a singular noun ends in s a second s may be added:

The pen of James *becomes*
James's pen *or*
James' pen

Apply these rules and you should never go wrong!

Watchit words!

When using the apostrophe s, care must be taken when using 'watchit words'. These are words which already show possession without the need for an apostrophe:

The cat hurt its paw
Is this yours?
Ours is here. Where is theirs?
I have his and hers

The 'left out' sign

Another use of the apostrophe is to show that a letter (or letters) has been left out of a word:

did not: didn't   I am: I'm

Such contractions are used frequently in conversation, but should not normally be used in business documents. The most frequently used contractions are:

do not: don't   have not: haven't   it is: it's   I am: I'm
let us: let's   had not: hadn't   shall not: shan't

Take extra care in ensuring you can distinguish between:

its = of it   it's = it is
whose = of whom   who's = who is

Lastly, some words are found to be in a state of flux, where their short-ended forms are in the process of replacing their normal forms. In such instances, the apostrophe is sometimes used to indicate the omission:

aeroplane: 'plane
telephone: 'phone

But the shortened version is now becoming acceptable without the apostrophe:

plane   phone   bus

and a word like perambulator is now likely to be seen as, simply, pram!

Punctuation assignments

1 Re-write the following, using the apostrophe s:

the supply of the month
the switchboard of the receptionist
the lights of the disco
the coats of the girls
in the time of three months
the news of the week
the coats of the women
the horses of the jockeys
the hats of the ladies
the pen of the clerk

2 Insert the apostrophe in the following to create their shortened forms:

could not	cannot
is not	I have
I am	we are
you are	will not
they are	who is

3 Re-write the following passage, inserting the apostrophes in the places you think they should be:

'Its a fine day,' said John, 'Lets go to the river for a swim!'
'Im all for that – the suns so hot! But dont forget the dogs lead or hell be running off again.'
'Wheres my swimming costume? Whos borrowed it?'
'Its all right, its in its place, next to ours in the cupboard. Have you seen the childrens inflatable boat?'
'Whose coat?'
'No, boat! Oh, it doesnt matter, Ill get it myself.'
'Wheres Ruth? In Peters car?'
'Yes, theyve gone on ahead to see if the gates unlocked.'
'Well, off we go! Last one ins a cissy!'

4 Re-write the following in their plural forms, using the apostrophe s:

the room of the girl
the rim of the glass
the cart of the ox
the toy of the child
the halter of the donkey
the basis of the formula
the wool of the sheep
the church of the pilgrims
the style of the dress
the handkerchief of the lady

Business letters 1

The business background

Before setting out to acquire the techniques of letter writing, it is important to appreciate the commercial background against which business letters are sent and received.

Basically, letter writers in commercial companies are extremely careful about what they allow to be sent out to clients or to other organisations.

Firstly, most companies have legal obligations and responsibilities. It would be most unwise, for example, to allow a letter to be despatched which contained deliberately misleading information about a product.

Secondly, once the letter has been posted, the sender is quite unable to change a single word or expression, which on reflection he may think rude or discourteous.

Thirdly, at the root of all business lies the seller-customer relationship. If a company is to keep its clients' custom, every care must be taken to ensure that customers gain a good impression of the company from the letters they receive.

Lastly, customers, suppliers, insurers or servicing agents will, inevitably, judge an organisation by the letters which it sends out. Allowing a messily typed letter to be despatched implies that its receiver does not warrant the effort needed to produce a flawless letter! Similarly, faults in expression, punctuation or spelling will have the same effect and convey an impression to the letter's receiver that its sender does not care to take more trouble. In addition, an aggressive tone in a letter will cause hostility in a customer and might make him or her close the account.

Thus the layout, content, tone and use of English in a business letter all have a vital role to play, if the letter is to be successful and do the job expected of it – whether to register a complaint, make a sale or provide an estimate.

The letter writing team

The production of a business letter is very much the result of teamwork.

First and foremost, a graphics designer settles upon a suitable design for the organisation's letterhead. The letterhead is the part of the letter which displays a company's trading name and postal address, its telephone number(s) and, if it is a large company, its telegraphic and telex addresses. In addition, many companies include a logo in their letterheads. This is a design which attempts to symbolise in a memorable way the identity of the company.

Next, an office manager has to decide upon the colour and quality of the paper on which the letterhead will be printed. Many firms take a great deal of care over choosing the colours of paper and letterhead designs, since they know that a good combination will produce a sense of either reliability or dash or reassurance in the receiver's mind, which will go a long way towards persuading him or her to accept the letter's message.

At this stage, the stationery is ready for use. Most frequently, of course, the text of the letter is dictated by the letter's author, either into a dictating machine for an audio-typist to transcribe or to a secretary who 'encodes' it in shorthand and then transcribes the shorthand into a typewritten message. Nowadays this process is also being carried out with word processors. In this way, each letter opened in an office is the direct result of painstaking team work.

The essential link

Of all the various forms of written communication used in organisations the letter is by far the most common. It provides an essential link between the executives and departments of an organisation and the many external customers, associates and suppliers who are necessary to the successful running of either a business or government department.

Layout of the fully-blocked, open punctuation letter

The easiest way to learn how business letters are set out is to study models. In the fully-blocked format, *all* the typescript parts of the letter start from the same left-hand margin. The body of the letter is punctuated normally, but in all other parts, punctuation is omitted to save the typist's time.

Letterhead components

The letterhead is the part of the letter which is produced by a printer and includes:

Trading name ①

Companies must state their registered trading name, and many try to devise a name which is easy to remember and which aptly describes the business.

Postal address ②

The postal address is set out in full, including the post-code. Note that the address may be that of a local branch. In this case, public companies are obliged to include the address of their registered office – often at the foot of the letter.

The telephone number ③

Companies include their telephone number as a speedy means of contact and, unless the STD prefix (e.g. 01 for London) is the same throughout the country, the name of the town or city is also supplied. Note also that larger firms also provide a telex 'address' in number form and a telegraphic 'address' as an abbreviated code word.

The logo ④

A logo is an emblem (often used as a trade-mark) which aims to illustrate graphically what the firm does. Commercial artists are often very ingenious in designing memorable logos.

Typescript components

The letter reference ⑤

Letter references are typed on letters and file copies to aid identification. Usually made up of the writer's and typist's initials, 'Our ref' is for the writer and 'Your ref' is for the letter which is being answered.

① **Speedy Stationery Services Limited**

② 10 West Road
Middleton
Southshire MS9 45K
③ Tel: Middleton 478964

④ SSSL

⑤ Your ref   PGT/JR   S 162

Our ref   KP/JT   FICL 24

12 July 19--

⑥ Mr P G Truman
Chief Buyer
Fidelity Insurance Co Ltd
24 New Street
TRENTON
Northshire   TR14 6NS

⑦ Dear Mr Truman

⑧ FREEFLOW CONTINUOUS COMPUTER STATIONERY

⑨ Thank you for your letter of 9 July 19-- in which you enquired
about the availability of continuous computer stationery.

I am pleased to inform you that my company has recently secured
an exclusive agency for Freeflow Continuous Computer Stationery.

The paper used is of good quality and is not prone to irritating
breakage by tractor feed sprockets.

I have enclosed a brochure from Freeflow which will provide
you with more detail on the advantages of continuous stationery.
Our current price-list is also enclosed and in view of your
valued past custom, I am pleased to extend to you an additional
discount of 10% on orders placed before 1 August 19-- for
12 or more Freeflow 5 kilo packs.

Please let me know if I may provide you with any additional
information.

⑩ Yours sincerely

P Preston

⑪ P Preston (Mrs)
Sales Manager

⑫ encs

⑬ copy to: G Knight Sales Representative Northshire

MODEL: FULLY-BLOCKED OPEN PUNCTUATION LETTER ANSWERING A SALES
       ENQUIRY

Recipient's name and address ⑥

It is necessary on business letters to include the name and address of the receiver of the letter (so that it is also retained on the file copy).

Recipients are sometimes only referred to by their job title:

The Manager
Accounts Department
Express Freight Limited

It is better to use the recipient's title and name, however, when it is known:

Mr Green   Mrs Brown   Miss White   Dr Black

and to include letters after the name if they are known. Notice the following conventions:

For men: R Green Esq BSc
For women: Mrs R Green BA
              Miss R Green Dip Ed

The salutation ⑦

There are two kinds of salutation most in use:

Dear Sir   Dear Mr Brown
Dear Sirs   Dear Mrs Brown
Dear Madam   Dear Miss Brown

Dear Sir or Madam *always ends* Yours faithfully
Dear Mr/Mrs/Miss Brown *always ends* Yours sincerely

The subject heading ⑧

Many business letters are headed by a brief statement of the letter's theme, often displayed in block capitals and given space above and below to make it stand out. Such a subject heading aids sorting of mail and retrieval from files.

The body of the letter ⑨

The body of the letter is constructed in paragraphs, which are spaced to make them easy to read. They are often kept short for the same reason. Remember that the body of the letter is *always* punctuated normally! In the fully-blocked letter layout, each paragraph begins against the left-hand margin.

The subscription ⑩

Sometimes called the 'complimentary close', the 'signing off' part of the letter is set out after a suitable space below the body of the letter. The two subscriptions most in use today are: Yours faithfully, used after Dear Sir etc, and Yours sincerely, used after Dear Mr Green etc (see above, The salutation). Sometimes, writers who know their recipients well use Kind regards or Best wishes after Dear Mr Green or Dear Jack.

Writer's name and job title ⑪

After a space has been left for the writer's signature, his or her name is typed in, to make sure that the recipient knows precisely how to address the sender in any subsequent letter. Married ladies often insert 'Mrs' after their names, though some do not, and may have to be addressed as 'Ms' in any follow-up.

The enclosure reference ⑫

The abbreviation 'enc' or 'encs' is often used at the foot of the letter to draw the attention of its recipient to the fact that something has been sent with it.

Copy(ies) to ⑬

When a copy of the letter is sent to a third person, then this fact is conveyed by displaying 'copy(ies) to' or cc at the foot of the letter.

When a manager, clerk or assistant wishes to contact an external organisation, he or she has to choose from a number of available options including making a visit, using the telephone, using telex or sending a letter. Choosing the letter provides the sender with a number of important advantages:

- printed letterhead, stationery and typescript give a good impression
- a written record is sent (the letter) and retained (the file copy)
- complex detail may be transmitted
- the letter may be legally binding
- the written message allows for re-reading and memory refreshing
- carefully constructed sentences ensure the message is clearly stated
- enclosure material – leaflets, brochures – may also be included

LETTERS FORM VITAL TWO-WAY LINKS

enquiring customer → sales department

stationery suppliers ↕ office administration

vehicle servicing garage ↔ transport department

equipment maintenance engineers ↔ production department

marketing department ↔ advertising agency

personnel department ↔ job applicant

suppliers of raw materials ↔ buying department

accounts department ↔ bank manager

company secretary ↕ shareholders

Components of the effective letter

A successfully composed letter is the result of care and attention being paid to its individual parts. Not only must the letter look crisp and elegant, its message must be concise and expressed in a suitable style – asking a customer to pay a long-overdue account requires a different skill from seeking an order from a potential customer. In learning, therefore, how to compose letters which will do their job effectively, care must be taken to acquire communication expertise in the following main areas:

- how to set out the letter
- how to structure its message
- how to adopt a suitable tone
- how to write it in acceptable English

Note: When typists set out a letter in the fully-blocked, open punctuation style, they observe rules about the number of line spaces to leave between the various sections of a letter. (See the model on page 49.) When setting out a letter in longhand, you should aim to leave such spaces clearly between each section, but should not try to adhere specifically to the typist's rules, since your handwriting will not be as small as typescript.

Examples of organisation's logos

The Coca-Cola Company

EMI

 PLESSEY

west sussex county council

Letter writing assignments

Set out the following letters using the fully-blocked, open punctuation system. Take care to ensure that your version is correctly punctuated and organised in appropriate paragraphs.

1 Design a suitable letterhead for the following letter and then set it out correctly:

your ref kp/jt 24 our ref pgt/jr s 162 16 july 19 – – mrs k preston sales manager speedy stationery services limited 10 west road middleton southshire ms 9 45 k dear mrs preston order for freeflow continuous computer stationery order no kh 1927 i was pleased to receive your letter of 12 july 19 – – together with the enclosed freeflow brochure on continuous stationery and your current price list having given the matter careful thought and after having discussed the prices and paper quality with both senior and junior staff i have decided to place an initial order with you for 12 packs thus qualifying for the 10% discount for orders placed before 1 august 19 – – would you therefore kindly make arrangements for the enclosed order to be processed as soon as possible particularly as we are already running short of existing continuous stationery supplies yours sincerely pg truman chief buyer enc

2 Set out the following letter (which includes the letterhead components) as a fully-blocked, open punctuated letter:

anglo office equipment ltd 12 west road crosstown southshire st5 3wd tel crosstown 765986 your ref sm/ df aoe 4 our ref jg/cd wb5 24 october 19 – – messrs white and brown 26 queens road newborough northshire ns16 3ak dear sirs your order four stowaway filing cabinets tg 94691 thank you for your letter of 21 october 19 – – ordering four stowaway filing cabinets two three drawer and one four drawer catalogue nos fc 64a and 64b i very much regret to inform you that there is likely to be a short delay in delivery as the production of the cabinets at the companys factory has been affected by a breakdown in the supply of semi finished materials from our suppliers normal production should be resumed however in fourteen days and delivery should be possible by the end of the month at the latest however should you require the filing cabinets urgently i should like to recommend our fastfind range which is a little more expensive but extremely elegant and reliable immediate delivery is guaranteed from our warehouse i have pleasure in enclosing a fastfind brochure and look forward to receiving your further instructions once more may i apologise for any inconvenience the delay may cause yours faithfully john goodwright order department enc

How a computer works

Entire textbooks have been devoted to explaining how computers work, so this section can only provide an overview of the essential features of computer equipment and how it operates, and should therefore be studied in conjunction with more detailed texts.

Basically, a computer represents a system for taking in, storing, processing and giving out information or data:

The input stage

Information is put into the computer (input) in a number of ways, most commonly by means of a keyboard, similar to a typewriter keyboard, in the form of words, numbers and symbols:

the order % * \ £ 1234 + – = [ ], etc.

Sometimes, however, the information may be sent in to the computer by electronically delivered means – via cables connected to other computers, telephone lines delivering messages packaged in languages the computer can understand, voice input and by Optical Character Recognition (OCR). OCR means the computer has a camera-like eye which can read visually presented information rather like the way a photocopier 'reads' the page it has to copy, although the technology which makes this possible is different.

The processing stage

When the information reaches the Central Processing Unit (CPU) of the computer it is stored in a series of electronic 'mailboxes' and may be moved around by the computer as it makes calculations, forms text or graphic designs, in response to the set of instructions it is currently working to. Some of the computer's memory capacity is permanently situated in the CPU and is activated every time the computer is switched on. Other instructions or memory are put into the computer's short-term memory banks whenever an operating disk or software applications package is loaded into the computer. When the computer is switched off, this kind of memory is instantly erased.

The output stage

While the computer operator is working on the computer

the text, chart or table being created will be displayed on the computer's VDU or screen. While under production, the data displayed may be moved about on the screen electronically, erased, modified or expanded by means of instructions given to the computer via the keyboard.

Most software packages – which are, in essence, the set of instructions which enable the computer and operator to perform specific tasks – include a set of 'Help' guidelines which can be accessed through a display panel on the screen at any time.

Thus the computer's screen is one means of accessing the computer's output. Often, however, a more permanent form of the output is required and thus a printer is customarily part of the computer's set of equipment. Once the operator is satisfied that the letter, graph or set of figures displayed on the VDU is correct and well laid out, a print command is given to the computer which results in the printer receiving a series of electronic signals which it converts into print by means of either a dot-matrix, daisy-wheel or laser or ink-jet printing mechanism. The printed output may be transferred either on to continuous stationery, mainly for internal use, or on to sheets of A4 paper fed either manually or automatically into the printer.

Other output devices include the photocopier, the facsimile transmitter and the telex transmitter which can now be used to accept messages created by the computer for direct onward transmission.

The feedback stage

Within the computer – activated either by its internal or software inputted memory – are a series of error checks which automatically advise the operator of an error or difficulty. Messages like this sometimes appear on the VDU:

Syntax error line 36
File not found
Disk drive error in Drive B
Abort, Retry, Ignore ?
Bad command or filename

In such instances the computer is providing the operator with instant feedback that something has gone wrong or cannot be activated. Thus a system of providing feedback – a means of informing the operator as to the effectiveness of the operation – is built into all computers. Additionally, most software packages have further feedback aids and assistors to help the operator to produce an error-free piece of communication or data processing. More simply, the operator may use the scrolling commands of a software package to re-read and check those parts of a text being created before the print command is activated.

However effected, the feedback process is invaluable in saving time and in pinpointing the source of a processing error.

The Micro Computer's Working Parts

① **The Visual Display Unit (VDU)**
The screen on which data is displayed

To mains supply

The Central Processing Unit (CPU) ②
Employing 2 floppy disk drives

The Computer Keyboard ③
Combining 'QWERTY', command and number keys

To mains supply

⑤ **Floppy Disk Software**

5.1 Operating Disk

5.2 Software Applications Disk e.g. Word Processing Disk

5.3 Formatted Work Disk To Store Created Files

The Printer ④
Here a dot matrix printer using continuous stationery is illustrated

The microcomputer's working parts

As we have already discovered, whether a computer is a mainframe, mini or micro, it will have common component parts carrying out the functions of:

inputting   storage   display   outputting

In the diagram on page 53, illustrating a microcomputer set-up (the jargon word is 'configuration'), these functions are carried out as follows:

input   via   keyboard

storage   via   central processing unit (CPU) housing the twin floppy disk drives

display   via   visual display unit (VDU)

output   via   printer – illustrated is a dot matrix, low cost printer using continuous stationery

operations via   5¼″ dual density double sided floppy disks used to load the computer with its operating system and software application package in use.

The keyboard

Microcomputer keyboards look very much alike nowadays and are constructed to include:

- a **QWERTY** keyboard with upper and lower case set out just like a conventional typewriter's keyboard

- a set of **command keys** usually situated to the left of the QWERTY keyboard which are employed to give the computer instructions while a package is in use

- a set of **number keys** set usually to the right of the QWERTY keyboard which may be used to carry out number calculations via the computer and which often double as keys which can move the cursor around on the VDU screen:

$$8 = \uparrow$$

$$4 = \leftarrow \qquad\qquad 6 = \rightarrow$$

$$2 = \downarrow$$

The right-hand side of the keyboard also contains other command keys which carry out functions such as deleting text, making possible text insertion and moving the cursor rapidly from start to finish of text created and so on.

The central processing unit (CPU)

The central processing unit is the electronic control centre of the computer. Here the keystroke depressions from the keyboard are converted into electronic pulses which act as instructions or commands across the computer's micro-circuits and, through the means of the computer's incredibly fast handling of electronic signals, can either transform a keystroke depression for the letter 'b' or the number '8' and display it directly on the chosen part of the VDU screen, or can carry out a calculation in a trice and *then* display the result upon the screen and so on.

The floppy disk software

The microcomputer illustrated is using 5¼″ floppy disks. Some microcomputers employ smaller floppy disks 3″ in diameter.

Three disks are normally needed to enable the computer to function:

1 A disk to store the instructions which activate the computer's working circuits. This is called a DOS disk where 'DOS' means Disk Operating System. This disk is inserted first in the left-hand drive: (Drive A) of the dual disk drive micro.

2 An applications disk. This disk stores the particular set of instructions and commands which go to make up, for example, a word processing software package or application but it might equally be a desk top manager, spreadsheet (a calculations package) or graphics package, depending on what job the operator wanted to perform. Equally, nowadays, it could be a package amalgamating all those referred to above!

This disk is loaded in Drive A after the DOS disk has been removed, for the act of loading DOS, or 'booting up' the computer has the effect of installing the instructions held on the DOS disk on to the computer's short-term memory (for as long as the computer is left switched on).

By the same token, the computer also accepts a 'copy' of the application package's set of instructions in its electronic circuitry to work from for as long as the computer is powered up.

3 The third floppy disk needed represents the operator's blank sheet of paper – a kind of electronic note-pad for holding the text or number work the operator produces with the aid of the DOS and application package systems.

This work disk has first to be configured or 'formatted'

so as to be able to accept the computer's data and is normally inserted in Drive B.

When the work is completed by the operator, he or she instructs the computer to 'save' the work created on a particular 'file' which has been named and which is then stored permanently on the working disk. The operator can recall this piece of work or file at any time simply by reloading the working disk in to the computer and asking for the particular file to be displayed. Also, the data on the file can be amended or edited while it is displayed on screen and a modified copy printed via the computer's printer.

The printer

Microcomputer printers nowadays come in various shapes and sizes and incorporate various ways of printing the computer's output. The major print delivery mechanisms are:

dot matrix   Text is produced by means of 'needles' punching dots on to the paper via the ribbon in the printer to form letters or numbers etc.

daisy wheel   The text is printed by means of individual letters, numbers, symbols etc. which are set at the end of a spoke-like printing head made to rotate very swiftly and to deliver the correct character to the ribbon for 'hitting' on to the paper – very much like a set of typewriter keys.

laser device   This printing mechanism effectively 'burns' or 'etches' the print on to the paper and can operate at very high speeds.

What the computer printer does is sit and wait patiently until the operator is ready and activates the 'print' command. At this moment the printer which is 'on line' or connected directly to the computer receives a stream of electronic signals which represent the data to be printed. The printer converts them into its own set of commands which in turn present the correct character of the daisy wheel to the ribbon for printing, or produce the appropriate dot matrix character tapped out through the printer's ribbon.

Printers either use continuous stationery which is carried past the printing head by means of a 'tractor feed' mechanism, or employ a feed arrangement for supplying A4 notepaper sheets, either singly or in a series.

Know your IT! Key words and terms

1 The system

analogue: conveys meaning via symbols and not numbers – see 'digital'

bit: short for binary digit and equal to a single on/off pulse in the computer; eight 'bits' make a 'byte' which is equivalent to a single character or number

byte: see above – equal to eight bits

chip: popular term for the micro electronic circuitry etched on to a 'silicon chip' or microprocessor

CPU: Central Processing Unit, where the electronics circuitry does the computing – usually housed in a microcomputer in the 'box' housing the disk drives

digital: having to do with digits or numbers – hence a computer working via numbers is said to be 'digital'

input: data or information inserted into the computer – see 'input device', the machine which does the inputting

kilobyte: strictly speaking, 1024 bytes of information – see also megabyte – 1 million bytes
commonly abbreviations are used:
      256 k
       20 mb

memory: this term is popularly used to signify the power of a computer – '600 k RAM' where **RAM** stands for Random Access Memory, which can be used to store information which has been created by the user prior to its transference on to disk for later use and access. Computers also have **ROM** – Read Only Memory – built into their micro circuitry to help them in their calculations and functions etc

operating system: computers work by understanding extensive sets of instructions which have to be installed in its temporary memory in the case of a micro by means of a 'DOS' disk, where DOS stands for 'Disk Operating System'; different computers have different operating systems but manufacturers are now tending to produce computers with compatible DOS systems to aid the widespread use of software

output: data or information which comes out of the computer – either by means of screen display, or printed on paper (hard copy), or as an electronic message for relay to another machine

program: note the special spelling – program – for 'one-off' set of instructions which instruct the computer in how to behave when it is running any applications package; in fact the package as the computer understands it is in the format of a 'program' written in a specific language which is converted into binary digits or bits

Extend your IT word power

Find out what the following stand for:

EPROM, gigabyte, 16 and 32 bit processors, 'high level' languages used in writing computer programs, a program 'bug', to 'crash' a program, a 'corrupted' program

Proof-reading

An essential office skill

In any organisation, the secretary or typist often has to proof-read documents before they are typed or printed in final draft form or posted, to ensure that they are free from spelling, punctuation or typing mistakes. This is why such staff need to acquire a thorough knowledge of grammar, syntax and use of English.

The ability to become a successful proof-reader is not attained overnight. As well as having a good knowledge of English usage and language rules and conventions, the proof-reader must develop an 'eagle-eye' and a painstaking approach. It is only too easy to overlook a mistake because of haste or carelessness. The following checklist includes some of the principal mistakes for which the proof-reader should be on the watch.

Spelling

Since most documents to be proof-read are typed, the errors in spelling which may be detected will arise, not only from the author's or typist's inability to spell a particular word correctly, but also from mistakes in typing, where pairs of letters may be transposed – sincerley for sincerely – or typewriting rhythms which prompt words like skillful for skilful to be typed because the typist has absorbed the rhythm of typing 'skill'.

Punctuation

It is easy to make mistakes of punctuation when composing written documents, especially when they originate from audio-dictation. If the dictator has not provided punctuation marks, the audio-typist may fail to notice that, for example, an apostrophe has been omitted from the written text. Similarly, hyphens and dashes are also easily overlooked.

Use of English

In style terms, some documents – especially those hastily composed – tend to use words or phrases close together which are identical and therefore repetitive. In such instances, it is necessary to re-word one of the phrases. Another aspect of usage is that of agreement. In proof-reading documents it is important to ensure that subjects and their verbs always agree in number and person.

Errors of typing

In addition to errors stemming from spelling, punctuation or use of English shortcomings, the proof-reader must also be on his guard to spot mistakes in typewriting. These may, as already pointed out, take the form of transposing letters by mistake. Also, double consonants may be inadvertently trebled – thankfullly – or single vowels or consonants incorrectly typed because of keyboard errors – typegriting, parapgraph, etc.

The development of accuracy and precision in proof-reading is a skill which employers are quick to notice and be grateful for – especially if the final draft of a report is intended for a company's board of directors, or a sales letter for an important customer. One last word of advice. You should always be your own sternest critic. Always proof-read every document you have produced before you send it and *never* slip into the habit of letting a document leave you knowing that it contains errors which you could have corrected!

Assignments

1 Proof-read the following extract from a business letter. There are 4 spelling errors and 4 mistakes in punctuation. List the errors then re-write the extract correctly.

I am writing to enquire whether your company stocks adjustible typists chairs which might prove suitable in my companys' general office, at present some forteen typists are employed in the office and off recent months I have received a number of complaints regarding the shortcomings of the chiars.

2 Assume you have to explain to someone quite unfamiliar with the conventions of fully-blocked, open punctuated letter layout how to set out just such a letter. Either: explain the layout orally to a partner (who should make a note of any errors or omissions) or write out the instructions as points in a logical order.

Discussion topic

Why do you think managers and secretaries set so much store in ensuring that a business letter is flawlessly produced? Is it only the *message* of the letter that really matters?

Research assignment

Find out how goods are documented from the time they leave the factory until the retailer despatches his payment for them.

Activities and Assignments

1 Make a list of the different types of resource which your library makes available.

2 Find out what newspapers, periodicals and magazines are stocked in your library which could be useful on this course. Make a checklist for the group.

3 Find out what computer based and viewdata facilities are available in your local libraries.

4 Find out where to obtain the information in your library and then write a short biography of Melvil Dewey.

5 With the help of any diagram or illustration, write an account of how the Dewey Decimal System works.

6 Prepare suitable notes and illustrative material first, then deliver a short talk to the group on one of the following:

- How can the spoken word be made interesting and its message be passed on effectively?
- How to make best use of the library
- How the Dewey Decimal System works
- What help are reference books to the student?
- An explanation of the three sectors of industry and how they relate to each other
- What business letters are used for
- How to set out a fully-blocked, open punctuated business letter

7 In small groups, discuss your approach and then design and draw up a checklist of instructions for new students on how to join your library and borrow books.

8 Write a clear account of how to use the apostrophe correctly. Illustrate your account with examples.

9 In small groups, draw up a checklist of Do's and Dont's for using the spoken word effectively. Compare your list with those compiled by other groups.

10 Write an account of the activities of the three sectors of industry.

11 As an individual exercise, design and produce a leaflet intended for new students. It should outline clearly the range of services which your library offers. Include any drawings or diagrams you think helpful.

12 List three materials produced by industries in the primary sector.

13 Name three services provided by organisations in the tertiary sector.

14 Explain briefly what you understand by the terms: vowel, consonant, diphthong. Give two examples of each.

15 Explain what is meant by the term cliché. Give three examples of a cliché.

16 List as many golden rules of speaking as you can remember.

17 List as many influencers of the spoken word as you can recall, and explain what you understand by each term.

18 List as many different main sections of the Dewey classification system as you can remember.

19 Explain the different use of the apostrophe in the following examples:

it's   children's   boys' books

20 Explain the meaning of the following terms used in letter layout:

letterhead	salutation	subscription
logo	subject heading	enclosure reference

21 Explain what is meant by the terms 'fully-blocked' and 'open punctuation'.

22 Explain the system for referencing letters.

23 After having carried out further research in your local library, write a short article of about 300–400 words entitled: 'What a microcomputer can do for you!'

Your article is intended for students who may own or have regular access to a microcomputer. Assume that your readers have little or no knowledge of how a microcomputer works or the scope of its activities.

24 First carry out your fact-finding and then give your group a three minute lecturette on one of the following:

How a floppy disk functions
How a dot matrix printer prints
How text is displayed on a VDU screen.

Unit 4

Perhaps the best definition of a work organisation is:

'A collection of people, working in groups, with various skills and resources – money, materials, equipment – in order to achieve the aims which they have set themselves.'

Such a rough and ready definition will do, not only for the grocer, who, perhaps, with his wife and a part-time assistant runs his small business, but also for the giant, multi-national companies such as ITT, Sony, ICI and IBM.

No matter how small or how large, work organisations all have one thing in common – they all need to be structured in such a way that the lines of communication are clearcut. If the decision-makers at the top of an organisation do not know what is happening on the shop-floor, or behind the sales counter, then important decisions will not be taken, and sooner or later, the business will fail.

The corner-shop grocer's organisational structure is simple and looks like this:

The small shopkeeper enjoys a number of communication advantages. He serves many of his customers personally and is able to supervise his assistant's work at all times. If his wife runs into difficulty over the book-keeping, then she has a direct line to her husband for help and decisions.

When a business grows, however, the lines of communication soon become longer and the messages are passed through more people. Similarly, in a retail organisation, the customers are much further away from the owner, who may never serve them, and barely ever see them.

(A) In such an organisation, the owner relies much more upon the ability of his staff to do a good job in his absence. Also, because he is not able to be in every branch all the time, more rules and regulations are needed, which staff have to

follow, to make sure that the business is run the way he would like it to be.

The next phase in the growth of a business is probably the setting up of an administration office, to take care of all the paperwork for buying, selling, government regulations, records, payroll and so on. This development has the effect of putting the owner still further away from his all-important customers.

In such an organisational structure, not only do messages have to travel much further up and down the organisation, they also have to travel across the organisation, for example, between branch managers or between office staff. It is easy to see why running a large business is much more complicated than running a corner-shop!

Efficient communication can be even more difficult in a large manufacturing organisation where specialist departments have been set up to do a specific job. For instance, a manufacturing company will probably have a research and development department to invent and design new products. It will also need a production department to make the products. Next it will require a marketing department to decide how, where and to whom to sell the

Organisational chart of a large manufacturing company

managing director

R + D manager   production manager   sales manager   marketing manager   accounts manager   buying manager

senior staff

supervisory staff

junior staff

other departments   customers   advertising agency   suppliers

staff totals: managing director: 1   heads of dept: 6   senior departmental staff: 17
supervisory and junior staff: 105

key: ◄──────►   just some of the lines of communication

products, an accounts department to look after the company's financial matters and a buying department to acquire as cheaply as possible all the materials the company needs. Each department will be run by a departmental head, with senior and junior staff, and every department will report to an owner or managing director. The organisational chart above illustrates the sort of structure needed in such a company.

(B) In such an organisation, all the staff need to cooperate and communicate effectively if the products which the firm makes are to be sold at a profit. Some departments, such as marketing and accounts, will be in direct contact with the customer and must relay his needs and problems back to the company's senior managers. Other departments, such as buying and marketing (again), need to keep in close touch with outside companies – suppliers of raw materials or advertising agencies providing advertising and packaging designs. Similarly, departments such as research and development and production will need to (C) liaise very closely with marketing to ensure that the products which are designed and manufactured are those which the consumer wants and which can be sold. It is not difficult to imagine, therefore, the strands of communication which criss-cross the company, linking senior and junior members of staff with each other and with customers or other companies providing specialist services.

The organisation pyramid

One of the most helpful ways of understanding the structure of an organisation is to think of it as a pyramid. At the top, the directors or owners look at all the informa-

tion on how the company is doing, and make decisions on how best to run it. Once these decisions, or policies have been made, the directors instruct the appropriate heads of department to put the plan into action. They in turn will brief the middle managers on what is needed, and then the (D) junior office staff or factory operatives will carry out the necessary action. This is not to say that only the junior staff do all the work – though they might think so sometimes. It does mean, however, that managers in the upper half of the pyramid spend a good deal of time supervising the work of others and checking that it is being done properly.

directors

heads of department

middle managers and supervisors

junior staff

The routes of communication in an organisation

Up and down the organisation

If the company is to function properly, it is very important that the decisions made at the top of the pyramid are correctly sent *down* the organisation, so that the staff expected to make them work know exactly what is expected of them. In the same way, it is important for senior managers to receive feedback on how their instructions are being carried out. Moreover, if things go wrong, or junior staff have suggestions or criticisms to make, it is equally important that such communications are able to be sent *up* the organisation and reach the ear of senior staff. Thus the two-way movement *up* and *down* the organisation of communication is essential if the aims and objectives of the company are to be achieved.

Across the organisation

As important as communication up and down the organisation is that which travels *across* it, at various levels. For example, junior sales assistants or clerks may need to work together to make a sale, or check some invoices. On the shop floor, assembly-line workers will need to work together smoothly in the process of making a motor-car or sewing-machine. At higher levels, heads of department may need to meet together to discuss the introduction of a new product, or directors may get together to decide to build a new factory. Without communication *across* the organisation, departments will have no idea what their counterparts are doing. Even within a department, sections or small working groups may work alone, telling no one else what they are doing. In such situations, suspicion and fruitless rivalry grow, and the all-important cooperation towards a common end is lost.

Diagonally across the organisation between departments

Though many messages travel up and down the organisation within one department – such as an instruction and feedback between a sales manager and his representatives – there are other situations when it is necessary for staff at different levels in the organisation, and working in different departments, to communicate. When this happens, it is important for the staff concerned to remember that they must act politely, since the senior staff involved are not in a position to *order* something of someone in another department. Correspondingly, the junior staff involved should be mindful of the need to show particular courtesy to people working outside their own department.

Organisations are people!

The single most important fact to remember about the structure of organisations is that they are not tidy diagrams on paper, with convenient arrows connecting their parts. On the contrary, organisations are people!

Moreover, the people who go to make up organisations do not vary much from company to company. They share all the good and bad which makes up human nature. Some will be friendly and helpful, others aloof and distant. Some will have a high regard for qualities like loyalty, honesty and hard-work, others will set bad examples, and be for ever looking for opportunities to avoid jobs or to indulge in gossip. Some people in organisations will be easy to get on with, while others will put a person's back up. Yet, whatever characteristics or attitudes people possess, the newcomer has to learn how to cope with them, how to seek the help of the upright, how to get along with the 'difficult', and how to avoid the downright bad influence!

Working in an organisation, then, requires not only specialist skills, such as shorthand, typewriting, filing or operating a computer or the switchboard; it needs a whole range of social skills – of appreciating how the people working at different levels in the organisation are likely to think and behave, of working out ways of 'rubbing along' with different kinds of people, of knowing when to remain silent, or when to show interest or sympathy. Similarly, in being 'sensitive to the feelings of others' the new employee must learn to make allowances for colleagues or senior staff who may be working under pressure, or who may not be personally responsible for the unpopular instruction – only detailed to see that it is carried out.

Mastering the meaning

1 Explain in your own words what an office does.

2 What communication advantages are enjoyed by the small, one-man business?

3 What communication problems emerge as a firm grows larger?

4 Why does the owner of a large organisation 'rely upon the ability of his staff to do a good job in his absence'? Line A

5 Why do you think a large commercial organisation is divided into specialist departments?

6 What is meant by 'to cooperate and communicate effectively'? Line B

7 Explain the meaning of the following words:

   (*a*) liaise   Line C
   (*b*) brief   Line D

8 What is the purpose of the lines of communication which go

   (*a*) up and down
   (*b*) across
   (*c*) diagonally up and down the organisation?

9 What effects may the less attractive aspects of human nature have on communication?

10 What challenges face the employee in 'rubbing along' with others?

Discussion topics

1 If it seems to be so much more difficult to run a large company than a small one, why is it that small companies strive to become big ones?

2 Do you think that people behave differently, say, at school or college than at home or work? Why might this be?

3 Can you think of any advantages a firm might enjoy by splitting up its work between different specialist departments?

4 Do you think it is fair to describe an organisation as a pyramid, with the most important people at the top? Or are all the people in an organisation equally important?

5 What personal standards should a new employee seek to hold to when starting a new job? Can you draw up a list suitable for *all* newcomers in *all* jobs?

Written assignments

1 Draw a chart to illustrate the organisational structure of your school, college or place of work. Show how different parts communicate.

2 Select one of the following departments, find the information you need, and then write an account of the sort of activities it performs:

production   marketing/sales   accounts

3 Find out as much background material as you can, and then write an account entitled either: 'A day in the life of a manager' or: 'A day in the life of a secretary'.

Research and discussion topic

Ask your older brothers, sisters or friends what they think are the main differences between being a student and working full-time.

Tell your group what you discovered. See if there is any similarity in the differences mentioned.

You *can* spell!

Suffixes

The specialist word given to frequently occurring endings which are 'tacked on' to various base or root words is **suffix**. Like its partner, the prefix, the suffix is used to change the meaning of the base word. For instance, words like 'break' and 'transfer' may have their meanings changed by the addition of the suffix -able: break<u>able</u>, transfer<u>able</u>. The addition of such a suffix now gives each word the extra sense of, 'capable of being broken, or transferred'. Some suffixes are added to words to make them describe a person:

-ant: account   accounta<u>nt</u>,   attend   attenda<u>nt</u>

and sometimes a suffix is added to a base word to convey the idea of, 'the study of':

-ology: psych<u>ology</u>   insect<u>ology</u>   bi<u>ology</u>   ge<u>ology</u>

The following checklist illustrates some of the principal suffixes used in English. You should add to this collection and ensure that you find out the meaning of the types of suffix you come across and how they are spelled and how they may affect the spelling of the base word.

Type of suffix	Nature of use	Examples
-able	to form adjectives having the meaning of 'able to be'	manageable portable washable
-an	usually to form an adjective or noun saying 'one who is'	Anglican Roman
-er	frequently to add to a base word the sense of 'one who'	painter waiter
	(note: take care in spelling to check whether the suffix ends in -er or -or since they are both very common)	
-ery	usually to form nouns	jewellery stationery brewery
	(note: take care in spelling to check whether the suffix ends in -ery or -ary)	
-ic	usually to form adjectives from words ending in -y	economic historic
-ism	usually to form an abstract noun	atheism baptism

-ist	to form the noun for 'one who is'	atheist baptist realist
-ious	usually to form adjectives from nouns ending in -ion	religious contagious infectious
-ity	to form nouns from base words	punctuality brevity necessity
-ly	to form adverbs	quickly slowly quietly
-oid	to form adjectives or nouns meaning 'like something'	humanoid
-ology	to form nouns meaning 'the study of'	psychology escapology

Suffix spelling tips

It would be fair to say that the majority of suffixes added on to base words do not affect the way in which the base word is spelled. This is certainly true of most of the words whose suffixes *do not* begin with a vowel. Yet, (inevitably!) there are so many exceptions to this general rule that the spellings of many words containing suffixes must be learnt by heart.

Examples

to maintain maintenance, to explain explanation, to occur occurrence

The following tips will help you:

1 Base words ending in -y usually change it to 'i' before the addition of -ness:

happiness loveliness

2 Base words ending in -l usually keep it when -ly is added:

principally exceptionally

3 Base words ending in -e usually drop it when adding a suffix beginning with a vowel:

to engage engaging, to revere reverent, senile senility

But be very careful with words adding -able. Sometimes the final -e is kept. When in doubt always check your dictionary.

4 When base words end in -ge, in order to keep the 'g' soft, the final 'e' is usually kept:

manageable courageous changeable

5 There are, sadly perhaps, a large number of words in English which have very different spellings for their different forms! The only sure way to conquer them is to start a collection in your vocabulary book. Here are some for a start:

to maintain	maintenance	to exceed	excessive
to explain	explanation	to argue	argument
to regret	regrettable	humour	humorous
to benefit	beneficial	brief	brevity
to occur	occurrence	to receive	receipt

6 The 'shun' sounding suffix is probably made up of either -tion, -sion or -ssion.

7 The 'shus' sounding suffix is probably made up of either -scious, -tious or -cious.

Spelling assignment

Each of the following questions requires you to think of a particular word with a certain suffix:

1 One who types is a ...?

2 One who runs a library is a ...?

3 One who edits is an ...?

4 A lady who looks after aeroplane passengers is a ...?

5 A place where people are buried is a ...?

6 Someone who travels by train daily to work is a ...?

7 A girl engaged to be married calls her intended her ...?

8 A reference book of human knowledge is an ...ia?

9 A reference book which gives the meaning of words is a ...?

10 Form a noun using the following words:

simple
punctual
monotonous
difficult
confusing

11 Form a noun from each of the following infinitives:

to dictate
to pay

to extend
to perform
to differ

12 Form a noun meaning 'one who administers'.

13 Form a noun meaning a collection of stories (clue: it ends in -ology).

14 From the word 'credit' form the noun which means 'one who is owed money'.

15 Form a word meaning valuable which ends in -ious.

16 If you are in a state of ecstasy you are ...?

17 Capable of being recognised is ...?

18 If something is tragic it is a ...?

19 Two words meaning 'extremely large':

    (*a*) ends in -ous
    (*b*) ends in -ic

20 If you allow yourself to be tempted, you have given in to ...?

Wednesday afternoon and Thursday morning

A case study

Wednesday afternoon

'Christine, I thought I told you never to type over mistakes! Look at this letter. It's perfectly dreadful! I certainly can't allow it to go out like that, can I?'

The voice of Miss Parkstone, office supervisor, carried across the typing pool, causing some of the girls to grin and exchange knowing smirks. Christine Dawson felt her cheeks burn as she blushed crimson.

'I'm sorry, Miss Parkstone – I was hurrying to catch the post.' Christine did not add that she was also hurrying to make sure that she left work on time. Her boyfriend, Derek, was picking her up at exactly 5.35 on the corner, and they were driving up to London on his bike to go to a pop concert.

'More haste, less speed,' remarked Miss Parkstone, stating the obvious. 'Though you're quite right, Mr Gulati does want the letter to go off tonight without fail.'

'But it's already 5.20,' replied Christine, 'and I ...' Her voice trailed off as she decided not to finish her sentence.

'Well, I should have thought you had more pride in your work. Now, just buckle down to it, it shouldn't take you long. There's a good girl. I'll be in my office. And – no mistakes this time!' Miss Parkstone strode off.

The typing pool was full of bustle and chatter, as the girls put the cover on another day's work at Westwood and Meaker, Manufacturers of Cooking Utensils and Enamelware.

'Don't do it for her! It's only 'cos she's got it in for you!' The suggestion came from Christine's friend Diana.

'Oh, she really made me feel small!' gasped Christine, whose nervousness was rapidly turning to anger as she saw the minute-hand of the office clock falling to the six. 'She's always so right and perfect! And anyway, the mistake was hardly noticeable!' But the heavy red ring of Miss Parkstone's biro around it clearly meant that another letter would have to be typed, since further efforts at camouflage would prove useless.

'Come on!' whispered Diana. 'Just leave it there! Grab your bag and slip out with the rest of us. She can't make you stay on! Serve her right!'

'All right,' decided Christine. 'Derek'll be waiting by now anyway.'

Thursday morning

'And when I returned, the letter was just where I'd left it, but there was no sign of Christine. I thought she'd popped out to the er .... Anyway, at 5.45 there was still no sign of her – she'd obviously just left without saying anything. Really, it was most annoying. I was here myself until seven, finishing off Christine's letter – among other things. But I knew you wanted the letter to reach Harlow's by the week-end. I don't know how I shall carry on if my authority is continually being flouted by untrustworthy 17-year-olds!'

'Very well, Miss Parkstone,' sighed Mr Gulati, 'you'd better ask Christine to see me at ten o'clock ....'

Assignments

1 How would you have handled the situation if you had been Christine?

2 How well did Miss Parkstone deal with the problem?

3 What do you make of Diana's part in the problem?

4 What would you say to Christine in Mr Gulati's place?

5 Compose a dialogue illustrating how you think the situation should have been handled. Record your dialogue and play it to other members of your group for discussion.

Grammar

The pronoun

As its name suggests, the pronoun is a part of speech which is used to stand in place of the noun:

He
~~John Brown~~ is a sales representative.

She
~~The receptionist~~ took the telephone call.

It
~~St Paul's Cathedral~~ is in London.

Pronouns are time-savers – they permit us to refer to a noun, which has usually been previously mentioned, in a shorter and simpler fashion:

George Bennett was shortly to give a talk to the sales

They
representatives. ~~The sales representatives~~ were looking

it   *he*
forward to ~~the talk~~ as ~~George Bennett~~ was a good speaker.

Types of pronoun

The personal pronoun

Pronouns which are used to refer to people (or pets, ships, objects, etc) are called **personal prounouns:**

I	you	he, she, it
we	you	they

When these pronouns perform different jobs in sentences, they are seen in their other forms:

Subject:	I	you	he she it
	we	you	they
Object:	me	you	him her it
	us	you	them
Possession:	mine	yours	his hers its
	ours	yours	theirs
Indirect	(to) me	(to) you	(to) him her it
object:	(to) us	(to) you	(to) them

The demonstrative pronoun

The **demonstrative pronoun** is used for drawing attention to or pointing out people or things:

this, that   these, those

Examples:

What is *that*? (book, tree, etc)
These belong to Jane. (records, tapes, etc)

In the above examples you can see clearly how the pronoun is used instead of an unstated noun.

The reflexive pronoun

Sometimes we wish to say something – to describe an action – where the action 'returns' on the doer:

I cut *myself*.
Peter hurt *himself*.

The -self suffix indicates that the pronoun being used to describe the doer of the action is **reflexive**:

myself, yourself, himself, herself, itself, ourselves, yourselves, themselves

The emphatic pronoun

The reflexive form of the pronoun is also sometimes used to show when the doer or receiver of an action is to be emphasised:

I *myself* will do it.
I asked you to do it *yourself*!

The interrogative pronoun

The **interrogative pronoun** is used to replace a noun in a question sentence:

Where is it?
Who did it?
What do you want?
Whose is the briefcase?

The principal interrogative pronouns are:

who, whom, what, where, when, which, whose

The relative pronoun

The **relative pronoun** is used when additional information is introduced into a sentence, which *relates* to a previously mentioned noun:

The customer *who* ordered the stationery will call back this afternoon.
The copy letter *which* you requested is not in the file.
The applicant *whom* you interviewed has decided to withdraw his application.

The major relative pronouns are:

who, whom, which, that

Note that the relative pronoun is sometimes left out of sentences for the sake of quickness, or because the noun immediately precedes it, thus making the meaning clear:
(which)
The message ∧ I took was for Mr Jones.

Assignments on pronouns

Identify the pronouns in the following sentences and state which kind of pronoun each is:

1 The manager asked to see them.

2 The secretary gave her the files.

3 The report is mine and I am prepared to stand by it.

4 This is my coat. Which is yours?

5 The managing director himself gave us the instruction.

6 What can I do for you?

7 Where is the telephone directory? It's on the shelf.

8 The minutes which you asked for have been drafted. Shall I type them myself, or would you rather do that?

9 The computer I particularly wanted is out of stock at the store that normally supplies us.

10 These are mine, and theirs are over there, but where are yours?

Somewhere in the above sentences is a pronoun which is 'understood' and which has been left out. Did you find it?

The spoken word 2

Giving and receiving messages

Often, employees, visiting clients or sales representatives make calls only to find that they are unable to speak to particular colleagues or company officials because they are either at meetings or otherwise unavailable.

In such a case, a third person – usually another member of staff – has to deal with the visitor's business and relay it to the absent person on his return. Sometimes the messages taken require urgent action. It is therefore important to master the techniques of giving or receiving a spoken message efficiently, so that action can be taken.

Check carefully through the list of points which both the message giver and the message receiver need to follow in order for the message to be conveyed clearly and without mistakes or omissions.

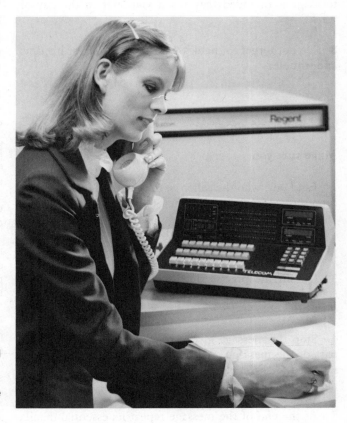

The receptionist in action   Courtesy of British Telecom

As a message giver

Make sure you

1 Pass your message to someone whose identity you have established – you may need to go back to them later on the telephone or by letter.

2 State clearly who the message is for. Give his name and job title to avoid mistaken identity – there may be several Smiths, Clarks or Joneses in the firm.

3 Impress on the message taker – if appropriate – that your message is urgent and supply a deadline by which an answer is required.

4 Express the details of your message clearly, *slowly* and

put your main points in a logical order. Remember that the message taker may be taking notes of what you are saying.

5 Repeat or spell any difficult names, addresses, numbers etc.

6 Make sure the message taker has fully grasped all the essential points of your message before you leave. Obtain feedback to make sure that this is so.

7 Remember to say where the person for whom your message is intended may reach you later in the day or week.

8 Do not forget to thank the message taker for his time and trouble.

As a message receiver

Make sure you

1 Find out: who the caller is; the organisation he or she represents; for whom his or her message is intended.

2 Check and make a note of the time and date of the call. Sometimes this information is very important.

3 Obtain the precise details of the message. Make a special note of names, dates, telephone numbers, quantities etc.

4 Stop the message giver whenever you fail to take in part of the message. Ask for the part you missed to be repeated. Ask for spellings whenever you are unsure of names, places, etc.

5 At the end of the message repeat its essential details back to the message giver. This will give him an opportunity to check that you have not missed anything out or misunderstood any part of the message.

6 Unless the message is very short and simple, be sure to *write it down*, first in rough notes and in a fair copy immediately the caller has departed. Do not allow the caller to leave until you are sure you have taken the message correctly!

7 Take *immediate action* to pass the message on to its intended recipient. It is easy to forget when you are busy.

Assignments

1 Design a message pad which would be suitable for taking down a variety of spoken messages from visitors and employ-

ees. You should use the message giver and receiver checklists as a guide.

2 You are a sales representative for a company which makes and sells: typewriters and related products; or a range of office stationery including printed letterheads; or vending machines which dispense drinks and snacks.

Devise names, addresses, telephone numbers, etc and a reason for calling upon a company. (It might be to arrange for a display of your products.) Another student plays the part of assistant to the sales manager – who is unavailable. Again, names and background should be devised.

Pairs of students can then role play the situation and a message can be delivered and taken down using the message pad devised in 1 above.

Note: It may be interesting for the visiting sales representative to write out the details of his call before the role play so that the message taken may be compared for effectiveness!

3 Form groups of 4 or 5 students. Each student should compose a message of about 100 words, containing names, dates, numbers, addresses, etc.

The messages should be passed on to the next member of the team, out of the hearing of the others, and so on, until it reaches the fifth member, who should write down the version passed to him.

When all the messages have been passed through the chain, the first and last versions should all be compared for accuracy!

(You may wish to pass some of the messages by word of mouth in the second, third and fourth links in the 'chain', and others by using a message pad in all five stages. It will then be possible to compare the degree of accuracy of both methods to see what help a message pad provides.)

4 There is the Christmas dance to be organised. Form groups of 4–5 students and pair with another group. One group is the Student Social Sub-committee, the other is either college principal, registrar, senior caretaker and restaurant supervisor; or school head, secretary, senior caretaker and kitchen supervisor.

Either group may communicate by exchanging written messages and the Social Sub-committee may also send a messenger to the staff group. During a period of, say, 40 minutes all the necessary arrangements should be made for the annual dance.

At the end of this time each of the groups should prepare a checklist of arrangements. In a general class discussion compare the sets of checklists and discuss the reasons for any problems that emerge during the activity.

Syntax

Direct and indirect objects

On pages 15 and 16, we learned that to qualify as a grammatically complete idea, a sentence needs to include at the very least, a subject and a finite verb.

We also learned that such basic sentences could be enlarged by adding on verb extensions:

SUBJECT   FINITE VERB
I   waited.

SUBJECT   FINITE VERB   VERB EXTENSION
I   waited   patiently.

Verbs which take objects

The next step in understanding how ideas are expressed in writing is to examine those ideas in which a doer (subject) performs an action (finite verb) on someone or something:

SUBJECT	FINITE VERB	DIRECT OBJECT
The bank manager	opened	the safe.

Here, the doer or subject is clearly 'the bank manager', and 'opened' the finite verb. The part of the sentence which 'receives' the action of the verb is called **the direct object**:

SUBJECT	FINITE VERB	OBJECT
Jenny	answered	the telephone.
The customer	was choosing	a birthday card.
Everyone	has enjoyed	the outing.

Verbs which take objects are called **transitive**, while those verbs which do not take objects are called **intransitive**:

Time *passed.*
Dawn *is breaking.*
Peter *sleeps.*

A simple test to check whether a verb can take an object, or whether it is intransitive, is to add the word 'it' after the verb in question:

The bank manager opened ... *it.*
Jenny answered ... *it.*

By no stretch of the imagination, however, can:

Time passed ... *it.*   Or
Dawn was breaking ... *it.*

make any sense!

Indirect objects

Another type of object is sometimes needed to express certain ideas:

The cashier gave *the clerk* the money.

Clearly, 'the money' is the direct object (he gave it). However, 'it' was given to someone – in this case, the clerk. In fact, 'the clerk' is really short for 'to the clerk' and is called the **indirect object**.

Syntax assignment

In order to check on your ability to handle subjects, finite verbs, direct objects and verb extensions, sort out the following jumbled groups into ten sentences which make sense. Identify in each sentence the subject, finite verb, direct object or verb extension.

First group

the managing director
modifying the design
henry watson
an all-out sales effort
the new receptionist
the retailer
the training manager
the typist
the demonstrator
understanding grammar and syntax

Second group

has been given
explained
will be arriving
will cause
is required
confirmed
was duplicating
speaks
gives
worked

Third group

his weekly order
tomorrow
a host of problems
the award of best salesman
confidence and authority to every student
the report of the conference
how the machine worked
conscientiously
clearly and fluently
from all sales staff

Syntax and grammar progress test

In order to check your progress in grammar and syntax, answer the following questions. After you have answered them all, check back through the preceding pages to see if you gave the right answers:

1 What are the essential parts of a grammatically acceptable sentence?

2 What does a verb extension do?

3 What does the word 'finite' mean?

4 How would you define a noun?

5 Explain the difference between 'concrete' and 'abstract' nouns.

6 List the different types of noun.

7 What is meant by the 'tense' of a verb? Give an example of three different tenses you know, using the verb 'to go'.

8 The postman delivered the mail.
The mail was delivered by the postman.

Write down the sentence which you think is using the verb 'to deliver' in the passive.

9 How would you explain what a direct object is in a sentence?
Compose a sentence containing a direct object and underline it.

10 What is an indirect object? Write down the indirect object in the following sentences:

I passed the message to Jenny.
He gave them the signal to start.

11 What is the job of the pronoun?

12 List the types of pronoun you can remember.

13 Write down an example of each of the pronouns you listed in 12.

Boost your spelling power!

Learn these key words by heart

Remember, an asterisk after a word indicates that it is very commonly misspelled:

access n, v	(accessible adj)
benefit n, v	(benefited past participle, beneficial adj)
conscious adj	(consciousness n)
definite* adj	(definition n)
exaggerate v	(exaggeration n)
friend* n	(friendship, friendliness n)
hero n	(pl heroes, f heroine)
independence n	(independent* adj)

movable adj	(movement n)
negotiate v	(negotiation n)

Check, in your dictionary, the meaning of any word you do not know and enter it in your vocabulary book.

Sentence building 1

One of the most important skills to master in continuous writing is the ability to construct sentences which not only convey meaning clearly, but which are also made interesting for the reader and which link ideas attractively.

In the early stages of learning to write continuous prose, young children tend to write their ideas as a series of short and simple sentences:

An outing to the seaside
We got up at six o'clock. We had a quick breakfast. Dad put the picnic-basket in the car. We all got in. We were all excited. We were going to the seaside! We had a long drive. I was sick. We arrived at the seaside at ten o'clock. The beach was not crowded. We found a place easily. We all went for a swim. We felt very happy. We were in a hurry. We changed on the beach.

Although the ideas in the above passage are set out very clearly, in a chronological order, the effect upon the reader is one of irritation, because each sentence is so short and each is constructed in a very similar way:

subject + finite verb + verb extension; or
subject + finite verb + object

This is because young writers find it difficult to manage more than one main idea at a time. Consider, however, the effect of making changes in the passage by joining some sentences together and by adding extra linking words:

An outing at the seaside
On the chosen day, we got up at six o'clock *and* had a quick breakfast. *Then* Dad put the picnic-basket in the car *and in a state of excitement* we all got in. We were going to the seaside! *During the long drive* I was sick *but* we arrived at the seaside at ten o'clock. The beach was not crowded *and so* we found a place easily. *In a happy mood* we all went for a swim. *To save time,* we changed on the beach.

The effect of the italicised linking words and phrases is to make the passage read in a more adult and fluent way. The information is conveyed far more attractively because the *rhythms* of the longer sentences are more varied and because the 'thud' of a falling sentence-end after each 8–10 words has been avoided.

Coordinating conjunctions

Despite their rather dreadful name, **coordinating conjunctions** are very simple words which are easy to use. The most common are:

and but next then so or yet

They are also found used in pairs:

either ... or neither ... nor
both ... and not only ... but also

The reason these conjunctions, or sentence-linking words are called coordinating is because they link together two (or more) simple sentences which convey main ideas of equal value. They could, if wished, stand alone as independent sentences. You can check this by comparing the two versions of the above passage.

Notice that each 'sentence' linked by a coordinating conjunction to form a longer sentence still contains a subject, finite verb and object or verb extension:

VERB EXTENSION	SUBJECT	FINITE VERB
During the long drive	I	was sick

SUBJECT	FINITE VERB
but we	arrived

VERB EXTENSIONS
at the seaside at ten o'clock.

Note: when two or more simple sentences are joined by a conjunction, they are then called **clauses**, and the longer sentence becomes a **compound sentence**.

Adverbial phrases

There is another way of extending meaning when building sentences, and that is to include a group of words (without a finite verb or subject) which provide more information about *when? where? how?* etc. Such phrases are called **adverbial** because they extend in more detail the meaning of the verb:

On the chosen day = *when*
During the long drive = *when*
At the seaside = *where*
In a happy mood = *how*
To save time = *why*

In the course of producing continuous writing, adverbial phrases are used a great deal to link ideas and to provide additional meaning:

on the whole as soon as possible
in the meantime whenever convenient
after some time in a while
as a result at present at the moment
in good repair with due care

Remember that adverbial phrases are generally introduced by words such as:

on in after before at with for over under
during whenever as

Sentence starters

Sometimes we wish to construct a sentence which either reinforces or supports the one which has gone before, or which seeks to introduce an idea which will lessen the effect of the preceding sentence:

John was late. *Moreover* his class had already left for the outing.
The manager decided to make economies in the office. *Furthermore* he intended to introduce savings in the expenses of the sales representatives.
The sales turnover of the shoe department was disappointing. *However,* it was more than offset by the excellent performance of the gift department.

Additional sentence starters which will serve to link adjoining sentences either by reinforcing or by lessening the effect of the first are:

nevertheless even so in addition on the other hand
still despite this fact

You should collect further examples for your own use.

Assignments

1 Study the following set of simple sentences and then make the passage more interesting by linking appropriate sentences with coordinating conjunctions chosen from: and; but; or; next; then; so; yet.

Learning to build interesting sentences is an important skill. It takes time and patience to acquire. The effort is worthwhile. First it is necessary to form clear, simple ideas. It is helpful to set them out in a rough draft. An examination of the sentences will show locations for linking words. Longer sentences are more interesting to read. They help to hold the reader's attention. Sometimes a short sentence is needed to convey an idea with a sharp impact. Prose passages may contain some short sentences. They may contain some long sentences. Much depends on the type of content of the passage. It is important to write in a varied sentence structure.

2 Compose a sentence for each of the following adverbial phrases to show how they may be used:

on the whole; as soon as possible; in the meantime; whenever convenient; after some time; in a while; as a result; at present; in good repair; with due care

Remember that each sentence must contain a subject and a finite verb!

3 Write two sentences. The second one should begin with one of the following words and be linked to the first sentence:

moreover; furthermore; however; nevertheless; even so; on the other hand; still; in addition; despite this fact

Write a pair of sentences for each starter word.

Here's the proof ...! 1

The following sentences each contain one spelling error. Identify the errors.

1 I have written to the Manager of the Norbury Hotel enquiring what accommadation he has available on 6 November.

2 There is unfortunately no acess to the roof from this floor.

3 The reps will definately be occupied elsewhere on that date.

4 Without exagerating, sales have trebled this month.

5 Is it really necesary to be an efficient proof-reader?

In each of the following sentences you will find an error of punctuation. Correct it.

6 Of all our branches, throughout the country, it is the best stocked boys department.

7 In five years' time, when I will be 28 will secretaries still use typewriters?

8 Yesterdays post was not taken to the Mail Room because Mary's off sick.

9 Transport, food, clothes, household goods, and raw materials will all be more expensive as a result of the increased price of oil.

10 This is the typists office. Is this yours? No, its the accounts office.

The following paragraph contains seven spelling mistakes and eight punctuation errors. Identify the errors and re-write the passage correctly.

The new Managing Director called a meeting of all employees – director's and factory workers alike. He explained that at the begining of the financial year when sales' had been bad proffits were down on buget. However during the sumer months trading had improved so all members' of the company would receive a bonuss for there eforts which had helped bring the company back into the black.

Information technology in organisations

For some ten years after the commercial introduction of the microprocessor in 1971, all kinds of organisations, involved in manufacturing, distributing, retailing, professional servicing and public administration, began to realise the tremendous advantages which IT could bring them. They began to design, build, sell or purchase a wide range of office equipment or production plant which incorporated computing and data processing features.

For several years, however, progress was slow in some sectors of industry since IT was new and unfamiliar and some firms and employees were reluctant to embrace the changes in their own work patterns or to carry out the re-training needed.

By 1980, however, it became obvious that the first trickle of IT change had become a fast flow and would soon become a torrent! Moreover, those far-sighted companies which had embraced IT straightaway were clearly seen to be reaping the benefits in increased productivity, sales and profits. Thus the race to become IT literate and IT centered in all kinds of organisations gathered momentum in the early 1980s and took a firm hold in the curricula of schools, colleges of technology, polytechnics and universities as the need for highly trained IT-competent personnel was recognised and acted upon.

The following chart illustrates some of the principal effects of IT in the way in which work is carried out in a range of activities spanning the major departments of larger organisations.

Employing IT in organisational departments

1 The accounts department

Computerised accounts
ledgers

The ledgers which keep the records of financial trans-actions of the firm – sales, purchases, goods returned for credit, stocks held, cash at the bank, records of overdue debtors, etc. – used to be maintained by hand and are now processed by computer which can carry out in a single operation all the entries associated with, for example, a sale or purchase.

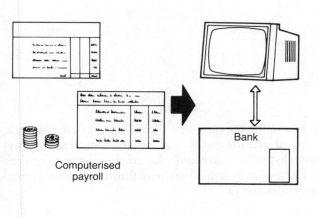

Bank

Computerised
payroll

The calculating, recording and making up of all employees' pay was also formerly carried out manually by cashiers and is now undertaken by computer by means of a payroll software package which will print out the appropriate pay slip, and likewise authorise a credit transfer for the correct amount to the employee's bank.

Management accounting
reports

Accountants also use the computer to provide helpful reports and analyses for senior staff to use and refer to in their planning and decision-making.

2 The sales department

Computerised stock control
and interrogation

Large organisations use the computer to handle incoming sales enquiries and to check directly whether the goods required are available.

The computer is also often used to monitor the performance of sales representatives – to check how well their actual sales are going in relation to a pre-set target or budget.

By using such services as British Telecom's BT Gold Service, sales representatives working hundreds of miles from their sales offices can send instant order confirmations or information requests to their own company's computer, and obtain immediate action or response. In this instance the sales rep will connect his or her own mobile computer to the firm's mainframe by means of BT's telephone lines.

3 The marketing department

Marketing analysis

In marketing the computer is used a great deal to analyse sales, advertising and sales promotion campaigns, to forecast what sales will be and what effects such as price rises or cost increases in the short-term future may have on company sales and profits.

4 The production department

Computerised design

Robotic welding
in car assembly

In the research and development of products, computers are used today to produce a wide range of designs and drawings. The software for such applications also enables VDU screens to display, say a motor-car design in three dimensions and to rotate it before the viewer's eye on the screen.

In the factory the computer, with the help of robotic arms and mechanisms is now able to carry out many manufacturing processes, tirelessly and faultlessly, which were frequently dull and repetitive. However, such developments have sometimes cost operatives their jobs, or at least caused them to be redeployed.

The process of minimising waste and faulty product manufacture has also been assisted greatly by the advent of computers which can be used to evaluate equipment electronically and even to sort parts into acceptable and rejected groups.

The initials CADCAM – Computer Aided Design and Manufacture, and CIM – Computer Integrated Manufacture are now household words in the world of manufacturing and production.

5 The personnel department

John
Bloggs
Records

As you will by now have come to expect, the employment, achievement, promotion, staff training and associated records of a company's employees are increasingly being recorded, stored and accessed by computer.

Such computerised records save much time; for example, in identifying a sales representative who speaks Spanish and has been on the firm's staff training course on its new drill, and can therefore assist the sales director with the visit of Spanish customers.

6 The office administration department

Computerised records
accessed via terminal
or microfiche process

The function of office administration is to process information and data and to ensure that sub-offices and branches in the regions in which the firm operates are provided with the range of office equipment, materials and services needed to enable them to function efficiently.

In this context, the computer is now widely used as a means of archiving or storing company records, of maintaining up-to-date details of companies selling office equipment or services, e.g. office furniture, window-cleaning and typewriter maintenance, and also their current prices.

Computerised
form design and printing

Computers may also be used to design forms and other routine documents which may be printed directly by an 'intelligent' photocopier which accepts the text of the form electronically, formats a master and prints the required quantity – all at the press of a button!

The advent of 'desk-top publishing' is now supporting office administration and communications. This is a computer based method of designing pages of text with an enhanced visual impact because of the facility to include logos, art-work and bold type-faces – all designed by the microcomputer operator with the help of desk-top publishing software packages which 'paint', draw and manipulate text and artwork.

The above chart is only able to provide a 'taster' overview of the kind of activities which have been transformed by the introduction of IT across the various sectors of industry. This transformation has not escaped the public sector, where accounts for rates and water, council house rent payments and electoral registers are all compiled and maintained with the aid of a computer.

Indeed so extensive is the computer's use in commerce, industry and the public service today that the country's social and economic fabric would very quickly disintegrate if all the computers in use were to be switched off together.

The chaos which would ensue is difficult to over-emphasise. For example, when the computer failed in one of the London Heathrow terminals everything came to a halt – no baggage could be checked in, no boarding passes issued, no planes could take off – until the computer came back into action; several hours passed before the terminal returned to normal.

If banks, fire-stations, factories, hospitals, super-markets and the like suddenly lost computer services, we should all realise rapidly how dependent we have all become on the power of the microprocessor and computer!

Computerised transactions in a large organisation

Suppliers
waste disposal firms
Stationers

Maintenance firms
Overall/towel rentals

STATEMENTS

Office equipment suppliers

INVOICES

Office administration department

CONTRACTS

Production department

Design companies

Public relations companies

SCHEDULES

Marketing department

Stationery stocks
Staff productivity
Equipment records
Analyses of market surveys
Schedules for advertising campaigns
Product modelling simulations

Purchase records/stock control
Production analyses
Quality control
Production planning

Manpower planning
Personnel records
Job appraisal records

SENIOR MANAGEMENT: reports, abstracts and analyses

DESIGNS

Personnel department

Newspaper companies

Employment bureaux

Advertising agencies, trade journals, newspapers

ANALYSES

Regional, district offices

Sales analyses
Sales force expenses
Sales forecasts
Customer enquiries

Financial reports
Certified accounts
Status reports in profits, costs, cash flow etc.

SPECIFICATIONS

Jobs centres

Manpower Services Commission

REPORTS

Sales department

Account customers

Accounts department

ESTIMATES

Suppliers
Inland Revenue
Chartered Accountants

Account customers

Company branches

TODAY, LARGE AMOUNTS OF INFORMATION, FLOWING INTO, OUT OF AND AROUND THE ORGANISATION ARE PROCESSED BY COMPUTERS.

Activities and assignments

1 Write an account of the problems of communication which arise as an organisation grows. Illustrate your account with any charts or diagrams you think helpful.

2 First do your research, then write an account of how your college or school is structured. Include a diagram. **Note:** you

will find it helpful to interview staff and students before preparing your rough notes.

Alternatively, present your account as a talk to your group, appropriately illustrated with a chart or diagram.

3 Find out and report back to your group about the kind of administrative tasks which your school or college is now undertaking with the aid of a computer.

4 Explain the meaning of the following suffixes:

-able -an -er -ism -ology -oid

5 Complete the following words:

monot... (boring)
administrat... (one who administers)
nece... (needed)
station... (letters, envelopes)
princip... (main, major)
lovel... (beauty)
arg... (disagreement)

6 Provide three examples of the personal pronoun.

7 Explain the difference between a reflexive pronoun and an emphatic pronoun. Supply two sentences to illustrate the difference.

8 Identify the pronouns in the following passage:

I asked myself why he did it. The theft, which was almost immediately discovered, was hardly worth the effort. Who would imagine Peter could be so silly? Only the previous day, he himself had been talking eagerly of the chance of promotion. Now that is out of the question, of course!

Make a list and state which type of pronoun each is.

9 You are the assistant to the personnel manager of a large firm. He has asked you to design a handout which will explain to junior employees how to take and give messages accurately and efficiently. Either as an individual, or as a member of a small group, compose a suitable handout, in not more than 300–350 words, including any appropriate illustrations.

10 Explain the difference between a direct object and an indirect object. Compose a sentence which contains both and identify them.

11 Explain the job of the coordinating conjunction. Give four examples of a coordinating conjunction.

12 Compose three sentences; each should contain an adverbial phrase to answer the question:

(a) when? (b) where? (c) how?

Underline the adverbial phrase in each.

13 Interview an older relative or friend in order to find out what the major aspects of his or her job are, the methods of communication which he or she uses, and how he or she fits into the organisation as a whole.
Compose an account of your findings in about 350 words. **Note:** you should change the names to preserve anonymity of interviewee and organisation. When your general group has completed the accounts, exchange and study them.
As a general group exercise, discuss the various problems of communication and personal relationships which occur in different occupations. Try to decide what types of job are most demanding in a communication sense.

14 From your dictionary extract three words which you think members of your group should be able to spell. Then, in teams of 3–5, hold a spelling tournament. Two points for each correct answer, one point if thrown open to the opposing team.
Make a checklist of all the words you could not spell yourself! Write them up in your vocabulary book and memorise them.

15 Choose a local company and pick one of the departments illustrated in the chart entitled Employing IT in organisational departments. Carry out research into the ways in which work has been affected by the introduction of IT, in the following way:

(a) Pair up with a fellow student and then, with the help of your teacher, arrange to interview the manager of the department you have selected about the changes which IT has brought about.

(b) Before you carry out your interview, with your partner draw up a checklist of the questions you want to ask and produce them neatly in typescript or handwritten form. Then enclose them with a suitable covering letter sent before your interview date to provide the manager with advance notice of the nature of your investigation. You can pose further follow-up questions during the interview.

After the interview, carry out one of the following tasks.

(c) Write a short account of your interview findings and duplicate it for circulation in your group.

(d) Produce your questionnaire as an overhead projection foil and then give your group a five minute oral presentation – include any further audio-visual aids you wish – about your findings.

16 First carry out your research, then write an illustrated account of about 400 words on one of the following.

(a) How a computerised payroll package works.

(b) What 'computer aided design' is about.

(c) Computers as record keepers.

(d) Forms – from design to collation by computer!

(e) What desk-top publishing can do.

17 In groups of 4–5 plan and carry out the following group project.

Prepare and present in any form you think most effective a 10–15 minute group presentation on the following topic:

How IT has changed the ways in which organisations function, from 1970 to the present day.

Project planning tips:
1 Decide who will be your group leader and have a decisive role in case of disagreement – but always try to agree by consensus.

2 Decide how you will tackle the title – can you cover *all* kinds of organisation? Would it be more practicable to select one type of organisation and deal with that as an all-purpose example?

3 Should you concentrate upon changes in equipment used or on how jobs are carried out?

4 How much detail can you afford to go in to?

5 To what extent would charts, OHP foils, handouts and other audio-visual aids help you to cover the ground and get your points across?

6 How best could you divide up the jobs in your group of:

  (*a*) carrying out the research

  (*b*) delivering the presentation

so as to share the workload and to make for an effective presentation?

When you are ready to give your group presentations, select a member from each group to form a judges panel to decide on the most interesting and effective presentation.

Note: If possible, you may wish to video-tape the presentations so as to keep them for revision purposes later in your course.

Unit 5

How the office works

The word office comes from Latin and today possesses a number of different meanings, including the doing of a service. In the context of business it came to mean a counting house where merchants kept records of their transactions and, in the 19th century, a room where clerks worked on documents and letters.

Today we would probably define an office as a place where information is acquired, stored and distributed according to the needs of different people within an organisation and depending upon the work of that organisation. The Office, Shops and Railway Premises Act of 1963 included in the activities of an office: administration, handling money, filing, typing and carrying out clerical work.

(A) Essentially the office provides a support service for the staff who carry out certain jobs within an organisation. For example, the role of an office for company sales

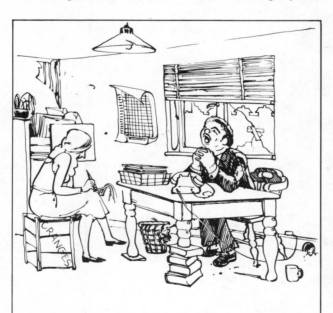

'. . . and you can finish the advert with, 'excellent opportunity to work with happy team in modern office surroundings' . . . .'

representatives includes processing their sales orders so that customers are sent the goods they order, paying the representatives' out-of-pocket expenses promptly, keeping car documentation up-to-date, relaying customers' messages to them quickly, and advising them how their sales figures compare week by week in relation to their budget, and so on. Thus in this example, the office enables sales reps to function effectively and happily. The following chart illustrates some of the major roles of an office as a servicing and supporting unit.

The office's major tasks

- Takes incoming messages – by telephone, telex, facsimile transmitter, computerised electronic mail or in the form of incoming post – and routes them to specified personnel.

- Produces various written documents on demand – letters, memoranda, reports, minutes, etc. for the initiating member of staff.

- Maintains an effective filing system, whether paper based and manually operated, or computer based and electronically filed. (B)

- Handles incoming customer, client or public enquiries and processes them via appropriate personnel.

- Completes and delivers various official and governmental documents and forms, e.g. VAT returns, Department of Employment records, etc.

- Maintains information and records about its own organisation's personnel for promotion, pay and sickness benefit purposes, etc.

As the above chart illustrates, the office is a nerve-centre (C) for the processing of information. And while some information processing, such as the filing of salesmen's expense claims, may be routine, other information, i.e. deciding whether or not to install a computerised network to handle the information flow of the office, could be crucial to its future success. Clearly, then, the office's staffing needs to be structured so as to enable both the routine and the 'one-off' kind of information processing to be handled with equal efficiency. Just as the organisation as a whole may be regarded as a pyramid in its structure, so also may the office of a particular department within the organisation:

office manager

3 senior supervisors

and

12 junior clerks, typists and data entry operators

The office manager

IT in the office

Ever since the typewriter replaced the quill-pen over one hundred years ago the processing of information has been made increasingly labour-saving and prompt as a result of the introduction of technology into the office. This century has seen the development of electronic, memory typewriters which heralded the introduction of word processing; the introduction of the Private Manual/Branch Exchange telephone switchboard to handle incoming phone-calls and internal extension calls; the facility of telex to send telephone-cable or radio-wave routed messages around the world, convertible into printed format on receipt; and facsimile transmission which made it possible to transmit transglobally pictures, diagrams, photographs and plans as well as text in pre-created page format. Moreover, today the impact of the IT office technology revolution is continuing to provide – almost daily – new miracles of information processing in the form of either office equipment hardware developments or computer software innovations.

The table on pages 81–84 provides an overview of the kind of office equipment and information processing facilities which have been brought into office work over the past 20 years or so.

The office manager

The person at the head of an office organisation, the office manager, has a very important job. There are many demands on his time and always he has to make sure that things run smoothly. As well as being responsible for up to 50 or 60 office staff he might have 450 branch offices throughout the country. These he would have to keep

stocked with sales documents such as receipt books, invoice pads, headed note-paper, and so on. Or, he may have to ensure that a company's 6000 employees all receive the correct pay at the correct time. Whatever he is doing the office manager must make sure that the company's objectives are being met, but that the costs are kept to a minimum.

Also, the office manager has to make sure that the work of the office has been properly delegated and is being efficiently supervised. Mistakes can be very costly and he very definitely takes the blame if things go wrong. In allocating and supervising the work of the office, he will need to keep a watchful eye on the personal relationships of his staff and be ever-ready to step in if there is a conflict or if morale becomes low. Clearly he cannot do all this himself, so he will rely on his senior supervisors to look after delegated responsibilities such as customer accounts, expenses or order processing.

The office supervisor

The office supervisor often acts as a staging-post or junction-box, since he will be given a job to do by the office manager. This will mean that the supervisor's staff will need to be briefed and instructions may have to be given carefully and in detail to ensure that what the manager said in broad terms is carried out in precise detail. Thus the supervisor will be in close contact with the filing clerk or audio-typist. Therefore, any problems at the bottom of the office pyramid will need to be spotted by the supervisor and reported to the manager. Equally, it will be up to the supervisor to tell the manager of any complaints or criticisms the junior staff may have. As you can see, it is important that an office supervisor is a good communicator who can establish pleasant yet productive relationships with staff.

Though problems will occur in an office on any day, much of its work is routine and recurs at regular intervals. For example, in an accounts office, customer account statements need to be compiled and despatched at the end of each month or trading period. In a transport office, company vehicles need to be licensed and taxed annually. Thus in every office, there are many activities which have been organised in a routine system, where a cycle of events is repeated daily, weekly or monthly. Though such routine work may lack glamour and excitement, it is extremely important and the supervisor well knows the need to keep such routine systems working smoothly!

The office junior

Because of the way offices tend to be structured, where responsibilities are divided into sections and further sub-divided as tasks and delegated to individual members of staff, the work of the office junior is likely to be very detailed, and only a small part of a much larger undertaking. A clerk, for example, may be solely concerned with maintaining the supply of a large office's stationery, or a typist may type only letters dealing with customer complaints.

Many junior members of staff will be in their teens or early twenties, and will therefore be learning about the work in their part of the office. But it is very important that office juniors take a lively and active interest in what is going on around them, so that they prove capable of assuming more responsibility when opportunities for promotion arise. In the same way, the go-ahead office junior will seek to acquire additional expertise on in-house training courses or day-release courses at local colleges. The following list includes some of the main activities which the office junior may perform:

opening and sorting the morning's post
sorting incoming invoices and bills
sorting incoming invoices and bills
producing quotations for customer enquiries
typing correspondence and documents
maintaining the filing system
making up monies to be banked
making up wage packets
running a switchboard
dealing with visitors
ordering stationery and office consumables
duplicating office forms and documents

As you can see, though many of these tasks are routine, there is not one of them which is not important for the efficient running of the office. Thus the office junior is very much at the 'sharp end' of the office's work, and employs daily the communication skills of speaking, reading, writing and listening. The work requires attention to detail and accuracy and an ability to get along cheerfully with fellow workers. Though the office junior may be at the base of the office pyramid, there is no doubt that, unless such work is properly carried out, the office would grind to a halt. And so the idea of the office junior holding up the rest of the office pyramid on his shoulders is not just a fanciful one!

IT equipment in the office

The pace of change and innovation in the design of IT based office equipment has never been faster than it is today. The instructions on pages 81–84 detail the major types of office equipment currently in use, but could easily need to be added to tomorrow with the advent of a new computerised communications tool!

Applications of a computerised office information system

Accounts
Sales ledger
Cost control

Word processing
Reports, letters, minutes, etc. — Electronic filing

Electronic mail

Facsimile transmission

Order processing

Sales statistics

Stock control

Sales forecasting

Payroll

National insurance

Personnel records

Modelling of markets

Computerised telephone PABX services — Teleconferencing viewdata, teletext

IT office equipment checklist

Equipment

Electronic typewriter

Desk-top computer

Facsimile transmitter

Features

automatic correction; text display panel; built-in memory; facility to act as computer printer

able to handle text and graphics production as well as a variety of software applications packages, e.g. word processing, spreadsheets, databases, etc.; can act as terminal of mainframe or minicomputer or as a 'stand alone intelligent computer' working from its own memory

used to send text, plans, diagrams, photographs, over long distances via telephone or radio transmission systems; transmitter converts text or diagram into an electronic signal and receiver turns it back into its original format

Courtesy of British Telecom

Telex

used for sending printed messages over telecommunications network; the text is produced on a typewriter-like keyboard and transmitted like facsimile messages; a printer at the receiving end prints out the text received electronically

Courtesy of British Telecom

Photocopiers

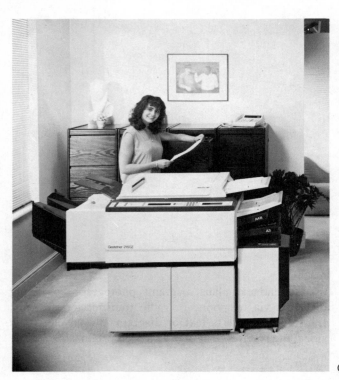

almost all photocopiers are now plain paper copiers and range from 'single sheet feed' desk-top models for 'one-off' copies to massive laser-driven printers used to print thousands of computer print-out pages per hour; colour printing and computerised text acceptance as well as optical character recognition of text are now features of photocopier technology

Courtesy of Gestetner

Printers

these range from simple dot-matrix computer outputs for internal use to sophisticated 'letter quality' printers with interchangeable print heads for variation of typeface and include features like: colour printing ribbons or toners, automatic emboldening, underscoring, centering, tabulating and graphics printing, etc. driven by computer programs

Computerised telephone systems

information technology has accelerated the pace of change in telephone technology; current features include extensive international direct dialling, IDD, computerised switchboards to 'hunt' for appropriate call acceptors, abbreviated dialling codes for often used numbers, telephone conferencing linking multiple users, 'camp on line' facilities to retry engaged numbers automatically and so on; British Telecom provide a wide range of specialist services including data transmission via modem, private line/network leasing, electronic mail message delivery, delivery of word processed messages (Teletex), video teleconferencing, etc.

Courtesy of British Telecom

Viewdata systems

BT's Prestel service provides 'tv' pages which can be scanned on a tv monitor and used either as a form of advertising or information distribution; some firms use them for internal training purposes and the system can be interrogated via computer keyboard and modem to send messages to viewdata transmitter – for example to obtain details of a polytechnic course of study.

Local and wide area networking and electronic mail

desk-top computers which used to 'stand alone' can now be linked to many others; used in various company departments (or even on the other side of the world) to access organisational information databases and to send messages from VDU screen to VDU screen – 11 seconds from England to Australia!

Your way ahead!

As the above examples clearly illustrate, IT electronic office equipment is now very sophisticated and rapidly taking over a host of office tasks, both routine and one-off.

If you want to get ahead and build a sound basis for a good career, the time and effort you devote to becoming 'IT expert' will be like a gold plated investment!

BECOME AN IT EXPERT!

Mastering the meaning

1 Explain the meaning of the following words and phrases in 'How the office works' on pages 78–80:

a support service   Line A
manually operated   Line B
the office is a nerve centre for processing information   Line C
pre-created page format   Line D
delegated   Line E
The office supervisor often acts as a staging-post or junction-box   Line F
attention to detail and accuracy   Line G
fanciful   Line H

2 Why is it so important for managers in organisations to obtain information on a regular basis?

3 What are the reasons for dividing the work of an office into sections run by office supervisors?

4 Why is it important that an efficient filing system is maintained in offices?

5 In what ways has the electronics revolution affected the way an office functions?

6 Why is the job of an office manager a demanding one?

7 Outline briefly the role of the office supervisor.

8 Why is the work of the junior of particular importance in the office?

9 Summarise in about 100 words the range of communication skills which are employed in the running of an office by both senior and junior staff.

Discussion topics

Discuss the following topics in a general session:

1 Would you like to work in an office? If so, give your reasons and state what sort of office you would like to work in. If not, explain why not.

2 What would you say are the most important skills and personal qualities needed in someone who works as a clerk or typist in an office?

3 Can you suggest any reasons why the office should have become the centre for much of the work that is done in companies or public service departments?

4 What changes do you think are likely to take place in the future in the way that offices function and are equipped?

Research assignments

1 Visit, by arrangement, a large office in your locality. Find out what its main activities are and how it has been organised to carry them out.

Draw a plan of the layout, and in 350–400 words write an account of what the office does.

2 By arrangement, interview a secretary in your school or college and write an account of his or her work.

Oral and written assignments

1 What sort of communications equipment do you consider essential in an office?

Draw up a checklist of such equipment and compose brief written notes to justify what you include.

Compare your checklist and notes with those produced by others in your group.

2 Find out what is meant by the terms 'office landscaping' and 'open plan office'.

Write an account of what are considered to be advantages of this type of office design. You should include any illustrations or diagrams you think helpful.

3 Talk to friends or relatives who work in an office. Find out what kind of emergencies can occur in an office.

Write a story about such an emergency and describe how it was dealt with.

Read the stories produced by others in your group.

4 First carry out your research, and then write an article of about 400 words to be published in a school-leavers' magazine. It should give the reader an idea of the type of work which takes place in an office and describe the sort of job a school-leaver might expect to get in an office.

5 Research *one* of the following, and then give a five minute talk to your group on the subject:

The role of the telephone in an office
The work of a word processor operator

What a filing clerk does
How an office may be organised and structured
How to handle callers to the office
How a computerised telephone system helps the office worker

Punctuation

The question mark

The direct question

The question mark is used in English to show the reader that a *direct* question is being asked:

'What is the time?' asked John.
Does anyone ever admit to being a gossip? Surely not, gossiping is something that other people do.

As you will have seen from the above examples, direct questions may be asked either within the inverted commas of direct speech, or they may be posed by the author in a piece of prose which directs a question at the reader. Such questions, which do not really expect an answer are called *rhetorical questions* and are used by the author to catch the reader's interest.

Direct questions are often introduced by key words such as:

what   where   when   why   who   how

To indicate that a question is being asked, the word order of a sentence is very often changed. In a statement, the word order is:

You have spoken to Jenny about the report.

In posing a question, the 'have' part of the verb is placed in front of the subject, 'you':

Have you spoken to Jenny about the report?

Notice that we also use 'do' and 'did' to show that a question is being asked:

Do you know where Jack is?
Did you see him today?

Whenever direct questions are being asked in direct speech, the question mark always comes inside the inverted commas and replaces any *other punctuation mark:*

'When is he arriving?' enquired Peter.

Remember also, that although the question mark acts as its own full-stop, in examples like that above, the 'e' of enquired is kept in lower case because the idea is all one sentence.

The indirect question

Sometimes questions are asked in direct speech and are later reported (in minutes of a meeting, for example). In direct speech a question may be asked:

'Mr Chairman, will Saturday 14th June be suitable for the next meeting?' asked Mrs Dixon.

Such a question, reported after a lapse of time would be written as:

The Chairman was asked by Mrs Dixon whether Saturday 14th June would be suitable for the next meeting.

We shall be dealing in more detail with such types of writing, known as **reported speech** in Unit 11. But notice that the question has been turned into a statement: it is true – this is what Mrs Dixon asked the Chairman. Therefore, no question mark is needed. Such indirect questions are often introduced by the words 'whether' or 'if'.

Also, direct questions such as:

'What shall I do next?' asked Jim.

may be turned into a statement in reported speech:

Jim asked what he should do next.

Again, as the sentence is a statement, no question mark is needed.

Remember

1   Direct questions always need a question mark.

2   Indirect questions in reported speech are usually statements and need no question marks.

3   In direct speech, the question mark comes *inside* the inverted commas, and replaces either a comma or a full-stop.

4   Rhetorical questions which act as direct questions require question marks.
(**Note:** it is generally considered bad style to use too many rhetorical questions in a passage of prose.)

Question mark assignments

Insert a question mark where you think necessary in the following sentences:

1 'Mary, have you seen the petty cash book.'

2 'What do you want it for' asked Jenny.

3 She wondered whether she should telephone Mr Jones, or wait until he returned.

4 The problem is simply stated. Why should anyone spend more time at work than is necessary. The answer is that some people are 'workaholics'!

5 Jenny asked Mr Jones if there were any more letters to be typed.

6 'If I do go,' asked Peter, 'will you come with me.'

7 Managers do not give enough consideration to the problem of secretaries who are over-qualified for the work they do. Indeed, I ask myself frequently whether some managers really care. Is there, then, a need to improve the secretary's career structure if he or she is to find true job satisfaction.

8 'Whether I go or not will depend on whether Penny comes with me.'

9 'What we want is fair shares for all.'

10 I doubt whether the key will fit.

'Tell them I'm on my way!'

A case study

Shirley Stephens, a junior clerk at Britalite Lamps Limited, works in the company's purchasing office. At present she is alone in the office during the lunch-break. Mr Hawkins, purchasing officer, has just left the office.

The telephone rings and Shirley takes the call:

'Hello? Who? Oh, Mr Simpson, production manager. You wanted Mr Hawkins? Well, he isn't here. He's out at the moment. Where? Oh, well, he didn't say, exactly, but I'm sure he won't be long. I see. You want him to ring you the moment he gets back. Oh, my name's Shirley. What? Oh, Stephens. Yes, I'll tell him it's important. Right.'

At this point Tony Gupta, from the accounts department walks into the office:

'Excuse me.'

'Yes?'

'I've come down from accounts. Miss Carter wants your expenses sheet for last month. Supposed to have been sent up last week.'

'Oh. Well that's Jim Riley's fault. He's at lunch at the moment.'

'Well, can't *you* give it to me? I've rung down for it twice already!'

'Well, I would, but Jim's got his own particular filing system. He's very touchy about who tampers with it. *He* knows where everything is, but I wouldn't know where to start looking! Oh, all right, I suppose I can try.'

As Shirley starts to rummage through Jim Riley's papers, a clerk from the mail room arrives:

'Got a memo here for Mrs Catchpole. Marked urgent!'

'Oh, well, put it down over there somewhere will you. I'm tied up at the moment trying to find a wretched expenses sheet. Now where was I? ... It's no good! We'll have to send it up to you this afternoon.'

'*Please* try to let me have it today. I can't get on till I've got it.'

Tony Gupta leaves and the telephone rings:

'Hello? Personnel? Oh. *Who* did you say? Carol Wainwright. Oh, Carol, I'm afraid not. Because she left about a week ago. Quite suddenly. How do you mean? Well it's not my job to tell you when people leave. If only people would give us a chance to get on here, without constant interruptions.... Yes, I'll tell Mr Johnson. Oh! Now I know why you don't know! Mr Johnson's been off sick for the past fortnight. Bunion's been troubling him again.... Well, Jean Parker does some of his work for him. Look, couldn't you give her a ring after lunch? Oh, all right, I suppose I could tell her to send you the details.'

Shirley rings off as Janet Goodson arrives from the company doctor's office:

'Hello, Shirley. How's things?'

'Don't ask! I've been rushed off my feet!'

'Well, I've just come from Dr Tanner. He's just had a call from the hospital. They've had a cancellation and could start the therapy treatment for your back. The appointment's for 2.30. You've just about got time if you hurry.'

'That's great news! Thanks! Tell them I'm on my way!'

With that, Shirley grabbed her coat and hurried off down the corridor, glancing anxiously at her watch.

Discussion topics

Discuss the following topics in small groups or in a general class session.

1 Read through the case study carefully. What shortcomings can you identify in the running of the purchasing office at Britalite Lamps?

2 How well did Shirley handle the callers and telephone-calls during the lunch-break?

3   What suggestions could you make for improving the way in which the purchasing office is organised and run?

Written assignments

1   Re-write the dialogue of the case study in the way that you think Shirley's conversations should have been conducted.

2   First check the section on message taking on pages 65–66, and then write out the messages which you think Shirley should have written to the members of staff.

Oral assignment

The following assignment should be role played in pairs. The dialogue may be tape-recorded by individual pairs of students and the various interviews played back for discussion by the class.

One student should play the part of Mr Hawkins and the other the part of Shirley Stephens. Mr Hawkins has called Shirley into his office to take her to task over the way she handled matters during the lunch-break. Shirley does not feel she is entirely to blame.

Know your IT! Key words and terms

2: Hardware

keyboard: the input device for inputting data into the computer's CPU (Central Processing Unit); commonly the keyboard comprises a QWERTY typewriter-like set of alpha-numeric keys, a set of functional or command keys (F1–F10) which input specific instructions depending on how they are used in any given software package, a set of number keys for inputting numbers for calculations and other keys for carrying out various editing jobs, like deleting data, moving the cursor around and so on.

the screen: often referred to as the 'VDU' or Visual Display Unit, it takes the form of a 'CRT' or Cathode Ray Tube just like the familiar one in your TV set. Electrons are 'fired' on to a specially treated material which forms the screen's coating so that they glow in the form of letters, numbers, graphic symbols etc.

screen words:
cursor   the rectangular 'blob' which shows where the next keystroke will be located.
menu   a set of options which can be accessed via the computer; for instance in word processing – indent, delete, reform paragraph etc.

status line   used in spreadsheets to remind the user of where he is and what aids he can access.
scroll   to move the screen up or down a set of information, like a tv camera moving over a large sheet of paper.
cell: an individual 'slot' for receiving data in a spreadsheet.

printer words:
on-line   connected to computer and able to act on print instructions.
impact printers   printers which 'hit' the paper by means of a form of metal pin (dot matrix) or metal key (daisy wheel).
founts/typography   words used to mean the kind of type face used to form the letters and numbers; note that some desk-top publishing equipment includes a wide variety of type faces available in its printer which can be varied at will for visual effect.
cps   characters per second; printers are measured by the speed at which they print, smaller daisy wheel printers reach speeds up to 60 cps, while larger printers print whole lines of text at a time rather than individual characters and are known as 'line printers'.
tractor feed   a term used to describe the way that 'continuous' or 'fan-fold' stationery is fed into the printer by means of two parallel sprocket wheels; see also 'hopper feeder'.

Extend your IT word power!

Find out what the following words or terms mean and explain them to your group:

the keyboard: the escape key, the home key, page up, page down keys, the end key, arrow keys;

the screen: windows, a light-pen, wrap-around, pixel, split-screen, overlay, touch sensitive screen;

the printer: embolden, laser-printer, intelligent printer, to spool, print queue, hopper feed;

general: terminal, peripheral, dedicated, stand-alone, shared-logic, hard-disk, Winchester, voice input, network, file-server.

You *can* spell!

Vowel sounds

A E I O U

The spelling of vowel sounds is not the easiest of skills to acquire. Few English writers or shorthand transcribers would contradict this statement; but it is, nevertheless, a skill which *can* be mastered with determination – and a good dictionary within arm's reach.

Perhaps the best way to learn the spelling of vowel sounds which are commonly used in English is to tackle the problem **phonetically** – by the way the vowels and vowel combinations sound. Inevitably there will be pitfalls; some vowel spellings sound the same but are spelled differently. But learn the 'rogues in the pack' and you will be surprised how easy the rest are to learn.

Helpful hints

1 I almost always comes before e except after c: believe; frieze; ceiling; receive; *but* seize; reign

2 A short vowel sound often indicates a double consonant coming next: hammer; bitter; cutting

3 A long vowel followed by a single consonant usually has an e after it: fire; bite; pipe; diner; ruler

4 Double vowels are usually: ee; oo (it is very unlikely that you will ever meet aa ii uu and then only in a foreign word) but remember that diphthongs link two different vowels – fear, broad etc

5 When a prefix is added which doubles the vowel, the vowels are sounded separately: cooperate; pre-eminent; coordinate; de-escalate

6 Most words ending in y, change the y to an i if the word is made longer: lovely: loveliness; lonely: loneliest; happy: happier

A helpful practice is to collect the various spellings of vowel sounds you encounter and to record them in your vocabulary book to commit them to memory between lessons.

Vowel assignment

Complete the spelling of the following:

def...t	(conquer)
compl...te	(full, finished)
m...t	(water round castle)
sp...te	(nastiness)
s...te	(of furniture)
p...rs...	(follow)
l...te	(guitar-like instrument)
sl...t	(small, slim)
fl...	(e.g. of a chimney)
igl...	(Eskimo house)
h...r	(one who inherits)
w...r	(controls river flow)
g...rdle	(belt)
gla...r	(frozen river of ice)
sph...re	(globe)
p...r	(stare intently)

enorm...s	(very large)
nutri...s	(good food value)
scrump...s	(delicious to eat)
misch...s	(naughty)
gl...r...	(look angry)
t...r	(round trip)
g...dy	(brightly coloured)
hum...r	(wit, jokes)
fero...s	(savage)
...rial	(radio mast)

Boost your spelling power!

Learn these key words by heart

Remember, an asterisk after a word indicates that it is very commonly misspelled:

accidental adj	(accidentally adv)
budgeted v	(budget n budgetary adj)
committee* n	(commit v commitment n)
desperate adj	(despair v)
eighth adj, n	(eight n, adj)
financial* adj	(finance n financier n)
guardian n	
lose v	(losing* adj)
noticeable* adj	(notice v, n)
occur* v	(occurred v occurrence n)

Do not forget to enter in your vocabulary book any words with which you are unfamiliar, either in terms of spelling or meaning!

Business letters 2

Structuring the letter

1 Introductory paragraph

Provides theme and context
The opening paragraph ① of a letter (see page 90) introduces the theme and puts it into a context or background. In this case, John Chandler acknowledges that he has received Penny Johnson's letter inviting him to act as stage manager. Opening paragraphs are also used to refer to essential people, events or things to which the letter will refer.

2 Middle paragraph(s)

Provide detailed information

Having introduced the theme ②, John goes on to confirm the dates and times of the rehearsals of 'South Pacific', as they have a bearing on the next part of his message. John points out ③ that his need to resit his GCSE mathematics examination has involved him in attending the College of Technology on a Wednesday evening – a day and time which clashes with rehearsals. As a result, he has to decline the invitation ④.

Thus the middle paragraph(s) of a letter develop its theme and provide the relevant details and particulars. The number of paragraphs used will depend upon the complexity of the letter's subject, but notice that in letters, paragraphs are kept fairly short, and deal with one topic at a time.

In bringing his letter to a close, John offers, as an alternative, to help out by assisting with the play's publicity.

3 Closing paragraph(s)

Provide action statement and courteous close

Thus the concluding paragraph of a letter makes a clear **action statement** ⑤, where the writer indicates what action he requests or expects of the recipient. Some such statements include a deadline. Lastly, some letters are concluded by a courteous sentence ⑥ to act as a means of signalling the end of the message.

Note: John Chandler goes to some trouble to compose a polite and helpful letter even though he is having to decline the invitation.

No matter how elegant or crisp the typewriting or handwriting of a letter may be, it will not have its intended effect upon the recipient unless its message is carefully planned and logically structured.

The first step in planning the structure of a letter is to ask oneself the essential question:

What is my aim in writing this letter?

Producing letters in business is an expensive process, and it is therefore important to ensure that the matter could not be dealt with in another, cheaper way.

The following are some of the reasons for writing business letters:

- to enquire about the price of goods or services and to find out about delivery times
- to complain about shortcomings or defects in goods or services
- to put right such complaints from customers
- to provide sales quotations or estimates
- to collect debts from account customers
- to sell a product or service to new or existing customers

---

46 Park Road
Hightown
Midshire HT12 5MS

12 September 19--

Miss P Johnson
Honorary Secretary
Hightown Drama Club
HIGHTOWN
Midshire HT4 2MS

Dear Miss Johnson

① Thank you for your letter of 10 September 19-- inviting me to act as stage manager for the Club's forthcoming production of 'South Pacific'.

② In your letter, you mention that rehearsals will take place on Wednesday and Friday evenings between 7 00 pm and 10 30 pm, and that the three weeks commencing 5 December 19-- would be taken up with a week's rehearsals and a fortnight's production of the play.

③ As you may be aware, I took a number of GCSE examinations last June and, unfortunately, failed the mathematics examination. As this particular subject is important to me, I have enrolled at Hightown College of Technology in an evening class on a Wednesday evening, leading to a resit examination at the end of November.

④ Much as I would wish to accept your kind offer to act as stage manager, I feel I must decline, as I should not be able to devote the amount of time needed to carry out the responsibilities of the position as I would wish, and as the standards of the Club require.

⑤ I should like to take this opportunity, however, of wishing the Club every success in the venture and shall certainly support it by helping with publicity and ticket sales.

Please let me know whom I should contact to help with the publicity.

⑥ I look forward to hearing from you.

Yours sincerely

John Chandler

The aim or aims of a letter will depend on the reasons for it being written. The complaining customer may feel it is better to express a complaint in courteous language if this results in securing a prompt replacement. Here, to express annoyance rudely would certainly not have the desired effect. Similarly, a polite but tersely written letter from a company accountant may result in a reluctant customer settling a long-outstanding account. Thus the aim of the letter will not only govern *what* is written, but *how* it is written – the creation of an **appropriate tone**.

The three stage approach

The next step is to select and organise into a sequence the main points to be included in the letter. In order to do this, it is helpful to think of the letter's structure in three main sections:

1 Introduction and background
2 Development of information
3 Action-stating conclusion

The opening paragraph

Many business and public service letters are given a subject heading. This helps the reader to see immediately what its subject is. Nevertheless, it is important that the opening paragraph puts the letter into a clear context, by indicating why the letter is being written:

I am considering taking my family to the south of France for a holiday this coming summer....

Thank you for your letter of 5 April 19— in which you request a quotation for....

Occasionally, it is important to provide in an opening paragraph, background information to help the reader to grasp the significance of the coming detailed information.

The middle paragraph(s)

The middle paragraph or paragraphs are used to develop the subject-matter of the letter. A sales office, for example, might seek to provide the main details about two or three desk-top computers in response to a customer's interest. Alternatively, a builder's letter providing a quotation might supply the breakdown of the cost of building a home extension. Since the main detail of the letter occurs in these paragraphs, it is important to ensure that the points of information given are presented in an order which will aid the reader to understand them easily. In longer letters, a main point may be dealt with in each of

a number of paragraphs. Remember that it is always helpful to make a checklist of the letter's main points before writing it out. This ensures that nothing important is omitted and also that it does not wander off the point. *Before you start to write*, you should make sure that the order of points in your checklist makes good sense.

The concluding paragraph(s)

Since most letters expect some sort of action from their recipients, it is essential that the writer makes a clear and courteous statement near the end of the letter to indicate what help he needs, how the customer may order a new product, what is expected to put a complaint right and so on. It is important not to be vague, but equally, not to place impossible demands on the recipient.

Many letter writers like to close their letters with a polite sentence in keeping with the tone of the letter:

I should therefore be grateful if you would look into the matter.
Please do not hesitate to contact me if you require any further information.
I look forward to hearing from you.

Notice in the first example the correct form of the verbs – should ... would and *not* would ... could.

Not all letters need such a close; a final demand for the payment of a debt might be better left with its final sentence being:

Unless payment is made within seven days of the receipt of this letter, I shall be compelled to put the matter in the hands of the company's solicitors.

In this way, the final statement of intent remains sharp and effective.

Specimen letter layout: semi-blocked, closed punctuation style

Letterhead: designed by graphics artist – trading name, postal address, telephone number ①

Letter references ②
Date: note the position ③

Recipient's name and address: note the inclusion of commas and full-stops, but that the post-code is not punctuated. ④

Salutation: note punctuation ⑤

Subject heading: note its centred location ⑥

Supatemp Agency Limited ①
12 New Street, Newtown, Midshire MN4 57K
Tel: Newtown 76943

Your ref: JK/JT ②
Our ref: BL/SR

8 May, 19-- ③

Mrs. J. Kean,
Office Manager,
Plastex Limited,
3 East Way,
NEWTOWN,
Midshire. NT4 6RG ④

Dear Mrs. Kean, ⑤

TEMPORARY OFFICE STAFF ⑥

Thank you for your letter of 4th May, 19--
enquiring about the engagement of temporary office
staff during your company's summer holiday period.

⑦

I have pleasure in enclosing a brochure which
provides full details of the range of services my
agency is able to provide, and should be pleased to
discuss them with you at any time.

Yours sincerely,

B. Lee
Director ⑧

enc. ⑨

Body of letter: note that each paragraph is indented and separated by a double space from the next. ⑦

Subscription, signature and job title: note that these are located to the right of the 'centre line' and that there is *no* punctuation after the author's name and job title. The subscription ends with a comma, however. ⑧

Enclosure reference: note that this is at the bottom left of the page, and is shown as an abbreviation by the full-stop. ⑨

Be careful!

Take care not to confuse open with closed punctuation – they don't mix! Also, the body of the letter is *always* properly punctuated.

Letter assignments

1 Three weeks ago you purchased a portable radio from The Hi Fi Centre, 10 High Street, Oldtown, Northshire 0T3 6NS. The following are the details of the purchase:

Model: Sonica II
Cost: £42.50
Sales Receipt No: HF 9456
Guarantee Card No: SII KJ 14587

When you proudly sought to show off the radio at home it kept on emitting a whistle, which came and went on two main stations.

You took the radio back to Hi Fi and a sales assistant promised to look into the matter for you. That was two weeks ago. Despite promises made to you over the telephone, nothing has been done.

Write a suitable letter to Mr Jackson, the branch manager to complain about the matter.

2 When members of your group have completed assignment 1, exchange your letter of complaint with a friend. Compose a suitable reply to put the complaint right. You should assume that the Sonica II radio sold in assignment 1 was the last one you had in stock and that the model has just been discontinued. Use your initiative to suggest a means of resolving the complaint. Note, your letter should include a suitable letterhead and be set out in an appropriate format.

3 Your family wishes to take a holiday next summer. You have been asked by your parents to write to Goldendays Travel Agency, 43 Richmond Road, Middletown, Southshire MT14 6SR to enquire about a holiday in a resort of your choice. Before you compose your letter, think carefully about the information the travel agency would need to be given.

4 Take one of the letters written by a fellow student in assignment 3 and compose a suitable answer. You should think carefully about what sort of information the receiver would need to know and what actions would need to be taken. You may invent details of holiday resorts, prices etc to make your letter authentic.

5 Imagine that your college or school has offered a travel scholarship to one of its students. The scholarship will provide a wonderful opportunity for the student to spend two weeks in a foreign country of his or her choice, staying in a school or college similar to your own and living with a family. Write a letter to your Principal or Headmaster applying for the scholarship and giving reasons for your application.

Talking point

Many organisations prefer to use the fully-blocked, open punctuation style (see model on p. 49) as it is easier and quicker to use. *All* the typescript entries in the fully-blocked layout start from the left-hand margin. Also, the omission of full-stops and commas in the inside address can save as many as 30 key strokes when typing the letter and its envelope. However, some firms still prefer to use the semi-blocked, closed punctuation style. Which do you prefer?

Sentence building 2

Using more conjunctions

As you have already learned, simple sentences may be made more varied and interesting by joining them together with coordinating conjunctions – and, but, then, next, yet, etc.

Sometimes, however, sentences are constructed which link a main idea with a dependent idea:

MAIN IDEA	DEPENDENT IDEA
Jack arrived late	because he missed the bus.

In this sentence, called **complex**, the main idea is joined to the dependent idea by the conjunction 'because'. The two parts of this longer sentence are referred to as the main clause and the dependent clause. (Remember that a clause needs both a subject and a finite verb.) The clause, 'because he missed the bus' *depends* on the main clause for its meaning. Clearly one could not write a sentence consisting only of:

Because he missed the bus.

The reader would feel irritated because he would not have been given the main consequence of 'because he missed the bus.'

There are a number of conjunctions in English, referred to as 'subordinating conjunctions' which may be used to introduce dependent clauses, which extend or modify the meaning of a main clause:

MAIN CLAUSE	DEPENDENT CLAUSE
Susan passed the examination	*although* she found it difficult.
The manager dictated the letter quickly	*in order that* it would not miss the post.
This is the salesman	*who* called to see you.
'Where is the report	*which* I requested?'
I shall wait	*until* you come.

The following is a list of some of the most frequently used subordinating conjunctions:

because; as; since; that; which; although; even though; though; who; what; when; where; why; how; if; whether; while; unless; before; after; until; as soon as; however; whatever; whenever; so that; in order that; with the result that

As well as linking a main clause with a single dependent clause, the subordinating conjunctions may be used to link three or more ideas together in the following way:

MAIN CLAUSE + DEPENDENT CLAUSE + DEPENDENT CLAUSE

MAIN CLAUSE +	DEPENDENT CLAUSE
It does not matter	*how* the job is done

+ DEPENDENT CLAUSE
so long as it is finished today.

and again,

The duplicator had been poorly maintained, *with the result that* copies were faint and smeared *whenever* they were run off.

'I am sure we shall meet our sales target, *even though* competition will remain fierce *until* the Christmas trading period finishes.'

By using the subordinating conjunction to make short, simple sentences into complex, longer ones, it is possible to link ideas together in ways that will not only make their connection clear – Jack's lateness was because he missed the bus – but will also provide the reader with a more attractive and interesting presentation of information than:

The duplicator had been poorly maintained. Copies were faint and smeared. This was true each time they were run off.

Another way of providing a varied sentence structure for the reader is to *start* the complex sentence with the dependent clause:

Though the leaflet was crisply printed, its message was not particularly persuasive.

'*While we have been resting on our laurels*, our competitors have been increasing their sales at our expense.'

This technique increases suspense and impact because the reader has to wait until the end of the later main clause to obtain the meaning of the sentence. Thus whatever comes last is given most emphasis.

Assignments

1 Link the following sets of sentences by means of one (or more) subordinating conjunctions:

Note: you may need to make some *slight* changes to the wording of some of the sentences.

(*a*) You are not permitted to travel for half fare. You are over fourteen years of age.

(*b*) The sales assistant was unable to refund the money on the garment. It had been worn several times. It looked in need of washing.

(*c*) The telephone demanded his attention. He tried to carry on writing the report.

(*d*) I have an important matter to attend to. I do not wish to be disturbed. Disturb me only if it is really important.

(*e*) Carol tried hard. She could not read Mr Black's handwriting.

(*f*) The list of account customers was required urgently. Peter decided to leave it until later. The request to go to the chief accountant's office seemed more important.

(*g*) They may try hard. It will take the new company many months to build up good connections with local retailers.

2 Study the following passage carefully, then write it out and insert a suitable conjunction in each of the given spaces and construct it in an appropriate number of sentences:

It is not always easy to construct sentences ... are interesting ... the writer is not careful, he may bore the reader with a succession of short sentences. On the other hand, he may baffle the reader with a tangle of clauses, ... the meaning of his long, complex sentence is lost. ... the writer wishes to make a strong impact, it may be best to insert a short sentence among a series of longer ones. Alternatively, he may choose to introduce a complex sentence with a dependent clause ... the reader is kept in suspense ... he has read the entire sentence, including the main clause which comes last. ... the writer constructs a sentence ... begins with a dependent clause, he may choose to separate it from its main clause with a comma. ... this practice is by no means compulsory, it does have the effect of causing the reader to pause and so to increase the impact of the following main clause.

Here's the proof ...! 2

The following sentences each contain a spelling or a punctuation mistake. Correct them.

1 Will you take the minutes at the finance comittee meeting?

2 A letter should conclude with 'Yours sincerly' when it begins with 'Dear Mr or Mrs'.

3 Would you arrange for all my calls to be transfered to extension 212, Miss Burton?

4 The memorandum was omitted from the delegates' envelope.

5 The cost accountant drew up the management accounts'.

6 Each recipient should be informed of the timetable rearangements.

The memorandum

'Good heavens!
It's a memo from Parkinson in research
and development on the 21st floor!
Says pigeon will wait five minutes in
case of reply . . . .'

The memorandum – frequently referred to as a memo – is a form of 'internal letter'. It is only sent to people *within* an organisation.

Memoranda are used to send instructions or directives, to provide information, to make requests or suggestions, or to confirm facts and agreements originally agreed orally.

As in the case of the letter, managers usually need to keep a copy of a memorandum so the typist will use either carbon and flimsy paper, or sets of chemically treated paper. Alternatively the original may be photocopied. In a growing number of offices today, however, such memoranda are stored electronically in a computer's memory and may either be found and displayed for re-reading on a VDU or converted into a 'hard copy' print-out according to need.

There are two usual sizes of memorandum sheet – A4, about the size of this page, and A5, half the size of A4. The shape of the A4 sheet, deeper than it is wide is called **portrait**, and the A5 sheet, wider than it is deep, **landscape**. However, various companies and public service departments do use memorandum stationery of differing sizes, depending on company preference. For example, some firms use memo-pads smaller than A5 size for brief, handwritten messages. Yet other organisations employ chemically treated, paired memorandum sheets with tear-off sections, so that a sender may despatch and the receiver return a memorandum message, while both retain a copy of their respective message, which, being handwritten, saves the expensive time of two typists. Also, with the

growing use of inexpensive computer printers for internal message printing, memoranda and messages are being increasingly produced on continuous computer stationery, and are also often typed nowadays by managers themselves using their own desk-top microcomputers.

The memorandum layout

Most memoranda have pre-printed 'memoheads', like a letterhead, which display printed entries for completion by the author or typist.

MEMORANDUM		
TO Managing director	REF	AB/CD NWR 39
FROM Sales manager	DATE	12 October 19—
SUBJECT JANUARY SALES TURNOVER NORTH WEST REGION		

Different organisations display this information in various ways, but the aim is to ensure that the memorandum is clearly addressed and referenced for filing.

Sometimes both sender and receiver are referred to simply by their job titles – TO Managing director FROM Sales manager. Or they may be addressed as John Smith, or Peter Williams. Titles such as Mr, Miss or Mrs are not used. The reference will be similar to that of the letter, usually incorporating the initials of author and typist. The date layout is exactly the same as that used in the letter: 12 October 19—. The use of 12/10/19— should be kept for handwritten memoranda.

As with the letter's subject heading, the memorandum's subject entry is usually displayed in capital letters or initial capitals underscored and should indicate clearly the theme of the memorandum:

```
HOW TO USE STATIONERY ECONOMICALLY
```

The message of the memorandum is then set out either in fully-blocked or semi-blocked paragraphs. In the case of the A5 memorandum, the message may well be expressed within a single paragraph.

Additional components

Just as with the letter, it may be necessary to classify a memorandum as CONFIDENTIAL. Such classifications are usually displayed prominently at the head of the memorandum. Entries such as enc, encs or copies to, however, are normally put at the left-hand foot of the memorandum.

The memorandum does not include a signature. Some managers, however, like to initial their memoranda to show that the memorandum has been checked and may be safely despatched.

If a memorandum is longer than a single A4 sheet, then the conventions of letter continuation sheets are used on the second and third sheets etc. Also, when the message of the memorandum is long and its detail complex, many authors provide headings to introduce paragraphs or tables of figures:

```
Effects Upon Company Staff
The main effect which the proposed m
company staff is that it will be mo
unless steps are taken to ensure tha
```

Such display techniques help the message to be absorbed more quickly and easily.

Tone

It is as important to create an appropriate tone in the writing of a memorandum as it is when composing a letter. Just because the receivers of memoranda happen to be members of the same organisation does not mean that messages may be allowed to lapse into rudeness or careless familiarity. Of course, employees are likely to take particular care with the wording of memoranda intended for more senior staff, but the good communicator should be just as alive to the feelings of his equals and his subordinates in the organisational structure.

Consider, for example the effect of the following on their receivers:

Despite clearly stated company regulations, your departmental staff seem half asleep when it comes to providing information when it is needed....

Could you let me have the figures asap as Mr Brown's a bit up tight about the delay....

In accordance with departmental procedure, I am obliged to impart to you that your request for a day's leave of absence must, regrettably, be declined....

Miss Johnson has reported to me your continual late arrival in the morning and that you have offered her no excuse. Please try to arrive on time in future as it upsets the rest of the staff who start on time, even though I daresay you don't find commuting easy these days....

Tone setters

When seeking to create a suitable tone, it is important to consider the following guidelines:

The context

Is the memorandum simply supplying information?

Use factual, precise wording
Avoid slang and colloquial wording
Link facts logically

Is the memorandum making a request for help or cooperation?

Ensure politeness and courtesy throughout: may I ...; it would be extremely helpful if ...; would be appreciated ... etc.

Provide sound reasons for needing the receiver's help. Avoid 'demanding' words and phrases: must ...; unless ...; have to ...; you will .... Adopt instead: I should be grateful if ...; could you please ...; may I ask you to ....

Are you trying to persuade someone to your point of view or to accept a situation or to do something which may require extra work or effort? In this case, words which have a persuasive effect will be helpful:

in need of your particular expertise ....
... though demanding will greatly assist departmental efficiency ....
... once fully in use, the system will greatly ease the workload of all office staff ....

Find words and expressions which will prompt a sympathetic response.

The receiver

Always consider the personality and background of the receiver of the memorandum:

Avoid gobbledegook and jargon
Do not use specialist terms when writing to a layman
Consider your relationship with the receiver: Is she a senior member of staff? Is he an inexperienced junior? Does he work in another department?

Memorandum assignments

1 You work for Mrs D Webster, personnel manager of a large firm. She has arranged a meeting for 11.00 am tomorrow for her staff, to explain a new filing system for company employee records. To help her illustrate the new system, she needs an overhead projector. Mr Keen, training manager, possesses such a projector as part of his training equipment.

As she is busy, Mrs Webster has asked you to compose a memorandum to be sent to Mr Keen in her name, requesting the loan of the projector – the meeting is expected to go on until lunch-time. At present Mr Keen is out of the office and is not expected back until late this afternoon.

Compose a suitable memorandum, including memohead components.

2 Mr Wilson, your office manager, has become irritated recently about the late arrival in the morning of office staff. He spoke to you earlier about the problem as follows:

'They drift in in penny numbers, and this office doesn't really start until 9.15. It's just not on! Staff are expected to be at their desks and ready to work by 9.00 am. It's time they remembered their obligations to the company. Besides, it sets a bad example to younger staff. Mind you, I realise that some staff always arrive punctually. Anyway, I'd like you to produce a memo in my name to go to all office staff which will put a stop to this.

As assistant to Mr Wilson, compose a memorandum, including memohead, which you think would bring about an improved attitude to punctuality.

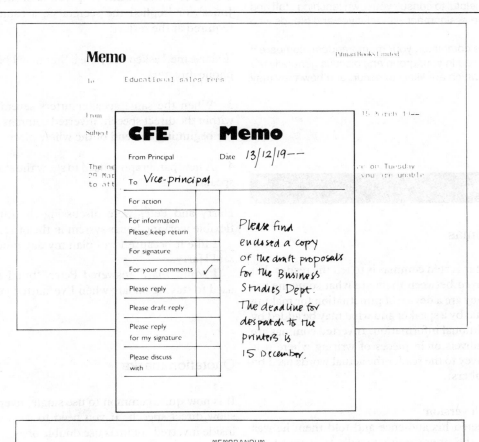

3 First do your research then compose a memorandum which will meet the requirements of the following situation:

Your department, the office administration department, is due to move three floors up in your company's head office building. The date for the move has been decided as Friday 21 June 19—. The staff involved are the office manager, his secretary, six clerks and two wp operators, together with yourself, his assistant.

The office manager has asked you to look into ways in which the staff could prepare for the move so that office business is not unduly disrupted and that the move goes smoothly on the day. He has asked you to draft a memorandum to go to all office staff, informing them of the move, and what actions they could take before the day to assist the re-location of the office.

You will find it helpful to consult your own teaching staff and also to discuss the assignment with relatives and friends who work in offices.

When you have completed your memorandum, compare it with others produced in your group and discuss generally the sort of problems which are likely to occur, and how they may best be solved.

Punctuation

Inverted commas

The main task of inverted commas is to tell the reader that the words displayed between them are what someone has actually said. They are a device of punctuation for making clear what was said by a speaker and what may be added by the writer as additional information. Inverted commas are mostly used in novels or in pieces of writing where it is important to convey to the reader the actual words used by one or more speakers:

Reported speech version
The speaker greeted his audience and told them he was pleased to have the opportunity to talk to them about developments in office communication.

Direct speech version
'Ladies and gentlemen,' said the speaker, 'I am very pleased to have this opportunity to talk to you about what is happening in the area of office communication at this time.'

The rules for using inverted commas

1 Inverted commas come first and last in the direct speech sequence.

In this sense, inverted commas act like brackets to enclose what was actually said. It is important to notice that they come *after* any punctuation in the direct speech:

'Ladies and gentlemen,' said the speaker ...
'What did you say?' asked John.
'I certainly did not!' retorted Jean.
Betty thought she ought to own up. 'I'm afraid I've mislaid the report,' she admitted.

Notice that when a question mark or exclamation mark are used *within* the direct speech, additional commas or full-stops are not used.

2 If a sentence of direct speech is broken by 'asked Mr Jones', or 'replied the secretary', a capital letter is not required at the restart:

'Excuse me,' asked Mr Jones, 'but may I borrow your telephone directory?'

3 When the same speaker utters several sentences, all within the direct speech, inverted commas are used only at the beginning and end of the whole piece.

4 A new paragraph is used to show the start of a different speaker:

Harry and Peter were discussing the introduction of a flexible working hours system in the office.
'I like it because I can plan my day much more easily,' said Harry.
'I admit that,' answered Peter, 'but I still cannot get used to staying on late when I've started late!'

Quotation marks

It is now quite common to use single inverted commas to show direct speech. If you need to use quotation marks inside inverted commas use double ones:

'Have you read "The Paperless Office" yet?' asked Ruth. 'At work I always try to remember the time proverb, "More haste, less speed",' said Harry. 'I don't always manage to put it into practice though!'

Assignments

Write out the following pieces, inserting all the necessary punctuation:

1 have you spoken to miss harrison yet asked mr thomas

2 jack could not let the opportunity pass im anxious that we set a firm date for the exhibition he said otherwise this meeting will have proved a waste of time

3 whatever you do called susan going out of the door dont forget to lock up before you go

4 the main sales feature is the removable hood emphasised the sales manager indicating the chart it can be put on or taken off in thirty seconds

5 the two secretaries were having lunch in the company restaurant on the third floor what sort of day are you having asked pauline helping herself to another biscuit oh not too bad answered jenny mr hawkins has been out all morning but hes due back at two thirty thats the trouble sighed pauline either there is little or nothing to do or the work comes in frantic bursts well time i was off

Activities and Assignments

The office

1 Imagine that your firm is about to move into a new office block. Your department, the general office, has been allocated one floor. It measures 20 metres long by 8 metres wide, with windows running down either side. Access is provided through centrally placed swing doors at either end of the floor. The office staff comprises:

1 office manager
1 personal secretary
1 secretarial servicing unit supervisor
8 secretarial servicing staff-typists, word processor operators
3 senior clerks
8 junior clerks
2 filing/records clerks
1 telex operator

You have been asked to design an efficient layout for the office, having regard to good communication. You may erect internal partitions where necessary.

In small groups, draw up a plan and indicate on it where communication tools such as computer terminals and printers, phones, typewriters, filing cabinets, telex equipment etc will be placed. Consider also the flow of staff in the office area. When you have designed your office, compose an account which explains why you chose your layout and what factors you took into consideration.

2 Imagine the office as it might be in the year 2000. Write an account of how you think it will function, and what sort of equipment it will be using.
Research the topic in your library first.

3 First do your research, then compose your notes and design any visual aids and then give a short talk to your group on one of the following:

How an office works
The role of office manager
What an office clerk's job is like
What an audio typist does
Equipment in today's office
The office of the future
How to take orally delivered messages efficiently

4 Choose one of the items of IT equipment from the table on pages 81–84 and carry out a research project on the 'state of the art' of its current use in offices. Either singly or in a small group, produce a project presentation for your class outlining how it aids communication practices and processes in organisations.

Dealing with messages

5 Compose an article of 350–400 words for your firm's house magazine. The article is intended for junior office staff and is to be entitled: How to deal efficiently with messages.

Letter composition

6 Your company, Delta Furnishing Limited, 14 High Street, Middletown, Southshire, MT4 6SH, telephone: Middletown 876540/5, wishes to purchase an electronic memory typewriter. Your suppliers are: Office Equipment Limited, 6 Western Avenue, Southam, Southshire SH12 4ST. You need a typewriter urgently which can produce different sorts of typescript. You want to know about costs, delivery and types of model. You expect it will be used a great deal.

Compose an appropriate letter, including letterhead and using the fully-blocked open punctuation format.

7 When you have completed 6 above, exchange your letter with that of a fellow-student. When you have researched the subject of electronic typewriters and found out about costs and performance, compose a suitable reply from Office Equipment Limited.

Sentence building

8 Write a paragraph which sets down guidelines on how to structure a letter effectively. Your paragraph should include a sentence starting with Although ..., another starting with However, ..., and another including the words 'in order that'. Make your sentences interesting to read but take care not to make them so long that you lose their thread.

Inverted commas

9 Explain briefly how inverted commas are used, then write a dialogue between a salesman and a customer about a complaint, to illustrate their correct use.

Memorandum and poster

10 Your office administration manager has asked you to compose two documents for display/distribution to departmental staff.

In the near future, a networked system of computer terminals linked to the company's mainframe computer is to be installed in the office. It will make the despatch and circulation of internal messages much swifter and simpler. The Training Unit will be providing a series of short courses to assist staff in learning to operate the system quickly and efficiently. Volunteers are needed from each section of the office to go on the first course.

Your task is to:

(a) produce a memorandum which will explain the situation positively and result in volunteers being forthcoming.

(b) design a poster for display on departmental noticeboards which will prepare staff for the installation and help 'sell' its advantages to all personnel in the office.

Your memorandum should not exceed 150 words and your poster should be A3 in size. Firstly find out about local area networks and then carry out the assignment. On completion, decide in your group who has produced the most effective memorandum and poster and why.

Unit 6

Working in groups

Since human beings spend much of their lives in one sort of group or another, it is important to understand what influences the way an individual behaves in a group, and also, how the group itself behaves towards other groups. Such an understanding is particularly important for a young employee joining a 'work group', or organisation. He or she will need to learn how to 'fit in' and to master the 'rules' which govern employee behaviour – whether the rules are part of written company regulations, or part of some unwritten, informal code of behaviour.

In human societies, the family is the most basic and important group. In it, children learn to accept authority with love from parents, to feel secure, to realise that other brothers or sisters have a right to an equal share of parents' time and attention. Nevertheless, as a result of human nature, there are, from time to time, conflicts, quarrels and jealousies even in the most happy of families. For example, an elder brother may resent the attention being given to a younger sister; two brothers may squabble over ownership of a toy; one sister may protest that another has had more than her fair share of favours or treats. Thus very basic human emotions such as anger, jealousy, envy or insecurity need to be recognised by parents in their children's behaviour and action taken to put matters right.

Such emotional upsets still occur, long after the children have grown up, and, as adults, have taken their places in offices, factories or shops. Owners and senior managers often take on a 'parental' role because, perhaps, two secretaries have fallen out, since the work of one requires that she has an electronic typewriter, while the other still has to work on an old electric. Similarly, a hard-working and successful sales representative may find his fellow representatives distinctly cooler towards him if he tops the bonus league or is promoted. An employee starting a new job may find one or two colleagues off-hand and 'snappy', (A) perhaps because they feel insecure about the arrival of a well-qualified and capable staff member whom they may see as a rival.

It is therefore important that experienced managers, responsible for the work of others, are quick to recognise the signals of tension or upset in the groups of people for whom they are responsible – before factory production falls away, or someone angrily hands in a resignation.

Yet, if it is true to say that all organisations – like all families – experience human relations conflicts some-times, so it is equally true that many organisations enjoy a happy and friendly atmosphere which the employees have created for themselves. Moreover, such atmospheres do not happen by accident, they are the result of constant hard work from all members of the group. The following chart suggests some golden rules for developing good group relations:

How to be successful in a group at work

Be sensitive at all times to the feelings of others

Try to see the other person's point of view

Never listen to or spread gossip about others

Accept the limitations of your present job. Don't envy those with more authority

Learn to work with others and not to want your own way all the time

Never show off or behave arrogantly or rudely towards others

Don't be jealous of another's success

Don't keep to yourself information that others need to know

Always be prepared to cooperate

The honeycomb effect

As we have already learned, work organisations are made up of interconnecting 'people-cells', where everyone works closely around and with others in a sort of honey-comb structure:

	sales office manager	
accounts office supervisor	sales office supervisor	personnel office supervisor
accounts office clerk	sales office typist	personnel office clerk

Thus the relationships which are formed between employees may be thought of as having three basic characteristics:

1 working with superiors
2 working with people more or less equal
3 working with subordinates

It is important to remember, however, that the terms 'superior', 'equal' or 'subordinate' have nothing to do with classifying people as either better or worse than others, but are used simply to indicate that the work they do within the organisation requires that they either do work for someone else, direct another's work, or liaise and work with someone of similar authority. Perhaps the basic reason for the pyramid shape of many organisations is that human beings need to be directed by an authority from above (which they accept) if jobs are to be done without constant argument or disagreement.

Working in a department

Most large organisations tend to be split into smaller sub-sections. A major reason for structuring organisations in this way is that people seem to work better in small groups in which each member knows the others well:

In the diagram of a sales department's structure, A, the sales manager has three section leaders, B, C and D reporting to him and managing:

1 sales orders from sales representatives
2 sales information and administration
3 large account customers

Each section has three subordinates:

1 E, F and G
2 H, I and J
3 K, L and M

In order for the department to work effectively, each member of staff must accept the nature of the structure and willingly work *within* it. This means that A must channel his requirements through B, C and D, who must in turn allocate the work to be done via, E, F and G, H, I or J or K, L or M. By the same token, the three sets of junior staff must channel their queries or confirmations back through B, C or D, who relay them to A.

Once this structure has been established, then a number of essential rules or procedures emerge which all thirteen staff members must respect:

1   A has the final say and is ultimately responsible for the department's work (including any mistakes or failures!).

2   B, C and D all have equal status and their work is essentially limited to the sections they control. All three report separately to A. None should 'tread on the toes' of the others by exceeding his given authority. For example, B should not take over large customer account work from C.

3   The junior staff in each section must report to either B, C or D respectively and ensure that they do not bypass the section head by always going straight to A.

4   A, though in charge of all functions, must not undermine the authority of B, C or D by bypassing them constantly with instructions for E, F, G, H, I, J, K, L or M.

The golden rules for harmonious work

Clearly, in a small department of thirteen people, there will be a good deal of liaison and close-working in 'overlap' areas between the three sections and it is never practical to suggest that people should work in 'watertight compartments'. Nevertheless, good staff relationships are built on the basis of everyone knowing clearly the answers to the following:

1 To whom do I report?
2 Who reports to me?
3 For what am I responsible?
4 Where does my authority begin and end?
5 Where do I take my problems?

Knowing for sure the precise answers to the above questions and keeping to the routes and procedures they represent form the foundation for good working relationships between people with different responsibilities and authority.

Working for a superior

In order to work successfully for a more senior staff member, an employee must first be sure of 1 above. It is not at all easy to report to more than one person simultaneously, since conflicts arise over who has the final say. Also, working successfully for someone else requires that the subordinate and his manager both know precisely what is expected of the subordinate – uncertainty leads to indecision and nothing being done.

Perhaps the most important factor in working for someone else lies in the cooperation which the subordinate must bring to the relationship. If he or she is surly and resentful of the manager's authority, then work will either be done poorly or not at all. 'Accepting' is central to 'working for'.

But much responsibility for success lies with the manager. If he or she is unfair, has favourites or bullies junior staff, then they have every right to complain. For example, E, F or G might be justified in taking up a complaint with A in the privacy of his office, if a difference with B cannot be settled. Such a situation may well tax A's ability as a manager if the working relationships in Section 1 are not to be soured.

As well as cooperation, satisfactory performance will be expected from the subordinate by the manager, who will be constantly measuring the quality of work done. For example, a typist will be expected to produce mailable copy even when working under pressure.

Thus the major expectations which the subordinate has to fulfil are:

1 Having a courteous and cooperative attitude
2 Being proficient in work done
3 Being able to meet deadlines
4 Passing on information received
5 Being resourceful and tactful
6 Giving loyalty and support

Directing another's work

Managing or supervising other people is not at all easy and requires much social skill. People are very complex machines and managers spend a great deal of time learning what makes individuals tick in order to get the best out of them. Managing has been described as 'meeting objectives through the work of others' and so a manager needs to have these qualities:

1 The ability to lead and inspire confidence
2 Fairness and impartiality
3 The ability to relate well to others
4 Possessing a ready and sympathetic ear
5 Loyalty towards subordinates

Working alongside others

In many ways this is the most difficult area of work relationships since the 'directing' or 'reporting to' roles are absent. The staff concerned enjoy equal status and neither *has to do* what the other wishes. Therefore both must believe in the need for cooperation as a means of getting the job done.

Sometimes problems get in the way. Two equals may become rivals for promotion. Envy may creep in, where each watches the other, in case he gains some privilege. Such practices only serve to create tensions and damage the climate of goodwill essential to harmonious work. Mutual trust is therefore the basis of relationships between equals.

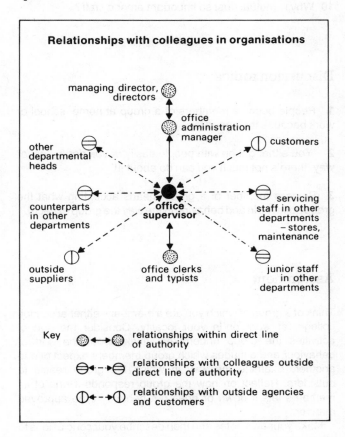

Mastering the meaning

1 Why is it important for a young person starting work to know how people behave in groups?

2 Why is it important for managers to spot early signs of tension between staff?

3 What sort of problems are likely to arise among people working side-by-side in an organisation?

4 What is meant by the word 'insecure'? Line A

5 What is the communication advantage of separating an organisation into sub-sections dealing with defined tasks?

6 What is likely to happen if people do not follow established routes and procedures for communicating?

7 What do you understand by the term 'honeycomb effect'?

8 What is meant by the expression 'watertight compartments'? Line B

9 What does 'meeting objectives through the work of others' mean? Line C

10 Why is mutual trust so important among staff?

Discussion topics

1 People become members of a group at home, school or work because they *need* to.

2 'You either get on with people easily or you don't – either way, there's not much you can do about it!'

3 Being a member of a group means accepting what the group believes in and behaving in the way the group expects.

Assignment

Think of a group of which you are a member – either at school, college, at work or in your locality. Consider the sort of activities the group undertakes, think about the sort of behaviour and attitudes which group members expect of one another. Examine the way in which the group reacts to outsiders. Reflect on how the group responds if one of its members lets it down or does not behave in the approved manner.

Make your own notes and then describe your conclusions to other group members – being sure to keep the group members suitably anonymous! Then try as a class to arrive at some answers to these questions:

Why do human beings tend to form groups either at work or at leisure?
What sort of requirements are expected of members of a group?
What advantages stem from being a member of a group?
Are there any disadvantages?
Can individuals learn how to 'fit in' to work or social groups?

Operating a word processing system

The equipment needed to operate a word processing system mirrors that required for any computer programming or applications work:

Hardware
- disk drive/central processing unit (CPU)

- visual display unit (VDU)

- keyboard

- printer

Note: the computer drive may stem from a mainframe, mini- or microcomputer. If from the mainframe or mini, then the word processing applications package or program will be permanently available and downloaded to the user's terminal on demand. Both operating and word processing packages stored on floppy disk have to be loaded into a microcomputer when it is switched on, or to use the jargon term, 'booted up'.

Software
- microcomputer operating system, e.g. PCDOS, standing for Personal Computer Disk Operating System stored on floppy disk

- word processing system – also stored on floppy disk if microcomputer version

- working disk for storing text produced in files

- back up disks: of the above for security and to avoid loss of master disks by mistake

- paper for printer: this may take the form of continuous stationery for internal office or personal use, or A5 or A4 stationery for letters, memoranda, etc.

Note: the word processing package to be used is invariably accompanied with a manual for reference and often with 'quick glance' cards listing key commands, or stickers to put on to individual keys to help the operator to remember when a key or combination of keys may be used to input a command.

Installation

When a word processing package is purchased it is customarily packed in a sealed box. The customer's attention is drawn to the legal consequences of breaking the seal, which include abiding by the manufacturer's conditions of sale relating to copyright and improper copying of the package – say to give to a friend. Indeed some manufacturers now have a means of preventing additional copies from being made by a special manufacturing device written into the disk. The licence which the purchaser acquires through purchase usually limits the operation of the package to a single machine and only permits security back-up copies to be made of the master package for daily use.

In order to install some packages, special procedures have to be followed from the user's manual once only, which usually include the formatting and legitimate copying of, say, five copies of the master. This is then stored away in a safe place and a copy employed for everyday use.

Blank working disks have to be formatted before they can be used and this process is to enable them to accept the computer's signals – effectively the text which has been produced on the VDU. The operating disk includes a set of instructions which are used to format other disks.

Setting up the microcomputer

Each computer possesses in its central processing unit various microprocessor circuits which are permanently installed on what are termed 'cards'. These are interconnected to enable the instructions stored on both the operating and word processing disks to be understood and acted upon.

Before the computer can be used, however, it has to have an operating system loaded into it and also to 'copy' or 'borrow' the instructions stored on the WP disk. Both sets are temporarily stored in the computer's memory circuits, but only for as long as the computer is switched on. Once switched off, the information on the disks disappears and has to be reloaded via the same floppy disks. Where microcomputers are used with larger memories or with hard disks (possessing far more memory capacity) then the operating and word processing systems (along with other systems such as databases, spreadsheets and graphics) are permanently stored on disk and no loading is needed. Thus you will see some computers with only a single disk drive for the working disk.

In brief, once the computer and printer's power switches are switched on, the following sequence of disk insertion into the disk drives is followed:

1 Into Disk Drive A (left hand side) goes first the Operating Disk. After the computer has persuaded itself that it is fully powered, and all its memory available and ready, the screen will display the disk drive sign: 'A>'.

2 This means that the computer is ready to accept the WP floppy disk in Drive A. Once this is installed in the drive, then the code to load its set of instructions into the computer is typed after the A> symbol. This results in the word processing package's page format being displayed on the screen once some housekeeping instructions have been followed.

3 The formatted floppy disk to store the files of text created is loaded into Drive B.

4 Before starting to produce a file, it is good practice to read the directory of the work disk in Drive B to see how many 'bytes free' remain available for use – much like checking to see how many blank pages are still unused in an exercise book. This check can be made at any time by recalling the B Drive: B> and keying in 'dir'

B> dir

The screen will display the series of code titles given to files already produced. These may normally extend to eight letters and may include digits. Certain operating systems will not accept specific keyboard characters and the user's manual of a given package will advise on how files may or may not be titled.

Setting up a file

When a microcomputer with dual disk drive is employed, then the WP package and the working disk sit side by side in Drives A and B. With a single disk drive, the WP disk has to be loaded and then withdrawn and its place taken by the working disk.

When using a dual disk drive, it is vital for the text to be created to be set up in a file which will be assigned to Drive B.

Again, the user's manual will explain this process and will display on the VDU the file (A or B) in use, together with the title given to the file in use, for example:

B: ABCLET23

might stand for the twenty-third letter being created to be despatched to the Arthur Black Confectioner's firm. Remember that it is always helpful to give files abbreviated titles which mean something rather than some arbitrary list of letters or numbers.

A typical word processing screen display will show the following information at the very top or foot of the screen:

FILE IN USE, e.g. ABCLET23 PAGE NO,
e.g. 2 LINE NO, e.g. 26 COL No, e.g. 63

Thus the user can see at a glance what file he is using, what page of text he is on (many WP packages visually display a warning of text about to extend to a second, third page etc.) and even what column his cursor (the flashing rectangle of light which indicates where the next letter or number is to be printed) is on in terms of a line or ruler able to accept up to 80 individual characters, the normal width of the text to be displayed on A4 or A5 paper.

The word processor's electronic blank page

Using a WP package is very much like having an endless supply of blank pages at your disposal on to which all kinds of display patterns of text and/or numbers may be formatted or designed, with the help of an extensive 'tool-kit' of keying and formatting aids – by courtesy of the WP package. The following diagram illustrates what a typical WP blank screen looks like before text is produced for display upon it:

Typically, the WP screen will display the following information for the user:

- given file title in use

- page, line and column numbers

- ruler line, including the location of any tabs set

- main help menu

- commands activated by command keys (F1–10)

- vertical line counter or graphically shown downward arrangement of blocks of text.

The ruler line acts very much like the ruler on a conventional typewriter which is used for setting tabs and margins (a tab is a point between the left-hand and right-hand margins which will act as a marker against which to

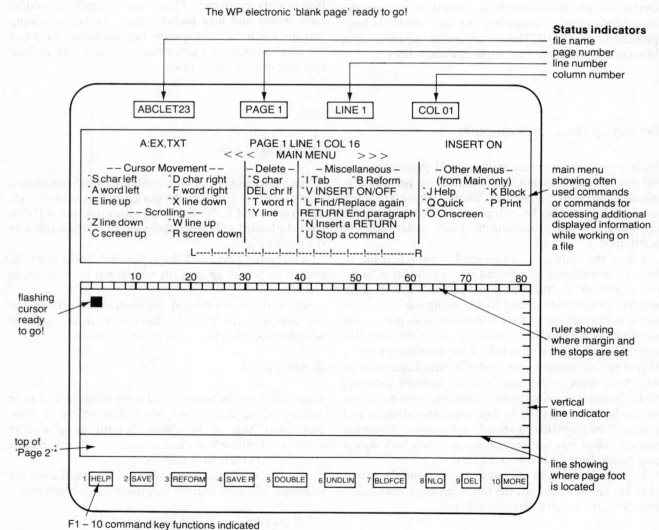

The WP electronic 'blank page' ready to go!

Status indicators
— file name
— page number
— line number
— column number

ABCLET23   PAGE 1   LINE 1   COL 01

A:EX,TXT   PAGE 1 LINE 1 COL 16   INSERT ON
< < <   MAIN MENU   > > >

– – Cursor Movement – – | – Delete – | – Miscellaneous – | – Other Menus –
^S char left   ^D char right | ^S char | ^I Tab   ^B Reform | (from Main only)
^A word left   ^F word right | DEL chr lf | ^V INSERT ON/OFF | ^J Help   ^K Block
^E line up   ^X line down | ^T word rt | ^L Find/Replace again | ^Q Quick   ^P Print
– – Scrolling – – | ^Y line | RETURN End paragraph | ^O Onscreen
^Z line down   ^W line up | | ^N Insert a RETURN |
^C screen up   ^R screen down | | ^U Stop a command |

L----!----!----!----!----!----!----!----!----!----!--------R

main menu showing often used commands or commands for accessing additional displayed information while working on a file

10   20   30   40   50   60   70   80

flashing cursor ready to go!

ruler showing where margin and the stops are set

vertical line indicator

top of 'Page 2'*

line showing where page foot is located

1 HELP 2 SAVE 3 REFORM 4 SAVE R 5 DOUBLE 6 UNDLIN 7 BLDFCE 8 NLQ 9 DEL 10 MORE

F1 – 10 command key functions indicated

Note: Experienced WP operators can blank out the main menu display if not required.

* This line only comes into view once text approaches the equivalent of the foot of an A4 page.

set columns of figures or words down the page). The computer keyboard has a particular key to send the cursor skipping across the screen to the next placed tab, marked:

|←

→|

The main menu is a checklist of often used commands for manipulating the text and will include the commands to be keyed in for displaying: for example, a 'Help' menu for users stuck or lost; the quick command for saving and printing text produced; the command for inserting words into established text or for moving blocks of text around a screen, and so on.

Some WP packages display continuously a set of quick commands activated by the 'F' keys situated on the left-hand side of most computer keyboards.

What the word processing package can do

Clearly the capacities of any word processing package will depend upon the amount of work which has gone into its design and the range of operations which its designers have written as program instructions. Whizz kid computer programmers are constantly improving WP packages to make them more 'user friendly': quicker and simpler to use, for the non expert user as well as the skilled WP operator or supervisor.

The following checklist illustrates what a typical WP package can do in order to create text and then to edit or modify it and to optimise the visual appeal of its layout or format on the page.

Functions of a word processing package

Text display
Striking any one of a computer's set of keys will cause a particular character to be displayed instantly on screen exactly where the cursor is flashing.

Cursor movement
Predetermined command instructions – single or paired keys to be struck – will cause the cursor to:

- move right, left, up or down either one space at a time or continuously until stopped.

- delete individual letters, words, lines or blocks of text on demand

- scroll (wind up or down like a car window) the text which has been keyed in so it may be checked or reviewed

- go forwards or backwards directly to a previously set position

- move directly to preset tab positions.

Formatting commands
In addition, the WP package enables the user to effect a number of quick commands which allow the text to be set as required on the screen page. Such format commands include:

- centering lines or phrases of text such as letter subject headings

- setting left-hand, right-hand margins and individual tabs

- clearing tabs and margin stops no longer required

- justifying text at right-hand side (spacing lines to achieve a tidy vertical line of letters down the page)

- reforming paragraphs which have become untidy after inserts, etc.

- setting text in single, double or treble, etc. spacing

Saving files
When the text is finished – or at regular intervals in a long piece – it needs to be 'saved' or copied on to the working disk as part of the set up file. Commands to do this are customarily part of the WP package.

Printing
Once the text is in its acceptable, final format it is ready to be printed and this is carried out by means of a print command.

Note also that print commands which can underscore words or lines of text, embolden particular headings or set particular blocks of text in capitals, etc. can be located at exactly the required spot in the text as it is being keyed in. Though their effect may not be visible on screen, the printer will pick up the commands while the print head is running.

Other features
Many WP packages have built in features aimed at making them more useful and versatile to the user. These may include:

mail merging – the ability to produce duplicated letters via the printer with individualised names and addresses of pre-listed intended recipients.

This feature extends to enabling the WP operator to key in fresh text at predetermined points in an otherwise standard letter.

spelling dictionaries – many WP packages have the capacity to correct any word which has been mistyped or misspelled in error. This is made possible by the inclusion in the WP package of, say, the correct spelling of some 200 000 words which the computer can almost instantaneously compare against the keyed-in word and correct if need be, before the text is printed.

But this is no reason or excuse for giving up on your spelling efforts!

finding text – some WP packages have the facility to find particular words or phrases in a trice within a long piece of text, perhaps for alteration or substitution by the user.

Major applications of word processing

As you can well imagine, once the initial fears of the new technology had been overcome and the techniques had been mastered, copy typists, secretaries and personal assistants jumped at the chance of having their own WP equipment. Imagine the boredom involved in re-typing a 20 page report some four or five times as successive versions are amended and recast before the boss considers it acceptable for despatch to the board of directors! With a word processor, instead of having to re-type a whole page of text to get rid of five well-spaced mistakes, only the mistakes themselves need attention, the WP package's ability to re-paragraph text and to re-justify whole blocks of prose makes time-consuming typing a chore of the past!

The following table illustrates some of the major advantages of word processing facilities in the office:

Document	Advantages of WP for document production
Reports	Numerous redrafts quickly accommodated and time thus saved: current computing facilities permit spreadsheet, database and graphics material, etc. to be transferred from interconnectable software for inclusion in WP file under creation.
Sales circular letters	Regular sales letters can be despatched via mailmerge facilities to listed clients and customers, where each has his or her name and address included as an integral part of an individually printed letter with a resulting improved response from its recipient.
Minutes	Draft minutes may be passed to a committee's chairman and any arising amendments inserted with a minimum of delay in getting the minutes out to members after each meeting.
Forms, routine reminders and instructions, etc.	All kinds of forms may be designed on VDU, and a master printed for photocopying on demand. Updating or modifying a form's structure is easily effected. Instructions or reminders sent to personnel at regular intervals may be promptly recalled from floppy disk storage and printed out after any necessary small updatings have been made.
Records	Records may be set out in virtually any keyboard based format and recalled for additions and amendments to be made at will. Space-taking filing cabinets are no longer needed and cumbersome paper is saved. Recalled records may be viewed via VDU, or a hard copy printed out if required.
Manager's notes and memos	Word processing and electronic mail network systems have made it possible for managers to send many of their messages to colleagues directly themselves, while secretaries or assistants gain more time to do other, equally important tasks.

Know your IT! Key words and terms

3: Software

disk/diskette: usually refers in microcomputer contexts to the floppy disks used to store applications packages or operating systems upon; generally these come in 5.25 or 3.5 inch sizes; manufacturers try to make them so as to contain as much information as possible, hence their specifications like 'dual density, double sided' etc. Floppy disks store data on tracks rather like LP records, but not in a single long line of sequence like the single track of the LP, but in sectors;

diskcopy: to copy the data held on one disk on to another either for security or as a working version;

to format: to prepare a disk for accepting data from the computer;

to boot up: to switch on the computer and install its DOS operating system and applications package, etc;

write-protect notch: a notch or rectangle cut into the side of the floppy disk which enables it (if not covered over by a sticky label) to be over-written or erased;

user-friendly: a term used to describe applications packages which are straightforward, helpful, and easy to use;

icon: a symbol shown on screen to depict an instruction which the computer can respond to; for example, a dustbin to signify the 'delete' or 'get rid of' function; such icons are used in conjunction with the cursor and mouse to input instructions;

back-up copy: a copy of a program disk or working disk made as a precaution in case either master copy becomes corrupt or its data is erased in error – an absolute must if you are to avoid fits of rage or floods of tears when hours – or even weeks – of work are lost in a split second!

Extend your IT word power!

Find out what the following words or terms mean and then explain them to your group:

a warm boot and a cold boot, copy-protected, menu-driven, error messages, integrated software, to boilerplate, a grand-father disk, to cut and paste, a file, a field, to merge.

Using the telephone

The modern miracle

It is almost impossible to imagine today how commerce, industry or the public service could carry out their tasks and transactions without at some time resorting to the telephone:

'Better give Mr James a ring and check ....'
'To save time, I thought I'd give you a call ....'
'I'm calling in connection with your order for ....'

Yet we tend to take the modern miracle of the telephone very much for granted. The average businessman soon becomes irritated if his dialled call does not put him into immediate contact with a selected individual among, say, Greater London's 11½ million inhabitants. Similarly the many telephone services which British Telecom maintains – emergency calls, directory enquiries, transferring of calls and person-to-person long-distance calls etc – are often used with little or no thought for the skill of the tele-communications engineer or servicing staff which makes them available.

Despite our frequent use of the telephone both at home and at work, many of us fail to use the telephone effec-tively, or to make best use of the many back-up and support services offered. Yet the ability to use the tele-phone successfully – whether as a call maker or call taker – is an essential communication requirement. Mastery of the telephone system will help the new employee to solve problems, maintain good customer and colleague relation-ships and to carry out efficiently many of the daily exchanges with other people which form much of the work of the office.

Two major systems

Basically, there are two ways in which telephone calls may be made or taken at work. The first way is via the tele-phone which is directly connected to the British Telecom exchange network and which is called 'an outside line'. This type of telephone is often found in small businesses – and the home. The second way is via a switchboard system which acts as a link between a number of internal exten-sions and British Telecom exchanges in the outside world.

When using the 'outside line' telephone, it is simply necessary to lift the receiver, dial the required number and to wait for the person at the other end of the line to hear the telephone ringing and to pick it up. There are, of course good practices to keep in mind and these will be dealt with later.

If the call to be made is local, then just dial the number found in the local telephone directory:

Reading 578631

If, however, a call is to be made over a longer distance, then it will be necessary to use the Subscriber Trunk Dialling code (STD) before the number:

0734 578631 (0734 is a Reading STD code)

If no STD facility exists, one has to contact the operator.

Larger cities and towns may have the same STD code throughout the country (London's is 01) but it may sometimes be necessary to consult the local STD code book. It is now possible to dial direct to an extensive range of foreign countries, using International Direct Dialling codes, (IDD).

For a smaller business, a single outside line may be sufficient to cope with the flow of incoming and outgoing calls, but for larger organisations a different system is needed. In a large head office, for example, there may be as many as 200–300 office staff, all needing at some time to make and take calls. Many will be using the telephone system simultaneously. For this reason it became necessary to develop a 'mini telephone exchange' or switchboard to handle the much greater flow of calls.

Such a switchboard acts as a link between the users of internal extensions located in individual offices and the outside world. Some switchboards are manned by full-time operators who carry out a wide range of duties, including the routing of incoming calls and obtaining outside numbers for office staff. Such switchboard systems are known as Private Manual Branch Exchanges (PMBX). A similar but more streamlined service is available – PABX (Private Automatic Branch Exchanges). Incoming calls are more directly routed to internal extensions, and office staff can, with selected handsets, dial direct to the outside world. This lessens the load of the switchboard operator. With the advent of computerised switchboards it is now possible to dial direct to an individual internal extension without the assistance of the switchboard operator.

When using the direct outside line, it is important to remember that it connects *directly* with the outside world. When the telephone rings, therefore, *anyone* could be on the line – a customer, your boss, or even the managing director! Similarly, when making an outside call, you will be representing your organisation – the receiver of your call will judge your organisation by the way you speak and the way you handle the call. In order to use an outside line efficiently, you will need to know how to use a telephone directory and STD code book. You will also need to know when it is possible to telephone more cheaply – time is money! Similarly, when using an internal telephone extension, you will need to know how the company system works – how to obtain the switchboard; how to make an outside call; how to transfer an incoming call to another extension; how to use the internal telephone directory. Whether using a direct outside line or internal telephone extension, you will also need to know what is good telephone practice, including how to use a telephone message pad. Moreover, each organisation will have its rules and procedures for taking and making calls, and you will need to know what actions to take. Some firms, for example, require all outgoing and incoming calls to be 'logged' with details of time, nature of call, receiver, etc.

TELEPHONE MESSAGE PAD

① TIME 11.15 AM   DATE 12/5/8–

MESSAGE FOR MR SHARP

② CALLER MISS KAY PETERS (PROP.)

③ ADDRESS EXCEL OFFICE SUPPLIES LTD
14 · WEST STREET
MIDDLETOWN SOUTHSHIRE MT46KN

④ TEL NO. MIDDLETOWN 78462 Ext. 16

⑤ MESSAGE Moderna Photocopier
Model MET4 not arrived. Delivery to customer promised this afternoon. Could fetch from our warehouse.

⑥ MESSAGE TAKEN BY: Jenny Short

| WILL CALL BACK | ⑦ PLEASE CALL | ✓ |
| WANTS TO SEE YOU | URGENT | ✓ |

Example of a telephone message pad

① Dates and times may prove to be essential information.

② Important to supply caller's name clearly and in sufficient detail.

③ Discretion must be used in deciding whether or not to take down the postal address.

④ Telephone number and extension where used are essential.

⑤ The message should be clearly written and supply the essential points of the message. Do not over-compress the message in note-form or it may be misunderstood.

⑥ Always identify yourself as the call taker. You may be asked to supply additional information.

⑦ Such 'tick boxes' help to emphasise important aspects of the message, such as the need here for urgent action and immediate personal contact.

Golden rules

Call making and taking:

The following 'Golden Rules' will help you to become a successful telephone user:

As a call taker

1 Always keep a message pad and pencil handy by the telephone. Delays in finding something to write on cost time and are inefficient. Scraps of paper are easily lost or not recognised as message sheets.

2 Always confirm to the caller your name, job title or your department. Do not hide behind anonymity.

3 Make sure early in the call that you obtain the caller's name, job title, telephone number and organisation. Such information is essential if you need to contact him later, or need to pass on a message.

4 Before you pass a caller on to your boss or a senior colleague, be sure to ask politely the nature of his business. Your senior staff may not always wish to speak to callers and they must know what the call is about before the caller may be told that they are 'in' or 'available'.

5 Take care to note the essential items of the caller's message. Do not be afraid to ask for repeats or spellings when you are unsure. Ask the caller to proceed more slowly if you are taking down a complex message.

6 At the end of the message, repeat its main points as feedback to the caller to ensure that you have neither misunderstood nor omitted anything important.

7 Check that you have the points in 3 above before the caller rings off.

8 Be courteous at all times. It is easy to sound brusque or curt on the telephone. Tell the caller that you will pass on his message or take the necessary action.

9 After the call, convert your brief notes into a fair copy on a fresh message pad if the caller's message is intended for an absent third party and check that everything has been clearly stated.

10 Always pass on messages and take any follow-up action immediately. It is only too easy to forget when something else crops up.

As a call maker

1 Decide what your main aims are *before* you make the call.

2 Make a checklist of your main points *before* you start your call.

3 Have any relevant documents to hand which you may need to refer to. This will save time and you will appear efficient.

4 Have pad and pencil ready to take any notes.

5 Make sure if possible whom you wish to speak to before you start. Otherwise you may repeat your message to several people unnecessarily.

6 *Always* obtain the name of your calltaker – you may need to follow up your call or to check progress.

7 Never guess at telephone numbers – always check. Millions of wrong numbers are dialled each year at great cost.

8 When connected, announce yourself, your company and say to whom you wish to speak. It helps to know people's extension numbers as this saves an operator's time, if you cannot dial through yourself.

9 When delivering your message, speak clearly and do not gabble – the call taker may be writing it down.

10 Give spellings of names, addresses etc. Also repeat invoice or telephone numbers.

11 Make sure the call taker has understood the essential parts of your message. Get him to repeat it to you, if need be.

12 Avoid distractions and interruptions while making the call. You may miss something vital.

13 Remember to thank the call taker for his help. Courtesy costs nothing and is essential at all times.

14 Carry out any follow-up actions before you forget – it is easy to be distracted by the next job or visitor.

15 Remember that using the telephone is expensive. Use the cheaper times; call back rather than be kept waiting.

Assignments

1 Consider the following greetings:

'Hello?' 'Stores here.'
'Harrison.'
'Miss Jones, Personnel.'
'Mr Cook's secretary, good morning.'
'Homecraft Limited, can I help you?'

In discussion, decide what sort of initial greeting is most appropriate when answering a call on:

    (*a*) a direct outside line
    (*b*) an internal extension
    (*c*) a company switchboard

Make up three examples to illustrate your answers.

2 Telephone Call Role Playing

Each student should prepare a situation for telephone role play between a call maker and a call taker. Necessary details of the situation, the names and addresses, telephone numbers and extensions of the people and firms involved should be devised. Next, two copies of the essential details of the situation should be made, one for the call maker and one for the call taker. If telephone training equipment is available, the situation may then be played out.

The following situations may provide a helpful start:

(*a*) You made arrangements with a local travel agency for two tickets to be waiting for you at the box office of a theatre some 30 miles away. You paid for them in advance at the agency. When you arrived at the theatre with a friend, your tickets were not there and no-one knew anything about it. You had to pay again. The next morning you decide to telephone the agency!

(*b*) Your company is thinking of purchasing a new type-writer. You are not sure whether you should buy a less expensive electronic model or go for one with an extensive memory. You decide to telephone your local office equipment specialist.

(*c*) Your mother works part-time for a local insurance company. Last night she had a nasty fall and is now in hospital. Yesterday she brought home some papers from the office to work on. You telephone the insurance company at 8.45 am to inform them of the accident.

If it is not possible to use telephone training equipment, you should consult with a partner and between you write out the dialogue of the call as you think it should proceed and then compare dialogues.

You *can* spell!

Consonants

Consonants are those letters which are not vowels (a e i o u).

Helpful hints

1 Single syllable words ending with a single consonant before a vowel, double the consonant when a suffix is added: big bigger; flat flattest

2 Words ending in a consonant followed by an e, drop the e when a suffix is added: flame flaming; drive driving

3 The suffix -ly is added to all base words: beautiful beautifully (but dull dully)

4 A soft g is followed by an e; gorgeous; George; garage

5 *Not* a rule but a guideline:
A short vowel before a consonant very often indicates that the consonant is doubled: hămmer tāmer, băbble lābourer, slŏpping slōping

The silent consonants

Be sure you note each word you meet which begins with a silent consonant. The most likely are g h k p w. For example: gnome; honest; know; psychology; write.

The 'sh' sound

Be especially careful when encountering the 'sh' sound, since it is made with a number of different consonant and vowel combinations:

action conscious anxious delicious fresher connexion (connection) attaché

Spelling assignment

Complete the spelling of each of the following words:

tele … ne	(to give people a ring)
… ead	(make bread with hands)
susp … s	(wary, doubtful)
consc … s	(hard working)
o … d	(happened)
ne … y	(needed)
fr … ile	(easily broken)
r … t	(used to play tennis)
a … ire	(obtain)
g … y	(study of countries)
s … e	(grab hold of)
l … e	(not tight)
u … e	(only one of its kind)
c … ee	(working party)
e … s	(make someone feel awkward)
e … l	(perform extremely well)
l … e	(taken on holiday)
… nkle	(crease line in face)
sp … s	(roomy)

People who need people?

A case study

If a visitor from another planet were sent on a mission to survey the species on Earth called humans, one of the major sections of 'its' report might well include the following observation:

Observation

'The species is made up of two sorts of creatures, one heavier and taller, the other shorter and lighter. The heavier and taller creature thinks it is the dominant one, but careful observation has shown that in reality it is the shorter, lighter one. It is this one which goes into their Creation factories to construct the young of their species.

'They inhabit the planet in vast numbers. We estimate some five billion of the species at present. They must rely on each other totally, since they like to live in enormous hives. Whatever they do, they do in groups. They have eating/sleeping complexes which they occupy in groups of three to twelve, though some of these dwelling complexes rise high into the atmosphere of their planet and are filled with many hundreds of them!

'Their production complexes are sometimes even larger and they have twice-daily wars getting into them and out of them. Some of the species are destroyed in these wars, which take place on their transport ribbons, along which they travel in lethal tanks at high speeds. They call these dangerous weapons 'cars' and 'buses'.

'Once in each seven days, as many as 50 000 all gather in an enormous open-air church to worship their gods. These gods are dressed in brightly coloured garments. Their church ritual consists of trying to put a round object into a net-like structure. These structures are placed at either end of a flat, green holy area and are fiercely guarded. When the object is placed in this most holy area, the worshippers go mad with ecstasy and cries of religious delirium echo round the church. There is also a black clothed devil who tries to stop their act of worship. When they fight to stop him, he banishes them into a black tunnel as a sacrifice and they are never seen again. Many millions watch these acts of worship in their home dwelling complexes on scanners, while drinking holy waters.

'As was noted, they seem to cooperate most cunningly in groups to build their hives and cultivate their nourishment. Yet even in this cooperation, they can be strangely aggressive.

'It would be well to warn mighty Mikron that, should this species ever become civilised, they could, one day, pose a grave threat to the Galaxy! Our ship com-

'Thousands of Earthlings travel hundreds of their miles to see such a holy object worshipped!'

puter, however, has projected that the species could destroy itself as a result of jealousies arising between different groups – especially since much of their effort is directed to developing horrible weapons to do just this!

'All in all, a most peculiar species.'

Recommendation

'That the planet, Earth, be kept in Galactic isolation and the species remain under observation in the faint hope that they may, one day, evolve sufficiently for contact to be made.'

AKRON

Discussion assignments

1 If you were a visitor from outer space, what conclusions would you draw about the ways that human beings behave in groups?

2 Do you think it is true that human beings like to live, work and play in groups? If so, what reasons can you give for such human preferences?

Written assignments

1 Imagine that Akron was ordered to make contact with humans and could speak our language. Write an account for him, explaining the advantages which humans think stem from working in groups.

2 How many different types of human group can you think of? Make a checklist and compare it with those drawn up by other students in your group.

Summarising

How to master an essential skill

For most of us, the word 'précis' or 'summary' has about as much appeal as 'washing up' or 'mowing the lawn'! Much of our dislike of the techniques of producing a précis or summary probably stem from our experiences at some time or other of having to reduce a dry or dull passage to a version only a third or so as long. It was difficult to see the point of the exercise.

In the world of work, however, no one can afford to waste time or effort in a task which does not have a direct relevance to the activities of the shop, office or factory floor. Similarly, the time of all staff is precious. Senior executives need to be given only the important key facts of, say, a meeting or a sales deal. In fact, employees working at all levels of an organisation are *constantly* sifting and selecting the *essential* items from the mass of information they handle, so that their customers or colleagues are not overburdened with piles of documents or never-ending dialogues. If staff did not use their summarising skills continually, the work of the organisation would soon be bogged down and would eventually founder and collapse under the weight of needless paperwork and long-winded oral messages.

The diagram illustrates some of the main office activities in which the skills of summarising play an important part.

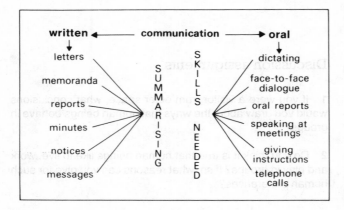

Summarising the spoken word

When delivering an oral summary – of a conversation with a visiting sales representative, or of an item of business in a meeting – it is necessary to make a mental selection of the main points *while speaking* and to ensure that the words uttered are clearly structured and fluently delivered. Listeners soon become irritated by frequent 'ums' or 'ers' and find it difficult to follow the thread of meaning when someone says:

'Oh, no, sorry, before that he said ...'
'Did I say he offered to take it back to the factory for inspection? Oh, well he did ....'

The ability to make oral reports or summaries of events for a superior or colleague who was not present must be studied and learned. Often experience of what the boss needs to know will help, but so also will the development of active listening skills – during a meeting or conversation – and the practice of logical structuring of key points, so that the oral summary has a clear beginning, middle and end and includes only those points which are important and directly relevant.

Summarising the written word

When summarising the written word, the principles are virtually identical. The task is, in fact, simpler, because the text of the original passage remains constantly in view and there is more time usually in which to produce a shortened version. Also, written messages tend to be written in elaborate and sometimes roundabout ways because their authors are anxious to put a point across in great detail or repeat it more than once to give it emphasis, and are, therefore, easy to simplify.

Consider, for example the following sentence:

Although the journey from work was not particularly long, the train was crowded with commuters and other travellers and when the office manager eventually arrived home, he felt tired and drained.

This sentence contains some 31 words. Of these words, the key ones are:

journey from work, not long, train crowded, office manager arrived home, tired drained

There are 13 *key* words. Other words like 'particularly', 'commuters and other travellers', and 'eventually' all help to make the sentence more interesting and to make its meaning more precise and detailed. However, if we were required to reproduce the key ideas of the sentence, we could write:

The office manager's journey from work was short, but his train was crowded and he arrived home feeling tired.

This shortened version contains 19 words, but a more polished and refined version is possible:

Travelling on a crowded train, the manager's short journey home from work left him exhausted.

Though the omission of the word 'office', and the substitution of 'exhausted' for 'drained and tired' may change the meaning of the original sentence somewhat, its sense remains the same, and its meaning has been broadly conveyed in less than half the words of the original.

When considering the summary of a collection of sentences in a paragraph, it will be necessary to identify the *key points* of the paragraph in much the same way as the key words of the sentence were located:

The new young typist glanced nervously around the busy, open-plan office, and stood at the door, not certain where she should go. Almost at once, a smartly-dressed man wearing gold-rimmed glasses rose from his desk and walked over to her, with a welcoming smile on his face.

'Good morning,' he said, 'I'm Peter Harris, senior clerk, and you must be our new typist. Miss Jenkins, isn't it? Do come with me, and I'll show you to your desk.'

'Oh, thank you, Mr Harris. I was wondering where I should go,' answered Penny gratefully. She was escorted to a pleasant position near a window, and on her desk someone had thoughtfully placed a small vase of fresh flowers.

117 words

Making notes

The paragraph contains six key ideas, which may be expressed briefly in note form:

1 Penny Jenkins – new typist – stops at office door
2 Not sure where to go
3 Peter Harris (senior clerk) rises – greets her warmly
4 Escorts PJ to desk
5 Desk pleasantly located by window
6 Fresh flowers on desk – put there thoughtfully by someone

The rough notes contain some 39 words.

If we assume that the original paragraph is to be summarised in about a third of the length of the original, then the rough notes are probably too generously written, since it usually takes as many words again to transform notes back into complete sentences. Since the target length of a summarised version is to be 40 words, it may be necessary to reduce the notes further, before attempting a first rough draft.

It may be necessary to re-phrase ideas like 'not sure where to go' and 'put there thoughtfully by someone' so that they are expressed more economically. Similarly, 'by the window' may be left out.

Notice that the rather lengthy wording of the direct speech exchange between Peter Harris and Penny Jenkins has been expressed much more simply by 'greets her warmly' and 'escorts PJ to desk'.

When summarising a passage, it is generally better to put over the *sense* of the original, than to try to use either the same words or sentence structures. Of course, it is necessary sometimes to make use of specialist words, where a great deal of meaning may be contained within a single word.

Writing a rough draft

A first rough draft of the summary may emerge as follows:

Penny Jenkins, the new typist, entered the office hesitantly, unsure of where to go. Immediately Peter Harris, the senior clerk, greeted her warmly and escorted her to her desk, which was pleasantly located. On her desk someone had thoughtfully placed a vase of fresh flowers.

45 words

A little careful pruning is needed to shorten the rough draft by some five words. Notice that the rough draft has been set out on alternate lines, so that any alterations may be made clearly:

Penny Jenkins, the new typist, ~~entered the~~ office *hesitated at*
the office entrance
~~hesitantly~~. Immediately Peter Harris, th~~e~~ senior clerk,

greeted her warmly and escorted her to her desk, which
, and on which
was pleasantly located. On ~~her desk~~ someone had thought-

fully placed a vase of fresh flowers.

The final version

The final version of the summary appears, then, as follows:

Penny Jenkins, the new typist, hesitated at the office entrance. Immediately, Peter Harris, senior clerk, greeted her warmly and escorted her to her desk, which was pleasantly located, and on which someone had thoughtfully placed a vase of fresh flowers.

40 words

If the original paragraph had been part of a longer story or article, then it would need a title. A suitable one might be:

Penny's First Day at Work

If you compare the summarised version with its original, you will notice that certain parts have been omitted, since they were not considered absolutely essential. Ideas like 'busy, open-plan' have been left out as have the references to Peter Harris's smartness and glasses. Ideas like 'with a welcoming smile on his face' have been conveyed much more briefly by 'greeted her warmly'.

The Acid Test!

The Acid Test of writing a good summary is whether it *reads fluently and stands by itself.* Sometimes summaries suffer because the ideas expressed are disjointed – the sentences do not flow and are not connected. Occasionally, the meaning of a sentence may be quite unclear since it has become 'overloaded' – the summariser has tried to make it convey too much meaning in too few words.

The 7 point summarising plan

In order to produce a successful summary, it is necessary to follow a plan. The main stages are:

- check aims
- understand original
- select main points
- produce rough draft
- write out final version

In more detail, the stages of the plan are set out below. Study them carefully and follow their sequence. You will find then that summarising is an engrossing skill – and that a lot of pleasure comes from producing an accurate and workmanlike piece of writing!

1 aims Be sure you know what you are required to do. Are you to produce a shortened version of all the original's main points, or are you expected to make your selection from certain parts of the original only?

Be sure, then, whether you are to produce a précis or a selective summary – it will all depend on the instructions you are given.

2 understanding the original Before you attempt to summarise the main points of the original, it is *essential* that you understand its meaning – both in terms of its words and phrases, and in the way in which its points are structured. A good practice is to read the original carefully two or three times:

- to absorb the general meaning
- to check the meaning of any unfamiliar words or phrases (use your dictionary!)
- to check the way the points are developed. Are any paragraphs or sections more important than others? What is the beginning, middle and end? How are major ideas linked?

original
(An article on office equipment)

précis | **summary**

A 'miniature' version of the original, faithful to all its main points | May select information about a <u>part</u> of the original.

3 give your summary a title Like a letter's subject heading, your title will serve to outline the theme of the summary and you can use it to measure each selected point for importance and relevance.

4 select the main points Go through the original methodically, and in your own words, make notes of each important point in a checklist. Check each point against your title for importance and relevance. Make sure you leave out anything trivial or outside your given instructions. Avoid any repetitions. Generally, avoid illustrations and examples which only support or reinforce main points.

5 check your list of points When you have completed your notes of the main points, check them carefully against the original. It is easier to insert an additional point or to cut one out, *before* you attempt a first rough draft. Bear in mind that your notes will probably expand to twice their length when re-written in complete sentence form.

6 write out your rough draft Before writing out your rough draft, think carefully about the most effective way in which to produce your summary. Should it be in continuous prose? Should it be a series of section headings with numbered sentences for quick reference? Should any of the information be displayed as a table or diagram?

Your aim should be to choose the layout which will best enable the summary's reader to use it effectively. For example, a summary for use in a meeting is best set out schematically, with numbered points for quick reference.

Write your rough draft on alternate lines, so that any alterations are easy to make.

If you have a word limit, aim to exceed it slightly. It is easier to cut words out than to insert them in a rough draft.

Check the rough draft for spelling, punctuation and grammar mistakes. Check for word length.

7 write out your final version You are now ready to write out your final version. Be careful not to miss out any words or lines when copying your rough draft. Check that you have not omitted any apostrophes, commas or question-marks, etc.

Supply your title and, if need be, the source of your original and its date of publication. (Someone reading your summary may wish to refer to the original.)

If your summary has been produced as a schedule or report, etc, it may be necessary to write a covering memorandum or letter to send with it to your boss or a senior staff member.

Remember!

The summarising skill is used *daily* in every office, whether in composing a letter or memorandum or whether drawing up a notice or bulletin. It is also essential when drafting minutes or writing a report. It is vital, of course when taking down a telephone message.

You can be quite sure that the skills you develop using the above **7 point plan** will stand you in good stead!

Boost your spelling power!

Learn these words by heart

Remember, an asterisk after a word indicates that it is very commonly misspelled:

niece n	(nephew n)
occasion n, v	(occasionally adv)
physical adj	(physique n)
psychology n	(psychological adj)
quiet* n, adj	(do not confuse with quite)
receive v	(receipt n)
seize v	(seizure n)
tendency n	
weird adj	
withhold v	(withheld v)

Do not forget to enter in your vocabulary book any words with which you are unfamiliar, either in terms of spelling or meaning!

Summarising assignments

Summarise the following:

1 Jack read the letter's message with great care.

in 5 words

2 The manager asked if he could be given a summarised version of the article, which was about word processing.

in about 11 words

3 Janet opened her morning's post and quickly came upon a letter from a customer who was complaining about the delay which had occurred in delivering to her office a floppy disk storage unit which she had ordered.

in about 25 words

4 'It's all right for you!' said Peter irritatedly to Penny. 'You don't have to see the customers yourself when mistakes have been made in calculating the amount due on their monthly statements!'

in about 18 words

5 Write a précis of the following article in not more than 130 words.

Though many of us receive business letters as a matter of routine, the production of a letter which is both attractive and effective combines the skill of a surprising number of people, some of whom will never meet!

First, a paper needs to be manufactured which will feel appropriately crisp and smooth to the touch. It will also need to take both the printer's inks and the imprint of the typewriter or computer printer without smudging or running.

Next, a graphic designer will need to produce a trade name, postal address, logo and possibly telex and telegraphic addresses in a suitable letterhead, which conveys an image to the receiver of the activities of the letter writing organisation.

At this stage, the notepaper is ready for the attentions of the letter's author and its typist. The person who 'writes' the letter may, in fact, never put pen to paper, but may dictate the message, either with the help of a dictating machine, or to a secretary who uses shorthand. The author will need to consider who is to receive the letter, the nature of its contents, and the right tone to adopt. The message must be carefully constructed and clearly expressed. At this point, the message may be transcribed – typed or word processed – on to the notepaper. The typist must take every care to ensure that no errors in transcription occur, and that the conventions of letter layout are followed.

Lastly, there are the carriers of the letter to consider – the office messengers, mailroom staff and postal service employees. Without their care, the letter may never reach its destination.

The production of a letter, then, is never routine – it is the result of a complex operation in which the creative and technical skills of literally dozens of people are combined!

300 words

6 You work as assistant to the personnel manager of Vulcan Engineering Limited. Your firm is in the process of introducing computerised equipment in both its factories and offices. The personnel officer wishes to print an article in the company's house magazine, *Anvil*, to make the personnel more aware of microprocessor technology. He has therefore asked you to produce a summary of the following article in not more than 140 words, which outlines what a microprocessor is, and what advantages it will bring to factory and office work.

The microprocessor, which has been developed by the electronics industry, has revolutionised the ways in which people work in shops, offices and factories. It has also affected greatly the ways in which they spend their leisure time, whether watching television, playing electronic games, or even cooking a favourite meal.

Also referred to as silicon chips, microprocessors are, in fact, a kind of miniaturised computer. They are about the size of a thumbnail and, with the help of chemical and photographic technology, many thousands of circuits may be built into a 'chip' about half the size of a postage-stamp, and about half as thick as a match-stick. And they are incredibly cheap to produce, costing pennies rather than pounds!

Microprocessors are able to store and to process information, both in number and written forms. They are the 'brains' behind pocket calculators, digital watches, desk-top computers and robot manufacturing machines in factories. Moreover, they are able to handle information with incredible speed and accuracy.

The microprocessor may be used to put an end to boring and repetitive work in factories and offices. Jobs such as spot-welding car body parts together are already being carried out by equipment 'untouched by human hand', and time-consuming tasks like working out the payroll for the company's employees, or calculating and printing the monthly statements for account customers are also jobs which may be rapidly performed by microcomputers, using microprocessors.

The possibilities for improving the quality of people's jobs and the range of their leisure and social activities are very exciting, provided that the 'microprocessor revolution' is carefully controlled and guided.

The top planners in government, industry and the trade unions will need to work hard together, however, if the miracle is not to become a disaster. Without care and compassion, dull and boring work may immediately be followed for many by an equally monotonous existence spent on a low income in long-term unemployment.

318 words

Grammar

The adverb

The adverb is a very frequently used part of speech. It has the important ability to make the meaning of a sentence more detailed and precise:

The salesman spoke –
eagerly
persuasively
slowly
quickly
with confidence
in an assured manner

As you can see from the above example, adverbs can either take the form of a single word or a group of words, known as adverbial phrases. The illustration above shows how different adverbs change or modify the meaning of the finite verb 'spoke', to give the reader a more detailed idea of how the salesman spoke.

The -ly ending

Most single-word adverbs in English end in -ly:

nicely   effectively   rapidly etc

It is important, however, not to confuse them with other words ending in -ly, which may be acting as adjectives:

She was wearing a *lovely* hat.

Also, there are a number of words which can act as adverbs and which do not end in -ly:

The athlete ran *fast*.
Janet speaks *well*.
The archer aimed *low* to allow for the wind.

In most instances, adverbs, as their name suggests, serve to alter or modify the meaning of the finite verb in a sentence:

spoke   eagerly
ran   fast
aimed   low

Sometimes, however, adverbs may be employed to change the meaning of other adverbs or adjectives:

	ADVERB	ADVERB
The office manager dictated the letter	*very*	*rapidly*.

	ADVERB	ADJECTIVE
The	*extremely*	*tall*

man stooped to walk through the entrance

Adverbs provide answers to a number of questions:

How? He answered the question *easily*.
When? I reached the station *in good time*.
Where? The ball dropped *into the pocket*.
To what extent? The shorthand was *quite* difficult to read.
Question posers *Where* did it appear?

The value of knowing

One of the values of being able to recognise words used

adverbially is that mistakes may be recognised easily and so avoided:

John types quick. ~~quick~~ *quickly*

He looked at her ~~cool~~ *coolly* and ~~confident~~ *confidently*.

I can walk more ~~slower~~ *slowly* than you.

She talks too ~~quiet~~ *quietly* for me to hear her.

Pat talks most ~~clearest~~ *clearly* of all.

Jenny listened as ~~careful~~ *carefully* as she could.

Adverb assignments

Write down the word or word groups being used adverbially in each of the following:

1 The clock ticked very quietly.

2 The tide rose fast and the swimmers were rapidly cut off.

3 I asked you politely, but you rudely ignored my question.

4 The particularly difficult question came last.

5 At what time did he go?

6 Feeling tired, the exhausted traveller went to bed early and rose late.

7 The winger scored a lucky goal three minutes before time and was mobbed rapturously by his team-mates.

8 She answered him in a brisk fashion and told him that the manager was unable to see him.

9 He eyed her sleepily but before she could say another word, he was snoring loudly!

10 An extremely urgent telex message has just been received.

Punctuation

The hyphen, dash and brackets

The dash and the hyphen are sometimes easily confused and so it is important to understand clearly the very different tasks which each performs as a punctuation mark.

The hyphen

Basically, the hyphen may be regarded as a link which joins two or more words together, or which joins parts of the same word together. Sometimes in English, different words may be linked together so strongly, that to all intents and purposes, they may be treated as one word:

The sales manager produced a *well-informed* report.
The motorist approached a *left-hand* bend in the road.
She fed the coins into the *parking-meter*.
The doctor recommended a month's *rest-cure*.

It is not always easy to be sure when words should or should not be linked with a hyphen, and so the best advice is to consult the dictionary whenever in doubt. However, one tip may be helpful. When unsure, try to express the idea of the sentence, using each of the words to be hyphenated singly:

The manager produced a well report.
The manager produced an informed report.

Since the first of the two options clearly does not make sense, if 'well' is to be used, it should be linked to 'informed' with a hyphen to make the two words into a single idea.

The other use of the hyphen is to show that a single word has been divided at the end of a line of print:

The typist picked up the file of documents and began to look through it.

Typists follow clear instructions on the appropriate way to hyphenate words which carry over line endings.

The dash and brackets

One of the most common uses of the dash is to add an additional thought or idea to the end of a sentence:

It is advisable to check carefully that the enclosure reference is included in a letter to be sent with brochures or other additional documents – otherwise its recipient may fail to notice that enclosed material has been left in an opened envelope.

'I'd like you to stay on for an extra hour tonight to type an urgent report – that is, if you don't mind.'

Though the use of the dash is perfectly acceptable in such structures as those illustrated above, it is important that you do not allow yourself to lapse into the 'dashitis' style of lazy punctuation:

Went to tea at Rodney's yesterday – Had a lovely time! – *Everyone* was there! – Even Penelope Dykes-Smith! – And, You Know Who! – I'm really over the moon about him – He talked to me all the time – And – You'll *never* guess! – He's taking me to dinner tonight at Emilio's!!!

Another task which the dash performs is to act as a pause indicator, which also shows that an idea has been inserted into the structure of the sentence:

Put two teaspoonfuls of brandy – or more if you can afford it – into the Christmas Pudding mixture.

Here, the dash shows that a 'second thought' has been added into the middle of an already constructed sentence. Sometimes this function may be carried out by brackets:

The first exercise is shown on page 9 (more experienced swimmers should consult the checklist on page 18) and beginners are advised to practise each movement separately before linking them together.

Brackets may also be used to provide a brief reference in this way:

The results show (Appendix II refers) that employees are evenly divided on the question of introducing a flexible working hours system.

Assignments

Insert hyphens appropriately in the following:

1 This custom built car has hand made upholstery.

2 The office intercom works on a two way switch.

3 The boss's blue eyed boy is really a good for nothing.

4 The firm's news letter is produced on a small printing press.

Insert dashes or brackets appropriately in the following sentences:

5 The letter is fully-blocked though I have nothing against that but I do object to the mistakes in punctuation and spelling.

6 The method more fully explained in chapter six is quite straightforward.

7 The chairman or chairperson if you prefer heads the committee structure.

Activities and assignments

Organisations

Group Discussion Topics:

1 Why do people tend to form groups in organisations?

2 How does a person become a member of a group and 'fit in' to it?

3 Why do organisations tend to be structured into departments and staff put into different grades of authority?

4 What are the essential facts a newcomer needs to know about his job? What happens if he doesn't find out or is not clearly informed?

The telephone

5 Research your information first, then write an account (with a diagram) to explain how the telephone system works in a large organisation.

6 Make notes of *five* support services which British Telecom makes available to commercial telephone users. Then, describe these services orally to your group. (You may wish to use visual aids to assist your account.)

7 Design a leaflet intended for newly-appointed junior office staff providing them with tips on how to use the telephone effectively.

8 First carry out your research, then give a presentation to your group on the range of facilities offered by a computerised telephone system in a large organisation.

Summarising

8 Make a checklist of as many activities at work as you can think of where summarising techniques are employed, when *a* the spoken word, and *b* the written word are used.

9 Read carefully the section in this unit which deals with working in organisational groups. Then make a summary of its main points in not more than 150 words. Write your summary in your own words, avoiding those of the original where possible.

The adverb

10 Explain briefly what an adverb does. Compose three sentences, each one containing an adverb. Underline the adverb in each sentence.

11 Identify the adverbs in the following piece:

Quickly Jack opened the envelope. His fingers searched anxiously for the letter inside. His trembling hands opened the notepaper and his eyes flicked with quick jerks as he scanned the page. He had been offered the job!

The dash and the hyphen

12 Explain the difference between the dash and the hyphen. Compose two sentences, one containing a hyphen and the other a dash to illustrate their correct use.

13 Punctuate the following passage:

turn left at the first cross roads then take the next right hand turning the next is a cul de sac so look for the telephone box on the corner of the first side road when you have turned right youll see a grocers shop called quickturnover on your left drive on until you reach the second set of traffic lights and then turn left oh and check that theres a post office immediately on your right on your right about three hundred metres further on youll see the man o war public house the hotel is just beyond it

Spelling: consonants

14 Complete the spelling of the following words by inserting the correct consonant(s):

—ilately	(love of stamps)
re—e—ee	(judge or umpire)
—ave	(jack in card game)
con—ien—us	(hard-working)
—eme—ery	(burial place)
—aw	(nibble)
a—e—	(measure or examine)
di—a—ear	(vanish)
—es—e	(like boxing, in a ring)
re—e—able	(unfortunate)

Wordprocessing

15 (*a*) Your present job is assistant to Mrs Kay Jenkins, who runs a busy office services bureau in the cathedral city of Norminster. Over the years she has established a long list of regular customers and, because of this, has tended to neglect the need to move with the times into IT and WP. However, now that competition is increasing, she has decided to purchase a microcomputer with WP facilities and has asked you to do some fact-finding for her with these words:

'Would you please find out what represents best value in the market at the moment, given the work we do – typing letters, reports, etc., preparing masters for photocopying, curriculum vitaes and so on. Then set out for me in an easily digestible and readable format what sort of equipment and what word processing software package we should opt for.'

If at all possible, carry out the production work for this assignment using a word processing package.

(b) Using a word processing package, create the following form letter which your boss, the Accounts Manager of Fordhampton Engineering Products Limited of Fordhampton House, Hamble River Road, Fordhampton, Hants, SO26 9EZ tel: Fordhampton 785436–8 wants to have on hand for despatch to customers with overdue accounts:

'Now let me see, we'll need to be able to send this to individual customers, so you'll need to take that into account. Also, you'll have to provide a subject-heading which displays the appropriate account number, amount overdue and for which monthly accounting period.

'Also in the letter you'll need to leave some space to include precise details of the total sum overdue and the statement or statements' number which relates to it, as well as the number of weeks the sum has been due for payment.

'Lastly, the letter should end with an alternative closing sentence depending on the length of time payment has been due and the sum involved – you could either ask for immediate payment according to terms of sale, etc. or go for the jugular and say that if we don't get the money within seven days we'll put the matter in the hands of our solicitors!'

Either singly or in small groups, compose a suitable form collection letter via WP package for your Accounts Manager. Remember that set pieces – sentences – can be set up in individual files and recalled from store to the file under production, and that letters can be created with blank lines set out for the subsequent inclusion of personalised text.

(c) Using a word processing package, produce an article of about 550 words entitled *The advantages of word processing in the office*. Your article should seek to use the layout facilities of the package to best advantage. As your article is a first draft, produce it on alternate lines.

When you have produced your print-out, pass it to a paired, fellow student who has the following brief:

'You are working as one of your college/school magazine editors. In front of you you have an article of about 550 words, entitled: *The advantages of word processing in the office*. Your editor-in-chief has asked you to cut it down to not more than 350 words and to include a paragraph about the importance of secretarial studies students acquiring WP skills, to make it more relevant to the college/school readership.

When you have made the appropriate hand-written amendments, pass it back to your pair for him/her to produce a final draft via WP. Then decide which article produced in your group should actually be offered for publication in your school/college magazine!

(d) With access to word processing facilities, set up a regular newsheet or paper of interest to your class or departmental students. See what support you can find to enable you to produce your newsletter during the lunchtime or after lessons.

Telephone case study

'Just a minute!'
Jean sat behind her desk, waiting for her nail-varnish to dry. Suddenly the phone rang.
'Hello?', she enquired.
'Oh, good morning, I'd like to speak to Mr Wilkins, please.'
'Oh. He's out. Won't be back until four – he's had to go to an important meeting about a merger or something.'
'Oh, I see. Well, could you take a message?'
'Yes. Just a minute! I need a pencil and paper. Right. Fire away!'
'Would you say that Mr Thomas of Fastflow Washing Machines called to see him about the new....'
'Hang on a sec! Jack, put the parcel over there, would you. Thanks. See you tonight? Yeah, looking forward to it! Sorry, Mr Tomkins, you want to talk about what was it again?'
'Oh, no, on second thoughts, I'll call Mr Wilkins after four o'clock.'
'Righto. Goodbye then.'
Replacing the receiver, Jean noticed she had chipped her nail, and, biting her lip in irritation, she reached for her nail-varnish once more.

Discussion topic

Study the above case in small groups and make a checklist of the shortcomings you detect in Jean's handling of the call.

Then, *individually*, write out a version of the dialogue of the case study which you think shows how the call should have progressed.

Lastly, compare your dialogue with those of your fellow group members and check which one your group considers the most effective.

Unit 7

Persuasive communication 1

One of the most frequent aims of the communicator in business and public service is to *persuade* as well as to inform. Though some situations – the writing of a report or the passing on of a message – may only require that the important information is conveyed in a factual way, many other instances occur when the sender of a spoken or written message needs to use persuasive skills.

For example, a manager may wish to persuade a group of factory workers to work overtime; an executive may ask his secretary to stay after normal finishing time to complete an urgent letter; or a salesman may seek to convince his customer that he should order extra supplies before a price increase. In other words, every day people at all levels of industry or commerce need to use their powers of persuasion if they are to carry out necessary tasks and meet given objectives.

This is particularly true in the marketing and sales departments of organisations, where special efforts must be made to sell goods to wholesalers, retailers or consumers. For instance, an advertising campaign may seek to persuade a housewife that a certain brand of soap powder washes better than other brands on the market. The campaign may be built around the slogan that,

KRYSTAL BRINGS THE WHITE BACK INTO WASHING!

Various advertisements, whether television commercials, roadside posters, leaflets or placards will seek to convince sometimes sceptical housewives to switch to Krystal – perhaps since it possesses some unique ingredient, or because it is particularly 'kind' to delicate fabrics.

Alternatively, the manufacturers of a breakfast cereal may strive to sell, not only the food value of the product, but the fact that it is fun to eat:

All the family loves Crackaflake cereals – they make break-fast fun, while doing everyone a power of good!

In another context, the makers of women's tights may use a sales letter approach to persuade retailers that a new range is well worth stocking:

The new line of Sheerline Eleganza tights are most attractively displayed in a space-saving, free-standing merchandiser. The easy, self-serve design of the merchandiser makes it so simple for your customers to select their own size and preferred colour. All you need to do is ring up the sale! Moreover, our sales representative will call regularly to ensure that you are never out of stock. With Sheerline Eleganza, we've taken the legwork out of your tights sales problems!

'Frankly, sir, I think you've made a very wise choice. Fits like a glove! You'll find the material won't ruck when you sit down. Of course, we can take the trousers up just a trifle, to give you a modish cut over the instep...'

In advertising, every effort is made to combine the impact of shapes, colours, images and word-pictures to put across a 'message' which will persuade someone to buy.

Marketing experts use various communications media in a carefully planned way to transmit an advertising message via television or radio commercials, newspaper or magazine advertisements, roadside hoardings or leaflets and brochures. In this way, all the impact of colour, shape, and the spoken and written word serve to emphasise the persuasive content of the advertisement.

Gold and red colours combined with elegant script, for example, are often used to convey a sense of luxury when selling chocolates or perfume, while greens, blues and white lettering are used to give a sense of freshness or cleanliness, as in food or washing products.

In this way advertisers attempt to connect their products with our deeply-rooted ways of judging values and our long-term experiences of the products.

Another persuasive technique is to provide the would-be customer with good reasons why a particular product should be preferred to others – by selling its 'benefits':

> SPARKLE washing-up liquid will bring a bright lustre to all your china and cutlery. It shifts even cold and burned-in grease, and costs no more than ordinary washing-up liquids. Change to Sparkle and you'll see a difference!

> Sun-Searcher Holidays *guarantee* your holiday satisfaction! All our hotels are vetted by our specialist tour inspectors. Only the most sun-favoured resorts win a place in our Sun-Searcher Holiday Plans, and once you have chosen your own sun-kissed holiday haven – your problems are over! Our highly-trained teams of couriers are constantly – yet discreetly – on hand to help you get the most from your precious holiday time, with suggestions for day-tours or evening visits, and they can handle your holiday problems – from safety-pins to baby-sitters!

> If blue skies, warm sand and clear seas are *your* holiday dream, ring Freefone 01-800-9000 and Sun-Searchers will make your dream come true!

The need to persuade as well as to inform is also important *within* organisations. Nowadays, companies employ large staffs, often working in distant locations. Managers know that staff morale and goodwill are all-important, if production, sales or office efficiency are to be maintained at high levels.

Consequently, a great deal of effort is put into the way that internal communications are designed and produced. Some firms employ communication managers to ensure that notices, bulletins, house magazines and the like are of a high standard. The way that staff acquire information is considered to be extremely important – it is much better to read a clear notice or receive an informative circular letter than to pick up rumours on the firm's 'grapevine'. Similarly, staff are much more likely to respond positively to directives or requirements if they are expressed in a way that causes acceptance rather than resentment:

> **Your company needs you!**
> So … *always* wear your safety-helmet! We just cannot afford to lose your expertise and experience. Besides, we rather think it suits you!

Here, a construction company is seeking to remind its building workers to comply with the requirements of the Health and Safety At Work Act, but has expressed the need for safety in such a way that the staff feel important to the firm. Also, the implied humour of the last sentence is much more likely to lead to the helmets being worn than a 'wear it, or else!' tone.

Alternatively, an organisation may wish to develop the skills of its office staff in using the fast-developing range of electronic office equipment. Rather than make staff take training courses, a more voluntary commitment may be preferred – so that the decision comes from the staff themselves:

All office staff   **4 May 19—**
Office skills are changing – fast!
The advent of the microprocessor or silicon chip has brought tremendous developments in the tasks which a wide range of electronic equipment can perform. Micro-computers, word processors and data processing terminals have now become familiar office tools in many companies.

How do *you* rate your ability to use such a range of office equipment?

Your own career development and promotion prospects may well depend on your ability to move with the times!

Mr Owens, the company training officer is keen to talk to anyone wishing to upgrade and develop keyboard, data processing or programming skills.

Ring Extension 293 today – it could mean the start of a more challenging and satisfying tomorrow!
Ref: JO/TG
Authorised: Comm Mgr 4/5/19—

The above notice has been carefully written to ensure that a positive and encouraging tone is transmitted to the office staff, and good reasons – career development and promotion prospects, linked with job satisfaction – are put forward to persuade the reader of the value of finding out more. The staff do not *have* to apply, and it may well prove that by seeking out the more motivated staff, a subsequent training programme is more likely to succeed.

Notice the other, essential ingredients of the message – it has a clear statement of the intended recipients of the message – all office staff; the date on which the notice was posted is included, together with a stimulating title, intended to make the reader curious and to want to read the notice's message. Also, the notice is given a reference for filing purposes and has been authorised by the company's communication manager before being displayed on staff noticeboards.

In addition to notices, posters have an important part to play in transmitting information within organisations. For example, a firm's social club may wish to advertise a forth-coming Christmas Dance to members of staff. A poster will create interest in the event and provide essential information about when, where, what, how much, etc.

In a poster such as the one illustrated, care must be taken to choose an appropriate colour for the poster paper, and printing which will create an atmosphere of enjoyment at Christmas time. Similarly, the graphics will aim to reinforce the Christmas party atmosphere and to be eye-catching at the same time.

Christmas dance poster

When designing a poster it is important not to over-crowd the available space with too much written information. At the same time, the essential information must be conveyed clearly. Here, the venue for the dance, the date and the duration of the event are all clearly given. It is not enough, however, simply to print the where, when and how long information. If tickets are to be sold, and interest stimulated, the 'key' ingredients – the dinner, band and disco, cabaret, tombola and Christmas draw must all be made to appear good value and to have a persuasive appeal to the Social Club membership. Since the cost of the tickets is very reasonable, the point is made that there may not be enough to go round – and this is turned into a selling point, by prompting staff to book early.

The result should be an eye-catching poster which persuades staff members to order their tickets from a named departmental representative without delay!

Mastering the meaning

1 Why do you think it is sometimes necessary at work for techniques of persuasion to be linked with the factual delivery of information?

2 Why is it particularly important for marketing and sales staff to have skills in persuasive communication?

3 What points made in the Sheerline Eleganza extract do you think would persuade a retailer to buy the new product?

4 Why do advertisers sometimes use a combination of media for advertising a product?

5 Why are certain colours used in advertisements?

6 What do you understand by the term 'selling the benefits of a product'?

7 Write down the words and phrases in the Sparkle and Sun-Searcher Holidays extracts which you think have a particularly persuasive effect. In each case say why you think the word or phrase is effective.

8 Why is it important to use techniques of persuasion *within* organisational communications?

9 What aspects of the 'Office skills are changing – fast!' notice do you think are effective in persuading staff to learn new skills?

10 What would you say are the important points to keep in mind when designing a poster?

General discussion topics

1 Is advertising necessary?

2 Do you think the techniques which advertisers use to persuade people to buy products are fair – or do they give a false impression?

3 What do you think is the most effective advertisement you have seen recently? Explain your reasons for so thinking.

4 If you were applying for a job, what information would you look for in a situations vacant advertisement?

5 If you were advertising, say, a clerical job, what information would you think it important to provide in an advertisement?

6 What do you think would be the effect if all advertising were to be banned?

Small group assignments

1 In small groups, imagine that you own a family business which retails records, tapes and a range of record and tape storage and cleaning equipment. You have just purchased a new shop in the main street of your town. It is due to open in five weeks' time.

Design a leaflet to be posted through the letterboxes of local residents to advertise the opening of your shop. Invent any necessary information you wish to convey. Also, using a tape-recorder, compose a thirty second radio commercial to advertise your shop's opening, which will be broadcast on your local commercial radio station.

2 Assume that your record shop is now open. Design an advertisement to appear in your local weekly newspaper advertising the range of products which your shop sells and providing sound reasons why people should wish to purchase from you.

3 The newly opened shop requires a sales assistant who must also help with clerical work. Design a display advertisement for the job which will be put in the local paper.

It would be helpful first to research similar advertisements in your own local paper.

Communication and reception skills

Although some people make the important duties of receptionist their full-time occupation, almost every office worker at some time or another acts as an unofficial receptionist.

The skills of reception are important. You never know when you will be left to 'hold the fort' or deal with an unexpected visitor or telephone-call.

The following sections summarise the main responsibilities of reception work so that clients, customers or colleagues are left with an abiding impression of courtesy and efficiency!

The reception area

It goes almost without saying that the reception area or foyer should appear smart and well-cared for at all times. The reception area and the receptionist provide an all-important first impression of the organisation for the visitor who will inevitably make value-judgments about a firm's efficiency, reliability and modernity by what he sees and hears around him upon arrival.

Consequently, foyer furniture, fixtures and fittings should always be kept well polished and dusted. Ash-trays should be frequently emptied and cleaned, and newspapers and magazines kept tidy and up-to-date – a firm which hoards old magazines may also do the same with outmoded ideas! Also, utensils for refreshments should be

kept clean and readily available. Some companies provide instant hot-drink dispensers for this purpose.

Desk tops and working surfaces, including workbooks and documents should always be kept clean and tidy and clear of clutter or personal belongings. In addition, the whole of the foyer area should be tastefully decorated and well-lit; and the caring receptionist will take pains to ensure that seasonal flower arrangements provide a pleasant, eye-catching feature.

In short, the reception area should always seem as though it had just been prepared for the next visitor – who is *always* a VIP!

The receptionist

Smartness, alertness, courtesy and initiative are the watchwords of the good receptionist. Top-flight organisations hand-pick their reception staff because they realise how important their functions are, whether in public/customer relations, message-relaying or security.

The receptionist should take a pride in his or her appearance: well-pressed clothes, well-groomed hands, attractive make-up or clean-cut features as well as carefully dressed hair will certainly not go unnoticed and communicate a great deal by themselves! Even more important is a ready smile and friendly turn of phrase – even in the middle of a crisis or at the end of a long day. In fact, the whole manner and bearing of the receptionist should clearly communicate at all times the kind of corporate (or company) image which the organisation wishes visitors to receive and hold in their minds.

The receptionist's job skills

In terms of job skills, the receptionist needs to be an expert in a variety of areas. Firstly, the telephone switchboard system must be thoroughly learned, together with the range and scope of any computer-based features, so that in-coming and out-going calls are quickly and flawlessly dealt with. The receptionist must also be able to 'keep cool' when the switchboard is 'jumping' and three visitors arrive simultaneously!

The receptionist must also take pains to get to know as many members of staff as possible, so that a personal touch may be added to routine communications:

'Good morning Mr Charlesworth, I have Miss Watkins on the line for you.'
'... Just one moment, I'll see if Mr Foster is available. He deals with our stationery.'
'Would you mind taking a seat? Miss Jones, the managing director's personal assistant will be down in a moment to take you to his office.'

The good receptionist
* smart appearance
* pleasant manner
* enjoys meeting people
* even-tempered and polite
* discreet and tactful
* shows initiative

Unexpected callers
You will need to find out
* the purpose of the visit
* whom they wish to see
* whether that person will see them

Arrange an appointment if necessary

Business cards save questions
They give
* the caller's name
* his or her position
* the company name and address
* the company's type of business

Do not give your signature without careful consideration
* Were the goods ordered?
* Are all the parcels present that should be?
* Is the packaging intact?

1 Keep a diary of expected visitors' appointments
2 Keep a register to record visitors' times of arrival and departure
3 Telephone the relevant person to say the visitor has arrived
4 Keep a list of frequently used internal and external telephone numbers and addresses
5 The receptionist may be required to combine other work with that of looking after callers
6 If the reception area is left unattended for any reason confidential papers should be placed out of sight
7 If there is some delay before a visitor can be seen, refreshments and reading matter should be offered

The reception area

or to deal with an emergency:

'Could you get Mr Weston, security superintendent, to reception at once please. I'm having difficulty with a caller who appears to be drunk!'

In the course of the job, the receptionist must know how to use a wide range of reference books and directories – the firm's internal telephone index, British Telecom telephone directories, Kelly's Directories, rail and airline timetables will certainly be among them. The receptionist may also have to transfer appointments made by staff into her own diary for future reference. This means she will be aware of all expected visitors and for reasons of security she may be required to record the arrival and departure times of all callers. No potential industrial spy or unwelcome visitor should be allowed to roam around design offices, laboratories or workshops unaccompanied.

Some firms expect the receptionist to supervise records of all outgoing telephone calls, so that they may be charged to the appropriate department. Moreover, telephone calls or callers may result in the receptionist having to take messages to be passed to relevant members of staff. And in case the receptionist should ever feel bored or lonely, many firms provide a telex or typewriter, so that non-urgent work may be typed in quiet periods!

The PA and secretary as receptionist

In many companies personal assistants and secretaries also carry out the duties of receptionist. From their outer offices, they can act as 'interceptors' of both visitors and telephone calls for the boss. In such instances, it is important for staff to remain courteous and polite – even when denying access to the principal because a visitor has called without an appointment, or because the boss just does not wish to see him!

In order to carry out such reception duties, the PA or secretary needs to obtain answers to a number of pertinent questions:

Who is the caller? Which organisation does he represent? What is the nature of his business? Is it urgent? Can I handle it or should I refer to the boss? Should I note down any particulars? Should I inform the boss of the caller's presence?

Answers to these and other similar questions need to be found before the caller may be ushered into the principal's presence or put through to his telephone extension. Throughout the process, constant tact and discretion are needed, rather than the rude bluntness of:

'Mr Jones can't see you. He's got an important account customer with him.'

Coping with the waiting visitor

Sometimes it is necessary for a visitor to be asked to wait in a reception area or outer office until the person he wishes to see is free. At such times, it is the duty of the receptionist to make the visitor comfortable and to ease the waiting time with remarks such as:

'I'm sure Mr Goodson won't keep you waiting long.'
'I'll just see if Mr Goodson has been delayed ...'
'May I offer you a cup of coffee while you're waiting?'
'Have you read this week's *Time Magazine*? It's in the rack beside you. I believe there's an interesting feature on ...'

'I'm only doing my job!'

A case study

Jane Oliver was thrilled when she landed the job of private secretary to Mr Peter Jameson, sales manager of Domestilectrix Limited, a wholesale company which sold a variety of domestic electrical appliances. For the first time in her life, Jane had her own office, between the outer sales office and Mr Jameson's own private office. Jane liked working for Mr Jameson, but he was demanding in the standards he required, and Jane was determined to impress.

Not long after her appointment, Jane was busily typing some letters, while Mr Jameson was holding an important meeting in his office. 'You hold the fort, Jane,' he had said, 'and don't disturb us unless it's absolutely necessary. We must finish planning the new range of discounts for the remodelled Frostite Freezers.' Jane was only too pleased to have a chance to attack the mass of correspondence on her desk.

'Good morning, I must see Mr Jameson – this is his office, I believe?' A heavily-built stranger stood in front of Jane, wearing a grim expression.

'Well, it's mine, actually. Mr Jameson's office is through there – but he couldn't possibly see you, he's busy planning a new discount structure for Frostite Freezers. Have you got an appointment?'

'Oh, I see. No, as a matter of fact, I haven't, but it's extremely important that I see Mr Jameson straight-away. Here's my card.'

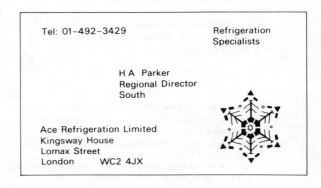

Tel: 01-492-3429 — Refrigeration Specialists

H A Parker
Regional Director
South

Ace Refrigeration Limited
Kingsway House
Lomax Street
London   WC2 4JX

'Ah, Mr Parker. Well, I'm sure I could help. What is it you wanted to see Mr Jameson about?'

'I'm afraid the matter is confidential – and extremely urgent. Would you please tell Mr Jameson that I should be grateful for a brief word.'

'Look, I'm sorry, but as I said, he's not available at the moment. Could you call back later? I'm rather busy with this correspondence at the moment.'

'Oh, really, this is quite intolerable!'

'Well, there's no need to raise your voice. I'm only doing my job!'

'Look, Miss Er, just tell Mr Jameson that I called and that I shall telephone him later.'

With that Mr Parker turned on his heel and left.

'The nerve of some people!' thought Jane, settling down to the letters once more.

About an hour later, Mr Jameson emerged from his office.

'Well, thank goodness that's got the discounts straight. I rather imagine that the cat will be among the pigeons when we start under-cutting the competition! Any messages, Jane?'

'No, except that there was someone from – oh, where did I put that card? Anyway he wouldn't say what he wanted, so I daresay it wasn't that important. I told him you didn't want to be disturbed.'

'Strange. Well, I must get down to accounts to see Mr French before lunch. You remember that I'm out all afternoon? But I should be back to sign the post.'

'That's all right, Mr Jameson, just leave everything to me!'

Assignments

1 In small groups, study the case carefully, and then make a checklist of the ways in which Jane may have handled the situation badly. Compare notes with other groups.

2 Compose the dialogue between Mr Parker and Jane in the way you think it should have progressed.

3 Design a checklist for effective visitor reception.

4 Draft a letter from Mr Parker to Mr Jameson complaining about the way he was treated.

Business letters 3

Tone

The tone of a written document stems from a combination of factors. First there are the aims and objectives of the written message: whether to sell a product or to recover a bad debt. Then there are the needs and expectations of the receiver of the document and the relationship between writer and recipient, such as retailer and customer. Lastly, there is the reason for writing: trying to put right a customer's complaint, or to hasten the delivery of urgently needed spare parts. Tone, then, is the result of all these factors. It gives the impression which the reader of the message receives, and it comes from the choice of words which the writer makes to express his message, and the structure of the sentences which convey it to the reader.

Aims and objectives

Does the document seek to:

- transmit factual information?
- persuade a customer to buy?
- urge a debtor to pay up?
- motivate a sagging sales force?
- discipline a wayward member of staff?
- answer criticisms or complaints?
- analyse and solve a problem?

The relationship between writer and reader

Much depends on the existing relationship between writer and receiver:

- is the receiver above or below the writer in the organisation's hierarchy?
- is the recipient a customer?
- is the recipient a member of staff?
- does the recipient report to the writer?

Profile of the recipient(s)

- what characteristics of the recipient will influence the way the message is received?
- is there one recipient or many?
- is the recipient young or old, male or female?
- is he an expert or layman?
- what attitudes or views does he possess?
- is he likely to be sympathetic, hostile or indifferent?

The needs of the situation

The tone of the document must respond to the needs of the situation:

- may the writer adopt a familiar or friendly tone?
- must the message be written in formal language?
- is the situation one in which the writer is informing? Or persuading? Or both?
- does the writer need urgent action from the recipient?

Choosing the right words

Once the writer has considered all the above points, he may then set out to use words which will best create the right tone. Sometimes colloquial expressions – 'Don't push it too far' – may be perfectly in order; at other times a more formal wording is needed – 'Do not attempt to sell the product too aggressively'. Occasionally the tone will need to be formal – 'Unless payment is made within seven days, legal action will be taken'. It is *always important* to ensure that the most appropriate words – the best words – have been carefully chosen.

Choosing the right sentence structure

The effect of sentences upon tone – whether short and sharp or complex and long – is also important to consider. The short sentence can be very effective:

> Company profits rose by 36% last year.
> Order *your* copy now!

But a succession of them can prove very dull and even irritating:

> Thank you for your letter of 14 July. You enquired about holidays in the USA. There are several we recommend. The first is in New York. It is for 7 days. It includes 3 sightseeing tours. It costs £650.00. The second is in Florida ....

Alternatively, longer sentences may be needed to explain complicated ideas:

> There are a number of selling points concerning the Hermes desk-top microcomputer which the sales force should bring to the attention of customers. The first concerns the computer's display screen which features normal black text on a white background – just like familiar notepaper. Further, the screen displays the equivalent of the full depth of an A4 sheet so that the user can always see the whole of the page of the letter or report being created. The second selling point is that with 20 megabytes of memory on hand, the Hermes' response time is always instant and the irritation of slow responses to commands is eliminated totally!....

A frequent problem with the composition of long and complex sentences is that the writer loses the thread of what he is trying to convey:

> Not having used your cordless, desk-top dictating machine, though I *am* used to dictating machines, which my company has used for the past fifteen years, which I think allows me to consider myself as someone rather more experienced than a newcomer to dictating practices.

Here, the writer has become hopelessly lost, trying to make too many points within the scope of a single sentence; he has forgotten what he set out to convey at the beginning of the sentence.

In short, the writer must seek at all times to *control* the length and structure of his sentences so that a clear and appropriate tone is conveyed through them. He should vary the mix of longer and shorter sentences, so that the message is easily understood by the reader, and at the same time is made interesting because of its varied rhythms.

What's in a word?

Study the following extracts from business documents and, in a general group discussion, decide what it is about the use of words which creates the particular tone you think each conveys:

> I should therefore be most grateful if you would kindly look into the matter.

> The repair-kit is so easy to use! You simply peel off the backing from a patch of the right size, press it firmly over the hole in your Junior Rowboat, reinflate, and you're ready again for more fun!

> As you will appreciate, the company warranty does not cover accidental damage, and I must, regretfully, inform you that I am unable to replace the camera. However, our servicing department is able to repair it for you at an extremely reasonable charge....

> Ken and I really enjoyed seeing you again at Gleneagles last week, and hope you had a safe journey back to Manchester. Mr Wilson will be calling on you next week to demonstrate our new industrial floor polisher....

> For the past week, the department has been absolutely frantic, trying to finalise the sales promotion presentation. I was hoping you might be able to give me a hand in designing a leaflet for the new satellite channel television – don't say no!

> ... so I am looking to everyone to make a solid effort to push sales up to our target during the last week of the month. You have done it before – in spite of the efforts of our competitors – and I know you can do it again, and crown another really superb sales performance!

> According to the provisions of the Employment Protection Act, it is my duty to issue this final warning, regarding your performance as a machine shop supervisor....

The letter of complaint

Notice that the *first paragraph* gives detailed factual information of the sales transaction, so that the complaint can be investigated quickly. It also provides the recipient with an early indication of the nature of the letter's message. The *middle paragraphs* provide further details of the precise nature of the complaint and emphasise the cost and inconvenience which the writer has incurred. The closing paragraph indicates clearly and firmly what action the writer expects from the retail store, and includes an *action statement*. Sometimes, letters of complaint provide a deadline such as 'within three days'. But in this first letter such an approach would be too strong. Notice that throughout the letter the tone never becomes aggressive or impolite; it is firm and clear so that the reader will not become annoyed by it, but rather, will wish to take urgent action to put matters right.

Structure

Opening paragraph ①

Note that all the details are provided so that the sale may be quickly traced – where, when, what, and document numbers.

Middle paragraphs

Here ② the writer explains in detail the nature of the complaint, and emphasises ③ that she does not consider herself in any way to blame.

Closing paragraph

It is important for the writer to state clearly what action he or she expects. Here ④ the emphasis is on immediate action to put the matter right. Thus an *action statement* is needed in the closing paragraph.

Tone

Opening paragraph ⑤

In a letter of complaint the opening paragraph sets the tone – polite but firm; the last sentence tells the reader what the letter's subject-matter is.

Middle paragraphs

The tone of this paragraph ⑥ is largely factual, but notice the effect of emphasising the care taken.

In this paragraph ⑦ the writer is at pains to demonstrate the result of the faulty iron – both in terms of the cost of replacing the skirt and the inconvenience of being without an iron. The effect is to bring home to the retailer his obligation to put matters right.

Closing paragraph

This paragraph includes the *action statement* ⑧ and its tone seeks to indicate the writer's sense of grievance by such phrases as 'without delay' and 'as soon as possible'.

---

6 Norfolk Gardens
Newtown
Midshire NT4 6TG

23 March 19--

The Branch Manager
Domestilectrix Limited
5 High Street
Newtown
Midshire   NT2 3AJ

Dear Sir

① On Thursday 21 March 19-- I purchased a Johnson Glida electric iron from your branch, model number HT456341, receipt number 094 for £27.42. The iron immediately proved defective when I tried to use it later that day. ⑤

② Before using the iron, I followed the instructions carefully about filling it with water and setting the temperature control correctly in order to iron my linen skirt. ⑥

③ However, as soon as I placed the iron on my skirt, it immediately scorched it, burning a hole in it and consequently ruining it. A replacement will cost at least £30.00. Apart from the damage to my skirt, I am now without an iron and so put to considerable inconvenience, since my job requires that I am smartly dressed at all times. ⑦

④ I should therefore be grateful if you would arrange for both the iron and the skirt to be inspected without delay and arrangements made to replace them as soon as possible. ⑧

Yours faithfully

Julie Dawson (Miss)

Boost your spelling power!

Learn these key words by heart

Remember, an asterisk after a word indicates that it is very commonly misspelled:

acknowledge v	(acknowledgment n)
bachelor n	(bachelorhood n)
disappear v	(disappearance n)
extreme* adj	(extremely* adv)
government n	(governable adj)
indispensable adj	
medicine n	(medicinal adj)
possess* v	(possession n, possessive adj)
replace v	(replaceable adj)
twelve adj n	(twelfth adj)

Do not forget to enter in your vocabulary book any words with which you are unfamiliar, either in terms of spelling or meaning!

The letter of adjustment

The structure of the letter of adjustment mirrors that of the complaint. The *opening paragraph* acknowledges the receipt of the letter of complaint and makes a suitable expression of regret. The *middle paragraphs* provide details of the actions being taken to remedy the complaint, while their tone seeks to emphasise the urgency and attention with which the complaint is being treated. The *closing paragraph* endeavours to keep the customer's goodwill – largely by its tone which emphasises the value of the customer's business. Remember that business in retailing is highly competitive and no firm wishes to lose its good name by failing to act quickly to right a complaint.

Structure

Opening paragraph ①

The writer first acknowledges the receipt of the letter of complaint.

Middle paragraphs ②

The writer sets out in detail the action he proposes to take in order to remedy the complaint.

Notice ③ that he does not commit himself until the company has inspected the iron and established that it, rather than its user, was at fault.

Closing paragraph

A restatement of apology ④ is in order together with an expression of hope that the action proposed (or taken) will be sufficient to make good the complaint.

DOMESTILECTRIX LIMITED
5 High Street
Newtown Midshire
NT2 3AJ
Tel: Newtown 89764/6

Your ref
Our ref   TF/AD

24 March 19--

Miss J Dawson
6 Norfolk Gardens
NEWTOWN
Midshire   NT4 6TG

Dear Miss Dawson

JOHNSON GLIDA IRON COMPLAINT

① I was extremely sorry to learn from your letter of 23 March 19-- of the trouble you have experienced with the Johnson Glida electric iron you recently purchased from this branch. ⑤

② I have made arrangements for our service engineer to contact you as soon as possible, so that he may call to inspect the iron and the damage done to your skirt. ⑥

③ Once the iron has been inspected and proved to be defective, he will be pleased to supply and test a replacement for you, which he will bring with him. Also, if you would kindly inform him of the replacement cost of your skirt, I will make arrangements on his return for a cheque to be sent to you for the full amount.

④ May I once again offer my sincere apologies for the inconvenience which you have been caused and express the hope that the action outlined above will prove to be to your satisfaction. The Company values your custom and I hope this regrettable incident will not prevent you from using my branch in the future. ⑦

Yours sincerely

T Franklin
Branch Manager

Tone

Opening paragraph ⑤

Notice that a suitably apologetic tone is created in the first four words to set the tone – to resolve the complaint and to keep the customer's goodwill.

Middle paragraphs ⑥

The tone of the middle paragraphs continues in its efforts to soothe an upset customer's sense of grievance. The writer seeks to show that he is dealing with the matter urgently and making every effort to remedy the complaint as quickly as possible.

Closing paragraph ⑦

The tone again is one of apology – the writer does not wish to lose the future custom of Miss Dawson, and the tone of the letter seeks to promote an image of the company as one which cares about customer relations and its good name.

Letter writing assignments

Choose an appropriate letter layout and compose a letter to meet the needs of the following:

1 Your firm, Watchtower Insurance Limited, 14–16 North Street, Middleton, Westshire MI6 9KL, tel Middleton 896723, purchased an electrically powered paper-shredding machine on 6 August 19— from Reliant Office Equipment Limited, 9 Western Terrace, Middleton, Westshire MI12 9TF. It was for disposing of confidential documents. When the machine was first used, it functioned perfectly, but after two weeks, it developed an intermittent fault, which resulted in its becoming jammed with paper. You telephoned the suppliers, and informed a Mr Peters about the problem, and he promised to supply a replacement. That was over a week ago, and you have since heard nothing.

Compose a letter of complaint to Reliant Office Equipment's branch manager, a Mr J Hopkins, which you think will help to resolve the problem.

2 As Mr Hopkins, write a letter to adjust the complaint from Watchtower Insurance Limited. When you investigated the matter you found that Mr Peters had gone on holiday but had forgotten to arrange for a replacement paper-shredder to be delivered.

Grammar

The adjective

Adjectives are describing words which are used to add extra meaning to an idea or to make the sense of a group of words more specific:

> The manager asked for the report.

The above sentence only conveys the idea of a business man wishing to receive a report on a subject we know nothing about. The addition of adjectives will enable the idea to be expressed with much more helpful detail:

> The *hard-pressed* manager asked for the *overdue sales* report.

Adjectives, then, are a valuable means of providing more detailed and more specific meaning to sentences. They are most frequently used to add meaning to nouns or to pronouns:

ADJ	NOUN		ADJ	PRONOUN
the	large	cupboard	the	same	one

Most adjectives come immediately before the noun or pronoun they affect, but sometimes they are to be found at the very end of sentences:

> Today the office is *busy.*
> The record sounds extremely *loud.*

Sometimes adjectives may be formed from the present or past participles of verbs:

> We were caught in the *pouring* rain.
> Oil gushed from the *fractured* pipeline.

Adjectives are used in a number of different ways:

- to describe or specify:
  the *huge* crowd   the *dark red* leather

- to state possession:
  my book   *your* coat   *their* lunch

- to pose a question:
  Which layout do you prefer?
  What name did he give?

- to indicate a quantity or number:
  seventy-six trombones   *no* trouble
  some replies   a *few* answers

- to 'point out' something:
  this letter   *that* lathe   *these* figures

When using 'this', 'that', 'these', or 'those', always make sure that the adjective agrees with the noun it is directly affecting:

This type

~~These types~~ of problem

The adjectives 'more' and 'most' are used to change the meaning of other adjectives:

This design is *more* effective.
The blue dress is *most* suitable for the reception.

When using 'more' and 'most', beware of falling into the trap of writing phrases such as:

more better   most quickest
more faster   most likeliest etc.

Properly used, adjectives help the reader to gain a clear and sometimes vivid picture of people, places and events:

The *wizened* street-trader grasped my money in her *wrinkled* fingers and passed me the jug with a *cracked* smile and a *croaky* 'Here you are, ducks!'

The *old-fashioned* office smelled *musty* and looked *dingy*. Overhead there hung a *stale* smell of tobacco, *duplicating* fluid, ink and glue. The effect of *old, peeling* wallpaper and *cracked* paint was depressing to say the least, and was only excelled by the *dreary* clacking of a *single* typewriter and the *occasional* sniff or cough of a *sombre-suited* clerk.

As the above examples illustrate, adjectives help the writer to create vivid pictures by supplying the reader with a sense of sight, smell, hearing or touch.

The most common abuse of adjectives is to overuse them, so that the reader is smothered by them:

The *old, broken, rusty* bicycle lay against the *sooty, stained* and *graffiti-covered* wall, where *yellow, green* and *speckled* weeds struggled to survive, cramped between the wall and the *narrow, wet* and *oil-covered* pavement.

The writer must learn to be sparing with adjectives and to select those he thinks most expressive:

The *rickety* bicycle lay against the *decaying* wall, surrounded by *rank* weeds which bordered the *wet, oily* pavement.

Adjective assignments

Identify the adjectives in the following sentences:

1 Every employee is asked to read carefully the important instructions regarding the revised fire-drill.

2 The newly-opened branch is proving to be extremely successful.

3 Which colour do you think would be most suitable for the third bedroom?

4 The driving rain completely obscured his windscreen and the probing headlights of the car failed to penetrate the dark, rain-swept lane.

5 Your pay-claim has been wrongly made out and you will have to submit a fresh one.

6 Write down the adjective(s) which may be formed from the following words:

patience, work, mistake, to read, care, effect, to agree, to deceive, infection.

Note: a very helpful practice is to collect the different words which may be formed from a root source:

to need: needful, necessary, necessity, needed
to practise: practice, practicable, impracticable, practised
to receive: receiver, reception, receptacle, receptive, receipt

In this way you will increase your word-bank enormously and also help your spelling!

You *can* spell!

Gruesome twosomes

An area of English spelling which always seems to cause trouble is that of the 'gruesome twosomes' – or even 'threesomes' – those pairs or triplets of words which sound the same but which are spelled differently. The technical name for such words is **homophones** – 'words which sound the same'.

The following list is made up of a number of such homophones which are met most frequently. Check through the list carefully and memorise the variations in the spellings. Then try to use them in your own writing whenever the opportunity occurs. This way you fully memorise them and add their 'scalps' to your belt!

air	heir
aisle	isle
anti	ante
arc	ark
ascent	assent
ate	eight
aye	eye
bale	bail
ban	bann
bare	bear
baron	barren
beech	beach
been	bean

born	borne	or	ore
bough	bow	quay	key
bury	berry	pain	pane
ceiling	sealing	pair	pear
cereal	serial	palate	palette
choir	quire	pale	pail
chord	cord	peel	peal
complement	compliment	peer	pier
council	counsel	plane	plain
course	coarse	pleas	please
cue	queue	poor	pour
dear	deer	principle	principal
deuce	juice	put	putt
die	dye	rain reign	rein
draft	draught	real	reel
due	dew	review	revue
dune	June	roll	role
fair	fare	root	route
fate	fete	sale	sail
feet	feat	scene	seen
fiancé	fiancée	scent	sent
find	fined	seam	seem
for four	fore	see	sea
forward	foreword	shake	sheikh
foul	fowl	shore	sure
frieze	freeze	sight site	cite
fur	fir	soul	sole
gage	gauge	sow so	sew
gait	gate	stationary	stationery
gill	Jill	steal	steel
gnu	knew	straight	strait
grate	great	swayed	suede
guerilla	gorilla	sweet	suite
hare	hair	tail	tale
heel	heal	taught	taut
hoarse	horse	tee	tea
hold	holed	their there	they're
hole	whole	thrown	throne
hour	our	tide	tied
lain	lane	time	thyme
leased	least	to two	too
led	lead	urn	earn
lightning	lightening	vale	veil
load	lode	wait	weight
loan	lone	way weigh	whey
made	maid	weather	whether
manner	manor	weir	we're
meat mete	meet	what	watt
might	mite	where wear	ware
mind	mined	won	one
morn	mourn	you yew	ewe
nave	knave	your yore	yaw
need	knead		
new	knew		
night	knight		
nit	knit		
no	know		
not	knot		
oh	owe		

Collectors' pieces

In addition, you should collect in your notebook examples of parts of words which sound the same, but which have different spellings. The following will give you a start:

acquire	a choir
attacks on	a tax on
better	debtor
dependant	dependent
height	tight
proceed	procedure
succeed	exceed
water	daughter
almost readable	all most readable

Homophone assignments

1 Check in your dictionary each of the above words which is unfamiliar to you and enter them in your vocabulary book.

2 Each student should choose five pairs of words (or triplets) from the above list and make up a sentence for each word. The rest of the group should listen to the sentence and then write down the correct spelling, gaining a point for each correct answer and a minus for each wrong answer. Any student composing a sentence with a wrong spelling of a homophone loses two points!

Similarly, advertising copywriters make much use of the exclamation mark in their efforts to persuade us to buy their products or services:

> CHANGE TO GREENBOW – A REAL MAN'S CIDER!

> Slip into Lounger casuals – and you'll never want to wear an ordinary pair of shoes again!

> ANTAXIN – GETS RID OF WEEDS – FAST!

Thus the exclamation mark helps to transmit a sense of exciting taste, luxurious comfort or quick and effective killing power.

Notice that when the exclamation mark is used in direct speech it has the effect of a full-stop, and does *not* require any additional punctuation – whether a full-stop or a comma:

> 'Help!' she cried.
> 'I'm coming!' he answered.

Remember also that the first word *outside* the inverted commas starts with a small letter unless a new sentence is begun:

> 'He's getting away!' called John.
> 'He's getting away!' Indeed, the burglar was already climbing the garden wall.

Punctuation

The exclamation mark

The exclamation mark is used to convey a wide range of emotions and feelings – excitement, anger, shock, humour, sarcasm, given orders, surprise and so on.

Playwrights, novelists and journalists use the exclamation mark to help the reader to grasp more readily the tone or manner in which something is said or written:

> 'Help! He's trying to kill me!'
> 'There, officer, that's your man!'
> 'Oh, Jane, say you love me!'
> 'Get out! And don't come back!'
> 'You! Take on Fleet Street all by yourself – don't make me laugh!'
> 'And so, you see, your efforts to defraud the bank of £80 000 all came to nothing – because you couldn't spell the name on the cheque!'
> 'Fantastic! A real treat! A laugh for all the family!'
> Well, the critics who were able to write such lavish praise about Noel Parker's new play, 'And So To Bed!' must have been sleeping right through it to the final curtain! I thought it was dreadful.

Special effects department!

You will probably decide, after working on the exclamation mark assignment below, that too many exclamation marks lose their effect. So, use them sparingly at all times. Like a stunning party dress or well-cut suit, the exclamation mark should be held in reserve for special occasions when you wish to create a particularly special effect!

Exclamation mark assignment

The following passage has been peppered with exclamation marks – some of which are quite unnecessary. Re-write it, and make any necessary changes in punctuation. You should include only those exclamation marks which you think are really essential in conveying the feeling in the passage:

'OK! Stand over there! Against the wall! And don't move a muscle!'

The bank staff shuffled over to the wall opposite the cashiers' windows! Three men with sawn-off shotguns in their hands and stocking masks covering their faces watched them intently!

'Right! You! Where are the keys kept!'

'I–I–I don't know!' stammered one of the clerks.

'Don't give me that stuff! C'mon! Give me the keys! If you know what's good for you!'

'Honestly! I really don't know where they are! Mr Hargreaves always ...!'

'Yeah! Go on! Always what!'

The trembling clerk glanced anxiously over at Mr Hargreaves, the manager!

'It's all right, Whitworth! I'll take over! The keys are locked in the top right-hand drawer of my desk! The key is on this ring!'

The bank robber grabbed them out of the manager's hand! And ran to the office!

Here's the proof...! 3

In each of the following there is one error of spelling or punctuation. Re-write the sentences correctly.

1   She accnowledged that Tom was group leader.

2   The telephone gave a wierd buzz and crackled into life.

3   Each visitor was recieved with due ceremony.

4   The Ajax sales representative had a psychologycal advantage over his competitor.

5   For that special ocassion – Moondew – a perfume *he* can't forget!

In each of the following there is one error of punctuation. Re-write the sentences correctly.

6   Paperclips staples and typewriter ribbon made a jumbled mess on the desk top.

7   'Stop,' The sentry shouted.

8   'It's that word processor – the one over by the window, which needs repairing?

Teletext, Viewdata, Prestel

A case study

Teletext is the name given to the system which permits a limited number of pages of text to be transmitted by TV broadcasting stations together with their program emissions; these special signals are transmitted using lines which are not being used for the ordinary video signal. A special decoding unit in domestic TV receivers permits selection and display on the screen. All the information is transmitted on a cyclic repetition basis by the broadcasting station without any need for communication back to the TV transmitter from the domestic receiver. There is bound to be some delay between choosing a particular information frame and the display of that frame on the screen; to minimise this delay a restricted number of frames are transmitted, only a few hundred.

Ⓐ

Teletext services are provided in Britain by both the BBC and ITA: Ceefax and Oracle. In addition to the separate information frames, some broadcast TV programmes are accompanied by a teletext display of spoken dialogue so that these TV programmes may be enjoyed by the hard-of-hearing.

Viewdata, sometimes called 'videotext', is similar in appearance on the screen but is an interactive service. Viewdata has been operational in Britain since 1979. The UK service is now called Prestel; it uses a slightly modified domestic TV receiver in conjunction with an ordinary public telephone line in order to provide an interactive computerised data retrieval service (see diagram). Generally similar systems have been designed in France and in Canada.

Ⓑ

Prestel service is provided in Britain by a computer network organised to store frames of information which are transmitted (over the telephone line) at 1200 bit/sec when requested by the customer. A reverse channel at 75 bit/sec is provided to allow the customer to select the frame required or to provide answers to questions set in the information frame itself. This bit rate is sufficient for manual keyboard operation.

The database information is provided by many specialist companies. Some pages of information have to be paid for, some are free. Some companies put information on the database on a restricted access basis, e.g. only Prestel customers from their own organisation are permitted to call up these particular frames.

One present major difficulty is that the viewdata systems used in different countries use different procedures, codes and signals and cannot interwork with each other: e.g. customers using British Prestel cannot access the Canadian Telidon system. The Prestel system was the first of its type to be developed and uses an 'alpha-mosaic' method of constructing letters from small squares of colour; that is why they seem odd to those who are used to normal TV definition pictures. Telidon, much later in the field, uses an alpha-geometric method of constructing letters, with lines and curves as well as squares of colour, so it is able to give an easier-to-read page of text and better diagrams than Prestel. Some countries are experimenting with hybrid view-data/teletext systems by which the interactive or 'command' signals from the customer to the computer are sent via a telephone line but the called-for page of information, text or picture, is transmitted by a radio signal, coded, stored and displayed only by the customer asking for this particular page.

Considerable activity is taking place in some inter-national bodies to define standards which would permit interworking between generally similar services around the world. Among the bodies involved in discussions are CCITT (International Telegraph and Telephone Consultative Committee), CCIR (International Radio Consultative Committee), ISO (International Standards Organisation), CEPT (Conference of European Posts and Telecommunications Administrations) and EBU (European Broadcasting Union).

Improvements are continually being made to Prestel services; one which will have a significant effect is Picture Prestel which allows the insertion of a still picture of colour television quality into an information page. The only restrictions which affect this are the cost of the extra memory required in each terminal, and the time taken to transmit the required amount of data on a low-bandwidth telephone circuit. When digital trans-mission systems and digital exchanges such as System X have been brought into wide-scale use it will be possible for high-definition Picture Prestel to be transmitted very much more rapidly than is now possible.

Prestel Gateway is an extension of ordinary viewdata services which provides for greater interaction with users and enables Prestel customers to obtain access to computer networks managed by other organisa-tions. For example, among the banking services available to Prestel Gateway users are:

Accessing statements and ordering chequebooks
Handling loan enquiries and showing repayment
 options
Stopping payment on cheques
Amending standing orders
Effecting transfers of funds

Airline and tour operators are among those who find Prestel interactive services most useful; it is possible now to display on the screen all possible alternative flights and for tickets on a particular flight and for accommodation to be booked, all by a single call.

Prestel users are able to do their shopping via super-market computers, examine the choice of available items, check prices, make a note of special offers and then order the goods, all without leaving the comfort of their own homes.

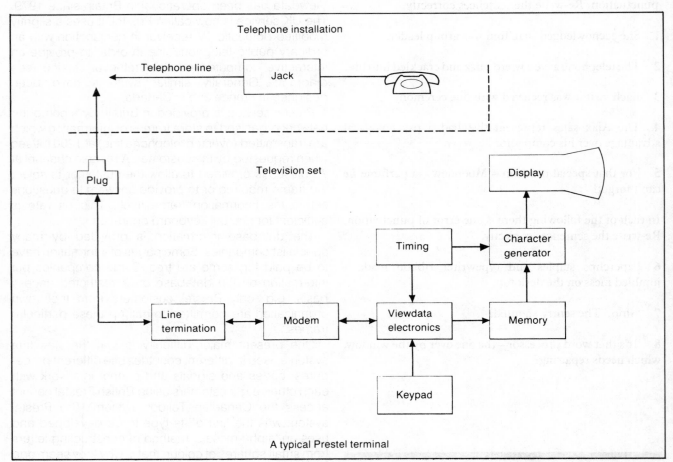

A typical Prestel terminal

Extract and diagram taken from *Telecommunications Primer* by Graham Langley

Assignments

Mastering the meaning

1 Read the article by Graham Langley, taken from *Telecommunications Primer* in your general class group and then carry out the following assignment:

With the help of your dictionary, write down in your own words the meaning of the following phrases:

together with their programme emissions   Line A

viewdata.... is an interactive service   Line B

to define standards which would permit interworking   Line C

it will be possible for high definition Picture Prestel to be transmitted very much more rapidly   Line D

Prestel Gateway.... enables Prestel customers to obtain access to computer networks managed by other organisations   Line E

A helping hand with the difficult bits!

A special decoding unit in domestic TV receivers – this is a part of the circuitry which enables the television to accept the Teletext signal, which is broadcast with the normal tv programme signals by BBC and ITV.

All the information is transmitted on a cyclic repetition basis – this simply means that the signals representing all the available teletext pages are being broadcast continuously in case an individual user wants to consult a particular page at any time.

An interactive computerised data retrieval system – this daunting phrase explains that, unlike teletext, viewdata is a system which is 'two-way': the user can read the displayed page, and with the help of a keyboard (see the diagram) send back to a central computer requests, via a telephone line, say, for a holiday brochure to be sent to his home address from the travel agency using the viewdata system to advertise on.

1200 bit/sec – this is a technical term for the number of 'bits' of data broadcast per second which form the signal which make up the pages on the television screen.

2 Sorting them out for yourself questions!

(a) In about 50 of your own words, explain the differences between the teletext and viewdata systems.

(b) What is the difference between 'alpha-mosaic' and 'alpha-geometric' methods for constructing the letters on the Prestel and Canadian Telidon viewdata systems? Which is preferable and why?

(c) What advantages would stem from a common international viewdata transmission system being set up?

(d) What benefits will the wide-spread introduction of System X British Telecom telephone exchanges bring to viewdata users?

(e) What services does Prestel Gateway provide?

(f) How can viewdata promote the growth of home-based 'teleshopping'?

Follow up research assignments

1 Find out how commercial firms are using viewdata and teletext to:

(a) help their businesses to grow
(b) to provide internal information to staff
(c) as a training tool

2 Find out what uses public service organisations are making of the viewdata Prestel system in the UK.

3 Find out what developments would follow the setting up of an international viewdata network via satellite telecommunications.

Handle with care

A case study

'Oh, do hurry up, Eric, the train leaves in ten minutes and Uncle George is getting into one of his moods about having to drive us against the clock to get to the station on time!' Mrs Greenaway's anxious call up the stairs brought an immediate response from her son, Eric.

'OK! OK! Keep your hair on! I'm just doing up the zip on me case – the newness hasn't worn off yet and I'm stuck at a corner.' Muffled bumps and thuds bounced down through the living-room ceiling echoing the truth of Eric's excuse, closely followed by a cry of triumph. 'Done it!' cried Eric. 'Wait for me, I'm just coming!'

A second, much heavier thud was heard on the upstairs landing accompanied by yell of anger and exasperation from Eric.

'What on earth's going on up there?' called Mrs Greenaway. 'Oh, do come on Eric, we really will miss the train at this rate!'

'Wretched handle's just come off the suitcase!' shouted Eric. 'I can't believe it, the blinkin thing's new. It's not as if I'd overpacked it or anything. Bet it's one of those cheap imported jobs!'

'Oh dear, oh dear, trust our luck!' Mrs Greenaway's brain went into overdrive, as it usually did in such emergencies.

'Eric, don't open it or anything, just get that long leather belt out of Dad's top drawer and strap it around the case where the handle is. We haven't got time to sort it out now, we'll just have to cope with it like that until we get to Majorca. Oh, and bring the handle with you.'

'Right you are. But wait till we get back. I'm going to give that manager at Bags Galore a right piece of my mind! It looks as if the metal rings holding the handle onto the case are made of metal that's too soft. Put anything into the case and 'Hey, presto!' the handle drops off! They're about as strong as cold spaghetti! Never mind, Majorca here we come – handle or no handle, eh Mum! And we can probably get a better case made of real leather at one of them markets!'

* * * * *

Two weeks later at the sales counter of Bags Galore, 24 High Street Weston, Midshire WE1 4HS Tel: Weston 794361.

Eric: Excuse me, miss, I want to see the manager about this Travella suitcase. Handle came off just as I was leaving for Majorca a fortnight ago, and I want my money back!

Assistant: It's Mr Simpson's lunch hour. Let's have a look at it. Ooh yeah, handle's come right off, all right. You probably overloaded it, you'll have to write to the makers, Travella Limited for a refund – address is on the inside of the lid. There, see it? Never had a handle come off a Travella before ... oh, course, you've got the Travella Lite model. We only usually stock the Travella De Luxe. Made of real leather they are. Still, handle on this one shoulda bin all right....

Eric: Look, I haven't got the time to argue the toss with you about the name of the bloomin case. I bought it two days before our holiday. Let me down first time I wanted to use it – just as we were leaving for Gatwick. Lucky for you we caught the train by the skin of our teeth or I'd be suing for a spoilt holiday like those people who got put on the wrong plane they wrote about in yesterday's paper!'

Assistant: No need to take it out on me! I didn't make the suitcase. You'll have to tell all that to the Travella people in Birmingham. Anyway, it's up to Mr Simpson to decide, and he's not here. Like I said. It's his lunch hour.

Eric: You haven't heard the last of this – not by a long chalk you haven't!

Making the case study 'come to life'

Four students should first read the case study aloud to the group, each taking one of the following parts:

Eric or Erica
Mrs Greenaway
Sales Assistant
Narrator

The reading group should get into the spirit of the event and play the roles as they think they would appear in real life, basing their oral deliveries on their experiences of such scenes at home or in shops and stores.

Next, each student should re-read the case study individually, so as to absorb all its information and each character's approach to the problem.

When you are ready, carry out each of the following tasks either singly or in a group:

Task 1

As either Eric or Erica Greenaway, write a letter of complaint to Mr Simpson, the Manager of Bags Galore following your recent visit to the shop to obtain a refund on the 'Travella Lite' suitcase.

Your letter should explain how the problem arose, the nature of the fault and how you would like the matter put right. Assume that you live at:
26 Appletree Lane,
Weston,
Midshire,
WE7 3AL

Write to Mr Simpson at the address shown in the case study, which is that of the Weston branch of Bags Galore.

Task 2

Pass your completed letter to a fellow student in your group. On receiving one of the letters of complaint, you should assume you are Mr Simpson the Manager.

Your position is that, despite the fact that Eric(a) has already made a visit to your shop, you must examine the suitcase before you can come to any decision. Write a suitable letter replying to the one from Eric(a) making this point clearly, and responding appropriately to any other points Eric(a) makes.

You should take into account the unfortunate timing of the mishap and the fact that retailers rely on customers who are happy with their purchases and who come back to buy more! Equally, products are only manufactured to cope with the demands of normal use and proper care and attention.

As this letter would be coming from a retail business, it should be typed and set out according to current letter layout convention.

Design a letterhead and logo for 'Bags Galore' as part of this task.

Task 3

The following questions should be read carefully and discussed by the students taking part in the assignment.
● 'When you buy a suitcase you are also buying reliability!' What do you think this statement is driving at?
● 'People don't just purchase products, they buy fun, a sense of security or of feeling good!' Do you agree? Is this statement relevant to the making of a complaint about a retailed product?
● How well do you think the assistant handled Eric(a)'s complaint? How well did Eric(a) communicate his/her sense of dissatisfaction? Can you make any suggestions as to how they might have done better?
● Do you think the assistant was right to request that Eric(a) write to the manufacturers of the 'Travella Lite' suitcase to convey the complaint?

Follow up assigments

Task 1

Find out as much as you can about one of the following and then either give a five minute oral report to your group about it, or produce a written report of about 300 words for your group to read and share:
● The Sale of Goods Act 1893
● The Fair Trading Act 1973
● The Citizens' Advice Bureau
● A County Council Trading Standards Department

Task 2

Either from your experience as a consumer/purchaser of retailed goods or from your experience of working full or part-time in a retail store (or from both) in a group of 3–4 students, draw up a set of written guidelines which you think would help sales assistants like the one who served Eric(a) to handle the customer's complaint effectively in the face-to-face situation.

Assume that your set of guidelines will be used in a retail store to assist new sales assistants. Remember that at some point the experience of a supervisor may be needed.

Task 3

In groups of 2–3 make contact with a local retail/distribution organisation and find out how they handle customer complaints. Report back (as a group) orally upon your finds, or write up an individual report of about 300 words.

Activities and assignments

Persuasive communication

1 Design a poster and notice for one of the forthcoming events in your college or school.

2 Imagine that you are a sales assistant, beauty consultant or car/motor-cycle salesman. Devise the selling benefits and advantages of one of the following products and then 'sell' it to a fellow-student acting as a doubtful customer:

a washing-machine; a hair-dryer; a hi-fi set; a perfume; a beauty kit; a sports car; a motor-cycle; a leather jacket; a party dress; a personal computer

Observers from the rest of the group should score the role plays and decide who was most effective.

3 Look at the 'situations vacant' advertisements in your local paper, then design an effective advertisement for one of the following:

Reliable Cars and Motor-cycles Ltd, 12–16 Western Avenue, Northbridge, Wealdshire NB2 3DG tel: Northbridge 765987:

(*a*) a trainee car/motor-cycle sales person, or
(*b*) a junior clerk in the general office.

Try to make your advertisement as realistic as possible in terms of pay, conditions of service, requirements, etc.

All completed advertisements should be displayed and group members should vote on the most effective.

4 In small groups, design a voting sheet to enable the advertisements to be judged. Make provisions for layout, wording, etc to be scored.

Communication and reception skills

5 Write an account entitled: How to be an efficient receptionist.

6 Make a checklist of **do's** and **don'ts** for a new receptionist joining a large organisation.

7 As assistant office manager of a large departmental store, draft a memorandum (including memohead) to all sales staff. It is to outline how they are to deal with customers telephoning or calling in to register a complaint.

Before writing make a careful list of the main points you think the memorandum should put across, and then ensure you adopt a suitable tone.

Grammar: the adjective

8 Imagine you have to explain to someone unfamilar with the subject what an adjective is and how it should be used effectively. Write a short account (or alternatively, deliver a short talk) which explains the subject clearly. Make up *your own* examples to illustrate your account or talk.

Spelling: gruesome twosomes

9 Use each of the following pairs of words in different sentences to illustrate their correct use:

site cite; compliment complement; review revue; lain laid; lie lay; dependent dependant

Consult your dictionary if you need to!

Punctuation: the exclamation mark

10 Write down three main rules to be followed in order to use the exclamation mark effectively.

Role play assignment

11 In small groups, write a script about a reception situation which goes wrong. Then, enact your script for the other members of the group, who should make notes and then suggest how events should have been handled. The following ideas may help you get started:

- a persistent salesperson calls without an appointment
- an angry member of staff calls to see your boss, who is 'unavailable'
- a customer arrives unexpectedly to make a complaint
- an important visitor arrives to see the boss who is not back from lunch

General oral assignments

In small groups (or individually), first make notes and then record a 3–5 minute talk on audio or video tape on one of the following:

- How to create an appropriate tone in written communications
- Writing an effective letter of complaint (or adjustment)
- What companies expect of their receptionists

You should consider how your group could use dialogue etc to help make the talk effective.

Unit 8

Non-verbal communication

What is non-verbal communication?

Broadly speaking, the term 'non-verbal communication' (NVC) refers to the ways in which people communicate with each other without using the spoken or written word. Sometimes NVC is referred to as body language, since it concerns the extremely varied and subtle ways in which people transmit signals with facial expressions, gestures or postures. Such signals very often reveal how a person is thinking, feeling or reacting in any situation.

The office clerk who emerges from the boss's office and pretends to wipe his brow with the sleeve of his jacket is clearly telling everyone in the office that he has just been 'hauled over the coals'.

Alternatively, a young girl waiting to be interviewed, who has folded herself tightly into a chair and who is constantly twisting a ring or handkerchief, is also clearly signalling her nervousness.

Indeed, we are transmitting and receiving non-verbal signals most of the time, except that we seldom stop to consider what is going on around us. Many people remain quite unaware of the NVC signals they are sending, while others, practised actors or public speakers, consciously use them to reinforce what they are saying.

The need to be able to 'read' NVC

It is important for all people who work with others – whether customers or colleagues – to become practised readers of NVC. Such an ability provides an early warning of potential problems ahead and also enables the perceptive communicator to offer help, sympathy, reassurance or tactful comments to others who may be anxious, angry, impatient or nervous. Once the NVC signals have been correctly read and interpreted, the communicator may respond with carefully chosen tones, selected words or appropriate NVC responses.

A case in point

For example, an angry customer, giving off NVC signals, may be calmed down more readily by a shop assistant who has correctly interpreted the signals and selected responses such as:

'Good morning, madam, something seems to be bothering you. May I be of some help? ... I see, yes, I can quite understand why you became so upset. I think I would have done too in the circumstances ... What exactly happened? I'd like to make a careful note ... Right, well I'm sure that the problem can be quickly remedied, and I'll look into it personally. Is there somewhere I can reach you later this morning? ...'

Expression   Gesture   Posture

R.B. JACKSON

Such a tactful and sympathetic response would make it difficult for the customer to remain angry. The request for particulars provides the customer with an opportunity to get the complaint 'off her chest' and to calm down by degrees. The personal involvement of the shop assistant and the promise of immediate action will also help. Moreover, while the alert shop assistant is speaking, he is looking for further signs of a lessening of annoyance – frowning eases, eyes become less slitted, colour returns to the face or angry spots fade from the cheeks. Similarly, stabbing fingers or clenched fists become more relaxed, breathing slows and the customer's voice becomes quieter or lower pitched and less jerky.

The above example shows how a knowledge of NVC signals may be used to warn someone of a likely problem in the offing, and also to enable a suitable effective response to be made. In other circumstances, such knowledge might let one decide to put off seeing the boss about a salary increase if he is clearly showing signs of irritation or frustration! Or it might enable one to go to the assistance of a junior colleague who is experiencing difficulty in handling a visitor or client.

There are any number of occasions in human relationships in which an understanding of the signs and signals of NVC may help the observant and alert communicator.

It is helpful to collect a catalogue of commonly occurring NVC signals, so that when next they are spotted, suitable action may be taken or responses chosen.

The table sets out some of the main NVC signals of anger or annoyance. There follows a number of other moods or feelings. Copy out the table and, in small groups, complete it by adding in your own details.

Feeling	Expression	Gesture	Posture
Anger	white face drained of colour, or reddened; brow frowning; eyes narrowed; lips thinned; sometimes being bitten; chin jutting out, teeth clenched; hard gaze	finger-stabbing; banging desk-top with fist; dismissive sideways swipes with hand; articles clenched tightly	body angled forward aggressively; arms held stiffly, legs in astride stance; tendency to stand up
Anxiety			
Nervousness			
Impatience			
Boredom			
Surprise			

You may add further feelings and reactions to the table as you meet them.

Non-verbal communication assignments

1 If you have access to a camera or video TV equipment, make a series of slides or a short film to show a range of NVC signals. You may also wish to add an explanatory commentary.

2 Select a particular mood or feeling and mime it using NVC signals for the rest of the group – who must guess the mood.

3 From magazines and newspapers, collect a series of photographs which display certain NVC signals; remove any written clues and then mount the photographs on a placard. The rest of the group should then hold a competition to decide who can correctly define the signals in the pictures. The results should be scored against a prepared solution checklist.

4 During the course of a single day, make a note of any particularly interesting NVC signals you see and what you think they indicated. Swap experiences in a general group discussion.

Discussion topics

1 Studying other people's NVC behaviour amounts to taking unfair advantage of them.

2 Can people pretend and transmit false NVC signals, or do such signals tend to provide a true indication of someone's mood or attitude?

3 A sharper awareness of NVC improves a person's ability to communicate effectively.

4 NVC signals are mostly the result of the observer's imagination!

Written assignment

Compose a descriptive paragraph which indicates clearly to the reader the NVC signals of someone who is either worried, excited or impatient.

Grammar

Prepositions

Prepositions are linking words; they link verbs to nouns:

He looked *over* the fence
I should be back *after* lunch

Could you finish the report *before* 3 o'clock?

We use a great number of prepositions:

at; across; in; into; by; on; upon; over; under; near; from; to; of; for; with; before; after; up; down; off, etc.

They are used with verbs to form particular ideas:

to look at; to look after; to look round; to look over; to look into; to look down on; to look up to

Each verb + preposition has its own meaning. There is no easy way to learn which preposition goes with which verb and noun, but your dictionary will help you. It gives examples of sentences using each preposition.

Sometimes, especially in speech, we do not link the preposition with its verb, but put it at the end of the sentence.

I don't want to give the job *up*.
He is not able to put his ideas *across*.

When, however, complex sentences are composed, with dependent clauses beginning 'who' or 'which', the preposition is placed in front of the pronoun:

That is a decision *with which* you must come to terms.
It depends on the reaction of the customer *to whom* you sold the goods.

although often in speech you will hear:

'That is a decision you must come to terms *with*.'
'It depends on the reaction of the customer whom you sold the goods *to*.'

It is said that the late Sir Winston Churchill made fussy language experts look a little silly when, having been taken to task about his use and location of prepositions, he replied:

'That is a practice up with which I will not put!'

Interjections

The final part of speech to be examined is the interjection. Literally its name means something like 'thrown in between', and is used to describe those words which writers use in dialogue mostly to convey the idea of pain, surprise, relief, astonishment etc:

'*Whew*! That was a close call!'
'*Hey* – where do you think you're going?'
'It is – *um* – what shall I – *ah* – say, a delicate situation!'

Comic characters like Billy Bunter were fond of uttering such interjections as, 'Ouch! Yarooo! Gurgh!' but they are about as rare as a £3.00 note in business documentation!

Preposition assignment

Complete the following by adding the correct preposition:

to account– unmindful– responsible– an insight– to contend– interested– to take exception– to take stock– concerned– to transfer– to negotiate– to substitute– to settle– on behalf– divided–

Boost your spelling power!

Learn these words by heart

Remember, an asterisk after a word indicates that it is very commonly misspelled:

achieve v	(achievement n)
compare v	(comparison n comparable adj)
disappoint* v	(disappointment n)
humour n v	(humorous adj)
irresistible adj	
omit v	(omitted* past part omission n)
prefer v	(preferred past part preference n preferable adj)
succeed v	(success n successful* adj)
surprise v n	(surprising adj)
vaccinate v	(vaccination n)

Do not forget to enter in your vocabulary book any words with which you are unfamiliar, either in terms of spelling or meaning!

Visual and number communication 1

So far, we have concentrated on the techniques of the spoken, written, NVC and graphic forms of communication. Yet there is still another form of communication to master – the technique of number and visual communication.

Accountants, sales managers, office administrators, local government officials and all their assistants and clerks make daily use of numbers and visual charts, diagrams, maps and plans in order to transmit a wide range of information. This is just as important as letters, memoranda or reports. Sales statistics, for example, help the retail manager to 'keep his finger on the pulse' of his branch's sales, while a profit and loss account recording income and expenditure enables the accountant to decide how his company's finances stand. The increasing use of graphics computer software packages in desk-top applications kits now enables the busy manager or assistant to express a set of figures either as a bar chart, pie chart or graph, according to best visual impact, and to incorporate the graphics created into, say, a word processed report.

This section will examine a range of tables, pie charts, organisational charts and plans and show how they may be used to convey facts and figures and relationships.

Tables

Consider the table below. It summarises the sales turnover of the three retail electrical stores which form Home Electrical Supplies Limited, Middleton, for the week ended Saturday 12 May 19—

HOME ELECTRICAL SUPPLIES LIMITED
Sales Turnover in £ sterling for Saturday 12 May 19—

Products	High Street £	West Street £	London Road £	Total £
Refrigerators	509.34	862.96	1293.06	2665.36
Radios	265.10	82.40	486.32	833.82
Hi-fi sets	693.41	180.96	332.75	1207.12
Mixers	129.84	89.90	186.53	406.27
Washing machines	696.30	325.72	945.20	1967.22
Irons	72.46	35.24	109.37	217.07
TVs	584.20	286.30	1104.90	1975.40
Miscellaneous	126.09	94.20	249.83	470.12
TOTAL	3076.74	1957.68	4707.96	9742.38

(Note that computers have made possible *daily* sales analysis by management.)

At first sight, the table presents the eye with a rather bewildering mass of figures. But once they are examined carefully, a number of important facts emerge. Remember that the table provides an excellent means of comparing one fact – expressed as a number – with another. Basically the table indicates:

More than   Less than   Same as   (and if we work it out) By how much

Most important, the totals expressed in a table serve as summaries of the information itemised in the listed columns. The table can be read both up and down, and across. Reading from top to bottom, the totals tell us the complete sales turnover for each branch, and then for the company as a whole (the sum of the three branch totals). Read from left to right, the totals in the far right-hand column give us the firm's total sales in each product: refrigerators, radios, hi-fi sets, etc. Thus the Weekly Sales Turnover Table breaks down the company's sales in a number of valuable ways: by branch, by product, and gives company totals.

Just to show how straightforward the information expressed in tables is to 'read', answer the following questions:

1 What is the total sales turnover of Home Electrical Supplies, Middleton for Saturday 12 May 19—?

2 Which branch has sold most? Which branch has sold least? What is the difference in their sales performance?

3 What is the total value of irons sold by the company in the week?

4 Which branch sold most hi-fi sets?

5 If you could use £500 to help one of the branches to sell mixers by advertising them in the local press, which branch would you choose? Why?

As you can see, once the figures are looked at singly, rather than as a mass, and once specific questions are posed, the table can give a great deal of useful information.

Now examine the table which represents the sales of radios in one branch for the first four months of the year:

Branch radio sales
Expressed in £ sterling

Brands	January £	February £	March £	April £	Total £
Wayfarer	1 296	1 064	987	831	4 178
Popular	492	476	483	497	1 948
Stereo X	1 497	1 534	1 672	1 771	6 474
Globemaster	1 191	1 084	1 132	971	4 378
Musicale	343	496	281	320	1 440
TOTAL £	4 819	4 654	4 555	4 390	18 418

This table gives us information similar to the first one, but it does still more. It provides us with valuable information about *trends*. For example, which particular radio is selling best over the four months? What is the accumulated value of its sales? And which brand is doing worst? Which was the best month for all radio sales? Which was the worst?

As you have already realised, this table reveals a trend which would worry the branch manager – sales are steadily *declining* during the four months, from £4819 in January to £4390 in April. Only one brand has increased its sales. Which one? Which one has done worst?

This type of table may also prove helpful in other ways. For example, suppose the branch made most profit from selling Globemaster radios, what instructions do you think the branch manager should give his sales staff for the month of May? Also, suppose you were one of the sales assistants, and you were given most commission for selling Wayfarer radios, what would the table tell you you should do?

Tables, then, provide a means of recording – and storing – a great deal of information in a small space. At the same time, they are not instantly 'readable' – it takes time to sort out the information contained. When we come to study graphs and bar charts, we shall see that in these media such information is much easier to 'read at a glance'.

Table assignment

During the week, collect as many tables as possible from newspapers and magazines and study them in small groups. Make a checklist of the information each conveys.

Pie chart

As its name suggests, the pie chart is a visual means of displaying number information using a circle, or 'pie', which represents a *known* total; parts of this known total are shown as 'slices of pie'. This form of visual communication shows clearly how the parts go to make up the whole, and the difference in size of each.

The above pie charts identify how the West Sussex County Council spent its income of £287.5m for the year 1986–87. As you can see, the largest expenditure went on employees' salaries and the rest of the income was spent under eight further budget headings. Without the inclusion of the percentage figures corresponding to each 'slice of pie', it is not at all easy to gauge from a pie chart what *proportion* of the whole is signified by an individual slice – particularly when there are six or so more or less equal. This is why many pie chart designers provide a percentage figure for each numerical slice entry.

IN 1986/87 THE COUNTY WILL SPEND £287.5m
How is it spent? (Gross Expenditure)

- Premises £18.0m
- Equipment & Supplies £19.8m
- Capital Charges £12.0m
- Student Awards £11.1m
- Highways £6.1m
- Services provided by other bodies £20.0m
- Other Expenditure (Including £10.5m for future inflation) £27.2m
- Police Precept £33.2m
- Employees £140.1m

Where the money comes from (Who Pays?)

- Government Grants
- Specific & Supplementary £28.2m
- Block £44.5m
- Charges for Services £34.5m
- Reserves & Balances £2.4m
- Ratepayers £177.9m

Courtesy of the West Sussex County Council

Assignment

Work out what the percentage is of £287.5m

(*a*) for each budget heading in the expenditure pie, and
(*b*) for each income heading in the income pie.

Remember, a circle has 360°. Since the known total is usually presented as 100%, then each degree within the circle is equal to 1% : 3.6° = 1%. Thus 25% × 3.6 = 90°. Half the pie chart's circular area will equal 50%, and a quarter 25%. Notice that it is difficult (without the assistance of an accompanying percentage figure) for the human eye to assess what smaller slices of the pie stand for. Another point to bear in mind is that too many slices in the pie make it difficult to read and interpret.

Pie chart assignment

Design a pie chart to illustrate the following information:

Employees budgeted for in 1986–87

1 Education: teachers   8746

2	Social services	2506
3	Fire and public protection	854
4	Highways	772
5	Library–7 archives	324
6	Miscellaneous (inc. central depts)	1012
	Total	14214

In your pie chart show the corresponding percentage of the whole for each sector of employees.

The database software package

Just as the word processing package has revitalised the production of text, so has the development of the database software applications package given the storage of data and information on easily retrievable computer files a tremendous boost. All kinds of company personnel are now able to tailor extensive memory and design resources to their own needs – whether by designing a standardised form for storing personnel information, a checklist of details about products for sale, or a series of electronic 'record cards' carrying the servicing history of a fleet of vans run by a large transport department.

So what exactly *is* a database software package, and how does it work? The following diagram illustrates the principles behind the division of data or information into a series of related tiers.

Within any department of an organisation, there will be a range of work areas which are sufficiently large to warrant a separately identifiable group of people to undertake them. For example, the sales ledger of an accounts department, the staff records section of a personnel department, or the market research unit of a marketing department. The work of such sections or units will be subdivided into various areas. For instance, the market research unit might have a member of staff working exclusively on the test marketing of new products, and another on customer reactions to dummy packs of various designs and colours. Within each of these subdivisions of the market department will be further sub-divided tasks – say, where a particular product's test marketing is done in three distinct towns, or where a particular product is tried out in three contrasting colour packs to test customer appeal.

In just the same way, a database is built up by creating major areas of interest and then subdividing areas which relate to them in a logical way. Databases organise major blocks or sectors of data firstly into FILES, where each FILE stands for a major item which is about one particular class of information. In the example above, the sales ledger, personnel staff records and market research activities could also serve as a suitable undertaking to be set up as a file. Notice that in the specialist terminology of databases, the term 'file' does not mean – as we have come to expect – a relatively small item of information on floppy disk, like a particular letter or memo, but a very extensive

The structure of a database software package

» Comparison with a suspension filing cabinet «

The 'file'
The entire filing cabinet's contents – provided they were about the same topic area – would equate to a database 'file'. [Note the different meaning of the term 'file' in database terminology.]

The 'record'
A record would provide data on a single subject – say a member of a company's personnel – and a number of records go to make up a 'file'.

The 'field'
Within each record there are various individual items of information set out. These are called fields – for example, the name of age of the company's member of staff.

resource of data: in ratio terms like the filing cabinet in the above diagram is to the letter in one of the hanging file holders within one of the drawers.

Indeed this is a good comparison to make, for we could say that the next tier of data downwards in the database, stemming from the FILE, and called the RECORD is rather like a single one of the suspended file holders in a given drawer. And lastly, that the final tier extending downwards from the RECORD, entitled the FIELD, is just like the single letter or memo stored within the suspended file holder. So remember this different use of terms and think of them always in DESCENDING order.

FILE – stands for a general area of data

RECORD – stands for one of many sub-areas of data

FIELD – stands for one item of information within the sub-area

In the case of the example given above, market research would be the file; the test marketing and checking of dummy product packs would be two separate records, and the specification, say, of the colours, dimensions and materials used for a *particular* dummy pack would be fields.

As you can imagine, such flexibility makes database software extremely versatile in organisational use, since almost any kind of data can be stored in a logical way making its retrieval very quick and, moreover, available in an exciting mix of ways.

To illustrate this point, let us devise a record which could be part of the pupil/student information file within your school or college. As you will have realised by now, if a database file is about a number of pupils or students, then a record will detail information about a single pupil or student. Even so, its design has to be standardised so that exactly the same category of information can be recorded for each person in a predetermined set of fields. Thus each record will consist of identical fields to be entered, such as,

FILE: Pupil information   RECORD: Personal details

1 STUDENT'S FULL NAME: ....

2 DATE OF BIRTH: ....

3 SEX: ....

4 CLASS CODE: ....

5 HOME ADDRESS: ....

6 TELEPHONE NUMBER OF NEXT OF KIN
                    WORK: ....
                    HOME: ....

full name, age, sex, home address, telephone number of next of kin and so on. Further, as you will also have noticed, some of these files will require, say, 30 or 40 character spaces, i.e. for the address, and some, like the

age, only two. The database record design has to take account of such factors, and also whether the data entered is to be in text or number, and if number, whether calculations will need to be made, such as totalling the number of boys or girls in the database if requested.

Thus our record as designed with the aid of a database software package might look like the one above.

This record might also go on to provide confidential details of any illness such as diabetes or epilepsy which it might be important for course tutors or heads of department to know about.

Now a most attractive feature of the database is its ability to extract data in a variety of ways from stored records. For example, in the record illustrated, it would be possible for a headteacher to check in a trice which pupils on the school rolls were in which class – by asking the database to display the records, of, say, Class VK. Alternatively, the records of any pupil suffering from diabetes or epilepsy could be brought out of storage very quickly.

Another record, for example, detailing examinations results, could just as easily identify which pupils achieved 'A' grades in Advanced Level French or which students were due to resit GCSE Geography – provided that this information had been set up on the records! Remember that a database is only as good as its updated 'housekeeping'.

Operating the database

Like any software applications package, the database will have a series of commands which have to be learned in order for it to perform as the user wishes. For example, records may be summoned up on display to have data recorded on them changed, added to or deleted. At any given time, a computer print-out of a given record or records may be taken. New individual records may be set up or obsolete ones deleted. The design features of the package will enable the user to set up forms or 'record cards' designed to meet a particular need. Most helpfully, whole files of records may be searched very quickly and specific information extracted. For instance, the two sales representatives in a sales force of five hundred able to speak Italian fluently, could be identified almost instantly if they were needed to assist an Italian businessman visiting the company. Again, database packages possess a 'sort' facility which enables all kinds of information to be provided as requested. For instance, account customers with overdue accounts could be listed in descending order, with the largest debtor coming first. Alternatively large personnel offices could sort several hundred names into alphabetical order, or age, or the date when each last took part in a training course, or, if it were appropriate – say in a laboratory context – the date each person last had a booster innoculation against tetanus. The following table illustrates just some of the applications for which database software packages are being used in a multitude of organisations today.

Uses of database software

Organisational area	Application
Accounts	names, addresses of account customers with details such as credit limits, discounts agreed etc.
Sales	customer profile records detailing firms' turnovers, cycle of rep's visits, products sold etc.
Production	checklists of which suppliers make what; details of customers' specifications for products in production, inventory details
Design	records of drawings and computerised designs with patent records etc.
Personnel	staff records, training course records, pay deal agreements, pension records etc.
Travel/tourism companies	'real-time' records of holidays arranged and flights booked etc.

The database in large organisations

The advantages of having a single database of information available to all staff (subject to security and level of grade restrictions) is now appealing to many national and multi-national firms. The advantages are that information need only be entered into the firm's mainframe computer once, that it can be made available to staff operating terminals hundreds of miles apart, or indeed on another continent! Such a development has been made possible by the net-working of computers and by the development, in the case of large organisations, of extremely large memory capacities in computers. Provided that the inputted data is not in error, thus 'corrupting' the database, then there are many distinct advantages to be had: information is 'up-to-the-minute' fresh and updated; it is almost instantane-ously available; it aids and improves decision-making on a local basis, and saves much time wasting and frustration. Needless to say, data processing managers have to be very well organised to ensure that the entire company's assets in terms of its information and records are 'accident proof', whether by fire, flood or thunderstorm!

'What made you apply for this post?'

A case study

Miss Jacqueline Singleton has been called for an interview for the post of junior clerk in the office administration department of Western Engineering Limited:

JK: Good morning. Miss Singleton isn't it?

JS: Yes. Good morning.

JK: My name is John King, personnel manager, and this is Mrs Pauline Hope, office administration manager. Oh yes, do make yourself comfortable. I hope you had a good journey...

JS: Not too bad, thank you.

JK: Fine. Well now, you have applied for the post of clerical assistant in our office administration department. As the details mentioned, the post has arisen because of the increase in the work of the department. You would report immediately to Mr Harrison, the senior clerk, and you would undertake a range of duties, including filing, some book-keeping, petty cash recording, invoice processing and so on.

JS: Oh, I see.

JK: Now I see you are currently following a business education course at Westleigh College of Tech-nology. What exactly does it involve?

JS: Oh, well, we do communication, typewriting, office studies, computerised accounting, word processing – that sort of thing. Oh, and there's an activities afternoon on a Wednesday. I'm doing car maintenance because I want to get a car when I'm seventeen.

JK: I see, and which of those subjects do you like best?

JS: I like word processing, and some of the com-munication. We do discussions, and case studies. The accounting's a bit boring some-times...

JK: And what is a case study?

JS: It's a sort of problem, I s'pose. You sort of have a topic with a problem in it which you have to sort out.

JK: Do you think case studies help you to learn?

JS: Sometimes. But sometimes our group just argues and we don't always manage to agree!

JK: Yes, well some problems occur just like that here it seems, sometimes! And what examinations will you be taking?

JS: I think it's called the National Business Institute's Stage II Diploma.

JK: Oh yes, of course. Are you going to pass do you think?

JS: Hope so!

JK: Well I'm sure you'll do your best. Now, Mrs Hope has some questions to ask you.

PH: Hello, Jacqueline. As you know, I'm the office administration manager and you would be working in my department. Now, when you're not busy studying, what sort of leisure activities do you enjoy?

JS: Well, I like badminton, and dancing...

PH: What sort of dancing?

JS: Disco mostly.

PH: Do you belong to any clubs at the college or a youth club?

JS: No. I go around with a group of friends. I'm going steady with someone.

PH: I see. Now tell me, what made you apply for this post?

JS: Oh. Um. Well, I suppose I need a job! My dad says Western Engineering's got a good reputation. He used to work here.

PH: Did he, that's most interesting. But what about yourself? What attracts you to office work?

JS: Well, I like working with people ... and word processing. I've always liked paperwork, I used to help me dad when he was a pools collector.

PH: Fine, and how about filing. With which systems are you familiar?

JS: Uuuum. Mm. Well, the usual ones, in filing cabinets and folders and computer filing. It's really great how quickly you can get to a file on a micro!

JK: Right, thank you Jacqueline. Now, is there anything you'd like to ask about the post?

JS: ... Not really. You seem to have covered most of the points...

JK: Right. Well, thank you very much for coming. I'll be writing to you in a day or so. Please see my secretary about your travelling expenses. Goodbye, and thank you again.

Assignments

In small groups, examine this case study. Would you have given Jacqueline the job? Did she interview well? What would you have said or done in her place? Would she get the job?

The interview

The interview is a very frequently used tool of communication – not only as part of the process of selecting someone to do a job, but in a host of other ways. Managers and officials need above all things, *information*, which is often in the possession of subordinate staff; sometimes staff members break company rules or regulations or develop personal problems which affect their job performance; at other times, senior executives make decisions which need

to be explained to other staff who have to carry them out. And so, though the job application interview is the first of the interviews which springs to mind, the interview is used in other, equally important ways:

- to select someone to do a job
- to promote an employee
- to discipline a member of staff
- to counsel or offer help to a member of staff
- to find out about, or to sell a product
- to pass on or to present information
- to seek information
- to sound out views, attitudes or opinions

Most interviews take place in private on a one-to-one basis between interviewer and interviewee. People are much more likely to 'open up' and to discuss a topic if they feel they are not being overheard or subjected to a sort of inquisition. Sometimes, though, a job interview may be conducted by a panel of three or four interviewers, who each ask different types of question and subsequently swap opinions on the basis that 'two or more heads are better than one'. Such panels do impose a strain on interviewees and many firms now prefer to interview on a one-to-one basis.

The interview is frequently used in the ways suggested above because human beings prefer to deal with others personally, and to establish a mutual understanding of one another often referred to as 'rapport'. In many types of interview, the interviewer is at pains to discover, not only facts, but the feelings and attitudes of the interviewee about a topic, such as the introduction of a new bonus system or the alteration of the holiday rota arrangements. This process of consultation by interview occurs much more often nowadays, because managers realise the importance of securing the active support of their staff.

The interview as a 'transaction'

Perhaps the best way to consider the interview is as a transaction, from which both the interviewer and interviewee gain something. For example, in a job interview the employer is 'selling' salary, prospects, working conditions and fringe benefits in order to 'buy' hard work, specialist skills, loyalty and integrity. Likewise the job applicant offers skill and experience in return for a satisfying, rewarding and challenging job, or, more accurately, *career*.

The skills of interviewer and interviewee

Such a process requires the development of oral, NVC and social skills. The interviewer needs to do his homework before the interview, to decide exactly what the job entails, and the qualities needed in the person to do it. He then has to look carefully at the documents of all short-listed candidates and form questions to find out more about their strengths and weaknesses, so that their suitability may be assessed. Moreover, at interview he has to do this in such a way that the candidate is kept at ease and remains willing to answer questions fully and freely.

For his part, the interviewee also has to prepare himself before the interview – to draw up questions about the job and firm which will influence his decision to accept the job, should he be offered it.

Such a checklist of questions will include:

What prospects does the post offer?
What are the arrangements for salary increases?
Will there be an opportunity for further education or training?
Will the job involve the opportunity for travel?

and to be considered but not always asked:

Would I enjoy working here?
Could I work with the people I have met?
Is the salary fair?
Are there opportunities to grow in the job?
Will I learn important skills here?

For his part, the interviewer usually rates the performance of each candidate against a checklist of required standards embodied in the following:

Checklist of what the interviewer is looking for
physique/health
appearance
intelligence
education/experience
qualifications
skills/specialisms
personality/character
circumstances

Assignment

Draw up a similar checklist of what you think the applicant should be looking for.

The job applicant attending an interview will need to be smartly turned out, polite and alert and ready to impart information about himself. The way he 'holds himself' during the interview, answers questions and poses his own will affect the way in which the interviewer assesses him. The interviewer is usually looking not only for someone to carry out the job on offer efficiently, but also for someone who will fit into the organisation generally and who displays potential for development and promotion.

Discussion topic

What factors do you think a job applicant should keep in mind when being interviewed?

The following list gives the major points which the job candidate should keep in mind and attend to before, during and after the interview.

How to succeed at interviews

Before

- Ask people in good time to act as referees on your behalf. *Never* take this permission for granted.
- Read application instructions on advertisements carefully – don't waste time on a long letter of application if first you have to send off for an application form.
- Check the advertised job prospects and its potential. Is it *really* what you are looking for, or merely a dead end?
- Consider the organisation carefully – its reputation, employee relations, location, etc.
- When short-listed for interview, confirm your acceptance promptly and then try to find out as much as possible about the firm.

During

- Above all – don't be late for the interview! You'll be flustered and the interviewer will be irritated.
- Check your appearance before entering the interview room.
- Control any nerves – deep breathing helps.
- Avoid 'fiddling' with clothes, rings, etc.
- Look at the interviewer posing the questions, and *listen* to them carefully – letting your mind wander can make you look silly if you have to ask for repeats.
- Don't mumble, gabble or restrict yourself to one-word answers – the organisation is spending a lot of time and money to give you a chance to promote yourself!
- Remember to pause at intervals to check whether you are expected to continue.
- Take your time over tricky questions.
- Try to think ahead and anticipate what will be asked next.
- Don't forget to ask *your* questions – they are just as important as the interviewer's.

- Remember to thank the interviewer(s) for your appointment.

After

- If you are offered the job verbally at interview confirm your acceptance promptly in writing.
- Let your current employer have your resignation in good time – by letter if that is the custom.
- *Always* part from employers on good terms – you may need another reference one day, or you may work for them again later in your career.

Remember: Don't try to 'put on airs and graces' at interviews – it's much better just to be yourself – after all, that is whom the company will be employing.

Interview assignments

1 Assume that you are a customer of Delta Departmental Stores Limited. You recently purchased one of the following:

a dress; a suit; a table-lamp; a briefcase; an electric alarm clock; a pair of shoes; a record; a cassette tape; a necklace; a bracelet

Invent a particular defect or shortcoming in the product (plus any other details about promises over the telephone etc) and, with another student role playing the sales assistant, simulate the scene where you bring it back to the store to complain.

Note: it is the policy of Delta for all customer complaints to be recorded in writing and for the details to be passed to the departmental manager for a decision.

2 Imagine that you are a senior supervisor in a large office. One of your employees is tending to arrive late in the mornings and this is causing resentment among other clerical staff. You have to call the offender into your office to discipline him or her. In pairs, role play this disciplinary interview. (**Note:** the offending employee should adopt a tone and should have reasons for lateness which are either more or less likely to be sympathised with!)

3 Assume that you are short-listed for one of the following positions:

audio-typist; clerical assistant; trainee motor-car or motor-cycle salesperson; sales assistant; receptionist

A panel of three students should devise:

(*a*) a display advertisement for the chosen post
(*b*) an application form for the post
(*c*) details of the post – pay, conditions of service, etc.

A series of candidates should:

(*a*) compose a letter of application for the post
(*b*) complete the application form
(*c*) devise a checklist of questions to ask

After both teams have completed their preparations, the interviews should be role played and ideally recorded on video-tape or cassette for later evaluation. The panel should award the job to the best applicant and give their reasons for preferring one application to another. Two groups of students should act as observers, one to evaluate the performance of the panel, the other the performance of the candidates. These teams should also give a report on their assessments.

At the end of the assignment, a general discussion should take place to determine what facts have emerged from the simulation, and what has been learned from it.

4 In order to gain an insight into the problems of interviewing people, devise a set of questions, and then conduct a survey by interviewing students in your department to assess their views on, for example, compulsory military service, solving the unemployment problem, participation in student association social activities, what sort of employment they will be seeking, etc. Such interviews could be conducted with a portable tape-recorder for later analysis.

Small student groups should write up the results of the survey and interviews in an account – perhaps for the college magazine.

Using database package assignments

Form small groups of 3 to 4 students and, with the help of a suitable microcomputer database package, carry out the following assignments.

1 Set up a database for the use of the students in your class which will provide each of them, as a potential user, with the following information:

(a) the name and address and telephone number of each student who has:

- records
- tapes
- paperbacks
- back numbers of specialist magazines

(b) which he/she is willing to either:

- loan,
- swap for a suitable alternative or
- sell for a displayed price.

Consider how you could design into this database file the means for your fellow students to arrange to inspect any of the items included, and how you are going to ensure it is kept up-to-date: this may need some form of input documentation and a rota of operators.

Compare your database with those produced in other groups and set up a final one, incorporating what your group considers the most effective features of each database created.

2 Assume that you are helping Harry and Rita Johnson in their Westbrook Stores business to introduce the micro-computer they have just purchased into their business administration. They have asked you to design a file which will make their stock ordering quicker and simpler to achieve. Harry explained his needs to you as follows:

I currently order my stock from some 27 different suppliers, believe it or not, with depots and warehouses they deliver from spread all over the place, and I'm always wasting time sorting out addresses and phone numbers, not to mention the fellers who I deal with. It would help me enormously to have an easy to follow checklist of what products I order from each supplier, their current retail prices, as well as my normal discounts with each supplier. I don't suppose I order more than 15 items from any single one. Also, it would be useful to include the agreed payment arrangements for each supplier – with some I get a handsome discount if I pay up on delivery, with others I have to settle up within 15 days of receiving a statement, and with others it's 30 days.

Oh, and by the way, if your database could list my suppliers by these product groupings it would save me a lot of time:

foodstuffs,
newspapers and magazines,
gifts and toys,
stationery and
household hardware.

Have a look at it with some of your computer mates and see what you can produce – you may also come up with some ideas of your own you could include!

Before attempting this assignment, re-read the case study: Westbrook Stores and Gift Shop go computer! on page 34.

When you have finished your database design, take a copy of it to a local small business retailer and ask him or her to what extent such a database would be useful, and how, in his or her opinion, it could be improved upon to suit that particular business. Report your findings to your group.

The 'Are you sure we studied that?' revision quiz!

1 Explain the meaning of as many as possible of the underlined following dictionary entries:

kid, <u>n</u>, & <u>vt</u> & <u>i</u>, (-dd-) 1 Young of goat; leather from skin of this, used for gloves and boots; the Kids or Kid, three small stars in Auriga; (<u>sl</u>) child, whence -d'y n; glove (<u>adj</u>) over dainty, avoiding everyday work etc 2 vt give birth to (~); (vi) give birth to ~. <u>ME</u> kide f <u>ON</u> kith f <u>Gmc</u> kithjam rel to <u>OHG</u> chizzi, -in

2 What functions do the following carry out in a sentence?

(a) subject (b) finite verb (c) object (d) verb extension

3 Which of the above are needed to construct the simplest kind of sentence?

4 How would you recognise a finite verb?

5 List the six stages of communication of a message from sender to receiver.

6 What is the difference between a common and a proper noun? How are proper nouns easily recognised?

7 Give two examples of collective nouns.

8 What do the following prefixes stand for:

anti contra trans poly mono

9 Compose a sentence in which the verb 'to type' is used in the passive.

10 What is the effect on style of using verbs in the passive?

11 Write down the past participles of the following verbs:

to bear to lie to break

12 What do the following abbreviations stand for:

pp ref sp eg pl

13 Identify the subject, finite verb and object in the following sentence:

The falling leaves covered the forest floor like a brown-coloured carpet.

14 What are the adjectives in the above sentence?

15 What are the names given to the three main sectors of industry? Explain what each means.

16 Explain the body processes involved in uttering speech.

17 Give four guidelines for effective speaking.

18 Explain how the Dewey Decimal System works in a library.

19 List five reference books which an office worker would find useful.

20 What are meant by the terms: fully-blocked and open punctuation in letter layout?

21 Write today's date as it would appear in an open punctuated letter.

22 Complete the following:

Dear Sirs ... Yours
Dear Miss Green ... Yours

23 How would you show that something had been sent with a letter?

24 What is the correct salutation for a partnership?

25 Write down the correct form for the recipient's name entry in a letter for an unmarried lady, Joan Smith, who has a Bachelor of Arts degree, and who is a member of the Chartered Institute of Secretaries.

26 What does the term 'logo' mean?

27 What does the word 'hierarchy' mean in the context of an organisation?

28 Draw an organisational pyramid for your school, college or place of work.

29 What do the following suffixes stand for?

-ology   -ist   -less   -hood

30 Write down the correct word to fill the blank:

The cat was washing – face.

31 What part of speech is the word you have inserted?

32 Write down five points each for the message taker and the message giver to keep in mind.

33 Which is the direct object in the following sentence?

I gave the postman the letter.

34 Write down four words used as connecting words which *start* sentences.

35 What is wrong with the punctuation of the following?

'I say, you over there!, cried Susan.
He wondered whether he ought to go.

36 Describe the functions of the opening, middle and closing paragraphs in a letter.

37 Identify the main clause and the dependent clause in the following:

I shall go although I don't really want to.

Since it is urgent, it will have to be copied immediately.

38 List:

three conjunctions linking main clauses
five conjunctions introducing dependent clauses

39 Put the following components of a memohead in an acceptable layout:

12 March 19—   Managing Director   Proposed Merger With Sentinel Insurance   VR/TG   All Office Staff

40 Explain briefly how you would 'boot up' a dual disk drive microcomputer.

41 List five advantages of using word processing facilities in an office.

42 What do the following initials stand for:

RAM   CRT   256K   mb   CPU

43 Outline five factors which should be kept in mind in order to work successfully as a member of a group.

44 Draw a diagram to illustrate the relationships an office manager is likely to have with other people at work.

45 List the components of a telephone message pad.

46 List the seven steps to follow in producing a summary.

47 Identify the adverbs in the following sentence:

He was running quite fast but they caught him easily.

48 List four instances when it would be appropriate to employ a persuasive tone in a written document.

49 What points need to be kept in mind when designing a poster?

50 What colours would you use in an advertisement to denote expense and luxury?

51 Outline briefly the duties of a receptionist.

52 List the main stages in the structure of

(a) a letter of complaint
(b) a letter of adjustment

53 What factors go to make up tone in a piece of writing?

54 What aspects of a recipient is it important to consider when writing to him or her?

55 What is likely to be the effect of using too many adjectives in a piece of writing?

56 Compose two sentences, one in direct speech, to illustrate acceptable uses of the apostrophe.

57 What do the initials NVC stand for?

58 List the three main sections of NVC which relay signals.

59 What signs would you expect to see in someone displaying:

    (a) impatience
    (b) nervousness?

60 Explain what a database software package is used for.

61 Complete the following by adding the correct preposition:

in accordance – different – further – filed –

62 What are the main uses to which numerical tables are put?

63 What is a pie chart? Draw one showing the proportions of $\frac{1}{8}, \frac{1}{4}, \frac{1}{2}, \frac{1}{8}$

64 In a word processing context, what do these words mean:

to scroll   word wrap   ruler display   help menu?

65 List as many different applications of the interview as you can remember.

66 What should an interviewee keep in mind during an interview for a job? Give a brief checklist.

67 Which topics so far studied do you feel you need to revise most urgently?

Spelling quiz

1 What is the most common rule for forming the plural of English words?

2 Write down the following words in their plural form:

quiz formula radius tomato fox bus ox knife scarf

3 Complete the following:

a ... o ... date   (to house)
emba ... a ... ed   (shy)
a ... ress   (where you live)
u ... e ... e ... ary   (not needed)
defin ... te   (certain)
o ... u ... ed   (happened)

4 Write down a word for each of the following definitions:

travels on land or water
bicycle with one wheel
study of rocks
not replaceable
study of gods
clinic for expectant mothers
lover of stamps
man with many wives

5 Form an adjective from each of the following:

wool
necessity
to permit (*not* permitted!)
to define

6 Write down a word for each of the following definitions:

a person who studies the economy
something which resembles a human
the state of having a king or queen
state in which one is very miserable
act of being baptised

7 Complete the following:

another word for an office: bur ...
goods in transit: fr ... ght
thin whippy sword: rap ...
very tasty: del ...
road going through: tho ... re
hard working: con ... us
stringed instrument: l ... te
to follow: p ... ue
after seventh comes: e ...
victor: con ... r

8 List three words, each of which contains a different 'silent' letter.

9 What other spelling makes an 'f' sound? Provide two examples in which it is found.

10 What is the rule for adding suffixes to words ending in -l?

11 What letter always follows 'q'?

12 Supply one or more words which sound the same as the following, but which are spelled differently:

sight
council
there
principle
ascent
need
where
wait
straight
stationary
taught
choir

Punctuation quiz

1 What is the full-stop used for other than to signify the end of a sentence?

2 Provide two different examples of the use of the comma in two sentences.

3 Re-write the following using apostrophes:

in the time of two weeks
the shoes of the ladies
the tickets of the women
the tails of the donkeys
the signature of the letter

4 Write down the contracted form of:

they are; we are; you are; does not; it is; shall not; who is; I am

5 Punctuate the following:

when will he be arriving asked the secretary
its a question of the extent of the planes delay answered the sales manager the airport information staff are not very well informed im afraid ah but theres the phone ringing now it could be them

6 Explain briefly the difference between a hyphen and a dash in punctuation. Compose two sentences which illustrate the difference in action.

The IT acronym quiz

This quiz is not as dreadful as its title suggests! The term 'acronym' simply means 'words which are made up of the initial letters of several words' – for example UNO = United Nations Organisation. Right! Off you go!

Write down the full versions of the following by supplying the word for which each letter stands:

OCR LCD LAN RAM ROM CAD CAM DP
PABX CCTV PSTN WAN BASIC COBOL VDU
CRT CPU

Find out what the following stand for:

COM CCITT MOWDEM LASER SATSTREAM EFT

Unit 9

The accounts department

The basic task of an accounts department is to process and record all those aspects of a company's business which (A) involve money – its financial transactions. Though most of us are familiar with money in the form of cash or cheques, an accounts department is concerned with worth or value in a number of other forms too:

property, buildings owned by the company
raw materials, stocks, products
stocks and shares
plant, equipment, fixtures and fittings
rebates – sums due in the future
goodwill – a value placed on an established network of customers

In order to provide the company with an efficient service in each of the above areas, the accounts department (B) will be divided into specialist sections, each dealing with a specific responsibility. For example, one section may deal with the processing of customer accounts or credit sales; here, each and every individual transaction with each customer has to be recorded on a set of documents – delivery note, invoice, statement, credit note, etc. (C) Another section may deal solely with the compilation of company payroll details – basic pay, overtime worked, bonus or commission due, statutory deductions including tax payable, national insurance and superannuation, net pay due and so on. Such work also involves keeping records of national insurance paid and company payroll (D) tax paid. Again, a further section may concentrate on cost control, to ensure that the outgoings of the company, whether in the form of manufacturing costs or office stationery and telephone costs etc, are kept within bounds.

The managers in the company's other departments – research and development, production, sales, marketing and so on, all need accurate up-to-date information to enable them to make sound decisions based on reliable (E) information. Another duty of the accounts department, therefore, is to maintain an efficient information recording and relaying system. Developments in electronic technology in the office – the use of data processing machines, (F) computers and telecommunication equipment over the past 15 years – have made the work of the accounts department much easier in many large companies. But it is also worth remembering that in small firms, much of the work of an accounts department is carried out by an all-purpose general office staff with the help of accounting computer software on micro- or minicomputer.

In terms of communication, a great deal of the work of an accounts department is expressed in number form and stretches across the many different activities of a company's various departments. For example, a balance sheet expressing the firm's financial standing has to be prepared annually for submission to the Inland Revenue and for the inspection of the company's shareholders. At regular intervals, detailed profit and loss accounts are prepared to show where the earnings of the company have come from – where the money has been spent and the profit that is left. Specialists called management account-

The functions of an accounts department

(G)

- Keeping records of all company financial activities so as to provide accurate details as required by company law

- Maintaining records and processing all payments made by the company to its suppliers, insurers, shareholders, landlords, Inland Revenue, etc

- Maintaining records and processing all payments to the company from its customers (whether cash or account), royalties on patents given, or licenses granted to other firms to make goods researched by the company, revenue from shares held, properties leased, sales of properties, etc

- Processing and recording details of company payroll (wages and salaries)

- Processing and recording cash held at the bank, petty cash outgoings

- Keeping up-to-date records of sales, costs and overheads so that profit (or loss) totals may be identified at frequent intervals

- Providing company managers with up-to-date information across the range of financial activities to aid them in making decisions ants kept a watchful eye on the way departments incur expenses, whether it is in manufacturing goods or advertising services. They prepare regular reports for the senior managers who run the company.

Though much of the work of an accounts department is routine, when it is viewed in the broad context of the company's performance – and sometimes its very survival in hard times – it is never dull! Indeed, one of the challenges facing accounts staff in the area of communication is the need to present number-based information to laymen clearly and simply. Otherwise, the problems and dangers of, say, a company failing to create sufficient ready cash weekly to pay its workforce may be understood too late, or the failure of a company to secure payment for goods supplied on credit may result in its bankruptcy. Above all, accounts staff need to be effective communicators in the medium of number – tables, charts, statistics, and graphs – as well as in the media of the spoken and written word.

The following diagram illustrates the broad range of activities which an accounts department is likely to be concerned with in a large organisation:

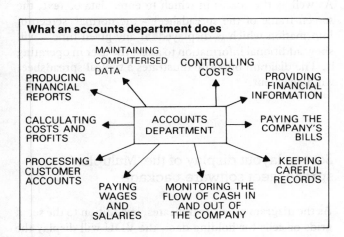

What an accounts department does

Mastering the meaning

1 In your own words, explain the meaning of the following expressions and phrases:

financial transactions   Line A
each dealing with a specific responsibility   Line B
compilation   Line C
cost control   Line D
Another duty ... is to maintain an efficient information recording and relaying system   Line E
telecommunication equipment   Line F
insurers   Line G

2 Explain the two different meanings of the word 'stocks' as used in the passage.

3 Explain briefly why it is that the work of an accounts department extends to every other department within a company.

4 Why is it so important for an accounts department to be in a position to make financial information readily available?

5 How can a management accountant make an important contribution to the efficient running of a company?

6 In your own words, outline the communication role of an accountant within a large company.

7 In about 100 words, outline what you consider to be the main functions of an accounts department.

Discussion topic

What is the likely effect upon company communication and information systems as used in an accounts department of the rapid developments in micro-chip based office equipment? Are there likely to be any dangers or problems arising from too much information being too readily available to company staff?

Assignments

1 The following words and phrases are frequently used in the context of accounts and financial matters. Choose two groups and, having carefully researched their meaning, explain them to the other members of your group.

auditor   plant and machinery
chartered accountant   fixtures and fittings

creditor   overheads
debtor   labour costs
days of credit
                           gross profit
cash at bank   net profit
overdraft
cash flow   capital
                           revenue
shareholder   reserves
investor
                           depreciation
invoice   written off
statement
credit note   budgetary control
                           stock taking
asset   inventory
liability
dividend   work in progress
                           integrated accounts package
                           audit trail
freehold
leasehold

2   In small groups, research one of the following topics (you may approach anyone who can help, after consulting with your teacher). Prepare a presentation of the information you have discovered for the rest of your group, using any visual aids or handouts you think appropriate.

    (*a*) What is a balance sheet?
    (*b*) What is a profit and loss account?
    (*c*) How does a company try to control its costs?
    (*d*) How are a company's wages and salaries calculated?
    (*e*) What are stocks and shares? How does a shareholder help to finance a company's activities?
    (*f*) How have computers made the accountant's job easier?

Operating a spreadsheet system

One of the most useful and indeed versatile of all the software applications packages so far developed is the spreadsheet. It is used in a wide variety of situations where the user wishes to record number or financial details and to manipulate them by means of various formulae which are built into the package. Additionally, the spreadsheet enables the user to create his own formulae – such as adding 10% to the value of all goods held in stock and re-calculating the stock's new value, and to obtain a print-out of the revised totals to form the basis of new prices to be given to customers and so on. As you can well imagine, the spreadsheet is an invaluable tool which assists both the small business person and the mighty multinational company executive alike!

As its name suggests, the spreadsheet is a kind of large sheet over which numbers, text or mathematical formulae may be displayed. In effect, the user has available a series of columns which extend from left to right and a series of rows which extend from top to bottom. The size of spreadsheets varies in this respect, and the following diagram illustrates the size of a typical spreadsheet used on a micro-computer.

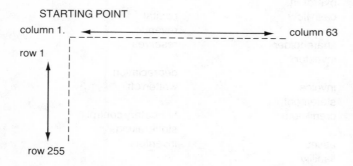

STARTING POINT

Imagine a rectangle of space which is some 63 columns wide and 255 rows deep as a large sheet of paper, which is made up of a grid of smaller rectangles, each one consisting of a single column width and row depth, as follows.

Thus a 'window' of the spreadsheet which can be displayed on a VDU screen would look as follows:

As well as the spaces in which to enter data or text, the screen frame of the spreadsheet – the normal 'screen of information which is displayed' at any given time – will show additional information to assist the user in operating it. The diagram opposite illustrates a typical spreadsheet window layout.

Screen layout display of the 'Multiplan' spreadsheet software package

As the diagram opposite indicates, in addition to the set of grids or cells for holding data, the VDU will display the following information customarily to assist the spread-sheet user.

1   Numbers or letters to indicate each column, for example 1, 2, 3 or A, B, C as far as 63 numerically or as AB, BB, CB etc. to signify columns beyond 26 (A to Z) etc.

2   Numbers to indicate rows going down the grid vertically indicating the location of each row of cells (say, 1–255).

3   An illuminated box or pointer to show which particular cell or grid is in use – that is, where any data will be positioned within the displayed frame.

4   A selection of commands set out as a 'menu' which the user can activate and employ upon demand, for example, to edit or amend a screenful of data, to delete an entry, to move instantly to another screen frame of data altogether – say columns 36 to 42 and rows 24 to 44, to change a formula, to print a screen and so on. Such a set of

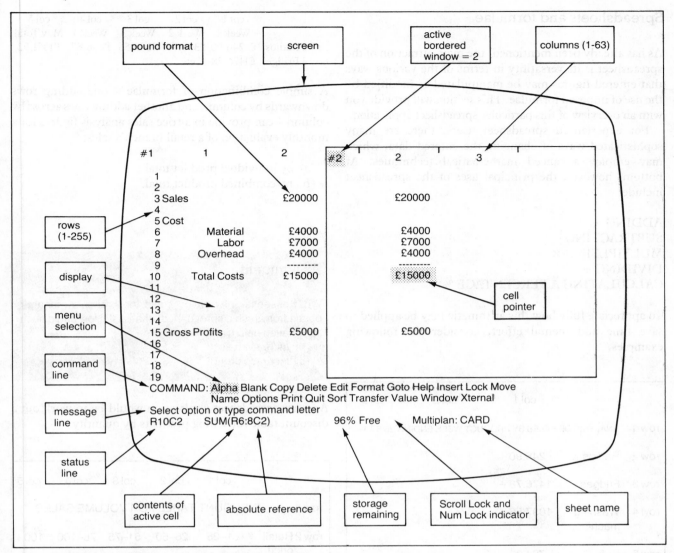

Example of the screen layout of a spreadsheet.
Reproduced by permission of IBM (UK) Ltd and Microsoft
Corporation USA.

commands would be referred to as a menu selection or command line. When a particular command is activated – say to edit a piece of text on screen, then a space or additional command line may be used to show the line of text or data being edited before it is transferred into the displayed screen frame.

5 Additionally the spreadsheet – usually at its foot – will display information on a message line. This line will remind the user of what he or she can do as a next step – it will act as a reminder or 'prompt' line, or may advise the user of an error in the operation of the spreadsheet.

6 A further line at the bottom of the screen frame is the 'status line'. This line is used to show the user where he or she is in terms of the spreadsheet – that is, in which row/ cell the pointer or illuminated cursor is located; what information the pointer is highlighting, and sometimes further helpful information such as the amount of available unused space on the spreadsheet; the title of the file

being created or edited; or what formula is being constructed to manipulate rows of figures etc.

7 In addition, the screen can, in a sense, be 'overprinted' at any time to introduce a detailed page of HELP prompts or to subdivide the screen frame into a series of 'windows' which display on screen data temporarily borrowed from other screen frames some distance from the one in use. While the 'overprinting' window command is in use, the original screen frame remains on screen partially visible. Some spreadsheets provide a number of windows of information taken from different parts of the package to be displayed simultaneously – either to act as a visible reminder of stored data for cross-reference, or to indicate how certain spreadsheet commands could assist the user.

The above outline of how a spreadsheet page is displayed on screen and how it may be used, has provided only a brief overview of the scope of the spreadsheet and you should now take pains to find out more about the use of spreadsheets in organisations during your visits to local firms and in your information technology lessons and lectures.

Spreadsheets and formulae

As has already been mentioned, the main attraction of the spreadsheet is its versatility in terms of the various ways that entered figures may be manipulated or modified by the use of imposed formulae. This section will provide you with an overview of this particular spreadsheet application.

For experienced spreadsheet users, there are many sophisticated ways of changing the entered data, which may employ advanced mathematical techniques. At bottom, however, the principal uses of the spreadsheet include:

ADDING +
SUBTRACTING −
MULTIPLYING ×
DIVIDING ÷
CALCULATING A PERCENTAGE %

To appreciate fully how this arithmetic may be applied to save time and mental effort, consider the following examples.

	col 1	col 2	col 3
row 1	ANALYSIS OF SALES BY PRODUCT WEEK ENDING 25:5:19—		
row 2	Radios	246.90 +	
row 3	Fridges	1476.78 +	
row 4	Washing machines	1097.56 +	
row 5	Hi-fi	784.23 +	
row 6	TOTAL	3605.47	

This simple example shows the spreadsheet's ability to add individual items and provide a total. Neither the plus signs nor the equals signs appear on the spreadsheet display, and the sum will have been set up by entering the data according to this formula:

$$R2C1 + R3C1 + R4C1 + R5C1 = R6C1$$

So far this does not exceed the ability of the humble pocket calculator, but the spreadsheet could, if required, add a further series of sales analyses for subsequent weeks in further columns across the page, so that product totals could be summarised by month, quarter and year, simply by including another formula in the calculation:

$$R2C1 + R2C2 + R2C3 + E2C4 = R2C5$$

and so on for each product.

	col 1	col 2	col 3	col 4	col 5
	Week 1	Week 2	Week 3	Week 4	May Total
row 2 Radios	£ 246.90	£378.79	£269.56	£456.67	£1351.92
row 3 Fridges	£1476.78	etc.			

A simple combination of formulae – one adding rows downwards by column, and another adding rows across by column – can provide in a trice sales analysis figures for a monthly evaluation of a retail branch's sales:

(a) by individual product total
(b) by combined product total.

Another spreadsheet application would be to work out a discount table for selling products by quantity.

	col 1	col 2	col 3	col 4	col 5
row 1	DISCOUNT TABLE FOR VOLUME SALES				
row 2 Retail price	1–25	26–50	51–75	76–100	100+
row 3	5%	10%	15%	20%	25%
row 4 Radios					
row 5 24.99	23.74	22.49	21.24	19.99	18.74
row 6 Fridges					
row 7 49.99	47.49	44.99	42.49	39.99	37.49

(and so on for other products)

The beauty of the spreadsheet in this context is that the formula which has set up the discounting of each product – radio, fridge, etc. – at multiples of 5% for quantities of goods in groups of 25, in this case 5%, 10%, 15%, 20%, and 25%, could easily be modified, say if the seller's buying terms improved, to recalculate at:

1–25: 12.5%   25–50: 17.5% and so on

Once the modified formula had been entered into the spreadsheet, all the individual prices would be re-displayed in an instant showing the new range of discounts! Thus the spreadsheet can calculate any given change in the command formulae extremely quickly. Such a capability enables the spreadsheet user to pose many useful questions based on, 'What if?'

For example:

- What if my costs increase by 15%?

- What if my turnover falls by £10 000 this year, how would this affect my gross profit?

- What if we produced 100 000 more tin boxes per week, how would (*a*) production costs increase overall, and (*b*) the wages bill rise, and (*c*) by how much would gross profit per tin box increase?

Of course, in order to obtain such useful information at the drop of a hat, complex spreadsheets need to have:

- Very large grids in which to store data.

- A significant amount of time and effort put into the inputting of the raw data per cell.

- A person skilled in creating the appropriate spreadsheet formulae.

- People able to interpret and manipulate the spreadsheet correctly and imaginatively.

Some major applications of spreadsheets

In business

- To monitor cash flow projections – that is, to check out in advance the consequences of anticipated income and expenditure per month for, say, the year ahead. Increases in stock costs or payroll or rent, etc. can be built into the program as they occur.

- To monitor budgets – the rate of expenditure of given budget heads like stationery, office equipment, transport costs, etc. can be deducted in a rolling plan from a given amount and the pace at which the allocation is being spent carefully watched and corrective action taken if need be.

- To calculate profit and loss monthly over a calendar year. The extent of sales and their cost, leaving gross profit can be monitored on a regular basis and the spreadsheet can supply hypothetical answers to a range of 'What if?' questions.

- To compare sets of figures quickly and easily. For example, via the windows technique, sales performance over a wide range of products can be quickly compared between: 'this year, last year'; 'this year so far as against last year in full'; 'this quarter as against the same quarter last year' and so on.

In public service

- To record costs of maintenance work done on county schools.

- To monitor the rate of costs involved in a major public works contract, i.e. building a new roundabout.

- To calculate the effects of raising the general rate to meet rising costs.

In effect, the applications which a spreadsheet can perform in the general area of 'number crunching' and financial operations are limited virtually only by the imagination of the user and his ability to construct new ways of getting the best from the spreadsheet's amazing calculating and data manipulating power!

Spreadsheet assignments

1 Contact local private and public sector spreadsheet users, in company, county council and district council offices and ask them to show you some of the ways in which spreadsheets are helping them in their work. Tip: likely user departments are: County Treasury, Planning and Surveyor's Departments and in the private sector, production, accounts, marketing and sales departments.

2 With the help of your teacher, construct a spreadsheet to carry out the following tasks:

To produce a simulated (or actual) analysis of the sales prices and cost prices of products sold in your refectory or school/college shop and to calculate the effect on prices of:

(*a*) an across-the-board increase of 17% in your purchase prices upon your gross profit

(*b*) the effect upon your gross profit of an increase of 12% in the sales price of your two best selling products.

3 With your teacher's help and authorisation, set up a spreadsheet to monitor the rate of expenditure of goods purchased in your department. For example, the range of stationery and secretarial consumables used up monthly in the Secretarial Studies Section. Your spreadsheet could be designed so as to provide a running total of revenue remaining after each individual purchase has been entered under a particular budget head.

During your course of study, if you maintain such a spreadsheet, you could provide very helpful information on the likely effect upon departmental expenditure of, for example, a 15% increase in the cost of typewriter cartridge ribbons, photocopying paper and so on.

Usage – agreement

Subjects and finite verbs

'Agreement' is the technical word which is used to describe the relationship between words which are so strongly linked grammatically that they must show that link by, for example, both being in the plural or both in the singular. Subjects and their finite verbs must agree in this way, as must also adjectives and the nouns they describe:

S   FV
Jane dictates clearly.

Since 'Jane' is singular, so also must be 'dictates'.

In sentences such as that above, the agreement is instantly recognised and the correct forms of subjects and verbs used. In longer sentences, however, which may contain both singular and plural forms of words, mistakes are easily made:

The meeting of the sales representatives, which normally take place in the conference room, have been cancelled.

Since the word 'meeting' in the above sentence is a singular subject, it must govern its finite verb, which must also be singular 'has been cancelled'. Similarly, the relative pronoun 'which' stands for the word 'meeting', and so 'takes place' must also be singular. Indeed it is the position of the word 'representatives' in the plural, standing nearer to the two verbs than 'meeting', which causes the confusion!

Adjectives and nouns, nouns and pronouns

Similar mistakes may occur in the agreement which should exist between adjectives and the nouns they qualify, or in pronouns standing in place of nouns:

These set of spanners are more expensive than those.

In the above sentence, the word 'set' is singular; consequently its adjective 'This' must also be singular. Similarly, the pronoun at the very end of the sentence stands in for 'set', and must also be singular – 'that'. The verb too must be singular – 'is'. The sentence should read

This set of spanners is more expensive than that.

Watch out also for the expressions which may be built around 'type' or 'kind':

Wrong: These kind of washers are rust-proof.
Right: This kind of washer is rust-proof.

We ... I, one ... you

Another common error in agreement occurs with the use of 'we' and 'I' in the same sentence or in adjacent sentences:

We are most pleased to accept your kind invitation, and *I* look forward to seeing you.

In using the pronouns 'we' or 'I', the writer must be consistent and stick firmly to one or the other.

'*I* am most pleased ... *I* look forward to ...'

Similar lapses in agreement are sometimes to be found in the use of 'one' and 'you' in the same sentence or passage:

One occasionally meets awkward customers, and then *you* need a good deal of tact!

Here, the word 'you' should be discarded in favour of 'one' for the sake of consistency. Indeed, 'you' constructions are almost always better avoided.

Pronouns taking singular verbs

Note that some pronouns always take a *singular* verb:

EACH *has* had a share of the reward.
NONE *is* left to give out.
NOBODY *wishes* to volunteer!
NEITHER *is* willing to stay late tonight.

'All', however, may be used with singular or plural nouns:

ALL *is* lost!
ALL *are* in agreement over the decision to cancel the dance.

Boost your spelling power!

Learn these words by heart

Remember, an asterisk after a word indicates that it is very commonly misspelled:

absorb v	(absorption n absorbent adj)
acquaint* v	(acquaintance n)
breathe v	(breath n)
bureau n -eaux pl	(bureaucracy n)
category n	(categoric adj)
centre/center v, n	(central adj centering v centred v)
deficient adj	(deficiency n)
desire v, n)	(desirable, adj desirous adj)
eliminate v	elimination n)
emphasize v	(emphasis n emphatic adj)
equip v	(equipped v equipment n)
feasible adj	(feasibility n unfeasible adj)
February n	
genius n	(geniuses pl)
grammar n	(grammatical adj)
honour v, n	(honourable adj honorary adj)
horrendous adj	
incident n	(incidental adj incidence n)
incipient adj	
lively adv	(livelihood n)

Do not forget to enter in your vocabulary book any words with which you are unfamiliar, either in terms of spelling or meaning!

Assignment

By arrangement, choose four of the above words. Compose a sentence for each, in which the word is used correctly. Compare your sentences with those devised by others in your group. This will help you to add the above list of words to your **active vocabulary.**

Here's the proof ...! 4

There is one mistake in each of the following. Re-write the sentences correctly.

1 Each of the delegates were given a folder.

2 Although I have given your request special consideration, we cannot allow you to have six weeks' leave this year.

3 By October it was plane that the sales budget would not be met.

4 At least mens' wear is showing a profit.

5 Magipaint spreads even.

6 Two cases of Magipaint will be delivered to you in three weeks time and the balance of the order will be despatched on the 8 August.

7 The accounts department computer was an apple.

8 We are withholding payment until all delivery faults are put right.

Communication media

Every day, people in commerce and industry are faced with the recurring problem of choosing the best medium in which to communicate a message.

Making such a choice is not always as straightforward as it may seem. Decisions are influenced by such basic alternatives as: do I speak to him, or write? Do I call a meeting or contact staff individually? Would my message be better conveyed in words or in a diagram or number table?

In addition, there are other factors which influence the choice of communication medium. How urgent is the message? Should its recipients receive it at the same time? Does the complex nature of the message require a detailed written analysis? Is a written record needed? Is the persuasive content of the message more likely to prove effective if recipients are seen face-to-face? How quickly is feedback required?

The choice of the most effective medium for any message will depend on what its essential aims and objectives are, whether to inform objectively, or to persuade.

The very nature of the message and its context will influence the choice of medium. For instance, counselling or disciplining would require a private, face-to-face interview, while a special offer on a range of goods will be perhaps best conveyed to customers via a circular sales letter. Reassuring an upset client, however, may call for a personal visit from a divisional sales manager.

Moreover, choosing the best way to send a message will ensure that it is well-received, accepted and acted upon in a positive way – the choice of medium is essential to effectiveness. Therefore the good communicator must resist the temptation to reach instinctively for the telephone, rush into the next office, or commit everything to writing. Indeed, the increasing variety of IT-based communications tools makes it increasingly important to think before acting. Consideration and reflection before action *always* pay dividends! Furthermore, it is also well worth remembering that, once put in an unsuitable medium, it is much more difficult to 'cancel out' the message and start again. A useful motto, therefore, is:

Think the matter through before choosing the medium!

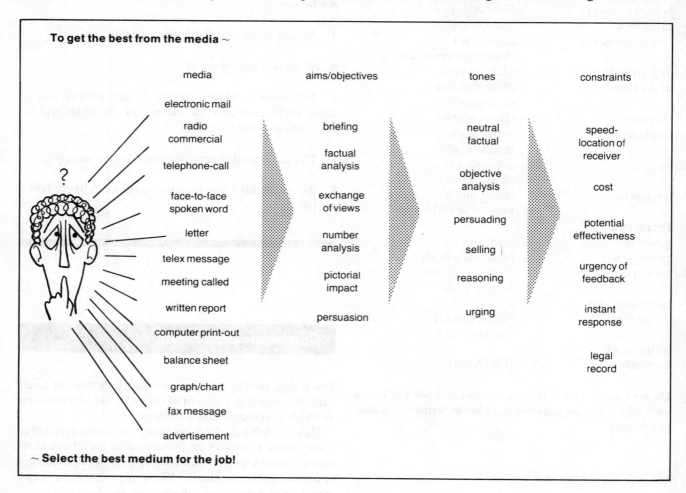

To get the best from the media ~

media	aims/objectives	tones	constraints
electronic mail			
radio commercial	briefing	neutral factual	speed-location of receiver
telephone-call	factual analysis	objective analysis	cost
face-to-face spoken word	exchange of views	persuading	potential effectiveness
letter	number analysis	selling	
telex message		reasoning	urgency of feedback
meeting called	pictorial impact		
written report	persuasion	urging	instant response
computer print-out			
balance sheet			legal record
graph/chart			
fax message			
advertisement			

~ Select the best medium for the job!

Media choosing assignments

In small groups, consider the following situations. Then decide which you think would be the most appropriate medium to use in conveying the message:

1 A sales representative, calling on one of his customers, hears accidentally that a competing firm is about to bring out a new product which seems to be a potential winner. What action should he take, using what medium?

2 While her principal is out, a secretary takes a message from an important client, who insists that he wants to speak to her principal urgently on a confidential matter. What action should the secretary take, using what medium?

3 The office manager realises that morale in his department is very low. There are rumours about a number of staff redundancies being imminent. What action should the office manager take, using what medium?

4 A regional sales manager discovers that the number of sales staff leaving one of his region's retail stores has become alarmingly high. What action should he take, using what medium?

5 A personnel manager overhears two of his staff talking in the staff restaurant. One of them, a highly valued employee appears to be 'fed up' and is actively considering leaving the organisation. What action should the personnel manager take, using what medium?

6 A message is received at an exporting company's head office; one of its overseas agents has just received a large order, but the delivery date is crucial and the prospective customer wants a definite date urgently. What action should be taken in the export sales department, using what medium?

Note: In some of the above cases, the effective handling of the problem may require the use of *more than one medium*. You should therefore decide in your discussions what would be the best way of resolving the problems outlined.

Punctuation

The semi-colon

The semi-colon is, perhaps, best regarded as a punctuation mark with a strength value between that of the comma and full-stop.

Nowadays its use appears to be in decline – largely because a number of writers tend to avoid it because they are not entirely sure how to use it correctly. This is a pity, because its use is basically straightforward and because it can prove an extremely effective punctuation mark.

A helpful way to regard the semi-colon is as a separator of main clauses. It places a particular emphasis on what comes last in a sentence.

As we have already learned, main clauses are virtually the same in structure as sentences, in that both possess a subject and a finite verb, plus perhaps an object or a verb extension. Consider the following two sentences:

The sales target of £3.5 million set this year was extremely demanding. This target was exceeded by the sales force by over 26 per cent!

Both the above sentences are quite capable of standing alone, yet the second is closely related to the first. It is, in fact, an extension of the first in that it conveys a welcome piece of additional information, which modifies the meaning of the first sentence in a surprising way – though the sales target set was demanding, it was not merely reached, but exceeded by some 26 per cent. Now consider the following single sentence:

The sales target of £3.5 million set this year was extremely demanding; this target was exceeded by the sales force by over 26 per cent!

The effect of combining the two sentences into one separated by a semi-colon is to connect the second main clause much more closely to the first. The pause of the semi-colon is shorter than that of the full-stop, and greater emphasis is placed on what is coming next in the second main clause as the reader hurries on to find out how the sentence will end. Putting the figure of 26 per cent right at the end of the second main clause, and hence at the end of the sentence, gives it a marked emphasis, since it represents the climax towards which the sentence has been heading. In other words, the sentence has been deliberately constructed – with the help of the semi-colon – to create a sense of surprise and suspense, the outcome of which is a pleasant surprise. The words 'extremely demanding' contrast sharply with 'exceeded ... by over 26 per cent'.

Consider, for example, the following sentence:

The manager finished the report at last; his wife was busy making a fruit-cake.

Clearly, such a construction makes no sense, since the two ideas expressed in the main clauses have no obvious connection.

Another use of the semi-colon is to link main clauses together which could have been connected by a conjunction which, to add to a sense of emphasis, has been omitted:

Tom Parker at last succeeded in closing the difficult sale; he decided to make no more calls that day.

The emphasis of the above sentence would be lost if the clauses were connected by 'and' or 'and so'.

Thus the main use of the semi-colon may be summarised as follows:

- The semi-colon is used to link main clauses,
- which are closely connected (they usually share the same topic and subject-word),
- so that emphasis is placed on the second clause because the pause of the semi-colon is not as great as that of a full-stop.

Examples of the semi-colon at work

The following examples show other ways in which the semi-colon may be used effectively:

Jones had left; the office staff revelled in their new-found freedom from his heavy-handed management.

She finished the letter; it was perfectly typed; let Miss Johnson dare to criticise her now!

There is a simple solution to this problem; either you resign, or I report you to the board!

Semi-colon assignments

Re-write the following sentences, inserting semi-colons wherever you think it appropriate:

1 the duplex computer displays edits stores and prints its programmed documentation and is instantly accessible yet it costs little more to rent per month than the average plain paper copier

2 communicating entails selecting an appropriate language it requires consideration of the needs of the recipient it depends on the selection of the right medium or channel to transmit it correct choices have to be made in each of these areas if the communication is to be effective

3 miss johnson is loyal discreet and conscientious i can thoroughly recommend her for the post

4 the use of a wider range of electronic office equipment and the introduction of increasingly complex electronic filing and recording systems place heavy demands on todays office worker it is therefore particularly important that relevant and practical office studies courses are developed in schools and colleges

5 a successful sales assistant needs to be enthusiastic tactful hardworking and loyal finding all these qualities in one person is no easy task

What is 'register'?

The word 'register' is used when considering the *style* of a communication. For example, is there harshness or softness, warmth or coldness, formality or informality? Slang words, for instance, would be regarded as having a very informal and familiar register:

Wotcha me ol' cock sparrah!
What a rip-off! Stone the crows!

While statements such as the following would be regarded as very formal and impersonal in their register:

The defendant wishes to register a plea of not guilty.
The Council regrets that it is unable to grant planning permission in this instance.

The chart illustrates how a desire for people to make less noise may be expressed across an extremely broad

register, ranging from an almost pleading tone through a fairly neutral request to an outright rude bellow!

In all we ever say or write, we are constantly making choices about the register of the language we are using. What will be perfectly acceptable as friendly leg-pulling in one situation may seem impertinent in another. Thus it is extremely important that sufficient care is taken to adopt an appropriate register in the language and vocabulary used. Otherwise offence may be given or an appearance of being 'stuffy', cold or over-familiar.

Right dress!

A case study

'Oh, Richard, would you step into the office for a moment, please.' Richard Williams, an eighteen-year-old clerk in the general office of Castle Insurance Company Limited put down his pen and strolled into the general office manager's office.

   'Yes, Mr Pearson?'

'Ah, do sit down, Richard, there's something on my mind I want to discuss with you ...'

'Is it the Kingston quotation? I'm working on ...'

'No, no, it's nothing like that, it's your general appearance that concerns me.'

'I'm sorry, I don't follow you.'

'You see, Richard, the company has a certain image to put across. As you know, we have a number of clients who call into the office regularly and staff are expected to look appropriately turned out at all times.'

'And you're saying I'm not?'

'What I am trying to say, Richard, is that your jean suit and open-neck shirts don't fit in with the sort of dress which I consider right. Then there's your hair. I know its the fashion these days for young people to adopt different hair-styles, but I think long, dyed hair is out of place in an insurance office.'

'I see. You think I'm some sort of disco freak, is that it?'

'No, not at all, Richard, I'd be the first to say that, given your – ah – style of dress, you always look fresh and cleanly turned out. It's just that what might be perfectly acceptable – even desirable – in a theatre or TV production team is out of place here. Look, I can see that you're taking this matter personally ...'

'How else am I expected to take it? I really don't see that my clothes or hair are any concern of yours, provided I do my job properly!'

'Yes, well, that's an understandable response – from your point of view. Let me try to put it another way. You must have noticed that the female staff here always wear dresses or skirts and not trousers or the like. There has never been any compulsion in this regard on the company's part. I imagine that newcomers take their cue from the older, longer-serving staff. And I think the ladies look much more attractive and presentable in this – ah – mode of attire. So all I'm saying is that you would do well to make an effort to meet the expectations of the firm with regard to your personal appearance. You see, insurance is a field in which customers expect a certain reliability, solidity and, yes, even a certain amount of tradition.'

'So you'd prefer me in a charcoal, pin-striped suit with short back and sides? Does this mean that I may expect a salary increase to enable me to buy more expensive clothes?'

'Look, Richard, there's no need to adopt that sort of tone. If you'd just stop to think about it, I'm sure you'd realise that my bothering to take the time to talk to you about this – delicate matter – is because I have a high regard for you and don't want to see your career prospects hampered ...'

'In other words, if I don't conform, I don't get on, is that it?'

'That's entirely a matter for you to consider. Now I've tried to put this matter to you in a helpful way, but I don't think you are prepared to see the problem *constructively* ...'

'Well, I don't see that there *is* a problem! I think the whole thing is my own personal business. Perhaps you'd prefer me to resign, if, as you say, I don't "fit in".'

'I'm sorry you're taking this attitude, Richard, and I don't think any purpose will be served by prolonging this interview. I've told you what is expected of you. It's now up to you to reflect upon it and decide what you wish to do. Now, if you'll excuse me.'

Later that morning, in a sandwich bar:

'Well,' declared Patricia Roberts, a fellow clerk, 'I think old Pearson's taking a real liberty! He's just an old fuddy-duddy, who's failed to move with the times!'

'I don't know, though, I think he's got a point,' answered Peter Jenkins, 'he's got *his* job to do, and some of our customers are pretty fussy ...'

'Well, I don't know *what* to do!' exclaimed Richard. 'It just seems an undue restriction on my freedom to dress as I please!'

Right dress! written assignments

1 In class or in small groups, discuss the following aspects arising from the case study:

(*a*) What would you do in Richard's place?

(*b*) Do you think that Mr Pearson handled the matter effectively?

(*c*) Do you think Richard's responses were justified?

(*d*) If you were a new female staff member, would you arrive for work after a few days wearing jeans or trousers? If so, why? If not, why not?

(*e*) Do you think it is justifiable for certain types of organisation to require staff to dress in a certain style? What justifications can you make for staff in certain organisations conforming to a certain type or style of dress?

(*f*) If firms do expect such conformity, should they make some provision for it in the salaries they pay? Can you think of any examples?

2 Assuming that the sort of dress to which Mr Pearson refers was made a condition of service for staff at Castle Insurance, compose a paragraph to be included in the Staff Conditions of Service Schedule outlining the requirements, which would be applicable to both male and female staff members.

3 Assuming that you are a company employee and also a representative of the National Union of Office Staffs, compose a suitable letter to be sent to the Managing Director of Castle Insurance Company Limited, Castle House, Broad Street, Castleton, Northshire CS3 5GF. It should ask for the current conditions of service regarding staff dress to be reviewed. Your letter should seek to make a case on the lines that fashions have changed, that young people find certain clothing expensive, and that staff recruitment is being adversely affected, etc.

Discussion topics

1 How much are people's judgments of others influenced by the way they dress?

2 'What you wear says what you are!' To what extent is this true?

<hr>

Communication as an 'all-round' skill

In any busy organisation, information is constantly flowing in, out and around, in virtually every mode of communication.

In every office, shop, factory or warehouse, the spoken word abounds, as instructions, confirmations, explanations, enquiries or reports are passed from one member of staff to another.

Similarly, the written word is used extensively to transmit and store messages in the form of letters, memoranda, minutes, reports or notices.

Number communication in the form of tables, charts, graphs or diagrams is used in the course of many tasks to communicate sales performance, production targets or profit margins.

Data keyboarded into computers and recalled via VDU display or as hard copy computer print-out is now a common place feature of offices, shops and factories.

In advertising and sales promotion, cartoons, photographs and drawings are devised to impart a visual impact in a variety of forms and colours to prompt customers to choose particular products or services.

Yet it is seldom in the course of the working day that communication takes place *within* a single communication medium or language. More often, staff are involved in using their communication skills in a *variety* of media or modes – oral, written, number, graphic – which interconnect and react with each other. For example, the secretary will often have to take dictation in shorthand, orally transmitted, and then convey it in the form of the typescript written word. The manager may receive instructions by the spoken word which result in his

producing a report using both written and number communication. The advertising designer may listen to ideas conveyed at a meeting and then convert the spoken instructions into a mix of pictures and printed words as an effective advertisement, or the sales manager may receive a large order almost instantaneously by electronic mail through services like 'Telecom Gold', from a remote phone box!

Moreover, in order to produce a particular communication – whether a talk to a group of sales representatives, or a detailed investigatory report, business people often need to extract information which is expressed in a wide range of communication languages and then to transmit it in yet another form best suited to the needs of the moment – a telephone conversation, reference to a filed letter and checking of a table of sales figures may lead to a sales manager composing a memorandum to his sales force advising them of the need to increase their sales efforts in the following weeks.

Thus the efficient communicator – at *all* levels in the organisation – must develop the ability to move with equal ease through the entire range of communication languages or media. This means developing not only skills of speaking, listening, reading and writing, but also the more demanding skills of:

Processing information from a variety of sources

Handling the range of information sources takes skill!

- Knowing where to find sources of information
- Being able to identify key points in a mix of data
- Structuring clearly the key points in a logical order
- Selecting the most effective format in which to present the information
- Choosing an appropriate tone and style to convey the message

<hr>

Ajax pumps

A multi-source assignment

The following extracts deal with a problem which Ajax Pumps Limited, Ajax Works, Westland Road, Waltham Grove, Westleigh, Midshire WS1 4KG, is experiencing with its employees parking their cars. Study the extracts carefully and then tackle the assignments that follow.

'It really is too much! I'm housebound and spend much of my day in my front sitting-room. On most days the light through the window is poor because of those wretched cars and vans parked all day long. No consideration. You'd think they own the street!'

Comments of an old-age pensioner to an investigating manager of Ajax, Mr J Simpson, made on Thursday 10 January 19—

5 CAR PARKING FACILITIES

The Chairman opened the discussion by asking whether everyone had read the report submitted by Mrs Castle, which had been previously circulated.

It was generally agreed that urgent action was needed to resolve the problem of parking of both employee and company vehicles.

Mr Sewell referred to the deterioration in public relations with local residents as a result of the extensive parking by employees in the residential areas near the works.

After a full discussion, it was agreed that the Management Committee should recommend to the Board that the Westland Meadows acreage should be purchased as soon as possible in order that work on extending the company car park might be started as a matter of urgency.

3.0 FINDINGS

3.1 Car Parking Facilities

The current provision provides parking places for 200 motor vehicles. This was entirely adequate when the company was first opened in 1970. Since then, however, the number of employees has risen from 450 to 1120 and the extension of the company's fleet of commercial vehicles has reduced available parking space.

As a result, access to and egress from the car park has become subject to bottle-necks causing costly delays and inconvenience both to staff and company commercial vehicle movements.

The marking out of parking grid lines has deteriorated over the years. Consequently, many staff park carelessly and the available space in the car park is being used uneconomically.

For some time, large numbers of staff have taken to parking in the streets in the vicinity of the works.

3.2 Extension of Car Park on Westland Meadows Land

With the purchase of the Westland Meadows acreage, it should be possible to construct additional parking facilities for a further 200-300 cars, and to provide additional parking space for company vehicles.

Extract from the Minutes of the Management Committee Meeting held on 24 February 19— Chairman: Mr Peter Wright, deputy managing director, Secretary: Miss Jane Parker, personnel manager.

Extract from the findings of a report on the proposed construction of additional car parking space, submitted to Mr Simon Wells, Managing Director, by Mrs Eve Castle, Company Secretary on 23 January 19—

'Hello, Fred? Charlie here. Look, I've an item I'd like included on the agenda of the next meeting of the Shop Stewards' Committee. I've just heard that the management are proposing to extend the company car park by purchasing some of Westland Meadow. It's absolutely ridiculous. The land'll cost at least £80 000! What we need is better plant in the works if our lads are to keep their jobs – you know how the orders are falling off – and it's the machinery we've got to work on! I think we ought to discuss the implications of this one and then take it to management. What do you think? ...'

Telephone call from Charles Wilson, shop steward, to Frederick Goodman, Convenor of the Shop Stewards' Committee, 1 March 19—

R.B.JACKSON

Assignments

1 Compose a letter to Mr Wells from Mrs Margaret Jackson, Honorary Secretary of the Waltham Grove Residents' Association, 5 Laburnam Gardens, Waltham Grove, Westleigh, Midshire WS2 9FG, complaining on behalf of local residents about the parking of cars in the vicinity of the Ajax Works.

2 Exchange your letter with a partner and then compose Mr Wells' reply.

3 Draft a memorandum from Mr Wells to all employees of Ajax outlining what the firm is doing to solve the car parking problem and what they should do to help.

4 Role play a meeting between the Shop Stewards Committee and management representatives to discuss the proposed expenditure of £80 000 on extending the car park.
  Arrange for minutes of the meeting to be taken, produced by a word processor and passed to the 'Senior Shop Steward' for editing. Send a copy to all participants and check their views on the accuracy of the minutes.

5 Design a notice to be posted on all works noticeboards setting out a revised procedure for parking cars.

Unit 10

Communication styles at work

Communication in a hierarchy

One of the most important things for the new office worker to keep constantly in mind, is that an organisation
(A) is a hierarchy. This means that the people who work in it have been given jobs to do, which are not only specialised,
but which give some of them authority over others, as well
(B) as responsibilities and accountabilities for ensuring that work is done effectively. The newly-arrived clerk or typist
in a commercial firm will 'slot in' to a level or step in such
(C) a hierarchy and find in existence a chain of command which extends downwards from a managing director,
through a head of department and a supervisor to the level at which he or she will operate.

One of the main reasons for most firms constructing their organisation in this way is the need to delegate work
and responsibility. At the top of the organisational hier-
archy or pyramid, experienced managers (usually directors) will be concerned with a broad overview of what
the company is doing and with measuring how success-fully it is meeting the objectives it has set itself. Clearly,
such managers do not have the time to follow minutely how each and every ledger entry is made, or how
accurately each typewritten document is produced. But they do have an endless appetite for information. Without
information from the lower levels of the organisation they are unable to make decisions.

Staff working in the middle levels of the organisation have two principal tasks. The first is to understand and
interpret the directives and instructions from the top, and the second is to motivate and supervise more junior staff
who will be assigned the varied and 'nitty gritty' jobs which thus arise. At the broad base of the organisational
pyramid, clerical, secretarial and administrative staff will carry out work in smaller, clearly defined areas within
specialist departments or sections. And without attention to detail, all firms would soon founder. (D)

Communication routes in an organisation

DOWNWARDS — Directives and instructions
- Requests for information
- Authorisations
- Advice and help
- Confirmations

UPWARDS — Responses to information requests
- Seeking of authority to act
- Asking for information
- Suggestions
- Criticisms

ACROSS — Exchanges of information
- Liaison with colleagues
- Cooperation with other departments
- Group projects and tasks

DIAGONALLY — Liaising and cooperation with staff at different levels in other departments

DOWNWARDS   UPWARDS

DIAGONAL

ACROSS

The direction of the message affects its style and tone

Using the right style

For the newcomer to the world of work, such a complex structure of human relationships is often hard to understand and at times confusing to follow. This difficulty is sometimes increased when newly-appointed staff have to learn to use effectively a wide range of different communication styles and tones. What may be perfectly acceptable as a style of oral communication with a colleague who works on the same level – 'Hey Pete! Bring me a cup of coffee as well, will you!' would probably not go down too well if called after the departmental head or finance director. It might be thought of as being much too familiar.

It is of course difficult to generalise, since some firms have evolved quite formal styles or climates of communica-tion; and some very informal ones. Nevertheless, it is ⒠ extremely important, whenever starting in a new job, that eyes and ears are kept very much open to learn what styles and tones of communication are appropriate in the organisation.

The effective choice of the right tone or style in which to express a message is absolutely essential if the aims of its sender are to be met. However, it is important not to confuse choosing an appropriate style with the temptation to be either arrogant or dictatorial when instructing junior staff, or hypocritically flattering when talking to senior ⒡ colleagues. No one likes the bully or 'yes-man'; insincere behaviour is quickly spotted and most people in organisa-tions find it distasteful. Moreover, abusing one's status or authority seldom works in the long run. If a supervisor or

The influencers of style and tone

FORMAL | INFORMAL

Employee dismissal proceedings

Annual General Meeting of shareholders

Management/ trade union negotiations

Board of Directors meeting

Communication of company policy

Selling/ dealing with customers

Departmental meetings and discussions

Carrying out an assignment with section colleagues

'Talking shop' over coffee or lunch with workmates

Influencers to the formal and non-familiar

Matters involving entire firm
Legal proceedings
Retaining of written records
Relationships with shareholders
Relationships with outside agencies and customers
Relationships between more senior staff and rest of organi-sation
Issuing of directives on policy

Influencers to the informal and easy-going

Relationships with peer group colleagues, chatting to workmates
Working with staff within section, department
Communicating in speech only
Carrying out routine tasks
Seeking help or a favour

The good communicator fits the style to the situation!

Ⓖ manager treats his staff harshly, he is bound to cause their goodwill and support to dry up. Though they may not show their dislike or annoyance openly, they will eventually ignore or flout the manager's orders since they no longer respect him.

Ⓗ In whatever communication style, then, we choose to transmit messages at work, it is vital that the outlook and feelings of the recipient are kept firmly in mind. An awareness of the nature of the relationship between sender and receiver will help to keep the communicator on the right lines. For example, to the salesman, even an awkward and difficult customer *remains* a customer and source of income to the salesman's company. However difficult he may find it, he must always treat the customer with a professional courtesy. Again, however much a manager might prefer the easy informality of a discussion in his own office, he must accept that taking part in an annual meeting of shareholders requires that he makes a formal rather than informal presentation of information. A good

Ⓘ communicator, then, is *always* sensitive to the needs of a given situation and adjusts his communication style accordingly.

The factors which influence the style and tone of a communication are many. Some are straightforward – *all* transactions with a customer are important and over-familiarity may lose an account. A board of directors is always anxious to convey its competence to its shareholders. Dealings with government agencies will need to be both courteous and correct. Important announcements may be undervalued if expressed in colloquial terms. At the same time, close working with workmates, section colleagues and departmental staff will tend to be conducted in more easy-going and informal styles.

Mastering the meaning

1 Explain briefly in your own words the following:

(*a*) hierarchy   Line A
(*b*) responsibilities and accountabilities for ensuring that work is done effectively   Line B
(*c*) chain of command   Line C
(*d*) all firms would soon founder   Line D
(*e*) eyes and ears are kept very much open   Line E
(*f*) hypocritically flattering   Line F
(*g*) flout   Line G
(*h*) source of income   Line H
(*i*) sensitive to the needs   Line I

2   In about 50 words, explain the reasons for an organisation being structured as a hierarchy.

3   Why is it so important for senior managers to receive a constant upward flow of information?

4   What do you consider to be the particular tasks of managers and supervisors in the middle 'layers' of the organisational pyramid?

5   Explain in about 50 words of your own the problems of a newcomer to an office-based organisation in learning what is acceptable style in different types of communication.

6   Why do you think that some organisations develop more formal styles of communication and others more informal ones?

7   Outline what you consider to be the reasons for a member of staff adopting a flattering approach in communications with his seniors.

8   Why is a harsh authoritarian likely to end up without much real authority in an organisation?

Discussion topics

1   'A poor choice of style in any given communication could lead to its total failure.' What do you understand by this statement? Do you agree with it?

2   'If you just act as your natural self, you can't go wrong!' Do you think it is possible to use a deliberately adopted style of communication or is it enough just to 'play it by ear'?

Punctuation

The colon

Writers in earlier times often used the colon (:) as a punctuation stop in ways very similar to those we have learned to use with the semi-colon:

And it is without all controversy, that learning doth make the minds of men gentle, generous, maniable, and pliant to government; whereas ignorance makes them churlish, thwart, and mutinous: and the evidence of time doth clear this assertion, considering that the most barbarous, rude, and unlearned times have been most subject to tumults, seditions, and changes.
The Advancement of Learning Francis Bacon 1605

In the above long sentence of 56 words, the colon in the middle acts as a pivot. Bacon makes his case for learning before the colon, and justifies learning after its use by citing riots and lawlessness as the mark of ignorant times. Interestingly in the above quotation, the colon has been given a more emphatic strength than the semi-colon which precedes it.

Nowadays, however, such a use of the colon has virtually died. And this is perhaps a pity, since the beauty and control of 'rolling prose' has given way to the 'zip' and 'snap' of much shorter sets of sentences. However, the colon still has its uses. You may have noticed one of them in the first sentence of this passage – its use to introduce a quotation or table centred in a passage of prose.

Another use of the colon is to introduce lists:

The following have been selected to play in the Sports and Social Club Soccer XI:
J Wilson (Capt)
P Jones
G Summers ... etc

The list need not be displayed as it is above, but may continue as part of the sentence:

The following were the contents of the defendant's pockets when arrested: one bunch of keys, a leather wallet, two handkerchiefs and 73p in coins.

Finally, note also that the practice of putting a dash after the colon :- has been discontinued.

Boost your spelling power!

Learn these words by heart

Remember, an asterisk after a word indicates that it is very commonly misspelled:

acquiesce v	(acquiescence n)
business* n	(pl businesses)
category n	(pl categories
	categoric adj)
disaster n	(disastrous adj)
error n	(err v erroneous adj)
fulfil v	(fulfilled past part
	fulfilment n)
grievance n	(aggrieved v)
hungry adj	(hunger v, n)
influence v, n	(influential adj)
lie v int	(lying pres part
	lain past part)
lay v trans	(laying pres part
	laid past part
manoeuvre v, n	(manoeuvrable adj)
onus n	
parliament n	(parliamentary adj
	parliamentarian n)
recognize v	(recognition n
may also be	recognizable adj)
spelled – ise,	
isable	
scarce adj	(scarcely* adv
	scarcity n)

technical adj	(technological adj
	technology n
	technique n)
underrate v	
video adj, n	(coming in as a verb)
Wednesday* n	
address v, n	(addresses pl
	addressee n)

Do not forget to enter in your vocabulary book any words with which you are unfamiliar, either in terms of spelling or meaning!

Assignment

By arrangement, choose four of the above words. Compose a sentence for each, in which the word is used correctly. Compare your sentences with those devised by others in your group. This will help you to add the above list of words to your **active vocabulary.**

Giving a talk

R B JACKSON

Perhaps the most frequent picture that springs to mind when the topic of giving a talk is raised is that of the distinguished expert – top manager, professor or civil servant – addressing a packed audience from a raised platform, surrounded by an armoury of visual aids equipment.

Indeed, many talks are given in that sort of daunting context, but equally, in commerce and public service, staff at all levels are sometimes called upon to 'give a talk' in much more informal circumstances. Yet the skills of communication in both sets of circumstances are very similar. Consider the following scenes which may occur daily in a host of firms:

Office Manager to assembled staff:
'Janet has recently returned from the data processing course and will now explain to you how the newly installed Dataflow 2000 works ...'

Regional sales manager at sales meeting:
'I know that some of you have been picking up rumours on the grapevine, so I've asked John to explain to you how the new commission scheme will help you to boost your salary ...'

Managing director, pausing in new landscape office, with VIP's, at Sandra's desk:
'Gentlemen, as you can see, the new open-plan office has created a lot more space and improved staff communication. Sandra here is one of our treasured shorthand typists. I wonder, Sandra, if you would mind outlining the way in which the new layout has helped you personally in your job ...'

As the above 'cues' indicate, talks may be long or very short, and given in formal, semi-formal or quite informal circumstances. They may be given solely to supply factual information, as in a briefing on the workings of a new piece of equipment, or they may seek to reassure and pacify while relaying factual data. Sometimes, as in Sandra's case, they may drop on someone like a bolt from the blue! At such times, the ability to 'think on one's feet' and to grasp instantly what is expected are vital communication skills. It is important, therefore, that all prospective office workers master the essentials of giving a talk – of relating information and opinion clearly, concisely and effectively.

All of us at some time or another – at school speech days or work presentations – have squirmed in our seats when confronted with a talker who is ill-prepared, who drones or gabbles and who fails entirely both to capture our interest and to hold it. In such situations, as part of a captive audience, minutes seem to go by for us slower than hours. Our minds wander, we 'switch off' and daydream and yearn for the sweet music of the words, 'Finally I should like to say ...' The challenge, then, facing every speaker or giver of a talk is to overcome the temptations in his audience to cease paying attention. The following chart illustrates what factors a talk giver should consider when preparing and delivering a talk and suggests a five-stage plan for ensuring that the talk will be effective and well-received.

The five phase plan

1 Obtaining a brief

What am I trying to achieve?
Who are my audience?
What do they expect?

When is the talk?
Where is the talk?
Why is the talk?

2 Researching the material

What do I already know?
What do I need to find out?
Where can I obtain information?
Who could I speak to?
What audio-visual aids would help?

How should I store the data I collect?

Do I have enough/too much/too little material researched and collected?

3 Organising the talk

How shall I sift and organise the data?

Where shall I start?
What system shall I use to develop and to sequence the main points?
How shall I lead in from one section to the next?
How shall I conclude the talk?

What sort of questions or queries are likely to emerge from the audience – am I prepared for them?

What parts of my talk shall I illustrate with audio-visual aids?
Which aids shall I use?
What equipment and AVA facilities will be available to me at the venue?

4 Delivering the talk

What general tone/style/approach shall I adopt throughout?
Are there any topical remarks, jokes, anecdotes my audience will respond to?
How shall I pace my talk and check its progression?
What form of notes/cards shall I use as memory aids?
How may I check from the audience that I am getting across to them?

5 Tidy up and follow up

Have I left the platform/table tidy for the next speaker?

What letters/telephone-calls or responses do I need to make to follow up any points arising from my talk?

At the outset, it is vital to establish precisely what is expected, to form in the mind a clear profile of the audience and what they hope to gain, and to be certain about dates, times, and the location.

Thorough preparation is the key to giving an effective talk! First, jot down what you already know – personal experience lends authority to a talk. Then research in files, libraries, and in discussions with experts.

Devise a system of storing data logically, as it is found, perhaps in a divided ring-binder, on cards grouped in relevant sections, or via word processing.

At this stage major decisions need to be made on what is essential and what is not needed. A skeleton plan must therefore be plotted to link each major stage of the talk into sections – the material must be sifted into topics or sections and the trivial data put aside.

Having made a plan, the points must be put into an abbreviated sequence – on numbered cards or displayed in capitals on 2–4 A4 sheets.

Duplicated handouts, overhead projector transparencies, etc must be prepared.

At the outset an appropriate style – lighthearted, serious, persuasive, factual – must be conveyed to the audience who will take their cue from you.

You should use the notes only as a memory-jogger and keep eye-contact with the audience to check for positive responses to your talk. Do not drone, mumble or gabble, and keep an eye on the clock to ensure your talk is evenly paced and all points covered.

Never forget two essential courtesies – tidy up after your talk and write any appropriate letters to thank for hospitality or to follow up enquiries from members of the audience.

Assignments

1 First find out how one of the following audio-visual aids works, then give a 5 minute illustrated demonstration of it to your group, using notes you have prepared:

Overhead projector and transparencies
Slide carousel and taped commentary
Closed circuit television and videotapes
Duplicated handouts

2 Choose one of the following topics. Research it carefully and draw up your notes, then give a talk to your student group for 10–15 minutes, including a question and answer session at the end:

- How to become an efficient communicator at work
- The office of the future
- My favourite person
- Succeeding as a woman at work
- Setting up in your own business
- Is there a future for the small business?
- Local job opportunities today
- Working in local government
- What I like to do in my spare time
- A better image – how to present yourself to others
- From school to work – a thinking person's guide

3 In a group discussion, compare notes on talks that you have listened to in the past. Produce a combined checklist of those aspects which you found effective in terms of the talker's delivery techniques, and those which you felt were either irritating or made you 'switch off'.

4 As a final assignment for this topic, write an article of about 400–500 words intended for clerical and secretarial staff entitled:
You never know when you may have to give a talk – so be prepared!

'I'd like a report on that ...'

One of the most demanding tasks – and indeed often the most time-consuming – facing the office worker is to submit a report for others to use either to:

GAIN ACCURATE INFORMATION
or to
OBTAIN INFORMED INSIGHTS
or to
ASSIST IN DECISION-MAKING PROCESSES
or to
HELP IN THE SOLVING OF PROBLEMS

The oral report

Most reports submitted at work, believe it or not, take an oral form. They are relayed by word of mouth usually to a superior who has requested information. In fact, it is quite easy at work to find oneself in the act of giving what is, in effect, an oral report without realising it, since the request from a superior frequently takes the form of a simple question in the course of conversation or discussion:

'How did yesterday's meeting go, Jim?'

'Oh, by the way, Ann, what did you think of yesterday's demonstration of the desk-top publishing equipment? Should we be thinking of buying it?'

The alert communicator soon realises that what is, in fact, being asked for through such questions is a brief but clear account or analysis of an event or process, which provides an absent superior with concise and unbiased information relevant to his particular needs. In addition, as the last sentence of the second illustration above indicates, report givers are often expected to be able to supply sound judgments or recommendations based upon a careful weighing of the various pieces of information researched or acquired.

As the example below illustrates, Alan displays the care and attention which he devoted to his role of substitute at the meeting.

He follows the order of the items discussed at the meeting and dispenses with those parts which he does not think sufficiently important – so he is having to use his judgment as he goes along, selecting only the main and relevant points as he sees them in the context of Mr Jones' and the sales department's needs and interests. Alan also structures his oral report to proceed from the most important to the least important – he realises that Mr Jones is a busy man and has no time for trivia. In addition, he is particularly careful to ensure that Mr Jones is made aware of action which is shortly expected of him, particularly since the instructions come from a representative of top management, Mr Jackson. Lastly, Alan checks that no further action is expected from him, so that he may dispose of the meeting, as it were, in his mental checklist of 'matters outstanding', and move on to his next job.

Logic not magic!

There is nothing magical about the ability to deliver effective oral reports. The secret is to listen alertly as a participator in all office business, to make careful notes, to develop a clear memory, and to practise delivering information in a fluent, organised and logical sequence.

Alan Spicer, giving an oral report of a departmental managers' meeting he attended in place of his boss, Mr Jones, sales manager.

'As you requested, Mr Jones, I sat in on yesterday's meeting for you, which Mr Jackson (deputy managing director) chaired. Only the production manager couldn't attend.

'Matters were very much routine until Item 5 on the agenda – "Proposal to form a Training Department." Mr Jackson set out the background which you know about. One important development has taken place, though, that affects us directly. It seems that the budget won't stretch to building a new training centre, so we're likely to be asked to give up our storage rooms on the ground floor. However, the main point was that all the departmental heads are in favour – Miss West submitted a summary of production's views. Mr Jackson asked the personnel manager to submit a detailed scheme for discussion at the next meeting. Heads were asked to submit suggestions to Mr Jackson by next Wednesday.

'There wasn't anything else particularly important, except that the introduction of the staff holiday rota arrangements were given the go-ahead.

'Under Any Other Business, Mrs Davidson complained about the poor response to the forthcoming Social Club Dance, so I've asked Julie to do her best to sell some more tickets.

'I think that was about it. Is there anything you'd like me to follow up?'

Example of an oral report

Clear beginning At the outset, Alan confirms those present and who chaired the meeting.

Development of essential and relevant points in the middle Aware of the scope of Mr Jones' interest, Alan skips over some early items of no relevance to the sales department – his report selects the particularly relevant points.

Confirmation of action Mr Jones must take himself He anticipates those areas in which his boss must make a response and provides the key details, and deadlines.

Descent to more minor points Alan also confirms that action may now be taken on the rota system.

Confirmation of conclusion and request for further instructions arising from the meeting Nearing the end of his report, which has gone through the same sequence as the meeting's business items, Alan relays details of action he has taken on his own initiative. He closes by asking if there is anything further he should do arising from the meeting.

The written report

Standardised reports

The most frequently used report in business is the standardised report. This type of written report is used to record and transmit information on a host of topics required at regular intervals. Examples of this include: the salesman's weekly report, in which he accounts for his customer calls, orders taken, expenses incurred and so on; the safety inspection report required daily, weekly or monthly in factories or workshops which checks machinery or equipment; and the progress report which a clerk of works on a building site may be required to submit to his architect to show that work schedules are being maintained. Since such reports are used regularly, they are usually made on carefully designed, pre-printed forms, on which the essential information is simply and economically entered in boxes or where an appropriate option is selected and identified:

Date of last inspection: 24/6/19--   Number of new customers visited: 17

Safety status of machine:
   Excellent ☐ Satisfactory ☐

Service within seven days ☐   Withdrawn from use on inspection ☐

Though such reports are quick and simple to compile, and though the design of the form prevents required information from being omitted, they tend not to cater for the complex answer, and are quite unsuitable for dealing with investigations into 'one-off' problems.

The investigatory report

Problems in organisations have a way of coming into view like the tip of an ice-berg – small indications of something being wrong are picked up at first, and then a subsequent investigation reveals a much larger bulk of the problem which had not been entirely recognised or perceived. Good managers and their staff therefore keep constantly alert for any signs of difficulty or trouble, and once they have picked up the vibrations of a problem – say two consecutive months of declining turnover in a retail store, or evidence of a falling off in staff morale, an individual member of staff or a working party is briefed to investigate the matter in depth and to report back. Such a report often includes recommendations on what corrective course of action to take.

Since no two problems are exactly the same, the format for this type of report must be flexible. Also, since the subject matter of the report will differ in each case, the writer must use his discretion in devising a suitable order or sequence in which to present it.

There are, however, some important principles, both of format and structure which need to be learned. Once these have been mastered, you will be able to cope with writing an investigatory report clearly and coherently, and to display your information in ways which help the reader to understand and digest it readily.

The following illustrates the main stages in preparing and compiling an investigatory report:

The five stages of report writing

1   Establish clear terms of reference
What precise instructions? Any recommendations? What deadline? Who receives copies?

2   Research information fully
Consult records. Talk to people involved. Observe practices, procedures. Refer to specialist publications. Check local, national trends.

3   Organise gathered information
Sift material into unified sections. Reject trivia, identify key points. Assemble sections in logical order.

4   Compose rough draft
Use schematic layout techniques. Prefer fact to opinion. Justify assertions. Check conclusions and recommendations are valid and practicable. Check use of English. Seek opinions of first draft. Make final revisions.

5   Submit final draft
Ensure deadline is kept. Retain file copy. Ensure confidentiality if report is for restricted circulation.

Effective schematic layout

Since investigatory reports tend to contain much detailed information, it is *essential* that the full range of the typist's display skills are used to help the report's reader absorb the contents quickly and easily. By proceeding from the more important to the less important, and by a helpful use of section headings in capitals, underscoring, indenting and number referencing your report will be appreciated by its readers.

The short informal report

This is a very straightforward type of written report, the approach of which may be used in a wide range of situations where the topic of the report is of a 'low to middle level' of importance in terms of company affairs, and where the information assembled is relatively brief – say about two sides of A4 paper.

The use of the short informal report is perhaps best restricted to departments or sections, and where the report writer is making a report to an immediate superior on matters corresponding broadly to the following type of topics:

Revising staff holiday rota arrangements

Overcoming wasteful use of stationery

Late arrival at work of junior staff

The proposed purchase of a paper shredding machine

Such reports may be divided into three major sections:

1   An introductory section
Here the report's brief or 'terms of reference' are set out, the request for any recommendations confirmed and any specified deadline mentioned. Additionally, any relevant background information which indicates why the report was requested may be supplied. Essentially, this first section puts the reader clearly 'in the picture' on the need for and the scope of the report.

2   An informational section
This may be variously titled – Analysis of Problem, Findings, Information, etc and comprises the detailed sequence of data and researched material relevant to the report's terms of reference.

In the short informal report, such information may simply be a set of continuous prose paragraphs. Often, however, the reader is helped if each paragraph is given a clear heading to attract the eye. Since the report is short, it is not usually necessary to use an extensive number referencing system, but it may be helpful to number paragraphs.

3   A conclusions/recommendations section
Here, the two or three major factors are concisely summarised, and any recommendations supplied. It may be useful to number each recommendation.

Style: Since this type of report is of a relatively 'low status' and passes most usually between close colleagues, the first person 'I' construction is perfectly acceptable. However, you will note from the model on page 184, the author does not over-use this construction, preferring to keep the style as factual and impersonal as possible, letting the facts speak for themselves.

The short formal report

This type of report has five rather than three sections, since it is more suitable for handling complex material and dealing with matters of a wider and, in company terms, higher status, value. For example, it might well be used to relay information in the following types of area:

Relocating the manufacturing arm of the company in the north west

Trade union recognition

The following examples show the main techniques of schematic layout:

```
1  D O U B L E   S P A C I N G
        C A P I T A L S
   Use for titles, title page
   headings.

2  USE CAPITALS FOR MAJOR SECTION
   HEADINGS

   Remember to be consistent
   throughout.

3  Use Initial Capitals Underscored
   For Sub-Section Headings

   Again, use these consistently
   within each major section.

4  Employ a consistent system for
   numbering each part of the report.
   You could use: A,B,C, or I,II,
   III, a,b,c, i,ii,iii, etc for
   sub-sections.

   Note: one economic and neat way
   to number report items is to use
   1.0, 2.0, 3.0, etc for each major
   report section, and then divide
   each major section into a series
   of referenced sub-points eg 3.1,
   3.2, 3.3, for each of, say, three
   sub-sections of the third major
   section, 3.2.1, 3.2.2, etc for
   any further sub-divisions of a
   sub-section.

5  USE OF SPACE AND INDENTATION

   Do not be a miser with space!
   Leave lines blank above and below
   major section headings – and sub-
   section headings.  Also, start
   sub-section entries and any
   further sub-divisions nearer to
   the right-hand side of the paper
   – indenting.  (See 'Short formal
   report model' page  182.)

Note: Computer printers and
exchangeable daisy wheels in
typewriters have further extended
the scope of eye-catching layout
with features such as emboldening
of headings and key words and the
use of differing type founts.
```

Introducing an export sales department

Adopting a flexible working hours system

This type of report tends to be displayed in more schematic detail, and requires a more extensive use of number referencing, since it may be of some 5 to 30 or more A4 pages long.

In skeletal form, the short formal report's structure is as follows:

Structure of short formal report

1.0 TERMS OF REFERENCE

2.0 PROCEDURE

3.0 FINDINGS
    3.1 First main section
    3.2 Second main section
    3.3 Third main section
        3.3.1 Sub-section
            3.3.1.1 Sub-point etc

4.0 CONCLUSIONS

5.0 RECOMMENDATIONS
    5.1 First recommendation
    5.2 Second recommendation etc

(see page 186 for illustration)

Style: Since this report is usually sent to middle and top management, its style is more formal than any report circulating within a section or department. The impersonal third person constructions therefore are used throughout.

Report writing style: helpful tips

1　Prefer an impersonal style
Though it is quite acceptable to use 'I' constructions in more informal reports, the intrusion of personality is best avoided:

Personal: I spoke to the foreman who said that …
Impersonal: Discussions with the foreman revealed that …

To convey a neutral and impersonal style, the use of the passive voice of the verb is particularly helpful:

Active: *I examined* company sales statistics …

Passive: Company sales statistics *were examined* carefully … ('by me' is omitted)

The use of third person 'it' constructions is also helpful:

It became evident … It would be necessary to … It is suggested that …

Third person noun constructions similarly convey a neutral, objective style:

The introduction of work study is likely to improve productivity.

2　Avoid familiar, colloquial language
The inclusion of familiar expressions and constructions will tend to prevent the report from being taken seriously:

He reckoned the training scheme was *pretty useless.*
The new process has caused *a load of* problems.

3　Use conjunctions and linking phrases to show the connection between ideas
Some connecting words and phrases have the effect of reinforcing what has just been written:

Moreover, Furthermore, Indeed, In addition,

while others temper, qualify or balance a previous statement:

However, Nevertheless, On the other hand, Even so, It should be remembered, however, Although, Even though, etc.

Particularly useful are those sets of joining words which introduce statements to prove, justify or substantiate an assertion with a fact:

because, as, since, with the result that

Output is certain to fall *because* essential parts are in short supply.

4　Choose words and expressions which convey a precise meaning
The following examples illustrate words which convey a precise and objective meaning:
analysed … rather than looked into
inspected … rather than looked over
alternative solution … rather than another way of solving the problem
cross-section of staff … rather than some staff at all levels
surveyed customers' views … rather than customers' views were checked out

5　Avoid longwindedness and multisyllabic words
Prefer the short and simple word to the long and abstruse:

Not: Management submitted the sales turnover figures to a rigorous analysis and perceived an unacceptable level of error.

But: Management analysed the sales figures and found them to be wrong.

6 Wherever possible let facts and figures speak for themselves:

Absenteeism has risen by 17.4% in the first three months of this year.

Over 90% of those interviewed, some 54 staff, agreed that …

Sales turnover last month was £19 560, a decrease of 6.4% on July's figure.

7 Avoid making assertions which you cannot justify with fact:

It is clear that at least a third of departmental staff prefer the old system.

– Who says so? Can you prove it?

8 Remember that reports tend to be submitted to senior staff – so do not bully them!

Not: The bonus scheme must be introduced immediately or else staff will look for other jobs.

But: The board is requested to introduce the new bonus scheme as a matter of urgency in order to retain valuable staff.

Golden rules

Keep it clear. Keep it factual. Develop the argument in logical steps and support opinion with fact as much as possible. Keep it short! Everyone has more than enough to read these days.

Report assignments

Oral reports

1 In pairs, sit in on your next Student Association meeting and follow carefully, making any notes you need of the business conducted.

By agreement, one student makes an oral report of the meeting to his teacher. The other student assesses the accuracy and summarising ability of his partner.

2 Divide into two or more discussion groups. Choose a topic of current interest to debate – for example:

How can a business education course best prepare students for careers in a rapidly changing society?

Student observers should be attached to each group, and having listened carefully to the discussion, give an oral report of the views expressed to a general group session.

3 First carry out your research, then give an oral report to your group on what to look for when shopping for one of the following:

a pocket calculator   a hi-fi set   a 'Walkman' tape player   a pocket diary   a practical wristwatch

Written reports

Compose a short informal report to meet one of the following briefings:

4 'I'd like you to look into the study habits and practices of the students in your group and to make any recommendations which you think would help them to improve their study techniques. I shall need your report within seven days.' (Assume your teacher gave you the above terms of reference)

5 'I want to set up a sort of "mini library" of English language reference books for our secretarial and clerical staff. I have the money to buy five books to start with. I'd like you to look into what is available on the market and recommend to me five books which would provide a broad base from which to build. I'd like your report within a fortnight.'

6 'I've noticed recently that our departmental telephone bills are increasing dramatically! Staff are clearly adopting careless and expensive attitudes to making outside calls. I want you to look into the matter and then recommend what could be done to encourage staff to be more cost conscious when using the phone, and how we might control the expense more effectively. Could you have the report on my desk a fortnight from today, please.'

Compose a short formal report to meet the terms of reference of the following case study:

Your company: Amore Cosmetics Ltd is a medium sized firm which manufactures and distributes a range of beauty products from a single office and factory complex.

Your role: You work as assistant to Mr Keith Renshaw, general office manager, in the company's general office, which handles the administration of accounts, sales, personnel and records.

Your problem: At present, the work of the general office is carried out on the ground floor of the administration building in several smallish partitioned rooms. None of the partitions is load-bearing, and the overall floor area is some 20 metres long by 15 metres wide. The work of the department is divided into accounts, sales, personnel, secretarial servicing and clerical services and records; each section has a section head and about 4–6 associated staff. Currently, conditions of work are cramped and communications poor. As a result, Mr Renshaw has asked you to investigate the possibility of changing to an open-plan general office, and to make any appropriate recommendations to him.

Model of a short informal report

```
CONFIDENTIAL

FOR:      Mrs K Pearson, Office Manager

TO:       Christine Fellows, Personal Assistant

REF:      CF/AB

12 August 19--

REPORT ON THE PREVENTION OF WASTEFUL USE OF STATIONERY  ①

1.0  INTRODUCTION  ②

     On Tuesday 28 July, you asked me to investigate the current wasteful use
     of stationery in the department and to suggest ways in which it might be  ③
     used more economically in future.  My report was to be submitted to you
     by Friday 14 August 19--.

2.0  INFORMATION  ④

     2.1  Stationery Use Investigated  ⑤

          The range of departmental stationery investigated comprised:
          headed letterpaper and memoranda, associated copy paper and carbon
          paper, envelopes, duplicating masters and copy paper, photocopying
          stationery and continuous computer paper.

     2.2  Stationery Associated with Correspondence/Internal Mail

          The suspected increase in wasteful practices was confirmed upon
          investigation.  I spoke to executive staff who confirmed that a       ⑥
          significant proportion of typescript was being returned for retyping
          because of careless errors and poor standards of correction and
          erasure.  Faulty proof-reading was also marring word processed text.

          Observation and discussion with secretarial staff confirmed that      ⑥
          clerical and executive staff in particular are using printed
          stationery and unused envelopes on occasion as message pads.

          Regarding envelopes, white ones are being used where manilla would
          serve, and much non-confidential internal mail is being sent in
          sealed envelopes.  No member of staff appears to be re-using envelopes.

     2.3  Duplicating and Photocopying Stationery

          The photocopier is in need of servicing and staff are wasting
          extensive amounts of paper as a result of a fault which creases the
          paper.

          Though the increase in photocopying is in line with departmental work  ⑦
          (an increase of 11% in the last quarter) staff are tending to photo-
          copy when offset litho printing would be more economical and to despatch
          individual copies for information purposes when a single circulated
          initialled copy might suffice.

     2.4  Increase in Stationery Costs

          I analysed the cost of departmental stationery, comparing this year's
          second quarter with the first, and this year's consumption to date
          against last year's.

          The stationery bill for the second quarter of this year is 29% higher  ⑧
          than for the first quarter (Jan-March £607.22, April-June £788.31).

          Allowing for increases in price, the department's stationery bill for
          this year to date against an equivalent period last year is some 18%
          higher - £3416.30 compared with £2895.60 last year.  This increase
          does not appear to be justified by an equivalent increase in the output
          of the department.  Moreover, the rate of increase is rising.          ⑨
```

```
3.0   CONCLUSIONS  ⑩

        The investigations I have made do justify the concern expressed about
        excessive waste of office stationery and its impact on departmental
        running costs.

        The increase in careless use of stationery is not confined to one section ⑪
        but is to be found, in different forms throughout the department.  If
        action is not taken immediately the department is unlikely to keep within ⑪
        its administration budget.

        I should therefore like to recommend the following measures for your
        consideration:

        3.1  A meeting with senior secretarial staff should be called to discuss ⑫
             the gravity of the problem and to obtain their cooperation in improving
             secretarial performance.  A refresher course could be mounted by the
             training department.

        3.2  Control of stationery issue should be tightened; sections should be ⑫
             required to account quarterly for stationery if this proves practicable
             in principle.

        3.3  Departmental policy on internal mail procedures and message recording ⑫
             should be revised and all staff notified.

        3.4  An appraisal should be made on the possible savings to be made resulting ⑫
             from the introduction of NCR pre-printed forms (memoranda etc) from
             restricting access to and use of photocopying facilities.  Also, the
             cost effectiveness of storing data on computer disk and micro-fiche
             should be closely examined.
```

Reference heads section

The report is clearly headed with the appropriate information for despatch and filing.

Note the use of the CONFIDENTIAL classification resulting from the nature of the report's information, since some staff are clearly open to criticism.

A report's title ① should always indicate briefly yet clearly what it is about.

Introduction section

This section ② establishes concisely: What? Who? When? Why?

Note that from the outset it is clear that the report will include recommendations for action ③.

Information section

The INFORMATION section ④ could be made up simply of continuous prose paragraphs, but the inclusion of sub-headings ⑤ helps to break down the information into more easily digested sections, which emphasise the particular areas of investigation Christine Fellows thought important.

Note that the first sub-section identifies and defines the range of stationery to be investigated. In so doing, an effort has been made to break down the range into logical groupings.

Much of the report's information relies on Christine's observations and discussions with staff ⑥ and, in the report, takes the form of assertions. Mrs Pearson would need to rely on Christine's judgment – it is important, therefore, that in reports ⑦ investigators are just and fair,

and as far as possible, support their assertions ⑧ by quoting facts, figures or clearly evident practices. This reassures the report's reader that the report is based on fact, rather than opinion or purely personal views.

To this end, Christine has taken the trouble to examine the department's spending on stationery over the past 18 months. Her factual financial evidence is hard to ignore, and has the effect of emphasising the need for urgent action. ⑨

Conclusions section

In the short informal report, the CONCLUSIONS section ⑩ provides a summary of the main factors ⑪ which arise from the INFORMATION section, and also relays to the reader any suggestions or recommendations ⑫ which may have been asked for.

Note: In more complex reports, these two aspects, of summarising the findings of a report and then of specifying recommendations are in two separate sections.

In terms of the report's visual impact on the reader, it might have been helpful for Christine to have headed each recommendation with a suitable 'label':

Secretarial Staff

A meeting with senior ...

Such display techniques are a matter of personal judgment, since there are, in fact, no hard and fast rules governing report format; it is a matter of using most effectively the display facilities of the typewriter and setting out information in a logical and clear manner.

Model of a short formal report

CONFIDENTIAL

FOR: P J Kirkbride, Managing Director   REF: HTD/SC/FWH 4

FROM: H T Dickens, Chairman, Flexible Working   DATE: 14 February 19—
      Hours Working Party

REPORT ON THE PROPOSAL TO INTRODUCE A FLEXIBLE WORKING HOURS SYSTEM IN HEAD OFFICE

1.0   TERMS OF REFERENCE

       On 7 January 19— the managing director instructed a specially set up
       working party to investigate the practicality of introducing a system
       of flexible working hours in all head office departments, and to make
       appropriate recommendations. The report was to be submitted to him by
       21 February 19— for the consideration of the Board of Directors.

2.0   PROCEDURE

       In order to obtain relevant information and opinion, the following
       procedures were adopted by the working party to acquire the information
       in the report:

       2.1   Current office administration literature was reviewed.
              (Appendix 1 Bibliography refers.)
       2.2   A number of companies were visited which have adopted flexible
              working hours systems and the views of a wide range of staff
              were canvassed.
       2.3   Current departmental working loads and practices were observed
              and evaluated.
       2.4   Soundings of likely staff responses were obtained from departmental
              managers and senior staff.
       2.5   The cost of introducing a flexible working hours system was
              considered.

3.0   FINDINGS

       3.1   <u>Principles of the Flexible Working Hours System</u>

              The essence of a flexible working hours system consists of
              establishing two distinct bands of working hours within a weekly
              or monthly cycle and of ensuring that staff work an agreed total
              of hours in the cycle.

              3.1.1 Core Time Band

                    During this period (say 10 15 am to 3 45 pm) <u>all</u> staff are
                    present at work, allowing for lunch-time arrangements.

              3.1.2 Flexi-time Band

                    Periods at the beginning and end of the day (say 7 45 am to
                    10 15 am and 3 45 pm to 6 15 pm) are worked at the discretion
                    of individual staff members in whole or part, allowing for
                    essential departmental staff manning requirements.

              3.1.3 Credit/Debit Hour Banking

                    According to previously agreed limits and procedures, staff
                    may take time off if a credit of hours has built up, or make
                    time up, having created a debit to be made good. Most
                    companies require that the agreed weekly hours total (in the
                    case of head office staff 37½ hours per week) is reached but
                    not exceeded, though some firms adopt a more flexible approach,
                    which permits some time to be credited/debited in a longer cycle.

              3.1.4 Recording Hours Worked

                    In all systems, it is essential that logs or time-sheet
                    records are kept and agreed by employee and supervisor
                    for pay and staff administration reasons.

3.2 <u>Discussions with Departmental Managers</u>

Most departmental managers were in favour of introducing a flexible
working hours system, anticipating an improvement in both productivity
and staff morale. The sales manager saw advantages in his office
being open longer during the day to deal with customer calls and
visits. Reservations were expressed by both the office administration
and accounts managers arising from the likelihood of increased
workloads to administer the system.

3.3 <u>Sounding of Staff Opinion</u>

Discreet enquiries were made via senior staff regarding the likely
response of staff at more junior levels.

3.3.1 Summary of Favourable Responses

Secretarial staff in particular would welcome the means of
tailoring their work and attendance to fit in with their
principals' presences and absences. Many staff would enjoy
working when they felt at their personal 'peaks'. Over 35% of
female staff are mothers with children of school age, and would
probably welcome the opportunity to fit their work around
family responsibilites and according to seasonal daylight hours.
Weekday shopping opportunities would be improved and travelling
in peak rush-hour times avoided.

3.3.2 Summary of Unfavourable Responses

Few staff at junior levels intimated an unfavourable response
but more senior staff were concerned about key personnel not
being available when needed for consultation etc. Older staff
seemed less enthusiastic and any introduction of flexible
working hours would need to be carefully planned and full
consultation carried out.

3.4 <u>Cost of Introducing a Flexible Working Hours System</u>

The increase in costs of heating, lighting and administration of
the system would be offset to some degree by a decline in overtime worked and the cost of employing temporary staff to cover
for staff absences, which may be expected to reduce. (Appendix 3
provides a detailed estimate of the cost of introducing and
running a flexible working hours system.)

4.0 CONCLUSIONS

In the working party's view, the advantages of introducing a flexible
working hours system outweigh the disadvantages. Head office service to
both customers and field sales staff would improve; staff morale and
productivity are also likely to rise. Administrative costs do not appear
unacceptable and senior staff have the necessary expertise to make the
system work. Of necessity, the working party's view was broad rather
than detailed and the introduction of any flexible working hours system
should allow for the particular needs and problems of individual head
office departments to be taken into account as far as possible.

5.0 RECOMMENDATIONS

As a result of its investigations, the working party recommends that the
Board of Directors gives active consideration to the following:

5.1 That the introduction of a flexible working hours system be
accepted in principle by the Board and staff consultations
begun as soon as possible with a view to establishing a time-
table for implementing the change.

5.2 That all departmental managers be requested to provide a detailed
appraisal of their needs in moving over to a flexible working
hours system and of any problems they anticipate.

5.3 That a training programme be devised by personnel and training
departments to familiarise staff with new working procedures
and practices.

5.4 That a code of practice be compiled for inclusion in the
company handbook.

5.5 That arrangements be made to inform both field sales staff and
customers at the appropriate time of the advantages to them
of the introduction in head office of flexible working hours.

Computer networks in information technology

In the early 1980s two buzz or jargon words were to be heard in offices and read in IT equipment magazines. They were *convergence* and *networking*. Both were linked and marked a new phase in the development of IT in a business systems context.

Firstly, the idea of convergence had been evolving since the dedicated word processor was succeeded by the more versatile desk-top microcomputer which could process text, access files, be used with a variety of application packages and, in short, be employed in a far wider range of tasks. But at first, and like the dedicated WP machine, the desk-top micro tended to be used in a 'stand-alone' mode – that is, entirely independent of and unconnected to any other equipment save its own keyboard and printer.

However, alert data processing and office managers in companies quickly saw the advantages in setting up office networks by which all the IT equipment in use could be interconnected. For example, if you could despatch the word processed text just created in electronic code along a wire to the photocopier/printing machine where it could be decoded and its page format interpreted and acted upon, the desired number of copies of, say, a report could be duplicated and, with accompanying equipment, collated and bound untouched by human hand! Indeed,

this is just what was designed and constructed by various talented office equipment manufacturers and referred to as the 'intelligent photocopier'. To return to our buzz word, the use of two pieces of equipment 'converged' into one continuous flow of action.

By the same token, individual microcomputers on desks located in offices far distant from one another were connected to the same mainframe, midi- or mini-computer in which was stored the vast database of information for the entire company or public service organisation. As a result, the microcomputer could be used, either as a stand alone unit, employing its own memory and software, or it could access information stored in the central computer and act solely as a 'dumb terminal', and use the power of operation present in the big mainframe or mini.

In addition, each micro owner could route electronic messages or mail via the mainframe to remotely located colleagues by sending them through the telephone line networks of British Telecom. And so our second buzz word came into common use – networking.

The proper term for a network set up within a relatively small area – say a multi-storey office block, a series of buildings on a campus or site, or in the same town, is Local Area Network (LAN). When the network is more widely established, i.e. within the UK or transglobally, then it is known as a Wide Area Network (WAN). The diagram below illustrates the way in which an organisation may link into a Wide Area Network and use Local Area Network connections in its local work.

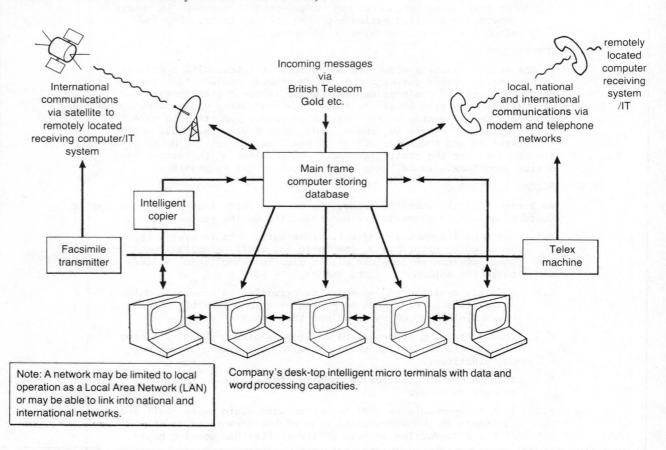

International communications via satellite to remotely located receiving computer/IT system

Incoming messages via British Telecom Gold etc.

local, national and international communications via modem and telephone networks

remotely located computer receiving system /IT

Main frame computer storing database

Intelligent copier

Facsimile transmitter

Telex machine

Note: A network may be limited to local operation as a Local Area Network (LAN) or may be able to link into national and international networks.

Company's desk-top intelligent micro terminals with data and word processing capacities.

The IT company network for local to global communication

There are three particular advantages of setting up networking facilities in an organisation. Firstly, a wide range of applications packages may be stored within a mainframe computer or a powerful, hard disk microcomputer which, in both instances, can download them or make them available to individual users connected to the network. Also, a printer or printers may be connected to the network and devices installed to minimise the time spent in users having to 'queue' to have their work printed.

The second and indeed very useful feature of the network lies in its ability to transmit and receive – almost instantly – electronic mail. By the mid 1980s, software houses and computer manufacturers were designing ever more effective yet simple-to-use packages. These enable their users to reduce the paper they have to read, file and despatch. Incoming electronic messages can be logged in by time and date and, in some cases, they can flash up their presence on a screen in use in between an operator's work on it, or activate a flashing signal on a keyboard. The receiver can either read and delete each incoming message, store it electronically, or obtain a print-out and send an answer in moments. And the returned message does not have to linger in an out-tray, mailroom and mailbag for hours or days! The package which supports electronic mail will often also provide the user with a computer diary which can be scrolled back and forth or skip to days in coming months, scan other users' diaries and yield the next date and time when, say, four busy executives are all able to get together for a meeting. In addition, it will keep all sorts of 'housekeeping data' such as often used telephone numbers, addresses, technical data etc. in a library for personal access and will send out simultaneously upon demand the same message to, say, fifteen section staff.

The third major advantage of the network is that it enables personnel, even at a far distance from a head office, to obtain up-to-the-minute information and to react to it. For example, the price of shares on the London Stock Exchange can be accessed by stockbrokers in small Scottish or Welsh towns and deals done just as readily as if they were sited in the City of London. Similarly, a sales representative in the far west of Cornwall can either drop into the local company branch office to check his electronic mail via computer terminal or even send in a sales order for prompt processing from a public phone box on a Cornish moor!

The advent, then, of converging of fully interconnected IT office equipment in either a local or wide area network has given a tremendous boost to speeding up communication, improving the quality of decision-making and saving both time and money. Of course it costs money to set up a network, but like factories, offices nowadays require a good deal of investment in modern electronic equipment in order to keep pace with innovative competitors.

Activities and assignments

Organisational structure

1 Find out what the expressions 'line management' and 'staff management' mean. Explain the ideas behind these concepts and point out to your group the difference between having a job in a 'line management' framework and in a 'staff' framework.

2 Design a chart which illustrates the line management structure of your college or school.

Communication climates

3 Interview one of your parents, relatives or a family friend on the subject of his or her experiences when going through the 'fitting in' period when starting a new job. Keeping your information suitably anonymous, report back to your group on what you discovered. Compare notes in your group and see if there are any common threads running through people's experiences which could provide you with helpful guidance for the future.

Tone and style

4 During the next week, collect a set of oral and written examples of a wide range of formal and informal tone and style in communications. For example, you could record extracts of radio interviews, collect newspaper cuttings and advertisements, or jot down remarks you hear. From your material, design a poster which shows the communications ranging from very formal to very informal. Indicate the *contexts* in which the communication was relayed. Display your poster in your classroom for your student group to view and discuss.

Giving a talk

5 Prepare carefully and thoroughly, and then carry out one of the following assignments.

Compose your notes and any suitable AVA material and then give a talk to *another class* in your school or college entitled:
HOW TO GIVE AN EFFECTIVE TALK *or*
HOW TO WRITE AN EFFECTIVE REPORT

Afterwards, describe to your group how your talk went – its effectiveness from your point of view, remembering that you were speaking to a group you did not know well, this time.

6 First carry out your research then, with appropriate illustrations, give an oral account to your group on how integrated computer software packages (WP, graphics, spreadsheets, etc.) are giving reports a much more stimulating and eye-catching format when printed. Note your presentation may also include colour pictures.

Spelling and usage

7 Correct the mistakes you spot in the following:

(a) Practise makes perfect!

(b) Lengthy sentance structures tend to loose me!

(c) The procecuting council winded up his case briefly but pursuasively.

(d) The vehical was stationery when hit in the behind.

(e) Ideally, I should like to persue a fully independent lifestyle, which I would have less obligations in and more personnel fullfilment.

(f) She was laying in the sun to long and consequentially has aquired a nastey sunburn.

(g) Alright! Whose borrowed my errasser without asking me permission.

(h) Its no good complaining, each of you are responsable for her own posessions. If you let other people lend your own things, youve only yourself to blame if their not returned.

Punctuation revision

8 Punctuate the following passage:

the report entitled overcoming high staff turnover has now received the personnel managers careful study mr stephens agrees with its major recommendations which he feels should be discussed at next weeks management committee meeting the need for the company to tackle the problem is urgent if staff continue to leave the firms employ at the current rate we shall to quote an apt if colloquial proverb find ourselves up the creek without a paddle I therefore recommend that you circulate the report to the following staff who are directly concerned with employee supervision miss wells personnel department mr hawkins office administration department mrs larkin accounts department and mr osgood sales department

Computer networks in IT

9 Explain briefly the meaning of the following terms:

dedicated word processor
stand alone
convergence of electronic office equipment
intelligent photocopier/printer
electronic mail
LAN   WAN

10 In your own words, summarise three main advantages which the networking of IT equipment can provide in organisations.

11 Find out which firms locally have access to a network and through your teacher make arrangements to interview selected user staff. Report your findings orally to your group.

12 Find out what it means in a large organisation to have a 'real time' database of information available for individual staff to access. Also, find out what precautions are taken in data processing departments to ensure that the database is not all lost in some power-cut catastrophe.

Unit 11

The factory

As we have already discovered, business organisations may be divided roughly into those which provide a service – retailers, banks, advertising agencies and so on – and those which manufacture goods. Such manufacturers range from the international giants with factories all over the world, to the small 'backroom' type of manufacturer who makes small and often highly specialised parts for a larger industrial firm.

Whether carried out in vast hangar-like factories or in small workshops, the process of manufacturing is complex and during the past 20–30 years has become much more so because of advancing technologies linked to micro-processors and laser beams.

The diagram shows the main activities which, together, go to make up what is often referred to as 'the manufacturing arm' of a company. As consumers, only interested in the 'end-product' of a good-looking, reliable, inexpensively priced motor-bike, car, television or washing machine, we all tend to take for granted the hundreds or thousands of people within any company. We forget the very extensive teamwork, communication networks and cooperation that are needed to transform an idea in a designer's head into a reality available from any one of thousands of shops and stores either in our home country or abroad.

One of the best ways in which to gain an insight into manufacturing is to consider stage-by-stage the various departments, sections or units which form the manufacturing arm.

Research and development

In competitive economies, where consumers are given a wide choice of goods or products, the research and development department is absolutely vital, and companies funnel often immense sums of money into laboratory or design research in order to bring a better product or an entirely new concept to the consumer. Mobile computers, anti-depressant drugs, cellular telephones and 'pocket' colour television sets are just a few of the revolutionary products which we take for granted today. In close touch with the research and development phase of manufacturing are the marketing staff, who are constantly monitoring what competitors are doing, and 'guesstimating' what consumers will be wanting to buy sometimes as many as five years hence.

Marketing liaison
'Next year we're convinced we need to be making X s as well as Y s to meet market demands, but it'll mean re-tooling!'

Research and development
'We turn ideas into prototypes!'

Sales liaison
'Is that the works manager? Oh, good! Well, we've just sold another 500 X s, but they want 'em by next Monday. Any chance?'

Purchasing and stores
'If we haven't got them, you can't use them!'

Toolroom
'We make the tools that make the goods!'

Work study, organisation and methods
'There must be a more efficient way...!'

Cost control
'Yes, but we still have to make them at a profit!'

The works
'Where it all comes together!'

Drawing office
'From rough designs to detailed specifications people can work to!'

Nothing gets made without a lot of communication and teamwork!

Prototype design

(H) Once an idea has been proved practicable in principle, it becomes necessary to build a prototype or 'first go' of the product to carry out extensive tests upon. At this stage, factory tool designers will be working closely with the prototype designers to ensure that the factory has the production facilities to make the new product. Sometimes new tools or 'jigs' are needed to make parts of the product.
(I) Sometimes manufacturing techniques which seemed viable at the early design stage have to be modified to fit into the scope of resources which the company has, either in terms of its existing plant and equipment or factory staff expertise. Where either is lacking, new plant or new experts may have to be acquired. But this costs money the firm may not have! Compromising is an art of successful manufacture.

Cost control

Keeping an 'eagle eye' on all the above developments will be the company's cost accountants – there's little point in designing and making a product which cannot be sold at a profit. The company's purchasing department has a key role to play, ensuring that raw materials or semi-made goods or finished component parts are of an acceptable standard but bought in at the right price. Similarly, the company's work study or organisation and methods staff will be minutely examining the techniques of production, both in terms of what equipment can do and what factory staff can do to produce goods as efficiently as possible.
(J) They will help to ensure that labour-saving and cost-saving techniques are introduced to keep production costs down and the quality of manufacture up.

Production

Bringing all this effort together are the works management staff, shopfloor supervisors and operative staff – 'the makers'. Planning here is essential, since it is very expensive to keep assembly lines closed and workers standing idle as a result of bad planning – some of the parts may not be available because insufficient stocks are held, or poor maintenance of a piece of machinery may lead to its breakdown in the middle of a production run. During
(K) production, expert staff who work in quality assurance will be taking samples of products and will inspect them to ensure that as few defective products as possible are made only then to be scrapped.

Also, in view of the very nature of repetitive production processes, managers need to ensure that staff are looked after and that their conditions of service are made as attrac-

tive as possible, so that poor morale does not affect the quality of the production process. Indeed this aspect is vital in all manufacturing processes, for when indifference leads to carelessness and slapdash standards of production, the entire company is heading for deep trouble! No-one wants to buy unreliable products and as orders dwindle, the very survival of the firm may soon be in (L) jeopardy. For this reason, many manufacturers have gone to great lengths to make the production process more satisfying for its workforce; in some instances the 'A to Z' assembly-line, in which operatives carry out only a small part of the making process, has been replaced by fully- (M) integrated teams making the entire product. They see and therefore take more pride in the end-product. Today, microprocessor and laser technology – manufacturing robotics – can take much of the drudgery out of manufacturing, but perhaps at the cost of causing redundancies of factory staff. This is a potentially grave problem which advanced technological societies have yet to resolve.

Marketing and sales

While the R & D and tooling processes are being carried out, the marketing and sales staff will not have been idle. From the very outset of manufacturing a new product, strategies have to be worked out on how best to market and sell it. Early samples of the product will be test-marketed to make sure that both design and packaging are effective; advertising campaigns will be created in order to generate demand for the product. The sales force will need to be trained in how to present and sell the product to distributors and retailers, and they in turn will need to be provided with posters, brochures, samples and special offer facilities, etc to merchandise the product at the point (N) of sale. Moreover, company accountants will need to ensure that the whole design, production, marketing and sales promotion activities are kept under strict financial control, to ensure that this complex activity results in an acceptable profit flowing back into the company.

Mastering the meaning

1 Explain briefly in your own words the meaning of:

international giants   Line A
'end-product'   Line B
to transform an idea in a designer's head into a reality   Line C
competitive economies   Line D
an entirely new concept   Line E

revolutionary products   Line F
constantly monitoring what competitors are doing   Line G
Once an idea has been proved practicable in principle   Line H
viable at the early design stage   Line I
labour-saving and cost-saving techniques   Line J
quality assurance   Line K
the very survival of the firm may soon be in jeopardy   Line L
fully-integrated teams making the entire product   Line M
to merchandise the product at the point of sale   Line N

2 Why do many manufacturers spend immense sums of money on research and development?

3 Why is marketing so closely involved with the research and development of a product?

4 What is meant by the statement at the end of the fifth paragraph, 'Compromising is an art of successful manufacture'?

5 Explain briefly the role of the cost accountant in the manufacturing process.

6 Why is work study important in production processes?

7 Explain why planning is a key factor in factory production management.

8 What happens when quality assurance fails to do its job?

9 In about 60 words, outline the reasons for works management needing to 'look after' operatives.

10 Explain briefly the role of marketing and sales in the manufacturing process.

Discussion topics

1 What communication practices do you think it would be helpful to use in manufacturing to ensure that such an involved activity is successfully carried out?

2 Why do you suppose that some factories have moved away from assembly-line techniques of production? What is likely to happen to production costs?

3 What social dangers may be associated with the introduction of robotics into manufacturing?

4 Should the consumer accept that mass production inevitably leads to inferior standards of quality and reliability, and that this is part and parcel of being able to buy very sophisticated products relatively cheaply?

Activities

1 By arrangement, visit a local factory and, having observed its work and talked to staff, write an account of what you discovered.

2 Seek out among your relatives or friends someone who can tell you what it is like to be:

(*a*) A works manager
(*b*) A toolmaker
(*c*) A works foreman
(*d*) A factory operative
(*e*) An apprentice in an engineering company
(*f*) A work study officer
(*g*) A cost accountant

Make notes of your conversation and report back in suitably anonymous terms on what you discovered.

3 Carry out your research carefully, finding out both the management and trade union viewpoint and then give an illustrated talk to your group on one of the following:

(*a*) The future of manufacturing.
(*b*) Is the closed shop justifiable?
(*c*) Is the idea of apprenticeship dead?
(*d*) Information technology in manufacturing – blessing or burden?
(*e*) A career in manufacturing administration.

Note: The talk may be researched and presented by a group.

4 Write an article intended for your local newspaper entitled: 'The challenges facing manufacturers today'.

Boost your spelling power!

Learn these key words by heart

Remember, an asterisk after a word indicates that it is very commonly misspelled:

aerial n   (aeroplane n)
chaos n   (adj chaotic)
discipline n, v   (disciplinarian n)
especial adj   (especially* adv)
forty n, adj   (fortieth adj)
hurried adj   (hurriedly adv)
inoculate v   (inoculation n)
lounge v, n   (lounging pres part)
marriage n   (marriageable adj)
opinion* n   (opinionated past part v)

pastime n
recommend* v   (recommendation n)
secretaries* n   (secretarial adj)
transient adj   (transience n)
unnecessary* adj
view* n, v
wield v   (unwieldy adj)
aggravate v   (aggravation n)
choice n, adj
dissatisfied   (dissatisfaction n)
    past part v

Do not forget to enter in your vocabulary book any words with which you are unfamiliar, either in terms of spelling or meaning!

Assignment

By arrangement, choose four of the above words. Compose a sentence for each, in which the word is used correctly. Compare your sentences with those devised by others in your group. This will help you to add the above list of words to your **active vocabulary.**

Storing data in research and development

Quality assurance

Analyses of tasks in work study

Computerised production processes

Information technology – integrates the whole manufacturing process!

Today many manufacturing organisations are proceeding to integrate their entire manufacturing operation through the application of IT in each phase – from early design models to the testing of finished goods. This technology helps to keep costs down and quality and sales up!

Computerised stock control and handling

Computerised planning of production runs and batches

IT in manufacturing

Just as the advent of IT has revolutionised office practices and office equipment design, so in the same way have computers and microprocessor-based tools transformed the ways in which products are designed, manufactured and tested for quality. Furthermore, IT is now intimately involved in the cost-effective distribution of goods from factory to retail store.

In the past ten years, many working practices in factories and workshops which have been followed for over half a century have been swept aside as highly sophisticated equipment has been brought into factories to make goods quicker, cheaper and freer from fault. This process, however, has not always been a respecter of persons and sometimes long-serving operators and machine technicians have suffered when their jobs have

One of the four robots on the automatic direct glazing system on the Montego line at Cowley fits a rear screen.

(B) been taken over by tireless, undemanding robots. On the positive side, it could be argued that robotics or Computer Aided Manufacture (CAM) is taking the mind-blowing
(C) boredom out of repetitive manufacturing processes; on the other hand, some parts of the UK have not seen an antici-pated blossoming of service industry job substitutes and
(D) repetitive but gainful employment is to be much preferred to demoralising unemployment. IT in manufac-turing, then, should not be seen simply as a process of introducing ever more efficient and economic production techniques, but as a two-edged sword, where an accom-panying challenge for governments, multi-national companies and local councils exists in finding alternative
(E) and dignified roles and opportunities for those displaced along the way.

Despite such worrying problems, however, the intro-duction of IT in manufacturing has proceeded apace principally because of the need for manufacturers to keep abreast of their competitors and to stay in the race in terms of continuing to make goods at a profit. If the firm down the road has introduced robotics and CAM equipment and is working shifts around the clock, other things being equal, it will make goods cheaper and with fewer faults. Unless fellow manufacturers follow suit, they are likely to
(F) go out of business, and so an almost irresistible pressure has arisen for them to join the IT users before it is too late.

The main areas in manufacturing in which the introduc-tion of IT has played an important part follow.

Impact of IT upon manufacturing

Manufacturing area	IT activity
Research and Design (R&D)	Modelling with computers. Simulating the actions/ operations of prototype products. Designing products by computer – CAD (Computer Aided Design).
Supplies/inventory/ stock control	Computerised control of purchasing amounts and frequencies, tied in with holding optimum stock levels and maintaining planned production.
Production processes & operations	Use of computer controlled equipment to make goods and carry out production operations automatically and within close tolerances.
Quality assurance	Use of computers to monitor testing of product processes along the way and to test finished products so as to minimise waste: electronic sensors can even test check car engines for hidden faults!

Management services: work study	Computers help work study officers to plan the most efficient methods of carrying out production tasks and how best to lay out production lines.
Works management	Computers are being employed increasingly to forecast production peaks and troughs so that neither jams or bottle-necks occur on the one hand, and plant and operatives do not stand idle on the other.
Cost accountants	Computers are helping cost accountants to keep a close and accurate check on 'work in progress', so that the costs of each washer, nut, bolt, bonus, wasted part, etc. are minutely monitored and controlled to keep the whole complicated production process within pre-set costs and budgets.

Talking point

Many traditional UK industries – ship-building, heavy engineering, motor-cycle manufacture, motor-car manufacture – have declined over the past 30 years. Optimists in industry and government have spoken of IT-based 'sunrise' industries which will take their place and thus provide alternative employment in jobless areas. What do you think these new 'sunrise' industries might manufacture? Do you think that the manufacturing industry is going through a temporary phase, and that the pendulum will swing back again to the virtual full employment of the 1960s, as new products are invented and introduced, or do you think that countries like Britain should concentrate more on alternative money-making sectors like tourism, banking and insurance, writing software programs, producing hand-made craft goods?

What future trends do *you* predict in *your* working life?

This brief overview of the impact of IT in manufacturing serves to show how extensive has been the acceptance of the computer and microprocessor-based equipment among far-sighted organisations. Very often, the benefits of introducing IT, i.e.

- improvements in design

- shorter development periods for new products
- cutting of manufacturing costs
- saving of money via smaller inventory
- saving on waste from defective manufacture
- saving on time and effort in production operations
- making more goods from the same investment, etc.

has meant that more orders have been obtained and goods sold, making the jobs of all those involved in the manufacturing process more secure and better paid.

IT in manufacturing assignments

Mastering the meaning
First re-read the section entitled 'IT in Manufacturing' and then either orally or in writing, answer the following questions:

1 In your own words, explain the meaning of the following words or phrases:

the cost-effective distribution of goods from factory to retail store   Line A

tireless and undemanding robots   Line B

the mind-blowing boredom ... of repetitive manufacturing processes   Line C

repetitive but gainful employment is to be much preferred to demoralising unemployment   Line D

alternative and dignified roles for those displaced along the way   Line E

an almost irresistible pressure has arisen to join the IT users before it is too late   Line F

2 Explain in your own words why the introduction of IT applications into manufacturing is a 'two-edged sword'.

3 What do you think are the attractions for the directors of manufacturing companies in installing robotics and Computer Aided Manufacturing systems into their factories?

4 How do you think the use of a computer could help to reduce the amount of stocks being held for use in the manufacturing process?

5 What factors do you think cause a factory's production lines to have either too much or too little to do at certain times of the year? How do you think IT could help solve this kind of problem?

6 If you owned a factory, would you want to introduce CAD-CAM? If so, what steps might you consider taking to minimise the loss of jobs which could arise?

Follow up assignments

1 By arrangement with your teacher in small groups visit a range of local factories where IT is being employed in the ways outlined in the above passage. Talk to personnel in the various manufacturing departments, i.e. R&D, Work Study, Production and so on and then carry out one of the following assignments:

(*a*) Write an account of the ways in which the introduction of IT has changed the ways in which the manufacturing process is carried out, highlighting any advantages and disadvantages you discover.

(*b*) Discuss in your group what you felt were the reactions to the changes which you found in the people you spoke to. Be sure to respect the confidential nature of any informal chats by keeping the sources of your information anonymous.

(*c*) After having carried out your researches during visits to local manufacturers, write an article for your college/school magazine entitled:

'The challenges of introducing IT into manufacturing'

(*d*) As a result of your direct experiences from visiting local manufacturing organisations, write an article for your college/school magazine entitled:

'The pluses of making a career in manufacturing'

Your article should cover the range of career opportunities appropriate to students in your group.

Talking point

Having seen production processes going on at first hand, do you think that people – as consumers – take too much for granted the inventiveness of designers and production engineers? What do you think could be done to publicise more effectively the important role in the UK economy which manufacturing industry has?

Grammar

The mis-related participle

As we have already discovered, there are two parts of the verb which may be used as other parts of speech:

running water
present participle used as an adjective

His *leaving* was expected.
present participle used as a noun (gerund)

Jenny's *broken* nail irritated her.
past participle used as an adjective

The *experienced* know when to keep silent.
past participle used as a noun

In addition, participial constructions may be formed from the present participle. They act in an adjectival way to describe in more detail a noun or pronoun:

Climbing the hill without a pause, they soon ran out of breath.

Here, it is a 'climbing-the-hill' they who are being described.
Such constructions may also be written in a past tense:

Having climbed the hill without a pause, they fell breathless on the grass.

Again, it is 'they' who are being described.
But consider carefully the following:

Going down the road, the tile fell on his head.
Eating faster than the rest, his plate was soon empty.
Having reached the office late, the telephone was ringing persistently for his attention.

In each of the above illustrations, the participial construction has been mis-related. It is not the tile which was going down the road, nor the plate which had a better appetite, nor the telephone which was late in arriving at the office! The confusion in such sentences arises from an over-compressed set of ideas which the author needs to expand in order to make the meaning clear rather than ludicrous:

As he was going down the road, the tile …
Eating faster than the rest, he emptied his plate before the others.
Having reached the office late, he found the telephone ringing persistently for his attention.

It is often a useful technique to vary sentence structures by starting them with such participial constructions, but the golden rule is:

After such constructions, *the very next word* must be the noun or pronoun being described.

Assignment

Re-write the following sentences correctly, changing their structure as little as possible.

1 Inserting the typewriter ribbon, which was a rather messy job as far as Tracy was concerned, the platen somehow became loose.

2 On finishing the final page of the report, the bell rang and it was time for the break Jim had been waiting for.

3 Having entered the column of figures carefully in ink on the page, a mistake in the last line caused Sheila to utter a heartfelt groan of dismay.

4 Dictating the letter at an impossibly fast speed in order to catch the 10.40 am train, the completely empty shorthand notebook of his new secretary entirely failed to catch the busy manager's eye, as he grabbed his briefcase and swept out of the office.

Gerund revision

Is there anything wrong with the following?

1 My mother does not like me coming home late.

2 As you requested, I spoke to them about them leaving the job unfinished.

3 Miss Jones doesn't mind us staying on late, provided that we switch the lights off and lock up before we go.

4 I can quite understand my supervisor insisting on high standards being maintained.

5 I wish to avoid you making the same mistake again.

Manufacturing assignment

The following words and phrases are frequently used in the context of manufacturing. Choose two of them. Carefully research their meaning, and explain them to other members of your group:

arbitration	British Standard
assembly-line	time-and-a-half
closed shop	guaranteed overtime
convenor	shopfloor

industrial action	shop steward
industrial relations	working to rule
job enrichment	official strike
mass production	unofficial strike
output	reject
flat rate	swarf
piecework	milling
shiftwork	grinding
heavy engineering	re-tooling
light engineering	jig
productivity	specification
robotics	

Using reported speech

Reported speech, sometimes called indirect speech, is the name given to the kind of writing which reports what someone else has said:

'I'm sorry I'm late. I missed the bus.' DIRECT SPEECH

He said that he was sorry he was late. He had missed the bus. REPORTED SPEECH VERSION

The above reported speech example has deliberately followed the direct speech quotation as closely as possible to show what happens to the person 'I' and the verbs 'am' and 'missed'. But it is important to realise from the start, that reported speech often paraphrases or gives the gist of the direct speech:

He apologised for being late. He had missed the bus.

The rules for writing reported speech are quite straightforward, provided that a careful eye is kept on one or two traps.

Rule one: persons/pronouns

Basically, the rule is that first or second persons, singular or plural become third person in reported speech:

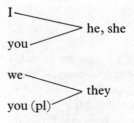

Personal pronouns already in the third person remain so. Note that the forms of the personal pronoun sometimes change:

'Would you like any more?'
He asked *them* if they would like any more.

Rule two: the tenses of verbs

The tense of the verb in direct speech goes 'one further back' in reported speech:

I write	he/she wrote
I am writing …	he/she was writing
I wrote …	he/she had written/wrote
I was writing	he/she had been writing
I have written …	he/she had written
I have been writing	he/she had been writing
I had written …	he/she had written (cannot go further back)

Notice that future tenses become conditional:

I shall write	he/she would write
I shall be writing …	he/she would be writing
I shall have written …	he/she would have written

The conditional is needed because it is an intention to write and we don't know whether 'he' actually did!

Rule three: the distancing effect

When people use direct speech – say in a meeting – the event is happening 'here and now'. When the meeting is reported at a later date, however, the discussion is in the past and took place 'there and then'. For this reason, a number of words and expressions need to be adjusted:

today … that day, now … then, here … there, this … that, these … those, tomorrow … the next/following day, yesterday … the previous day

Rule four: conveying the tone of the direct speech

If the reported speech writer is not very careful, the reporting may easily slip into a dull 'he said, she said, he said, she said', so it is important to vary the words that introduce the reported speech:

asked that, wondered whether, strongly denied that, confirmed that, suggested that, etc

In this way, the reader of the reported speech gains a better understanding of the tone of the direct speech.

Assignment

Re-write the following sentences in reported speech:

1 'I shall see you tomorrow'.

2 'Can you tell me when you will have an answer?'

3 'I certainly never said that!'

4 'Good afternoon, ladies and gentlemen, I am very pleased to be here today to talk to you about safety in the office,' said Mr Jones, the speaker.

5 'We shall be seeing him next Thursday, when the sales staff go to the conference,' said Mr Smith, the sales manager.

Meetings and committees

Most organisations, whether companies, councils or clubs, conduct much of their business through the medium of the meeting. Some meetings are held because the law requires it, others simply because the direct exchange of people's views and attitudes is felt to be the best way of arriving at decisions or solving problems. Meetings can range from the very formal, with complex rules of procedure, to the very informal, just guided conversations. Yet all meetings have one thing in common: to channel the group expertise of a number of people to achieve a set of goals or objectives. Though some meetings are called in organisations merely to impart information, usually referred to as briefings, most involve the participants in making of decisions as a group.

The active involvement of people in meetings helps to improve their commitment to a task or activity and also improves their morale – they are not continually being told what to do, but helping to decide what to do. For this reason, many organisations set up committees, working parties or study groups to investigate, recommend, put into action or to report back. Though costly and often time-consuming, senior managers often use the meeting for decision-making and communication because it enables experts to be brought together, encourages a feeling of involvement and helps to break down the 'us and them' barrier. And certainly, the old adage, 'two heads are better than one', still applies.

Many meetings are of a structured group of people called a committee. Over the years, the committee has been introduced into almost every area of commercial and public life. Its administration is shown opposite, and the roles of its members described on pages 201 and 202. Basically, a committee comprises a leader – coordinator, usually referred to as the chairman (or chairperson), an administrative assistant, the secretary, and a treasurer, who acts as a guardian of all financial matters. A senior committee member may act as vice-chairman. Committee members may have no special role, but in some committees, specific tasks are assigned and titles given such as publicity officer. Committees may have the power to carry out decisions reached and are then called 'executive committees', or they may only have the power to advise a more senior executive body, in which case they are termed 'advisory'. In addition, from main committees a series of subcommittees may be formed to carry out routine or 'one-off' tasks and are then called standing sub-committees or *ad hoc* sub-committees.

A meeting has been called ...

Statutory	... because the law demands it	shareholders', creditors', directors', councillors' meetings
Managerial	... to progress company affairs	to inform of policy, to brief, to delegate tasks, to discuss problems, to reach group decisions, etc
Creative	... to generate ideas, to open up new possibilities or avenues of action	to 'brainstorm' around the idea of what the firm could design, manufacture; to produce an advertising slogan, poster, etc
Negotiating	... to reach a solution to a problem acceptable to two sides with different interests	management and trade union to agree pay increases
General/public	... to report back to a group membership, or to air matters of public interest	Annual General Meeting of shareholders or club membership meetings; public enquiries into planning proposals

The 10 stages of committee meeting administration

		What?	Who?	Why?	When?
1	Minutes of the last meeting	Promptly after the meeting, the secretary expands the rough notes taken and produces a summarised account of the meeting.	Secretary drafts and chairman is consulted before duplication and despatch.	It is important that before despatching any summary of the meeting it is carefully checked for errors or omissions and to ensure its wording is not liable to misinterpretation.	Week One
2	Notice of the next meeting	Advance notice of the date, time and venue for the next meeting is sent to committee members, who may be asked to submit items for the agenda to the secretary. Minutes and notice are often despatched together.	Secretary draws up the notice – using either a pre-printed form, individual letter or memorandum depending on committee custom.	Notices should be sent out early to confirm the date, time, place of the meeting so that members have sufficient opportunity to prepare. For some meetings, the advance period of notice is set down by law.	
3	Agenda of next meeting – for committee members	Allowing time for items or suggestions to be sent in from members, the secretary drafts the agenda after consultation with the chairman. The agenda is sent with any other papers, reports or schedules which members need to refer to before the meeting.	Secretary in consultation with chairman (who has last word). If members are not to 'opt out', it is important that they feel involved in the compilation of agendas.	The structuring of the agenda needs care. Too long an agenda will result in members becoming restive. The chairman will wish to ensure that the agenda reflects the important issues to be discussed and so will insert these directly after routine items.	Week Two
4	Chairman's agenda drawn up	The secretary compiles an individual agenda for the chairman. It has the same headings as that for committee members, but also includes helpful reminders, notes or additional information.	Secretary for the chairman's exclusive use.	To chair a meeting effectively, the chairman needs to appear 'in touch' and authoritative at all times. Thus the chairman's agenda helps him via the secretary's often detailed knowledge of past and present decisions and attitudes.	Week Three
5	Correspondence	The secretary collects any correspondence related to the meeting, and makes copies for members if needed.	Secretary to outside contacts; outside contacts to the committee.		
6	Late arriving information	Any late developments or papers connected with the meeting are recorded or put in order.	Secretary for chairman, self, individual committee officers or all committee.	Inevitably, some information arrives late or needs to be included in items like 'Matters Arising'.	
7	Apologies for absence	The secretary receives and notes apologies from members unable to attend.	Committee members.	It is an essential courtesy to inform the secretary in advance if a member is unable to attend.	
8	Committee room prepared	Any seating preparations, stationery requirements or refreshment needs are seen to by the secretary before the meeting starts.	Secretary with company personnel or owners/landlords of hired rooms.	Business is better conducted and decisions better reached when the meeting is conducted in well-prepared surroundings	Week Four
9	Emergency spares of documents	Spare copies of agendas, relevant papers, minutes, a reserve chairman's agenda, etc. are prepared and taken into the meeting.	Secretary.	The chairman could be taken ill suddenly or called away, and the vice-chairman have to take over. Also, some members may need 'mothering!'	
10	Last minute conference	The chairman and secretary confer immediately before meeting to check any last minute amendments to notes, possible developments, etc.	Chairman and secretary.	It is sometimes necessary to anticipate problems or 'delicate' subject areas where feelings may run high.	

Once the meeting has been held, the secretary goes back to square one, to repeat the process over again for the next monthly committee meeting.

Committee members' roles

The chairman's role	to coordinate the work of the committee; to ensure that rules and procedures are kept to; to run meetings so that all members have a chance to air their views; to act as 'umpire' over disagreements; to steer the committee along avenues of decision-making; to ensure that documents and records are efficiently kept; to foster goodwill and working relationships among members; to act as the committee's leader and guide.
The secretary's role	to carry out the administrative work of the committee; to organise its meetings and to record the minutes; to liaise with the chairman regarding the general running of the committee; to keep committee members and associated parties informed; to act as the chairman's 'right hand'.
The treasurer's role	to monitor the committee's financial activities; to record all its money transactions and to submit regular reports to the committee and also annual balance sheets; to liaise with an external auditor who scrutinises the books; to advise the committee in matters of financial expenditure.
The committee member's role	to participate at meetings and do work delegated to him or her in the process of advising or decision-making; to attend meetings regularly and to offer information, views and responses either by means of voting or making views known to the chairman; to keep staff or interested parties he or she represents informed of the work the committee is doing and the decisions it has reached.

Special terms for meetings

Start your collection now!

Ad hoc for the particular purpose of

Advisory submitting suggestions or advice to a person or body entitled to carry out decisions and actions

Agenda a 'timetable' listing items for discussion at a meeting

AGM Annual General Meeting

Apologies for absence written or orally delivered excuse for not being able to attend a meeting

Chairman coordinator of a committee, working party, etc.

Chairmans' agenda like to ordinary agenda but containing additional information for guidance

Collective responsibility all members abide by what the majority decide upon at a meeting

Executive having power to act upon and carry out decisions

Ex officio by reason of an existing office or post

Honorary performing a duty without payment

Minutes written summary of a meeting's business

Motion a topic formally introduced for discussion

Nem con no one disagreeing

Opposer one who speaks against

Other business items discussed outside main business of meeting

Proposer one who speaks in favour of a motion

Resolution a decision reached after a vote at formal meetings – a motion successfully introduced

Secretary committee administrator

Sine die indefinitely

Standing committee one which has an indefinite term of office

Treasurer financial guardian

Unanimous all of like mind

A committee agenda

Ajax engineering sports and social club ①

The next committee meeting will take place ②
on Monday 23 April 19-- in the clubhouse
committee room at 7 30 pm

AGENDA ③

1   Apologies for absence ④

2   Minutes of the last meeting ⑤

3   Matters arising from the minutes ⑥

4   Finalising of soccer fixture list ⑦

5   Proposal to increase bar prices:
       That the current bar prices be
       increased by 10% to supplement
       club funds.

          Proposer: James Fox
          Seconder: Avril Saunders

6   Cleaning of changing rooms after
    matches

7   Any other business ⑧

8   Date of next meeting ⑨

Agenda printed on headed note paper ①

Preamble confirms date, time, location ②

Heading confirms nature of document ③

Apologies for absent members will be given by chairman to the committee ④

Usually circulated in advance, the minutes are checked to be true and signed by the chairman ⑤

Items progressed since the last meeting are relayed to the committee ⑥

The items of business the committee has met to discuss ⑦
   Note: agenda headings should make clear what exactly is to be discussed.
   Item 5 illustrates how a formal proposal would appear on an agenda.

Here ⑧ members may introduce any matter concerning the activities of the committee, but the discussion is kept short

A date is provisionally fixed for the next committee meeting ⑨

Note: Items 1, 2, 3, 7 and 8 are present on each agenda. They act as the 'links' between each meeting. The middle items, which will vary in number (here 4, 5 and 6) indicate the items of business which relate to that particular meeting. Some committees include a regular item 'Correspondence', if letters are frequently sent and received.

Extract from the chairman's agenda for the above meeting

CHAIRMAN'S AGENDA

1.   Apologies for absence

        Jack Brown is away in London

2.   Minutes of the last meeting

        The figure in Item 6 '£1522.23' is a
        typing error; it should be £1922.23

NOTES

*Ask members
to amend
their copies*

Producing the minutes

The most arduous job facing a committee secretary is that of writing the minutes. As the example on page 205 shows the minutes serve as a faithful record in summarised form of the business of the meeting.

Resolution minutes

Some types of meeting – those of boards of directors, for example – record only the decision reached, usually after a vote. The arguments, initial disagreements or conflicting views remain unwritten or unrecorded. Thus a lengthy discussion on the pro's and con's of keeping a barely profitable branch store open may be baldly summarised as:

```
5  NEWTOWN BRANCH
It was resolved that the company's
Newtown branch be closed with effect
from 31 May 19-- and the premises,
fixtures and fittings offered for
sale.
```

Such minutes usually include the word 'resolved' and may indicate the pattern of voting. Otherwise, the items, 'Apologies for Absence', 'Minutes of the Last Meeting', 'Matters Arising' and 'Date of Next Meeting' follow the pattern of narrative minutes. Note that in some formal meetings, the 'Matters Arising' and 'Any Other Business' items are not included, as a tighter rein is kept on what may be discussed.

Narrative minutes

Sometimes referred to as minutes of narration, narrative minutes tell more of the 'story' of what happened and who said what at a meeting. The main points of the background and discussion leading to a decision are recorded, and so anyone reading such minutes will gain a much fuller picture of a committee's work and views.

Narrative minutes are recorded in reported speech (see page 205). This simply involves referring to committee members in the third person – either by their office – 'The chairman said ...' or by name, 'Mrs Kent asked whether ...' When decisions are reached by a general agreement, rather than by a vote, expressions such as, 'It was generally agreed that ...' 'It was therefore decided that ...' are used to introduce the details of the decision. Further, to keep the record objective and neutral, the passive is often used: 'The secretary *was asked* to write to the Council to ...'.

Care must be taken when recording narrative minutes that verb tenses are appropriate and that the time interval between the actual discussion at the meeting and the later recording of the minutes does not lead to confusion:

He said he would contact the suppliers *next week*.

At the time this statement was made, 'next week' was true, but if the minutes were distributed and read a fortnight after the meeting took place, it would no longer be true; thus expressions like 'the following week' are more accurate.

Action minutes

Busy committees sometimes like to introduce a right hand blank column beside the minutes in order to put a designated committee member's name against a particular task to be carried out:

```
                                          ACTION BY:
6  ANNUAL FETE
The Secretary was asked to seek
approval to use the company Sports      Secretary
Ground again.
```

Narrative minutes assignment

Write out the following direct speech transcript of part of a meeting in narrative minutes:

Chairman:
Right, I think we should proceed to Item No 5, Christmas Dance Arrangements. Jim, would you like to bring us up to date?

Jim Barnes (secretary):
Well, as the committee requested, I wrote to the Kingston Disco organisers last week asking if they could play for us on the 22 December, but as yet I haven't heard from them. The room over the White Lion is definitely booked but we shall have to make arrangements for the bar pretty soon. Tickets should be ready for sale by next Wednesday 22 November.

Mrs Black:
Mr Chairman, could I ask that the tickets are distributed more promptly this year to departmental representatives. Last year we hardly had time to sell them and many staff were only approached a day or two beforehand.

Chairman:
That's a fair point. Jim, could you please see to that. What about publicity, John?

Mr John White:
No problems. The posters are ready to be put up and I've arranged for a small handout to be put in staff payroll envelopes next week.

Going back to the music side, though, I'm rather worried that we haven't got a group booked yet. I happen to know that the Brian Benner Quintet and Disco are free on the 22nd. Why don't we approach them?

Chairman:
The music is a key item, and I think John's suggestion should be taken up since Kingston Disco haven't replied. Would you contact The Brian Benner Quintet as a matter of urgency, Jim, and let me know the outcome as soon as possible – I take it that we're all agreed on that? Right, well, I think we can now proceed to Item No 6 ...

Example of narrative minutes

```
            AJAX ENGINEERING SPORTS AND SOCIAL CLUB

Minutes of the committee meeting held on Monday 23 April 19-- in the clubhouse
committee room at 7.30 pm

                        MINUTES

Present:  George White, chairman, Karen French, vice-chairman, Patricia
          Simpson, secretary, Lawrence Hopkins, treasurer, David Allen,
          Caroline Davis, James Fox, Avril Saunders, Jane Thornton

1    APOLOGIES FOR ABSENCE

     Apologies for absence were received from Jack Brown.

2    MINUTES OF THE LAST MEETING

     The chairman drew members' attention to the typing error in Item 6,
     Refitting of Shower Rooms.  The figure of £1522.23 should read
     £1922.23.  Members were asked to amend their copies accordingly.
     The minutes were then approved and signed by the chairman as a true
     record.

3    MATTERS ARISING FROM THE MINUTES

     The secretary reported that following the committee's request, she
     had written to Power Tools Limited to ask them if they would be prepared
     to sponsor the forthcoming sports tournament.  A reply was still awaited.

4    FINALISING OF SOCCER FIXTURE LIST

     The fixtures secretary informed the committee that there were only four
     fixtures still not arranged.  He had spoken to the secretary of Heaton
     Laundry Sports Club, who had promised to confirm within the week.  The
     fixtures secretary wondered whether the club would wish to meet
     Harrington Steel Rovers again, in view of the distance and cost
     associated with the away fixture.  It was decided to cancel the Harrington
     fixtures and the fixtures secretary was asked to write an appropriate
     letter.  The chairman requested that the finalised details be sent to
     the printers within the next fortnight, so that the fixture cards would
     be available to club members in good time.

5    PROPOSAL TO INCREASE BAR PRICES

     The chairman referred the committee to the proposal put forward by
     James Fox and Avril Saunders, 'That the current bar prices be increased
     by 10% to supplement club funds', and asked Mr Fox to speak to his motion.
     Mr Fox put forward a strong case based upon a comparative study he had
     carried out on neighbouring club bars and public houses, nearly all of which
     charged prices more than 10% higher than the club's.  Mrs Thornton was
     concerned that the increase might have precisely the opposite effect to the
     one desired, if fewer members used the bar facilities.  Mr Hopkins,
     treasurer, said that he supported the motion, since club funds were down by
     £122.00 when compared with last year's January to March quarter.  He
     emphasised the need for the club to ensure that it had sufficient money to
     pay regular bills which were being affected by inflation.  After a full
     discussion it was unanimously agreed that club bar prices be increased
     by 10% with immediate effect.
```

6   CLEANING OF CHANGING ROOMS AFTER MATCHES

The chairman informed the committee that complaints had been received from the Ladies' Hockey XI and the squash club players that on several occasions they had found the changing rooms left in an extremely untidy state after club matches held on Saturdays. The problem affected both the male and female changing rooms. Miss Davis confirmed the validity of the complaints regarding the ladies' changing rooms,. and felt that firm action was called for. It was decided that team captains should be responsible for ensuring that teams clear up the changing rooms after matches, and the secretary was asked to post an appropriate notice on the club noticeboard. The chairman said he would contact team captains personally.

7   ANY OTHER BUSINESS

Mr Allen raised the matter of the dangerous state of some of the chairs and tables in the club lounge. His wife had suffered a nasty cut and torn an expensive skirt because of a splitting chair leg. The chairman asked Mr Allen if he would make a careful examination of the lounge furniture and report back to the committee at the next meeting. It was agreed that the club would meet the costs of the repair to Mrs Allen's skirt.

8   DATE OF NEXT MEETING

The next committee meeting was provisionally arranged for Monday 21 May in the clubhouse committee room at 7 30 pm

signed:

Date: Chairman

Right! Let's make a start

A case study

The monthly committee meeting of Newtown Social Club. Present: Ron Dixon, chairman; Sally Pierce, secretary; Jack Slade; Eileen Johnston; John Turner; Peter Smith; Pauline Osgood.

Chairman:
Right! Let's make a start then! Jack, if you're ready ...? Oh, you haven't got an agenda ... No, I know, we were a bit late getting them out. Sally, have you got a spare? Oh, well perhaps you could share with Pauline? Good. Right. Apologies for absence. Fred Kemp can't make it. His wife's mother's come down with a nasty bout of 'flu in Leeds, and he's had to drive her up there, though, as he said, the car's not really up to it ...

Sally Pierce, secretary:
(breaking in) I think everyone's received a copy of the minutes Ron.

Chairman:
Ah, right. Anyone see anything amiss?

Eileen Johnston:
Well, it would be nice to see my name spelled right, if only once!

Sally Pierce:
Oh, sorry! My fault again!

Chairman:
Well, if you're all happy with the minutes, I take it I can sign them as a true record ...

Jack Slade:
No, hang on Mr Chairman, I'd like to go back on the discussion we had on the annual coach trip to London

next month. As I said, *I* think we should include a stop at Kew Gardens ... very educational *and* the admission's very reasonable.

Peter Smith:
Mr Chairman! Surely we're not going all through that again! I thought we'd made the arrangements at the last meeting ...

Chairman:
Yes, well Jack, I think we'll have to stick to what we decided. Perhaps next year ... Now, Matters Arising ...

John Turner:
I looked into the possibility of our booking the St Mark's church hall for the jumble sale next month but they're already booked for the 25th, so I spoke to Peter who said he would check at St Paul's with the vicar.

Peter Smith:
Oh, er, well, I've been pretty busy at the office lately ... I'll get on to it straight after the meeting. (whispering to John) Thanks a lot, mate!

John Turner:
(whispered reply) Sorry! I assumed you'd already found out!

Chairman:
Item Number Three, resignation of Mr Harris, bar steward. I'm sorry to have to report that Charlie's resigned and that we won't have a bar open next week unless we find a replacement as a matter of urgency ...

Pauline Osgood:
I didn't know Charlie'd resigned!

Jack Slade:
Yes, walked out in a huff I heard. Fed up with the way some members treated him!

Pauline Osgood:
Well, I'm not surprised. Take that Mrs Hitchcock for example. Always pushing in at the bar with her 'My good man ...'

Sally Pierce:
Why don't we approach Mr Rowbotham? He's retired now but still pretty active. He might be glad of the job.

Jack Slade:
What, George Rowbotham! You must be joking! I remember when he used to help out at the Dog and Duck. Hundreds of 'em laid out on the grass, dying of thirst!

Sally Pierce
All right! *You* think of someone, then!

Jack Slade:
Now there's no need to get hoighty toighty with me, Miss Pierce. Just trying to make a constructive remark, that's all!

Chairman:
Well, perhaps we'd better move on to Item Four, Renewal of the Curtains in the Club Room ...

(See page 208 for assignments.)

Activities and assignments

Manufacturing

1 First carry out your research and then write an account of how a large company runs its manufacturing process.

Usage

2 You have to explain to someone unfamiliar with the problem of the mis-related participle how it may occur in a piece of writing and how to avoid falling into the trap of introducing it. Illustrate your written account with helpful examples.

3 Explain briefly in a written account what a gerund is and how it should be used correctly in a piece of formal prose.

Spelling

4 Fill in the gaps in the following words to spell them correctly:

a ... nt ... ce   (someone you know)
bur ... x   (offices)
def ... nt   (lacking in)
f ... ible   (possible)
man ... vre   (put into position)
ad ... es   (places where people live)
a ... al   (used to pick up radio signals)
in ... te   (inject against illness)
un ... ry   (not needed)
a ... ate   (make worse)

Meetings and committees

5 Write an account to explain why the meeting is used as a medium of communication in organisations. Indicate what its advantages and disadvantages may be.

6 'The *last* place to go to get a good decision is from a Committee Meeting!' Discuss.

7 'A camel is a horse designed by a Committee!' What shortcomings of Committee work are implied in this remark?

8 First do your research, then give a ten minute talk to your group on the responsibilities of one of the following committee officers:

the chairman
the secretary
the treasurer

9 Find out as much as you can about the etiquette and procedure of meetings, then compose a list of do's and don'ts to help a newcomer to committee membership to make a good start.

10 In groups, assign appropriate roles to individual students, prepare notes and approaches, then role play one of the following meetings:

   (*a*) a public meeting to discuss the proposed plan to build a hypermarket on the outskirts of town. It may take trade away from local small businesses.
   (*b*) a student council meeting called to discuss ways of raising money for a local charity.
   (*c*) a student committee meeting which has an agenda including the following main items of business:
    4 Social programme for next year
    5 Abuse of the student common room
    6 Design of a handbook to help new students

In each of the above meeting simulations, students should be assigned to take notes and then to produce narrative minutes of the meeting. In (*c*), an agenda should be produced for the use of committee members.

Reported speech

11 Convert the following into reported speech:

Mrs Green: 'I am very concerned about the state of the printing room. Machines are being left uncleaned and without controls being properly adjusted after use. This has simply got to stop! And another thing – I shudder to think what the firm is paying out in terms of wasted photocopying paper and offset litho masters! Surely something can be done to put this right?'

Right! Let's make a start assignments

1 As a group, discuss what you think may be the shortcomings of this extract from the committee's meeting.

2 What guidance could you draw up to help:

   (*a*) the chairman of a meeting?
   (*b*) committee members?

3 Research the topic carefully and then write an account of the procedures which committees tend to adopt to ensure that meetings are conducted smoothly and efficiently.

4 In groups, re-write the dialogue of the above meeting as you think it should progress. Then, individually, write the minutes for your version of the meeting.

Unit 12

The job selection process

The organisation

1 Decision made that a vacancy exists
Staff may leave, or be promoted, or a department may grow.

2 Details drawn up of the type of job to be done and the sort of person needed
Many firms carry out a careful review of what and who is needed before advertising the post.

3 The post is advertised
Some posts are first advertised internally. Depending upon the type of appointment, a classified or display advertisement will be placed in either the local or national press.

4 Application forms and job details are sent out
Smaller firms tend to expect letters of application as a direct response from their advertisements, but larger organisations require an application form to be requested and completed.

5 Application forms and letters are sifted
Once applications are received, the company – usually personnel department – selects some six or eight candidates for interview.

6 References are taken up
The references of the short-listed candidates are taken up before interview. (But note that a candidate's current employers will not be approached without his permission.)

7 The interviews take place
Letters inviting candidates for interview are sent out and the interviews take place either with a panel of interviewers or as a one-to-one interview.

8 Confirmation of the appointment
The successful candidate may be offered the post at interview, or afterwards in a letter. At this stage references with a current employer will be taken up.

The candidate

1 Decision made to seek another post
People change jobs for a variety of reasons – boredom, lack of challenge, no advancement, etc.

2 Curriculum vitae drawn up
Many job seekers prepare duplicate copies of their personal details, education, work experience, etc which provides a 'potted history' of their careers to aid potential employers.

3 Advertisement answered
According to the type of advertisement, the candidate will either write a full letter of application, or send off for the details and application forms.

4 The application is made
The candidate despatches a copy of his curriculum vitae, completed application form and supporting letter of application before any deadline set. (**Note:** prudent job-seekers keep photocopied records of the application documents for subsequent reference.)

5 Acceptance of invitation for interview
A courteous letter is sent to the organisation accepting the invitation to attend for interview, confirming date and time.

6 Researching the organisation
Before interview, the candidate will try to find out as much as possible about the organisation, and prepare questions to ask at interview.

7 Attending for interview
The candidate seeks to make a good impression, having carefully prepared his ground.

8 Acceptance of the post
The candidate confirms in writing his acceptance of the post.

9 Resignation letter
Once the job has been offered and accepted, the candidate writes a courteous letter of resignation to his current employers.

Mastering the job interview

The prospect of applying for a job may seem daunting, yet we all go through the process several times in the space of our working lives. Practice certainly does help to make perfect, and the experience of having made a number of job applications – even when they have been unsuccessful – is of great assistance.

For many, however, the first job application represents the highest hurdle to have to jump. The following guidelines will help you to cope successfully with your next job application or to jump the hurdle of a first job-seeking attempt.

What sort of job?

Obviously, when jobs are scarce, the job-seeker may have to lower his sights and limit his ambitions to fit in with what jobs are available. Ordinarily, though, it is important to give careful thought to the sort of job, and in broader terms, career, which is appealing and which is likely to give long-term satisfaction. Drifting into any job without thought often leads to disappointment and to starting the whole job-hunting process all over again after a few weeks or months. The sort of questions to be asked are:

- Do I like working with people?
- Am I happier being left to get on with a task quietly?
- Would I like a job involving working with figures?
- Would I be happy constantly serving customers?
- Would I prefer a job with lots of variety, or do I work best in a familiar routine?
- What would I like to be doing in five years' time?

Preparing for job-hunting

When job-hunting, it pays to be well-prepared! One of the preliminary tasks to carry out is to compose and duplicate a curriculum vitae. This is a kind of personal data sheet set out in schematic form and organised into sections. It provides a concise account of a person's 'life story'.

The curriculum vitae

A curriculum vitae is normally divided into the following sections:

- Personal details: full name, age, sex, marital status, nationality, home address, telephone number.

- Education: names and dates of schools, colleges attended etc, and brief details of courses followed, with notes of any posts of responsibility or sports and social activities.

Examples of job advertisements

Model Agency

Requires a bright young person to learn all aspects of Agency work. Maths and English GCSE's and a good telephone manner are essential. Typing preferable. Starting salary £5,000. Write for an application form to Helen Dyer, 106 Watchet Road London, NW2 2WT

Advertising Jnr Sec
£5,500

We are looking for an excellent school leaver with good skills, plenty of personality, enthusiasm and well spoken to work for a smart and up-coming advertising agency. Duties will include client liaison, typing, WP, and computer operating. Will train on WP. Super friendly Co. Write with CV to John Bird, ACZ plc, 10 Barningham Road, Norwich, NR3 7SZ.

School leaver to train on computer, £5200 + bonuses. An excellent opportunity exists for a bright school leaver with GCSE's including maths and computer studies to join a young department within this well established company. Excellent prospects. Apply to Ron Albert, Vernon Smith UK Ltd, 53 Embridge Square, London, W1V 5FZ.

ACCOUNTS CLERK   £6,500
Well presented, articulate, young person with Maths and English GCSE required for general accounts position. Good prospects, BUPA and relaxed working atmosphere. Write to Miss Roberts, Computerland plc, Hatch's Road, Windsor, Berks.

- Qualifications: usually set out in chronological order, supplying dates, subjects, examining boards and grades.

- Work experience: names and addresses of past and present employers, stating post held and duties carried out. For people seeking a first post, it is helpful to supply details of any part-time work experience.

- Hobbies, interests: brief details of social activities, pastimes or hobbies.

- Circumstances: details of notice to be worked, willingness to move, availability, holder of clean driving licence, etc.

Having a set of curriculum vitaes prepared will save a great deal of time, especially when applying for a post where application forms are not provided.

- References: the next step is to approach people who are willing to supply a reference either about your work or your personal character. *Never* give details of a referee on an application form without first seeking his permission.

Once these steps are carried out, it is a matter of scanning local or national newspapers, trade journals or details displayed in job centres, or of registering with a local job centre.

Getting that interview!

In a sense, all the preliminary parts of the job application process are a preparation to enable you to walk smartly through the door of the interviewing room.

Once you have found an advertisement which looks interesting, you will need *either* to write a letter of application and send it off with your curriculum vitae, *or* write an initial *brief* letter requesting the further details and application forms mentioned.

Advertisements requiring the latter response normally state:

For further details of the post and forms of application, write to: Mrs K Thompson, personnel manager.

In this case, it is a waste of time composing a lengthy initial letter.

- The application form: application forms can sometimes cause a lot of trouble. A useful tip is to photocopy the blank application form and to carry out a 'trial run' on a copy, so that if mistakes are made, or items omitted, or boxes for information crowded and cramped, adjustments may be made on the fair copy to be returned.

Clearly some of the information asked for will already be set out on your curriculum vitae but this will not matter if it helps the interviewer to remember *you* among all the applications.

Letter of application

14 Westland Avenue
Newtown
Midshire NT34RT

Your Ref: AB/ID ①

12 June 198X

Mr A Brown
Personnel Manager
Starbrite Products Ltd
New Road
Westbury WT3 9QB ②

Dear Sir, ③

I should like to apply for the post of receptionist which was recently advertised in the 'Newtown ④
Echo', and enclose my completed application form ⑤
and curriculum vitae for your consideration. At present I am nearing completion of a full-time receptionist course at Newtown College of Technology. As my application form indicates, the course provides a thorough education in reception duties and emphasizes oral communication skills and computerised switchboard techniques. In addition, I have studied typewriting and word processing and expect to pass the examination in ⑥
both subjects in June.

I was very much attracted to the post, since I enjoy meeting and helping people and feel I have the necessary friendly but responsible outlook. Last summer I worked as a temporary clerk for two months at Lifeguard Security Ltd, where I gained valuable experience in operating a PABX computerised console and in dealing with ⑦
visitors and enquiries.

I shall be available at any time for interview and to commence work as soon as the summer ⑧
term ends on 29 June.

Yours faithfully

Caroline Ewing (Miss)

encs.

Points to note

The letter is handwritten on good stationery and carefully displayed and presented.

The given reference is quoted. ①

The recipient's name, title and address are appropriately set out. ②

The more formal Dear Sir – Yours faithfully salutation and subscription are preferred. ③

The letter starts with a formal statement of application for the advertised post. ④

Reference is made to enclosed documents. ⑤

The letter sets out to emphasise particularly those aspects of the applicant's education, qualifications, work-experience and personality which she feels are most likely to interest the personnel manager and to secure an interview. ⑥

Notice that Caroline makes deliberate reference to her experience of computerised telephone equipment. ⑦

The letter closes by stressing the ready availability of the applicant for an interview and also her earnest commitment to finding and starting a job as soon as possible. ⑧

- The letter of application: when the forms have been filled, it is often necessary to compose a detailed and supporting letter of application for the *particular* post advertised. Such letters are normally hand-written and are selective in the information they supply – there is little point in merely repeating what is on a curriculum vitae or application form. But there is a *great deal of point* in emphasising those aspects of your education, qualifications, experience and aptitudes which seem particularly relevant to the job advertised, whether the aspects be a knowledge of a foreign language, good shorthand/typewriting speeds, knowledge of ladies' fashions, interest in motor-cycles or whatever.

The letter of application, therefore, provides you with an opportunity to 'sell yourself' to a prospective employer by revealing your best side. But, remember, no one likes to read letters which seem conceited or boastful. The technique of projecting a suitable image of oneself is not easily mastered and requires practice.

Once the application details have been copied, the masters should be despatched in good time and the copies kept until, all being well, the all-important interview invitation arrives.

Research and prepare!
Once called for interview, it is very important that you find out beforehand as much as possible about the organisation. For large, national firms, the reference library will offer some help, but for smaller, local organisations, it is most useful to 'ask around' among relatives and friends, to gain some insights into the firm's reputation, stability and prospects for growth. Such preparation will help you to answer frequently occurring interview questions such as:

What makes you want to work for our company?
What attracted you to the post?

The next important task is to prepare the list of questions which *you* wish to ask at the interview. After all, an interview is two-way communication and just as employers will be wanting to establish whether they want you, so you should use the interview to make certain that you want to work for them.

Some information will be given in the job advertisement, though this is often very limited. There will be matters about which you will need reassurance. Normally, the essential information about conditions of service – hours to be worked, paid holidays, salary, etc are readily provided at interview – but the following types of question may help you to gain a better impression of the sort of organisation you may commit yourself to:

What are the prospects for promotion if I make a success in the advertised post?
Would there be any opportunities for me to receive further training and development in the post?
Does the company have a policy of promoting internally whenever possible?

Has the company any plans for future expansion (in the department where I might be working)?

Such questions may help you to establish whether the organisation has developed training schemes, whether there exist prospects of advancement for you and whether you would be joining a lively firm likely to expand and thus help you to develop in your career.

Being interviewed successfully

Even before the interview starts, a sound preparation like that outlined above will give you the essential self-confidence you will need.

Before attending for interview, it helps to go through the application documents you have kept and to make a list of the type of questions you think you may be asked. Questions about your education, work experience, hobbies and interests, future ambitions and aspirations are almost certain to be asked. It is also important to commit to memory those questions which you have to ask. It always sounds lame when the interviewer asks:

'Are there any questions which you would like to ask us?'

and you reply:

'Well, no, not really, you seem to have explained everything ...'

Appearance matters!
The matter of dress is always important. Though it may seem unfair, people do tend to make judgments about others whom they do not know well, based on their appearance. Looking smartly turned out will not in itself get you the job, but it certainly won't do you any harm. Over-casual dress may give an impression of being an untidy and slipshod sort of person, while being 'dressed up to the nines', and, in the case of young ladies, wearing too much make-up may transmit a 'flashy' rather than conscientious image.

Speak up and speak out!
In the limited time available, the interviewer is clearly trying to obtain a clear idea of both the job competence of the applicant and some impression of his personality – drive, enthusiasm, loyalty and sense of commitment. He can only do so by posing a series of questions and evaluating the answers given. The interviewee, therefore, must respond to the interview by giving clearly expressed and fluent replies. Mumbling and monosyllabic answers will create a poor impression – but so also will erratic gabbling without pause for breath!

The best course of action is to *listen carefully* to the question and then to compose a sensible answer given in a steady manner, all the while watching the interviewer's face for signs that you have said enough and should pause for him to make a comment or pose the next question.

If you feel you 'know your stuff' on a given subject, by all means demonstrate your expertise, but never 'woffle' or meander on when you find the going difficult. It is much better to be honest:

'I must admit I don't know the answer to that one.'
'So far I haven't had experience with that piece of office equipment.'

Coping with nerves
One of the problems which faces *all* interviewees, whether experienced or going for a first job, is how to cope with nerves. Remember that it is natural to feel nervous – and it even helps – because the mind often works faster and the senses are more alert when there is a challenge. Moreover, the interviewer will know just how you feel – he too has been interviewed – and will take pains to put you at your ease, since nervous candidates do not interview well.

It is important to control the effects of nervousness, since self-confidence transmits itself to interviewers positively, while nervousness in a candidate tends to make the interviewer feel embarrassed and guilty. Try to avoid speaking in short panting bursts by taking silent deep breaths to help you to relax and enable you to speak more fluently. Avoid giving off signals of nervousness such as ring-twisting, finger-twining and toe-tapping. It is helpful to assume a comfortable but not slouching position in the chair and to rest hands on lap when not making a supportive gesture.

Be yourself!
Lastly, be your natural self, without becoming over familiar – the firm should want to employ the real you! And, do not forget to thank the interviewer for his time and interest in your application.

Job application assignments

1 In groups, devise a checklist of the sort of tasks and responsibilities you think the Finer Foods clerical assistant would carry out.

2 As a group activity, design an application form to be sent to applicants for the clerical assistant post.

3 From the checklist devised above, compose a schedule providing further information about the post.

4 Decide upon the best information schedule and application form and give a copy of each to every member of the group.

5 Individually, complete the application form and compose a suitable supporting letter of application.

6 Organise teams to act as interviewing panels and applicants. Study the applications, then role play the interview for the post of clerical assistant. (You may wish to tape-record each interview.)

7 In a general group session, review what you learned from this assignment about the job selection process.

FINER FOODS LIMITED

Cash And Carry Specialists
require a

CLERICAL ASSISTANT

to work in their Newtown Food Centre

The successful applicant will need to be familiar with clerical procedures and able to work closely with customers and staff. Experience an advantage, but not essential, as full training given. Excellent prospects for advancement to office management. Salary according to age and experience. Special discount purchasing scheme. Luncheon Vouchers supplied.

For further details and forms of application, apply to:

Mr K Nesbitt
Personnel Manager
Finer Foods Limited
High Street
Midtown
Newshire MT3 5RT

Curriculum vitae assignment

8 Design and produce a curriculum vitae for yourself. It may either be an accurate record of your personal details and accomplishments, or you may invent any information you wish.

Discussion topic: What points should a curriculum vitae seek to emphasise?

Job resignation letter assignment

9 Assume that you wish to tender your resignation from the post of clerical assistant at Finer Foods Limited because you have been successful in obtaining a post as Assistant Office Manager at Taylor Transport Limited. Compose a suitable letter of resignation to Mr Peter Hopkins, your office manager.

You should further assume that you have been in the post for two years and, despite your hard work, it does not seem that any advancement or promotion are in the offing.

Job vacancy advertisement assignment

10 Design an eye-catching display advertisement for insertion in your local newspaper for one of the following posts:

- receptionist in a large insurance company's head office
- shorthand-typist to work in an accounts department of a medium-sized firm.
- junior secretary to work for the personal assistant of a sales manager in the fashion-wear business.

Try to make your advertisement as authentic as possible.

Here's the proof...! 5

There are 10 errors in each of the following paragraphs. Re-write them correctly.

1 Its a well known fact that tourism is one of Britains expanding industry's this explains why more and more school leavers aply for catering and tourism courses at there local colleges or for aprenticeship in the industry.

2 A well written buisness leter gives a good impresion of a firm. It proclaims it eficient and painstating in it's corespondance, which indicates a firm worth dealing with. The responsability for this good impression rests mainly on the secretarys shoulders.

Usage

Who or whom?

It's amazing the trouble that just one letter of the alphabet can cause! When should an 'm' be added to the word who?

If we wanted to solve the problem grammatically we could say, whenever it is acting as an object in a sentence:

OBJECT	SUBJECT	
Who<u>m</u>	did	<u>you</u>	see?

There is, however, a much simpler rule of thumb to apply in cases of doubt: if you can replace the word who/whom with the word 'him', then it *must* be whom:

Whom did you see?
Did you see *him*?

The rule also works in the plural:

The customers who/whom I spoke to all liked the new product.

Apply the rule: I spoke to them. Therefore it is:

The customers who<u>m</u> I spoke to.

Another tip is that if there is a preposition immediately before the word it must be 'whom': to whom, from whom, by whom, etc.

Less and fewer

These two words also cause trouble at times. The simplest way to ensure that you use them correctly is to think of 'less' as part of something that is normally impossible to split into separate parts:

There is *less water* in the tank this week.

Similarly, it helps to think of 'fewer' as something which can be split into separate parts:

Fewer fans attended this week's match because recently the team has been playing badly.

Assignment

Select the correct word in the following sentences:

1 The customer who/whom you served has complained.

2 Who/whom finishes first wins the prize!

3 I should like to introduce the young lady who/whom I spoke to you about last week.

4 We are selling less/fewer cars this month.

5 When there are less/fewer goods in the shops, the customers have less/fewer choice.

Boost your spelling power!

Learn these words by heart

Remember, an asterisk after a word indicates that it is very commonly misspelled:

aggregate n, v	
choice* n	(choose v)
dissatisfied past part	(dissatisfaction n)
excellent* adj	(excellence n excel v)
hypocrisy n)	(hypocritical adj)
install v	(instalment* n)
Mediterranean n	
penicillin n	
referred past part	(refer v reference* n)
separate v, adj	(separation n
	separately* adv)
until conj	
agreeable adj	(agreement n)
clothes n	(clothe v cloth n)
distributor n	(distribute v)
exercise* v, n	
hypothesis n	(hypothesise v
	hypothetical adj)
miniature n, adj	
permanent adj	(permanence n)
relieved past part	(relief n relieve v)
severely adv	(severe adj)

Do not forget to enter in your vocabulary book any words with which you are unfamiliar, either in terms of spelling or meaning!

Assignment

By arrangement, choose four of the above words. Compose a sentence for each, in which the word is used correctly. Compare your sentences with those devised by others in your group. This will help you to add the above list of words to your **active vocabulary.**

'Thank you for coming'

A case study

'Wish me luck, Mum!' With these words, Sally slammed the front-door and hurried to the bus-stop, just in time to see the City-centre bus disappearing down the road. Sally glanced irritably at her watch. 9.05. 'I might just make it,' she thought, 'if the next bus is on time. The interview's not till 9.45.'

At 9.43, Sally rushed through the glass fronted entrance, into the foyer of Global Associates Limited. She had just made it! 'Excuse me,' Sally panted at the reception desk, 'I've an appointment with Mrs Keen, the Personnel Manager at 9.45.'

Smoothly and efficiently, Sally was ushered into Mrs Keen's office suite and invited to sit near someone who was obviously Mrs Keen's secretary. Sally glanced admiringly at the secretary's polished desk and electronic typewriter. 'Just made it, luckily,' said Sally nervously. 'I suppose you must be Mrs Keen's secretary.'

'Yes, that's right. Mrs Keen won't keep you waiting long, I'm sure. Would you care for a cup of coffee meantime?' The coffee soothed Sally's nerves.

'What's it like working here? I mean really like? Do they crack the whip much?'

'Oh no, it's really very pleasant,' the secretary said with a smile, 'and I'm sure you'll find Mrs Keen very approachable.' With that, the telephone buzzed on the secretary's desk, and she said, 'Would you like to go in now, Miss Robinson. Mrs Keen is ready to see you.'

Sally opened the door gingerly and glanced round it into what was a large office. As she did so, a tall lady wearing a dark blue fitted suit rose to meet her.

'Ah, good morning,' she said, 'you must be Miss Robinson.' Sally shook Mrs Keen's hand and sat down in the chair opposite the desk. 'That's right, make yourself perfectly comfortable,' said Mrs Keen in a friendly voice, as she began to scan the papers in front of her. 'I hope you had a comfortable journey across town?' Sally fingered her hair, hoping it was still in some kind of shape.

'Well, it was a little hectic! You see, the bus I should have caught must have left early.'

Mrs Keen began to question Sally about her school and college education. 'What made you decide upon a secretarial course at the college?' she asked.

'Well, my mum thought it would get me a steady job in a pleasant office.'

'And what do *you* think?'

'Well, I always liked typing at school and I've mostly enjoyed the course at college – except that the accounts and commerce were a bit dull sometimes. Still, I'm pretty sure I'll get my hundred words a minute!'

'That's most interesting,' replied Mrs Keen. 'Now, what experience have you of word processing and photocopying?'

'Oh, well, quite a bit. You see, we have a super training office at the tech with all sorts of equipment – you know the sort of thing – networked micros, Prestel, fax, computerised telephone networks and colour copiers ...'

'Well, you do seem to have quite a repertoire,' said Mrs Keen. 'Tell me now, when would you think it best to use a photocopier for making copies, and when would you select an offset litho machine?'

'Ah, well now, let me see ... Yes! I think I should use the offset litho if there were lots of copies to make because it's cheaper. Mind you, it's not as easy to use as a plain paper copier. Personally I always prefer the photocopier – it's not so messy!'

As the interview progressed, Sally grew much more confident. In answer to a closing question about her personal ambitions, Sally replied, 'Well, I don't want a dead-end job. I mean, I want to be a top-flight personal secretary. I see this audio-typewriting job as a sort of stepping-stone. Besides, I don't want to lose my shorthand speed, and I'm not really sure that I want to wear ear-phones round my neck for ever, if you see what I mean?'

'I most certainly do,' said Mrs Keen. 'It's been most interesting to talk to you. I shall be writing to all the applicants very soon. Thank you for coming.'

'Not at all! Goodbye,' said Sally, feeling quite elated as she went out, and sure that the job was as good as hers already.

Assignments

1 Evaluate Sally's interview performance in groups and report back to your class.

2 In pairs, tape-record your own version of how you think the interview should have progressed. Play back your version to your class.

The role of the personnel department

Over the past 80 years the rights of employees in organisations have become much more clearly defined and acknowledged. Successive governments – sometimes prompted by trade unions and enlightened employers – have passed a number of Acts of Parliament to secure the rights of individuals in various areas while they are at work. These include the amount of personal space an individual is entitled to in a shop, office or factory, proper toilet and washing facilities for shop assistant and miner alike, due attention to health and safety precautions, the length of the working day and week, job security, grievance procedures to be followed and so on.

Correspondingly the task of co-ordinating the ways in which an organisation interacts with its employees in terms of:

- recruiting personnel

- providing induction, training and preparation for retirement

- appraising and evaluating performance

- employee counselling and welfare

- industrial relations

- formal grievance procedures to be followed

- dismissal procedures

- personnel records maintenance, etc.

has become much more complex and involved. As a result the range of activities of an organisation's personnel department has grown significantly. Today's personnel officer has to be proficient in all the areas set out above. He or she has to be a very versatile person – 'lawyer, agony aunt, trainer, skilled negotiator, diplomat and politician, a good judge of character and expert communicator' all rolled into one!

Very often the personnel manager has to convey unpalatable truths to a company's directors – say about employee unhappiness about new procedures set up in an office or factory. Equally he or she has to inspire the trust and confidence of employees who need to believe the manager is not just 'a boss's person' but someone who will listen to and accept arguments and criticisms as part of the upward flow of communication from employees to management.

In the case of many organisations, in both the private and public sectors, the personnel officer will be continuously involved in discussions and negotiations (for the management) with employees who are trade union members and officials. Acting often as the 'honest broker' in, say, a new round of pay talks, requires much expert technical knowledge and 'people skills' if expensive go-slows and strikes are to be avoided.

The 1984 Data Protection Act

A particular area of the personnel function which has been affected by IT is the setting up, maintenance and accessing of personnel records. Over the past ten or so years, many politicians, social workers, doctors and legal professionals became increasingly uneasy about the amount of information and data which organisations and institutions were putting on to computer about individuals, whether as customers, patients, wrongdoers, employees, taxpayers or simply as citizens of the UK.

For example, unknown to themselves, many consumers were being listed on credit information service organisations' computers as 'bad credit risks' – perhaps because they had refused to pay for goods which proved shoddy and defective and where the blame lay fairly and squarely with the retailer, who nevertheless 'reported them' to the information service's computer. When next such consumers sought to purchase on account or credit in another store at another time, the assistant might discreetly consult the store's computer terminal and on the advice displayed, diplomatically yet firmly refuse to give credit. Such practices were rightly deemed unfair and characteristic of the potential 'Big Brother' policing which computerised sharing of information might bring about.

Consequently, (and taking other worries such as people's confidential medical or criminal records being improperly divulged into account) the government in 1984 – an appropriate year in which to attack any 'Big Brother' developments! – brought on to the statute book the Data Protection Act. This piece of most important legislation was introduced to give each and every citizen closely secured rights of access to any computer database or listing which included information about him or her.

In a nutshell, the Data Protection Act obliges any organisation keeping identifiable data about their employees, customers or contacts to register the scope and nature of their computerised data records. Further, it gives individuals who suspect that data is being stored on computer by such organisations the right to inspect the 'Register of Data' kept by the appointed government Registrar's staff (in local offices, like the registry of births, deaths and marriages) in order to find out what is being recorded and how. Certain rights of confidentiality exist to protect the people who put the information on to computer but not so as to shield them from the consequences of any malpractice. Similarly, any data about people which is properly kept on computer file has to be protected by adequate security procedures. Some organisations – like the police – are exempt from the Act's requirements to give access to certain stored information if it is being held in the course of detecting crime.

The Act also makes a number of precise requirements of the user of computerised data and sets standards of integrity to be adopted.

Keeping legal – no simple matter!

As you can see from the above overview of the Data Protection Act, staff working in personnel departments – indeed in any department – need to possess a good deal of technical and legal information in order for them to comply with the law while doing their daily work. Ignorance of the law has for a long time been held to be no excuse and as the rights of citizens are increased and written down for all to see and know, so the obligations of every worker to be aware of and to conform to such legal requirements expand and become more complicated.

Indeed, most large companies employ a legally trained expert to carry out the job of company secretary which is centered upon providing advice and guidance on all the company's activities, so that the laws of the land are upheld and neither deliberately nor unconsciously broken.

Composing effective paragraphs

One of the most frequent traps into which unwary writers may fall is the tendency to compose prose paragraphs which are not put together in a unified way; they mix points or ideas which are not clearly related or connected in a logical sequence.

Consider, for example, the following 'paragraph':

An example of this is the trend of people today using their leisure time passively rather than actively. The development of television took place, in fact, over a number of years, with the Second World War intervening. One of the consequences of this is that people are generally less fit today than they were twenty years ago. The motor-car has made it easier for people to get out and about, and one answer must surely be to encourage people to stop merely sitting around, and to get out and pursue an active hobby or pastime.

If we read this paragraph two or three times, the gist of what the writer is trying to say becomes clearer. The problem stems from the fact that he has been jotting down ideas as they developed and that his brain has been working faster than his hand! The result is a disconnected garble of ideas which confuse and irritate the reader!

The following guidelines will help you to construct paragraphs which impart your message clearly and in a manner which will hold the reader's interest.

Essentially a paragraph is a passage or section of a piece of writing which deals with and develops a single topic in a unified way.

A very helpful comparison may be made with one of the Findings sections in the short formal report, which is made up of a section heading indicating its theme or topic, and a series of points which develop or illustrate the topic. The structure of a paragraph follows a very similar pattern, such as:

Plan before writing!

The key to an effective paragraph is careful advanced planning. Before any attempt is made to write it out, the paragraph's structure should be formed in outline. If we were to plan the above paragraph about people's leisure activities, it might look something like this:

Key point:
People today – passive not active leisure pursuits

Contributory points:
Development of TV caused people to sit and watch
Tho' cars enabled people – get out and about – still sitting
Result: people less fit than 20 yrs ago
So – need to encourage active hobbies

Already a clear structure and sequence is evident. Moreover, once the writer has a clearly formed paragraph plan, he can devote more time to composing polished sentences. Thus the paragraph may read as follows:

Today, people tend to use their leisure time in passive rather than active pursuits. Though the development of television took many years, the trend today is for people to spend many hours each week merely sitting and watching the 'silver screen'. Similarly, though the mass production of the motor-car has enabled many to get out and about, they are still doing so in comfortable seats! The result is that people are less fit today than they were twenty years ago, and so an urgent effort is needed to encourage people to get up out of their seats and to pursue an *active* hobby!

Another way of looking at the above paragraph's structure is as follows:

Key point:
A *bold assertion* – passive not active pursuits

Contributory points:
Support and justify assertion – TV and motor-car examples

Justifiable conclusion – people less fit
Action therefore needed – people should pursue active hobby

Logical structure

This way of looking at the paragraph's structure shows that it not only deals with a single unified topic separated into a **key point** and **contributory points**, but that it also has a clear beginning, middle and end which follow a logical process of thought.

Positioning the key point

Once the need to plan paragraphs before writing them has been accepted, a number of useful devices of style become available to the writer.

For example, the position of the key point in the paragraph makes a considerable difference. In the example about leisure pursuits, the key point is expressed in the first sentence:

Today, people tend to use their leisure time in passive rather than active pursuits.

Immediately, the reader can sense that the rest of the paragraph is likely to justify and expand this major statement. There are consequently few surprises in store, and the reader tends to absorb the illustrations and conclusions easily and readily.

Putting the key point *last* in the sentence, however, creates an entirely opposite effect of suspense leading to a climax which is not easily anticipated. Thus the reader is required to read the paragraph more carefully, so as not to miss the main point. Novelists use this device to keep their readers' interest, and to prompt them to read on:

His skin felt cold and clammy. Beads of sweat were trickling down his chest and back. He tried to prevent his eyes straying to the metal cell-door, but they kept flicking towards it just the same. His heart seemed like a swollen pump hammering in his chest. There could not be much more time left! Suddenly, the cell-door grated on its hinges as it swung open. A prison officer came swiftly into the cell. 'The Governor's just had a telephone-call from the Home Office. You've been reprieved!'

In this type of paragraph, the reader is kept – like the prisoner – in suspense right to the end of the paragraph's final sentence.

In a different context, such paragraph constructions may be used to end a piece of writing in an emphatic way:

The conclusions, therefore, are inescapable, the use of capital punishment cannot be justified on religious, moral or humanitarian grounds.

In short, the Flexiprint Computer printer is inexpensive to run, absolutely reliable, and beautiful to have around!

Some paragraphs may be constructed with a key sentence in the middle, with supporting points on either side. It is important in any piece of extended writing that you give careful thought to the way you structure your paragraphs, so that the reader may respond both to variety and intended effect.

KEY POINT OPENING

KEY POINT MIDDLE

KEY POINT CLOSING

Assignment

Compose a sentence using each of the above words correctly. Compare your sentences with those of others in your group. This will help you to add these words to your **active vocabulary.**

Paragraph composition assignments

Compose a paragraph of about 100 words on one of the following:

1 Key point opening: explaining how to leave a building in case of fire or emergency.

2 Key point closing: outlining the decision of your company to introduce vending machines for staff to get hot drinks during office hours.

3 Key point middle: a description of *either* a new brand of perfume *or* after-shave lotion.

Underline in your paragraph the sentence which contains your key point. Compare your paragraph with those written by others in your group.

Deceptive duos!

There are a number of words in English which set traps for the unwary! Sometimes they look or sound rather similar, sometimes they are thought to have a similar meaning. In fact, they mean something very different in each case. It pays to collect them and to make *quite* sure of both spelling and meaning. The following checklist will start your collection:

dependent	dependant
proceed	precede
continuously	continually
immoral	amoral
descent	dissent
induce	deduce
inedible	uneatable
immoveable	immobile
verbal	oral
succeed	secede
ingenious	ingenuous
economic	economical
uninterested	disinterested
infer	imply
oral	aural
readable	legible
lend	borrow

Know your IT! Key words and terms

4: IT in use

telebanking and teleshopping: two words destined to become popular as more consumers use viewdata systems to do their shopping or banking transactions at a distance and at a time to suit them; by such means customers can make changes in their banking arrangements and order goods displayed on screened pages of information via computerised interaction between shopper and shop.

computer hacker: an IT age criminal or at the least an intrusive pest! Usually a very clever computer user who can break into computers via modems and give instructions – for example to transfer money to an account he can access in a way which can be very hard to trace.

packet switching: sending batches of data very quickly to remote locations using telephone lines.

electronic mail: information sent from one computer terminal to another almost instantaneously by means of a Local or Wide Area Network.

EFT: Electronic Funds Transfer – a term used by banks to describe the computerised movement of money from bank to bank and customer to customer.

Extend your IT word power!

Find out what the following words or phrases mean and then explain them to your group:

radiopaging holograph bar code British Telecom Gold

cable TV Ceefax Oracle Prestel TTNS

Direct Broadcast Satellite interactive video

a Closed User Group a videodisk

Activities and assignments

Composition

1 Compose a set of sentences in which each of the following constructions is correctly used:

both ... and   either ... or   neither ... nor   not only ... but also

2 Compose a paragraph of about 100 words which includes four of the following sentence-starters:

Even so; Moreover; However; Nevertheless; Furthermore; Whether; As soon as; Having; In order that

3 Bearing in mind what you have learned about paragraph construction, compose an article intended for your school or college magazine on one of the following subjects:

What's new in teenage fashion?
My alternative to television!
How to cope with parents!
My kind of music

Your article should be about 450 words long and comprise at least four paragraphs.

Spelling

4 Fill in the gaps in the following words to spell them correctly:

(*a*)	agr ... ble	(friendly)
(*b*)	re ... ed to	(mentioned)
(*c*)	min ... te	(small)
(*d*)	e ... ll ... ce	(high standard)
(*e*)	di ... tis ... ed	(not happy with)
(*f*)	h ... p ... cal	(insincere)
(*g*)	man ... ble	(easily managed)
(*h*)	im ... ble	(impossible to move)
(*i*)	... oral	(non-moral)
(*j*)	in ... us	(extremely clever)

The job selection process

5 First carry out your research and then do one of the following:
either: as a talk to your group
or: in the form of a written account,
describe the nature and extent of the service offered to members of the public by:
either: a Job Centre
or: an employment bureau

6 With appropriate audio-visual aids, give a ten minute talk to your group on one of the following:

(*a*) How to cope with the documents involved in applying for a job
(*b*) How to be a successful interviewee
(*c*) How to write an article

Interviews

7 Role play the following situations in your group and then, in a general group discussion, try to establish guidelines on what are effective interviewing techniques:

(*a*) Gordon has arrived late for work three days running this week. His supervisor calls him into the office to get to the root of the matter, since it is affecting the morale of the other office staff.
(*b*) Betty works in an open-plan office where customers call quite regularly. Of late, her conversation has been loud and her language sometimes less than polite! Something has to be done, especially since her manager believes she is unaware of the damage she is causing the firm's public image.
(*c*) It is the time of the summer holiday leave in the office. Joan is one of the skeleton staff on duty. She learns that a cousin has suddenly decided to get married next Friday. She decides to ask her office manager for leave of absence.

Unsolicited letter of application

8 Assume your course finishes in two months' time. Instead of waiting for advertisements to reply to, you decide to send an unsolicited letter to a number of local employers to introduce yourself in the hope that they may decide to call you for an interview. Compose a suitable letter.

The role of personnel

9 Find out what a document used in personnel work called a job specification looks like. See if you can obtain copies of some real ones produced by local firms for examination.
  Having carried out your research, interview one of the following staff in your college or school:

the head caretaker
the school/departmental secretary
a refectory cook or assistant
a laboratory technician
a library assistant

  When you are confident that you have discovered the type and scope of the qualities and skills needed to carry out the job of the person you have selected, construct a job specification for his or her imaginary replacement. Let your subject have a copy and ask for an honest assessment of how accurate your job specification is. Apart from assessing your skill at analysing a job, the assessment will also give you an idea of how good you were at conducting your fact-finding interview!

10 Assume that you have been asked to write one of a series of articles for your school/college newspaper about the scope of jobs and career opportunities in various organisational areas. Carry out your further research and then write an article for school or college leavers entitled:

Working in personnel – agony and ecstasy!

Part of your research should be to interview a range of people working locally in various personnel functions. You may then be able to include some interesting direct quotations – with prior permission, of course!

Unit 13

One of the best definitions of marketing is:

The art of supplying the right goods (or services) to the right customer at the right time and at the right price, making the right profit.

A wise marketing man put it another way:

'Selling products that won't come back to customers who will!'

When seen in this light, it becomes clear why marketing is so closely involved in the work of each department – from research and development, to production, accounting, distribution and sales.

(A) Indeed, many firms are successful because they gear all they do to the needs and expectations of their customers. As one manufacturer of skis put it:

'We're not in the ski business, but the *fun* business!'

Marketing is, then, an essential function in firms which sell goods or services to the industrial market or to the consumer market. Yet the ways these two markets are approached are very different. On the one hand, a firm may be developing a product and designing its packaging
(B) and advertising display so that supermarket customers will buy it on impulse. In an industrial market, however, a team of specialists may take months to convince a
(C) sceptical team of purchasers that they should buy a piece of manufacturing equipment worth many thousands of pounds.

Whether meeting industrial or consumer needs, however, most marketing departments carry out similar functions.

Perhaps the best way to become familiar with the importance of the marketing function is to trace, step-by-step, how marketing is involved in the development and sale of a new product.

Let us assume that Fastsnacks Limited feels the need to extend its product range of sweet snacks. It may be because its existing main product has been on the market some time and that its novelty and appeal are fading.

Stage one

Market research

The market will be explored to find out what type of consumer is buying what kind of snack and what future trends are likely to be. Also, the firm will try to find a part of the market which may be ready for a new or different type of snack – to find a demand not already being met. This means identifying the potential customer. (D)

Stage two

Research and development

Armed with market research information, meetings will be held with the Fastsnacks research and development team, who will experiment with different kinds of filling and coating – biscuit, nut, nougat, chocolate, etc – and who will try to produce the sort of taste, chewing characteristics and handling features which the marketing team feel the consumer will find attractive.

Stage three

Product design and manufacture

Once a prototype product has been developed, the production department will take steps to ensure that their equipment can make it in bulk, and the accounts experts will ensure that it can be made profitably, which means that a decision has to be made on the selling price. Again, the marketing team will need to know what price competing products are selling at, and gauge how much customers are likely to be prepared to pay.

Stage four

Packaging and advertising

As well as developing the actual snack, Fastsnacks have to develop a wrapper and to plan an advertising strategy which will create a demand for an as yet unheard-of (E) product. Thus while production development is going on, so also is the advertising and sales promotion planning.

Stage five

Test marketing

Before committing itself to a name for the product, a particular wrapper design and an associated advertising campaign, Fastsnacks may try out several options in a range of 'test-marketing' operations. In this way, a representative sample of the customers expected to buy the product is used as a means of checking which combination of size, wrapping, brand name, advertising image, etc is most likely to succeed.

Stage six

Product launch

By this stage, 'all systems are go!' Fastsnacks decides upon a date on which to launch the product and has then to ensure that:

- the snack will be in the retail stores and shops ready for sale
- the material for advertising the product has been designed and produced – for example, television commercial, roadside hoarding, magazine advertisement, material for display in the stores
- production of the product is guaranteed to meet the anticipated demand

'Are you trying to tell me, Hoskins, that people are going to risk cutting their fingers on those ring-things and actually drink out of a can? Ridiculous! It'll never catch on!'

Come the day, there will be plenty of finger-crossing and breath-holding. For despite all their efforts, no organisation is able to guarantee that a new product will not flop. What is certain, however, is that without an all-embracing (F) and sustained marketing effort, a new product is much more likely to pass by, unnoticed and unremembered on its way to the museum of marketing disasters!

What marketing means

Working with R & D to evolve ideas for new products

Constantly monitoring the market for what prospective customers need or want

Anticipating (sometimes by several years) what customers will be wanting to buy and ensuring that the firm will be in a position to supply it

Carrying out market research to see how a product is received by customers; testing a prototype product in a sample market (G)

Working with an advertising agency to devise advertising and sales promotion campaigns to ensure that the public are aware of the product and stimulated to buy it (H)

Helping to ensure that sales representatives and dealers know how to sell the product, and providing them with supporting sales literature, placards, etc

Working closely with production to ensure that a demand created may be met from available supplies – it's no good making people want to buy what you cannot make enough of!

Taking care to ensure that the firm's range of products does not become too narrow or left behind by competitors' products

Mastering the meaning

1 Explain briefly the meaning of the following words and phrases:

(*a*) many firms are successful because they gear all they do to the needs and expectations of their customers   Line A

(*b*) customers will buy it on impulse   Line B

(*c*) a sceptical team of purchasers   Line C

(d) This means identifying the potential customer   Line D

(e) which will create a demand for an as yet unheard-of product   Line E

(f) all-embracing and sustained marketing effort   Line F

(g) prototype   Line G

(h) stimulated   Line H

2   What did the ski-manufacturer mean in his statement about being in the 'fun business'?

3   Explain the difference of approach to marketing in the industrial and consumer markets.

4   Outline briefly what you understand by the term 'market research'.

5   What are the advantages of 'test marketing' a product?

Persuasive communication 2

No matter what the job, everyone at work needs to be skilled in the art of persuasive communication. In a sense, the term 'persuasive communication' means using the resources of the spoken, written, pictorial or visual media to get others to do something you would like them to do when you cannot simply issue an instruction to be followed as a matter of course.

Many people at work, for example, undertake jobs or tasks which, strictly speaking, lie outside their contract or conditions or employment:

'Jane, I wonder if you'd mind staying on a bit later tonight? It's just that the Old Man's insisting that I have this report on his desk first thing in the morning! I'd type it myself, only you know what my 'hunt and peck' type-script looks like! I'll buy you a drink after – could you possibly manage it?'

Of course, Jane would be perfectly entitled to say that she had a previous engagement and was committed to leaving on time. Yet even if she was not 'otherwise engaged', her manager would still need to 'woo' her. He could not simply state:

'Jane, there's a report I need finished for first thing in the morning. You'll have to stay late, but it shouldn't take too long if you get stuck into it.'

Since Jane's manager realises that, he is in an 'asking', rather than a 'telling' situation. He takes pains to phrase his request as persuasively and as pleasantly as possible – hoping that Jane will feel it difficult to refuse! In other words, the skilled use of techniques of persuasion are needed if the report is to be finished on time. Very often,

secretaries will help their bosses out of a sense of loyalty and commitment to their jobs – but they still expect to be asked, rather than told!

Discussion topic

What is it about the first Manager/Jane extract above that is likely to make the attempt to persuade Jane to stay on late succeed?

The permutations of people and situations where persuasive communication skills are a crucial factor in achieving a desired goal are virtually endless in the world of business. The following examples will give you some idea:

- a salesman trying to clinch a sale
- a manager seeking an extra effort from staff to reach a sales target
- a personnel manager endeavouring to dissuade a disgruntled but key member of staff from handing in his resignation
- a clerk seeking a day off at a busy time in the office
- a secretary asking her boss for a salary increase
- management and union officials negotiating a pay increase
- a shop steward trying to persuade trade union members to vote for a return to work

As well as using spoken skills of persuasive communication, such skills are also frequently used in other communications media:

Written communication

newspaper advertisements
sales brochures and leaflets
letters to the press
unsolicited sales letters
press releases
articles in house journals
newspaper editorials
public information notices and circulars

Graphic communication

logos and trade marks
photographs and drawings in advertisements
television commercials
the use of different typefaces in printing – italic, gothic, etc
cartoons

It is also important to note the use of colour in persuasive graphic communication. For example, colours like gold, red and silver are used to convey a sense of luxury and expensiveness; while colours like white, green and blue are used to denote freshness, cleanliness or purity. Indeed, we are much more prone to persuasion by colour influences than we realise. Dentists and doctors, for instance, tend to use greens and blues in their waiting rooms because of their soothing and reassuring effects on patients; while discos and nightclubs are decorated in reds, blacks and golds to promote a sense of excitement and occasion.

When the various techniques of persuasive communication are used together, linking the spoken and written word and graphic communication, their effect is much more immediate and convincing. It is for this reason that the colour TV commercials which are broadcast nightly to millions of living rooms are so effective.

Using the spoken word persuasively

The ability to use the spoken word effectively depends upon bringing together a number of related factors:

choice of vocabulary
speech rhythms and delivery
non-verbal communication signals

Consider vocabulary. Although we refer to our language as English, it might be more precise to speak of 'languages'. As we have already learned, there is a good deal of difference between the more formal modes of some written communications and the more familiar and easy-going patterns of the spoken word. This difference is particularly noticeable in the use of spoken persuasive communication.

In order to appreciate this fact fully, it is necessary to go back to the roots of the English language, which embodies three main elements:

Because of invasions of Romans, Danes, Norsemen, Anglo-Saxons and Norman French, various dialects were found in different parts of the country. Latin was kept for the business of church and government; Norman French was the language of the ruling classes. Indeed, it was not until the beginning of the 14th century that the language we speak began to emerge – not so much from the French and Latin, as from the colloquial dialects which contained words of Saxon and Norse origin for everyday items. In contrast, words of Latin and Norman French roots were used to denote more abstract and administrative ideas.

Thus in a sense, there grew into modern English two strands of language. The one, with Saxon or Old English roots, which was used to describe the ordinary and everyday world, and the other with latinate or Old French roots, which was more theoretical and used in legal, religious or administrative circles. As a result, the words which tend to have most emotional effect upon us are those which have been in constant use by the working people in their everyday lives, while those words used to define abstract or theoretical ideas do not touch us so readily. It is therefore no accident that in persuasive spoken communication, the short, simple words of Saxon and Norse origin abound.

Table of word roots	
Old English roots	*Latin/Norman French roots*
mother	maternal
father	paternal
son	filial
daughter	
home	domicile
fire	conflagration
house	residence
field	estate
loving	amorous
death	extermination
fairness	pulchritude
sword	lance
knight	cavalry
horse-riding	equitation
feast	banquet
fine	resplendent
old age	senility

The table clearly illustrates that words of French and Latin origin are generally much less familiar to us and are much longer than those coming from Old English. In persuasive communication terms, not only do the shorter Old English words spark off a much more emotional response in the listener, they are also much more immediate and simple to understand. For this reason, both poets and advertising copy writers – who alike are seeking to sway the heart rather than convince the head – tend to use vocabulary with Old English roots rather than the more abstruse latinate equivalents.

In order, then, to use the spoken word to persuade, it is necessary to consider carefully the choice of words to be used and to avoid those words as a rule which are:

Latin in origin (or French)
multisyllabic
abstruse in meaning
neutral or factual in effect

With regard to speech rhythms and delivery, it is important that the message conveyed appears alive and vital rather than dead and monotonous. For this reason, it is essential that emphasis is given to key words in the way they are uttered, and that the voice rises and drops appropriately to signify the asking of a question, say, or the ending of a sentence. Actors and politicians who make their livings by using the spoken word are skilled in the techniques of delivery, and it is true that in meetings and assemblies, the *way* a point of view is expressed is just as important as its meaning.

Consider, for example, the two following extracts:

> Ladies and gentlemen, it gives me great pleasure to have the honour to address you this evening on such an important occasion, when I know that you will collectively be recalling the illustrious history of our celebrated and august Society, founded as you will all doubtless recall in the year 1892 by a few far-sighted and public-spirited educationalists, prompted by their abhorrence of the profound lack of educational opportunity which existed in the then ...

> Good evening all! That's right missus, you can wake up now, the star turn's begun! Here, that's enough of that cackling up in the balcony – I *am* a star turn you know. What! Now listen. You're lucky to have me. Oh, yes, the manager was saying to me just now, we've got a rough lot out there tonight! Yes, missus, not the usual sort we like to get in here, you know – he said it's the weather – most of 'em only come in to eat their fish and chips in the dry!

In the first extract, the speaker would be lucky to have anyone in the audience still awake by the time he finished his first sentence, since its length, the words used and the manner of their delivery make any message appear monotonous and virtually empty of meaning. In the second extract, a comedian in a live theatre is beginning his 'patter' and aiming to get and hold his audience's attention before proceeding to deliver his string of gags and jokes.

Assignment

In a general group, analyse the vocabulary, structure and tone of the two extracts and try to establish why the one is more likely to succeed than the other.

Of course, not all persuasive communications can be delivered as if part of a comic sketch. What is true of all attempts at persuasion, however, is the need to achieve both the following:

to pitch the message at the right level
to establish rapport with the receiver

The matter of pitch is most important. By pitch is meant the transmitting of the message in a style or tone which best suits the occasion and which neither baffles the receiver, nor talks down to him.

The term rapport is used to convey that sense of friendliness and goodwill which has to be created between the sender and recipient of the message.

Consider, for example, the following extracts and identify what it is about them which is likely to make the element of persuasion effective:

> Harry, I know you've done your share of cleaning out the stockroom, but Nick's off sick today, and the boss is bringing one of the directors round tomorrow on a tour of inspection. I'd appreciate it if you would give it a careful check over, because if I leave it to you, I know it'll be tidied properly.

> I quite realise that the improvements to the staff canteen were promised to be carried out during the current financial year. At the time, management gave the undertaking in good faith. As you all know, however, this has proved a most disappointing year for sales, and orders are well down on last year. As a result, there simply isn't the money available at present to carry out the necessary repairs. But I am sure that everyone here accepts the need for the firm to control its outgoings most carefully if we are to survive the current recession ...

> Listen, Carol, I know Mr Hendricks is not the easiest manager to work for – but he'll provide the work experience you need to get on here. Yes, I agree that he can be abrupt and overbearing at times, and, yes, say things which can be hurtful and upsetting. But I'm absolutely sure that's just his way. He never *means* to be rude or domineering. And another thing, the Apex Contract has given all of us a lot of extra work in order to meet the deadline. And with the managing director overseas, Mr Hendricks has been under a good deal of additional stress. Now you just dry your eyes and go and freshen up in the Ladies. I'll have a word with Mr Hendricks. Don't worry, he won't know we've spoken. And remember – he has a high regard for your secretarial qualities. You just stick up for yourself! Give as good as you get, and you'll have him eating out of your hand!

Using the spoken word persuasively assignments

1   The accident rate in your firm's offices is rising alarmingly. As a result, you have been asked to give staff a five minute talk on how to avoid accidents at work. Your aim is to persuade them to take more care in the way they operate and use equipment. Draft your notes, then deliver the talk.

2   Role play one of the following involving a customer and a sales assistant:

(a) a female customer is in a hair-dressing salon and hesitating about whether to have her hair cut and re-styled.

(b) A young man is undecided about purchasing a black and white or colour TV set for his flat.

(c) A young couple at a second-hand car dealer's are having second thoughts about buying a small car or, instead, purchasing a new motor-cycle.

3 One of your fellow students is feeling rather depressed in the middle of the course and thinking of quitting. Role play a sequence persuading him or her to see the course through.

4 In groups of 5–6, hold a meeting to discuss the following items of business:

(*a*) The means of raising £500 to save the Student Association from becoming insolvent.
(*b*) That the Student Committee take immediate steps to introduce a programme of voluntary help for the aged in the local community.
Proposer: A N Other
Seconder: A N Other-Another

Note: In each of the above assignments, it would be helpful to tape-record the dialogues/discussions for subsequent analysis and evaluation by the student group.

5 In a general group session, draw up an agreed checklist of the factors which go to make up effective spoken persuasive communication.

6 In small groups, devise a suitable radio commercial aimed at advertising one of the following:

(*a*) a new teenage boutique about to open in town
(*b*) a new disco club which has recently opened in the district
(*c*) a leisure centre which the local council is about to open in the town
(*d*) a situation vacant for a clerical assistant in a local government office
(*e*) a pop concert which will be taking place in the Town Hall next Saturday evening.

When you have researched your script and suitable sound effects, tape-record your commercial and play it back with the others devised by your group. Decide which is the most effective and why.
Note: Your commercial should not exceed one minute of broadcasting time.

Using the written word persuasively

Whether an organisation is a company in the private sector, or a part of local or central government in the public service, many occasions arise when written communications are sent with the definite intention of per-suading.

Clearly all forms of advertising writing fall into this category as do the compositions coming from a firm's public relations department which may send news or press-releases to local or national newspapers and specialist trade journals. Though the messages need to be newsworthy, they will also be put in such a way that the public image of the company is presented in a good light.

Similarly, the copy for advertisements needs to be written in such a way that the product or service on offer is presented to the consumer in a stimulating, fresh and exciting way, so that the desire to buy is generated.

Additionally, within an organisation, there will be numerous instances when memoranda, notices or posters will be designed or composed with a persuasive intent. For example, in factories there are many different types of poster on display which are intended to remind staff of the need to take care and avoid accidents; in the hotel and catering industry notices and posters will emphasise the need to maintain high standards of personal hygiene. In many sales departments, regular memoranda are sent to field sales representatives to boost their morale and to encourage them to meet monthly sales targets. And, as we have already discovered in the accounts department, letters of collection have to be composed which will encourage customers to pay outstanding debts, while keeping their goodwill – no mean feat!

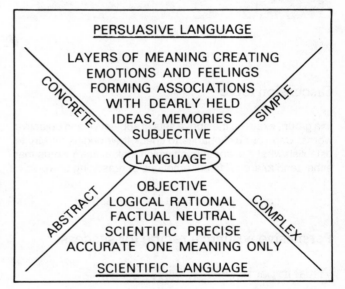

The diagram illustrates the two different kinds of written language which we can identify and use on two very different occasions. When the written word is being used to convey factual data and information, the writer will, naturally, seek to use those words and expressions which transmit a precise and exact meaning, devoid of any emotional overtones. Such is the language of reports, briefings, factsheets and information schedules. When, however, the writer wishes to change attitudes, to promote a desire to buy or to put people into a friendly and receptive mood, then the language used will not so much be factually precise but will appeal to the emotions and make associations with the reader's 'feeling' rather than 'thinking' mind.

Examples of subjective words

sparkling fresh cool pure tingling lovelier
tender young smooth happy bright
sunshine warm glow power tough strong
hard stout dainty delicate slim slender
home haven hearth farm supper safe

Examples of objective words

output target production capacity fraction
percentage ratio decimal net profit cost
price margin retail wholesale distribution
transport heat-resistant shatter-proof brittle
compute calculate multiply divide warranty
guarantee

Discussion topic

In a group, examine the above sets of subjective and objective words. Use your dictionaries to check their origins and try to establish what it is about each which makes them words that either tend to appeal to our emotions or reasoning powers.

Persuasive writing: a recipe for success

Visual impact

In producing an effective piece of persuasive writing, there are a number of important factors to consider. Firstly, the written document will need to appeal to the reader's eye. This means that the following components of the document will have a strong effect:

- the size of the paper
- the quality of the paper used
- the impact of colour – of paper and print
- the typography used
- the inclusion of graphic symbols, trademarks or logos
- the use of space around printed parts of the message to emphasise important parts and break it down into easily absorbed sections

Indeed, recent research has shown that up to 25% of a message's impact is due to the above factors!

Meaning impact

However, no amount of visual impact will serve if the meaning of the message is not properly looked after. Therefore the following aspects of composing the written word need to be given careful attention:

- careful consideration of the context in which the message is to be conveyed – selling, confidence-building, motivating, attitude-changing, etc
- regard for the reader's characteristics, personality and background – 'what makes him tick', and establishing of rapport
- appropriate choice of words – simple, direct, subjective, familiar, friendly, etc, avoidance of many multisyllabic words
- careful sentence and paragraph structure – avoiding over-long sentences, too many dependent clauses; avoidance of over-long paragraphs, where the reader flounders in a 'sea of prose'
- conveying a suitable tone to the reader – understanding, sympathetic, helpful and considerate, polite and courteous, etc, avoidance of 'talking down' to reader or of baffling with jargon and technicalities
- use of eye-catching headlines and section headings to arrest attention and stimulate interest
- a structure which is simple and easy to follow

Presentation impact

The final persuasive 'package' needs to have a presentation impact. In other words, care and attention need to be given to:

- delivery in good time
- getting names, titles, qualifications of recipient(s) right
- ensuring that the document is flawless – no messy erasures, smudges, etc, no punctuation or spelling mistakes
- ensuring that data is up to date and correct

The action statement impact

Since most persuasive communications are aimed at getting the recipient to *do* something, whether to purchase a product or to go out and sell harder, it is vital that the part of the message which conveys what is to be acted upon is clear, emphatic and written in a way which will make the recipient *want* to act – after all, this is the whole purpose behind the piece of writing, around which the message's visual, meaning and presentation impacts are centred!

Using the written word persuasively assignments

1 A senior partner of Johnson, Haines and Beckett, solicitors, 4 East Parade, Middleton, Newshire, MT4 6BG, telephone, Middleton 876584/6 requires a shorthand-typist to work as an assistant to his personal secretary. Hours are: Mon–Fri 9.00 am–5.30 pm, one hour lunch break; three weeks paid holidays, usual fringe benefits, and starting salary around £5500 pa. Might suit a school/college leaver.

Design a suitable display advertisement for the post to appear in the local weekly newspaper.

2 Family Foods Limited, a nationwide supermarket chain is about to open a new store in Westerton, Midshire, at 109/113 High Street. The firm is anxious to ensure that as many local residents as possible are aware of the superb shopping facilities and range of food products. You have been asked to design a leaflet to be posted through residents' letterboxes which will advise local people of the time, date, hours of opening, range of goods, shopping advantages, etc. Using graphic, visual and written persuasive communication techniques, design a suitable leaflet.

3 At a cost of £750 000, the Newtown Borough Council has almost finished building a brand new Community Youth Centre at 5 Parkside Road, Newtown, Wealdshire NT2 WS4.

The Centre will be managed by Chris Barnes, an experienced Youth Leader (telephone Newtown 567342) and the premises will include facilities for discos, table-tennis, drama, badminton, billiards and snooker, a snack bar and meeting rooms, etc.

The council is keen to see the centre fully used and, as an assistant to the council's information officer, Mrs Patricia Simpson, you have been asked to design a brochure to send to schools, colleges and clubs in the area to persuade teenagers to join in the Centre's activities. **Note:** the Centre aims to cater for young people between the ages of 13 and 19.

Either singly, or in groups, design a suitable brochure.

4 Liaise with your school or college's student committee and arrange to design, print and distribute posters or notices for a forthcoming social or sports event.

5 Design a suitable poster for display in a training office, workshop or laboratory to remind student users of the need to take care and avoid causing or being involved in accidents.

6 Design a poster to be displayed in your school or college aimed at preventing litter and to encourage staff and students to be more conscious of the need to care for their environment.

7 Consider carefully the current course you are following, and the type of students it aims to help. In groups, design a promotional 'kit' which could be sent to any potential student enquiring about joining the course next year.

How a sales brochure communicates

In a general session, study carefully both the wording and the illustrations of the Hermes sales brochure on page 230. Identify those words or phrases which you think particularly effective in conveying the attraction of perfume and in explaining how it should be used.

Assignment

Either individually, or in groups, design a sales brochure aimed at promoting the sale of *one* of the following:

a hair shampoo a toilet soap an after-shave lotion a toothpaste a perfume a talcum powder a men's hair lotion/spray

'What's he got that I haven't?'

A company wanted to make a small, technical change in the pension arrangements for its staff, which for legal reasons required each employee to sign a form accepting the change.

Everyone duly signed – except Charlie, who had run the stationery store for years. Charlie's immediate boss took him on one side and spent half-an-hour explaining that it was only a technicality and that it wouldn't affect his pension rights in any way. 'No!' said Charlie, 'I'm not signing the thing on principle!'

Eventually, Charlie's boss referred him to the personnel manager, who devoted an hour-and-a-half explaining to Charlie why he should sign the form and then forget about it. 'Danged if I will!' said Charlie. 'It's the principle of the thing! I won't!' And with that, he stalked back to his store.

Ten minutes later, his telephone rang. His presence was immediately required in the managing director's office!

Three minutes after being ushered into the MD's office, a smiling Charlie emerged to be greeted by a curious crowd from various offices. 'Did you sign it, Charlie?' asked the personnel manager.

'Course I did!' answered Charlie.

'Well,' went on the personnel manager. 'I spent nearly two hours with you going over the form and you wouldn't sign it for me. Yet within a couple of minutes, the MD's got you eating out of his hand! What's he got that I haven't?'

'Simple!' answered Charlie. 'He shoved the form in front of me and said that if I didn't sign it there and then, I needn't bother to come in to work tomorrow – and no one had explained it to me that clearly before!'

(With acknowledgements to unknown source)

History of Perfumes

It was in the East that perfume, originally offered to the Gods in religious rites, first became used by oriental women for perfuming the body.

In the middle of the 15th century, the fashion for perfume began in France, and with Grasse as the world centre for flower cultivation and distillation, and Paris as the world centre of fashion, the scent industry flourished.

But it was around the end of the last century, during la 'Belle Epoque', a brilliant era of luxury and elegance, that the perfume industry as we now know it really developed.

The great French couturiers entered the perfume field creating magnificent fragrances and placing France ahead of all others in the international perfume market.

Today, perfume is used all over the world. It has now become an indispensable fashion accessory for the feminine woman.

Pulse Points

Remember

1 Whilst the same perfume can be used in all seasons, more perfume should be used in cold weather, but less often.

2 An eau de toilette or parfum de toilette can be sufficient for daytime use, but a perfume is a richer essence more suitable for the evening.

3 Do not change perfumes during the same day, except after bathing.

4 To make the most of your perfume use either complementary or unscented soap.

5 Preserve your perfume by keeping bottles away from sun and heat.

Assignment

In a general group discussion study carefully both the wording and graphic illustration of the Hermes sales brochure. Identify those words or phrases which you think are particularly effective as persuasive communication. What does the graphic illustration contribute to the brochure's total effect?

Writing a letter to the press

Every week local newspaper readers feel the need to 'write a letter to the press'. Sometimes letters are full of indignation about a local event – car parking charges have risen, or the town centre is becoming a 'litter bin'.

Alternatively, a company or departmental official will feel obliged to answer criticisms which have been levelled at a local firm or public department. For example, there may be long queues at the main post office every day, or a local chemical firm may be pumping waste into the local river.

Whatever the motive for writing, the letter columns of local newspapers are usually filled each week with letters which seek to influence the opinions and attitudes of local residents. Indeed, the letter column service given by the press is a very important one in terms of local democracy and freedom of speech.

Letters written to local newspapers are usually addressed to the editor and begin with a customary 'Dear Sir', although some newspapers follow the tradition of starting letters they print with 'Sir'.

Whether as a local resident, local government official, or worker, one never knows when the need to use the columns of the local paper may present itself. It is therefore helpful to study some of the letters printed in such papers, and to practise composing letters to the press.

Assignments

1 Collect a set of back numbers of your local newspaper and study the topics written about, the approaches used and the tone of the writing. See if you can establish any common features or patterns which may emerge.

2 Imagine that in your town there is only one cinema, The Plaza. The cinema is owned by a local organisation which intends to close it down and to sell the site for office development. The nearest cinema is ten miles away in Appleford. Lately, the cinema has concentrated on showing 'adult' films. Apart from the cinema, there are few other leisure amenities in your town.

Write a letter to the local newspaper opposing the proposed closure and seeking support for the retention of The Plaza as a cinema.

3 As a local teenager, you are 'fed up' with the way that other residents blame young people for rowdyism and increasing vandalism. Assume that in your town there is very little for young people to do in the evenings and at weekends. Write a letter to the local press which puts the teenager's point of view and which asks for something positive to be done.

Grammar

The split infinitive

When writing – especially in haste – it is easy to split the infinitive.

What this means is that a word or phrase is put *between* the word 'to' and the infinitive form of the verb:

She had to *quickly* finish.

The correct word order should be:

She had to finish *quickly*.

It is usually adverbs which 'push' between the inseparable infinitive form to + verb. But sometimes a group of words is inserted in this way:

It is then not difficult to *very simply and easily* release the lever.

Again, the adverbial phrase should go after the infinitive and object at the end of the sentence.

In using the spoken word, we very frequently split infinitives – and no one seems either to notice or to mind. In using the written word, however, more care and accuracy is needed – and indeed, expected!

Should or would?

The two conditional forms of 'shall' and 'will' often cause difficulty because we use them indiscriminately, sometimes using 'would' when 'should' is required.

The reason goes right back to Anglo-Saxon times, when the form of verbs changed according to their person. Today English still echoes this verb structure:

VERB: to be

	future tense	*future conditional*
I	shall	should
You	will	would
He She	will	would
We	shall	should
You	will	would
They	will	would

Thus the first person, singular or plural almost always takes 'should':

I *should* be grateful if you *would* come.

But notice: when a firm intention is meant, 'would' is used:

I *would* go if I had the money!

'Should' is used to denote 'ought':

I *should* go, but I intend to stay.

Notice also the way that 'shall' and 'will' are reversed in the first and second person to transmit a sense of an order or positive determination:

Cinderella, you *shall* go to the ball!
I *will* go, and you won't stop me!

Lastly, do not confuse 'could' with 'would'.

could – can: to be able
would – will: to be, to do

For example:

I should be pleased if you *could* mend it.

does not mean the same as:

I should be pleased if you *would* mend it.

So, remember to treat 'should', 'would' and 'could' with care and you will write what you mean to say!

Here's the proof...! 6

Re-write each of the following paragraphs correctly.

1 'It gives me great pleasure to welcome you to Harridges. Each year we recruit ten trainees, and I always hire the best. You have all followed courses at local colleges emphasising the importence of marketting – I hope you shall be able to apply that nowledge here.

2 Will you please arrange to call on these people in about ten days time to show them our currant fabric samples. I hope to be in the area next week and will call on Mr Robinson, who I know well, you should recieve a copy of my report before you go there.

3 I am extremely worried by the amount of stationary that is being wasted – this is not a cheap item and we are all ready substantialy over-budget for the year. Would you please try to conserve stocks in the future and for internal male please re-use old envelopes?

Boost your spelling power!

Learn these words by heart

Remember, an asterisk after a word indicates that it is very commonly misspelled:

all right*	(*never* alright!)
colleagues* n	
dossier n	
deterrent n	(deter v)
essential adj	(essentially adv)
intelligent adj	(intelligence n)
minutes* n	
planning* pres part	
repetition n	(repetitive adj)
severe adj	(severely adv)
usual adj	(usually* adv)
note: unusual adj	
amateur n, adj	
college n	(collegiate adj)
exigency n	(pl: exigencies n)
irrelevant adj	(irrelevance n)
murmur v, n	(murmuring pres part)
potential n, adj	
shining pres part	
similar adj	(similarity n)
preceding pres part	(precedent n)

Do not forget to enter in your vocabulary book any words with which you are unfamiliar, either in terms of spelling or meaning!

Assignment

By arrangement, choose four of the above words. Compose a sentence for each, in which the word is used correctly. Compare your sentences with those devised by others in your group. This will help you to add the above list of words to your **active vocabulary.**

Fastsnacks Limited

A group project in persuasive communication

Form groups of 4–6 students. Each group should assume that it is the marketing team for Fastsnacks Limited. Study carefully the section on pages 222–223, Marketing, and having found out the principles and processes of marketing and advertising, carry out, *as a team*, the following assignments. When you have completed the tasks (*in secrecy*) hold a series of presentations in the general group to explain and display your approaches to launching Fastsnacks' new product.

Assignment 1

Hold a meeting to decide the following:

- Which age-group and income group will you aim your new product at?

- What sort of snack will you develop and produce, bearing in mind what is already on the market?

- What sort of price do you envisage it selling for to the customer? Again, bear in mind competition.

You should decide upon a chairman to coordinate your decision-making, and also arrangements should be made for the meeting to be minuted, and the minutes should be circulated before assignment 2.

Assignment 2

Assuming that you have decided upon the market you are aiming at, and a product has been developed with clear characteristics, you will now need to meet as a group and to plan your advertising strategy. You should therefore decide upon a different chairman, who will coordinate the following tasks you will need to carry out:

- Decide upon a name for your product.

- Design a coloured wrapper for the product and prepare an illustration of it for your presentation.

- Assume that you are going to advertise the product nationally for three weeks, coinciding with the launching of the product in the shops.
  You will need to decide what advertising media you will employ – TV, radio, roadside hoarding, magazine advertisement, etc.
  You have to produce three different but related advertisements. For example, a radio commercial, a magazine advertisement and poster on a bus.
  Decide which media you will use, and make brief notes explaining why you reached your decisions. Then devise and produce *three* advertisements in three different media ready to use in your presentation.

Assignment 3

As part of your programme to launch your product successfully, you have decided to compose and despatch a circular sales letter to your many retail dealers, to tell them about your new product, and to persuade them to stock it in some quantity prior to your national launching of it.

- Design a letterhead for Fastsnacks, including a suitable logo.

- Compose a suitable letter to the dealers from the sales director, and have it typed on your letter paper for the presentation.

Assignment 4

As part of your sales promotion campaign, you have decided to make a special offer linked to your new product to encourage your potential customers to buy it and try it. You have therefore opted to produce an A5 leaflet containing details of the offer, which will be inserted in a magazine, comic, paper,

etc which your potential customers are known to buy.
   Design a suitable leaflet, detailing the nature of the special offer.

Assignment 5

Your overall strategy and specimens devised and produced in assignments 1, 2, 3 and 4 must be coordinated and made ready for your presentation. Each group member must present part of the presentation, and you should plan it carefully for maximum effect – you have to 'sell' your ideas to a sceptical board of directors!

Tactful communication

Inevitably, in the course of business or social life, events occur which require tactful and sensitive handling. For example, calming down an irate customer needs a great deal of skill – knowing what to say and how to express it, using non-verbal communication expressions and gestures aimed at soothing and steadying. Again, a manager may have to tell one of his staff that he has not been selected for a departmental promotion. Similarly, a member of a sales administration section may have to write to a customer to say that an urgently required piece of equipment is in short supply, and so on.

   It is therefore important that we give due attention to the development of skills of tactful and diplomatic communication, whether expressed in the spoken or written word. After all, it may help you to get that increase in salary, or to avoid a clash with an upset colleague!

Tactful communication assignments

Using the spoken word

1   Role play a situation where a manager has to break bad news to one of his clerical assistants who works hard and has been with the firm several years. He/she has not been promoted to senior clerk in the department

2   A lady customer purchased a pair of fashion shoes yesterday to wear at a charity ball given by the city's mayor. When she was dancing with him, the heel on the right shoe broke off and caused her a great deal of embarrassment. She arrives in high dudgeon in the Ladies Shoe Department to register her complaint, clutching two shoes and a heel. It is lunch-time and only one sales assistant is on duty. Role play the ensuing dialogue between customer and assistant.

3   A relative newcomer to the office, Jean/Jack Goodson, has settled in well and has shown ability and capacity for hard work. Other staff in the office, however, are beginning to grumble about his/her habit of engaging them in lengthy conversations, which they find distracting and which interfere with their work. Jean's/Jack's supervisor decides that it is time to have a private word on the subject. Role play the conversation which follows.

Note: If possible, the simulations should be tape-recorded for subsequent analysis either by the participants, or with their permission, by the student group.

The following chart indicates some of the main aspects of tactful communication:

Golden rules

1 Choose your words *carefully*!
If your recipient is likely to be upset, disappointed, irritated or deflated by your message, he will be particularly sensitive to the form and impact of its language. It is therefore important not to use words, expressions or gestures likely to make a difficult situation worse.

2 Take care with your timing
It is easy to be insensitive in the timing of a message. If, for example, a member of staff had just been disappointed in a promotion application, it would be quite tactless to inform him at the same time that his application to join a training programme had also been turned down, if such bad news could wait for a few days.

3 Structure your message appropriately
Also, when conveying bad news or an unwelcome decision, it helps to lead into it gently, and to try to present it in as positive a way as possible. Compare the following:

'You've had your overtime this week, lads! Not enough jobs on, so you'll just have to put up with your basic pay!'

'I'm sorry, lads, we've had a good month so far, but I'm afraid there's no overtime working available this week. I'm pretty sure there will be next week, and I'll let you know in good time.'

People can either be let down gently, or have the rug ripped from under them!

4 Use appropriate NVC signals
When talking to someone on an occasion needing tact, remember that your face, hands and body are always communicating something while you speak, so remember to match your NVC signals with your spoken message.

5 Know when to keep quiet!
Often, the best communication in difficult situations is silence. As a wise communicator once said: 'I've often regretted it when I've opened my mouth, but never when I've kept quiet!'

Case study

Mike Weston has recently received a letter from the chairman of the Social Club Committee in the firm where he works, inviting him to take on the chairmanship of a sub-committee being formed to organise the Social Club's Annual Christmas Dance. Mike has other commitments and does not wish to accept the invitation. So he writes what he hopes will be a suitable letter to decline the invitation:

Dear Richard,

It was most kind of you to think of me as a possible chairman for the Sub-Committee to organise this year's Annual Christmas Dance, especially since it is always considered to be the 'high-spot' of the Club's year.

However, regretfully, I must decline your invitation. At present, as I believe you are aware, I am very much committed to the final year in my evening class course in office administration. In view of the increase this year in homework assignments, I do not feel I could carry out the demanding role of chairman as thoroughly as I would wish and the task requires.

I do appreciate your invitation and shall certainly do all I can to promote the dance in the department.

Yours sincerely,
Mike Weston

Discussion topics

1 What aspects of the letter's structure and wording help Mike to 'say no' gracefully?

2 Are there any parts which you would change, omit or add?

3 Is Mike's excuse for not accepting a suitable one?

4 Would it help if Mike were to suggest in his letter someone else whom Richard might contact to be chairman?

5 Should Mike have ended his letter by wishing Richard every success in finding a chairman and running the dance?

6 What features of the letter's three paragraph structure help to convey the bad news in a courteous and acceptable manner?

You've got to have 'IT' to sell it!

A case study

'You know, Charlie, if we don't do somethin' pretty miraculous straightaway, we've had it! I've just been going through last month's sales reports, and we're not just going through a down-turn in demand, as far as I can make out, there *isn't* a demand – not for what we've got to sell, anyway!' With these doom-laden words to greet her, 'Charlie' or Charlotte Harvey as her mother preferred her to be known, walked into her boss's office for their weekly review of what had to be done and in what order.

Charlie's boss, Harry Shooter, was the hard-working if traditionally-minded sales manager of Leisurelex Wholesale Limited, a company which sold a wide range of electrical and electronic products in the home use leisure market to smaller retailers outside of the bulk-purchasing chainstores and hypermarkets. Leisurelex sold portable radios, 'Walkman' tape players, hair dryers, coffee grinders, compact hi-fi sets and television receivers, manufactured by foreign manufacturers comparatively unknown in the UK, and thereby serving the cheaper end of the home appliance market. Leisurelex employed 12 sales representatives, each with a sales territory in the area of Britain known generally as the Midlands. To back them up was a rather anti-quated sales department, situated on the ground floor of a head office three-storey building on the outskirts of Birmingham, built in the optimistic 1950s, and which had seen barely a brush load of paint or new furniture since!

'And look at this lot!' Harry let a handful of expenses returns, memos, order confirmations and sundry pieces of paper fall through his hands on to an already littered desk. 'I'm not even keeping up with the daily load of bumpf that comes our way, never mind getting the additional business we need in a hurry! And if that's not enough, the duplicator's on the blink and that d**n phone hasn't stopped ringing all morning!'

'Oh, Harry, you've really got the Monday morning blues today,' consoled Charlie, while admitting to herself that he had good reason to be depressed. Business was indeed bad. The sales reps were failing to get orders and everyone was blaming everyone else.

Some said that the sales catalogues and brochures were out of date and prices always behind the latest adjustments. Others blamed the sales reps for not passing on their orders promptly so that retailers rang in to cancel having transferred their requirements to other wholesalers. Yet others said it was because the retail customers weren't given enough support on the qualities and selling points of often excellent but little known products and therefore didn't know how to sell them effectively. A different school of thought pointed out the large stocks of goods quietly mouldering in the Leirsurelex warehouse and highlighted the money being wasted on over-stocking – perfectly good products were being overtaken by later models marketed more aggressively and which sold out straightaway.

'You know, Harry, I think we should do some fast homework on IT. I think IT's our only chance for survi-val,' said Charlie, after some deep thought.

'What the devil are you talking about? Homework on IT is the only chance for IT to save us! I think you've finally gone bananas!'

'No, Harry, I..T.. standing for Information Technology – you know, computers, electronic mail, intelligent printers, Prestel, desk-top publishing, the whole bag!' exclaimed Charlie in a rush of enthusiasm for her new-found solution.

'Hm, IT. Well, perhaps you're right. I thought I'd have retired before I had to grapple with computers ... but you may have hit the nail on the head before it's too late. What we need is a feasibility study done straightaway to see just how and where IT could get our sales operation turned round and back on the right tracks. Sit down young lady and tell me all you know, while I make us some coffee!'

Assignments

1 Consider the case study carefully in groups of 3–5 students and then carry out the following:

 (*a*) Make out a checklist of the ways in which IT applications introduced both in the head office sales department and out in the sales territories could help solve Harry's problems.

 (*b*) After group discussion and consultation, devise a plan of campaign – assuming that Harry and Charlie have con-vinced their directors of the need to invest in IT equipment – aimed at securing an improvement in the ways in which Leisurelex sales are won and administered.

Here are a few ideas for starters:

With what IT techniques and equipment could the sales reps receive up-to-the-minute sales information in leaflets and catalogues?

What IT services run by British Telecom could the sales reps use to get their orders and requests to the sales department quickly and effectively?

Your plan should tackle the following areas and give a clear idea of priority areas:

● processing sales orders

● monitoring stocks

● sales literature and sales promotion/advertising

● administration of sales reports and sales intelligence

● recording buying terms and discounts etc. negotiated with customers

● storing sales details, specifications, ordering procedures etc for some 75 different product lines

● setting up circular sales letters and promotional leaflets sent regularly to some 500 customers.

Each group should present its plan to the class in the form of an oral presentation, using whatever audio-visual aids it thinks most effective.

Follow up assignment

2 Make arrangements to visit a wholesale business or distribution firm and see how they are using IT applications to help keep their sales healthy and growing.

Report back to your group on what you discover.

Activities and assignments

Discussion topics

1 A printer working in a small printing works is one day asked to print a booklet which puts forward precisely the opposite of his own, strongly-held political views.

Does he refuse to print it?

2 A manager with a 'roving eye' one afternoon asks his secretary to ring his wife at home to tell her he will be working late at the office. But his secretary knows he will, in reality, be taking out a female member of the office staff on a secret date.

Does the secretary agree to make the call? How would you react in her place?

Persuasive communication

3 As a group, collect a series of the following:

● full colour advertisements from magazines and supplements
● specimens of unsolicited mail delivered to your home
● leaflets and brochures from public institutions like libraries and post offices
● taped radio commercials or video-taped TV commercials

In smaller groups of 4–5, analyse a set of advertisements and present to the general group your findings about their effectiveness in terms of their graphics, colour, typography, working, etc.

4 By arrangement, visit a local store or shop and interview the manager on the techniques he or she uses to advertise the store locally.

Write a report of your findings for the group.

5 By arrangement, visit your local council offices and interview the information officer or public relations officer on the range and scope of the job.

Give a short talk to your group, summarising what you found out.

Marketing

6 When a local retail organisation next puts on a sale, make a careful study (in small groups) of the techniques adopted to promote it both outside and inside the shop or store. By arrangement, collect examples of sales promotional and advertising material, and produce a kit to accompany a briefing you give to your group outlining the ways in which the sale was promoted.

Unit 14

Visual and number communication 2

In every office, at some time or other, the need arises to display numerical information in a visual form. Clearly, departments such as accounts, sales, marketing and production will frequently express information in the form of tables, charts or graphs. But the need to convey number information clearly and simply arises in every department of private or public organisations. It is therefore essential that the office worker becomes familiar with this means of communication and confident in his ability both to devise visual communications involving numbers and to interpret them correctly.

As we have already learned in Unit 8, tables and pie charts are often used to display number communication. But perhaps the most useful and most frequently drawn up form of number communication is the line graph.

The line graph

Though it may, at first sight, appear somewhat daunting, the line graph is, in reality, an extremely simple form of number communication to devise and interpret. Most line graphs used in business take the form of a grid:

Information is plotted on the grid in a way which tells the reader what happened at a given point. Very often, the graph plots quantities against time. For example, a retail store may sell a certain number of washing machines each month. The manager may wish to keep a careful eye on his sales turnover in washing machines, and may therefore devise a line graph which records the number of machines sold by the end of each month.

In the line graph, then, we have quantity plotted along a vertical axis (from bottom to top), and time plotted along a horizontal axis (from left to right). We can see that in April the manager sold 25 washing machines, and in October, 30.

A more developed form of such a line graph can be used to compare the sale of washing machines in the current year against sales made in previous years.

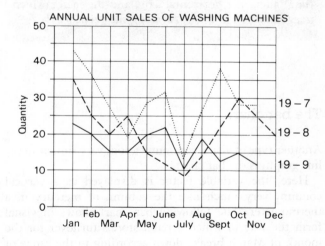

Thus the line graph not only acts as a means of storing information, but also as a means of comparing one set of facts or figures with another in a way which is easily interpreted.

An additional feature of the line graph is that from it, it is possible to predict what is likely to happen in the future.

In the following example the output of the factory fluctuates. It does not move upwards at a smooth rate. But it *does* go on moving steadily upwards over a period of time – here, over the course of the year. As a result, the line graph's upward trend as plotted makes it reasonable to suppose that the output will continue broadly in the same upward climb in the first few months of the following year. In this way, the graph helps the factory manager to carry out forward planning on the basis of what has been happening in the past.

Such information would be much more difficult to extract from a table of figures, as its visual impact would not be as immediate as the graph's.

> **Plotting rule**
>
> *Always* plot the factor which does *not* change (e.g. time) along the horizontal axis, and the factor which *does* change (e.g. quantity) along the vertical axis.

The bar chart

Another type of visual communication, very similar to the line graph, is the bar chart.

Here, the variable factor is displayed as a vertical column, very much like the column of mercury in a thermometer. The following bar chart shows in visual form the way in which a retail store's turnover for the month of March breaks down according to the range of products sold.

The bar chart provides a good visual impact for contrasting the respective quantities, sizes or amounts of items which are measured by a common unit. Here the unit is pounds expressed on a scale in hundreds of pounds.

Note that in order to give a true picture, the columns – TV sets, hi-fi, washing machines, etc – must all be of the *same width*. And in order to catch the eye, it is helpful to

give each bar in the chart an individual colour, or as here, contrasting shading.

The bar chart may also be used to compare and contrast items of the same kind measured against, for instance, different periods of time or different sources:

The use of the bar chart to illustrate comparative totals is ideal, *provided* that the number of items to be compared does not exceed, say, five or six. Any more than that and the chart is difficult to read. Also, if there is not enough contrast or difference between the totals displayed, a bar chart will be difficult to interpret.

Golden rules

1 Choose a sufficiently large scale.

2 Always ensure that vertical and horizontal axes are clearly headed, so that the units being used are readily understood, whether pounds sterling, or unit items sold, etc.

3 Display clearly the appropriate time period – year, quarter, month, etc.

4 Give the graph or chart a bold and accurate title.

Pictograms

Another way of giving impact to the visual presentation of numbers is to use pictograms. Here, the number information to be conveyed is combined with drawings or symbols which are easily recognised and understood.

For example, four and a half million tonnes of wheat production might be represented thus:

Again, the comparative production of motor-cars in different countries of the world might be displayed as follows:

The pictogram provides an arresting visual image for comparing statistics. For example, if we assume that home ownership rose from 100 000 in 1975 to 350 000 in 1985 in a given region, then the 350% increase could be presented thus:

One of the dangers, however, of using pictograms in this way is that the human eye is not very good at estimating the comparative sizes of irregular shapes. It is therefore tempting for the unscrupulous statistician to present visual information in pictogram form in a way which appears to over-emphasise increases. For instance, the reader could be forgiven if he thought the 1985 house above was five times bigger than the 1975 one, instead of only three and a half times bigger.

Percentages

One of the most common ways to express a proportion or share of something, is as a percentage:

Fastsnacks have 43% of the sweet market.
'Our target is to increase turnover by 10%'.

'Per cent' means 'part of a hundred'. So a number with a percentage symbol % after it means that it is so many parts of a hundred. For every hundred sweets bought, Fastsnacks made 43 of them. If turnover last year was £100 000, the target for next year is £110 000.

Working out a percentage

Percentages are very easy to calculate. Of course, if there is a percentage key on your calculator there is no problem; if you haven't, follow this method and you should have no difficulty:

Example
What percentage of 350 is 45?

Advantages and disadvantages of visual communications media

Inevitably, there are advantages and disadvantages in using the various forms of visual communication which we have studied. The following table summarises the principal factors involved, in the light of which the communicator has to make his decision – whether to devise a graph or to use a table, whether to incorporate number information in a pie chart or pictogram and so on.

	Advantages	*Disadvantages*

Table of numbers	Capable of storing a great deal of detailed information – especially in micro-film/micro-fiche form
	    Number information extremely accurate, e.g. numbers to 4 decimal places: 196.0534
		Difficult to interpret readily when many columns or items are recorded
		    Difficult to identify trends, and to see peaks and troughs in tables
		    Generally poor visual impact

Line graphs	Excellent for identifying upward and downward movement; good for comparing 3–4 items in a corresponding time-scale
	    Good at indicating trends
	    Lends itself to colour presentation
		Visual impact suffers if graph overloaded with more than 4 or 5 lines
		    Not very accurate – it is difficult to read off totals from vertical axis in any fine detail

Bar charts	Excellent visual impact
	    Good for comparison between a few products, items, etc
	    Good for colour presentation
	    Good for relaying data via transparency if items are clearly different in total size or amount
		Difficult to interpret if many items are to be compared and if the scale of the vertical axis does not show a significant difference in totals – the items from any distance (e.g. on a transparency) look almost equal

Pie charts	Good for showing shares of a *known* total
	    Especially useful if there are appreciable differences between totals
	    Good for colour presentation
	    Note: the total involved *must* be known if proportions are to be presented in pie chart form
		Difficult to interpret size of any given 'slice of the pie' since the 100% total is equated with 360 degrees of the circle. Thus a 12.5% share would be represented by 45 degrees etc
		    Poor visual impact when the shares of the total are many and similar in total – the pie chart takes on the appearance of a cart-wheel!

Pictograms and diagrams	A good way of presenting statistics simply and in a visually attractive way	Tendency to over-simplify information and pictograms can distort data visually

45 as a fraction of 350 is $\frac{45}{350}$

so as a percentage would be $\frac{45}{350} \times 100\%$

$$= 12.85\%$$

Fastsnacks turnover for one week is £35 000. Their turnover for the month is £125 000. What percentage of their turnover was earned in that week?

$$\frac{£35\ 000}{£125\ 000} \times 100\% = 28\%$$

Sometimes we may know something as a percentage, but want to work out what it is in real terms. For instance Ajax Pumps' gross profit may be 27% of turnover – but how much profit did they actually make? A retail store increases all its prices by 10%, so what is the new price of that washing machine?

Example
What is 12.5% of 290?
Divide 290 by 100 to find 1%

$$\frac{290}{100} = 2.9$$

so 12.5% is 12.5 × 2.9

$$= 36.25$$

The price of a washing machine is £245. The shop selling it wishes to increase the price by 8%. What is the price increase?

1% of £245 is $\frac{£245}{100}$

8% of £245 is $\frac{£245}{100} \times 8$

$$= £19.60$$

Percentage assignments

1 Calculate what the number 24 is as a percentage of 96

2 Calculate what 150 is as a percentage of 3000

3 Calculate what 333 is as a percentage of 666

4 Calculate what 14.2 is as a percentage of 58.63

5 What is 60% of £1345.00?

6 What must a customer pay if he is given a 33.3% discount on £500?

7 What is 110% of £650?

Fractions into percentages

Harridges department store earns its income in the following way:

Ladies' fashions:	4/10
Men's outfitting:	1/6
Electrical goods:	6/20
Food hall:	1/10
Haberdashery:	1/30

These different fractions make it very difficult to compare one department with another. It would be much easier if each amount was given as a percentage.

To convert a fraction to a percentage, just multiply the fraction by 100.

$$\frac{4}{10} \times 100\% = 40\%$$

$$\frac{1}{8} \times 100\% = 12.5\%$$

We can now work out as a percentage, what proportion of its income each department of Harridges makes:

Ladies' fashions:	40%
Men's outfitting:	16.67%
Electrical goods:	30%
Food hall:	10%
Haberdashery:	3.33%
	100%

Fractions into percentages conversion assignments

1 Express $\frac{5}{16}$ as a percentage

2 Express $1\frac{3}{4}$ as a percentage

3 Express $\frac{23}{32}$ as a percentage

4 Express $\frac{3}{9}$ as a percentage

Graphics software packages

Hard on the heels of the word processing, database and spreadsheet software applications packages has come the graphics software package – or rather packages, as there are a number now on the market. The reason is not hard to find. Once managers and text production staff had become familiar and confident in using the above trio separately, they very soon came to realise the advantages – in eye-catching presentation, time saved and flexibility – of integrating the data thus captured.

Ingenious programmers devised means by which the individual packages for word processing, database recording and spreadsheet calculations, could be brought together so that a single document could be created in which text, number and carefully set out alphanumeric data in fields could be presented in a continuous flow of information on the page, even though three distinct packages had been used to create it.

By using various manipulating devices, such as the 'mouse', to move blocks of data around the VDU the integrated package user soon became adept at 'stepping in and out' of the various software packages which formed the integrated pack. As a result, the graphics package which had tended to be restricted to managers producing data for transforming into colour slides or OHP foils came into its own – especially if the computer printer was able to print in colour, thus reproducing the visual impact of the graphs, charts and diagrams demanding attention on the colour monitor. In fact, another valuable data creation and presentation tool had been added to the integrated package armoury.

Graphics packages tend to include the following range of diagrams, all of which may be constructed from inputted number and references:

- line graphs
- bar charts
- pie charts
- three dimensional barcharts
- pictograms

- maps
- headed tables
- scatter graphs

as well as various, more specialised graphics features for users like statisticians, geographers and the like.

The following illustration provides an indication of the range described:

It is interesting to note that many graphics packages incorporate a wide range of graphics creation features such as:

- The ability to modify the inputted data so that the displayed pie chart, for example, is immediately transformed into a bar chart (using the same data): thus the user can decide which format best communicates the given data.

- The ability to use different print styles for headings and references shown on the diagram – either to provide a friendly or formal visual effect.

- The capacity to edit saved graphs as information changes or is updated.

- The flexibility of changing the colours forming the graphic design so as to maximise impact or to make best use of contrast. The display of up to 16 different colours in colour graphics software is now commonplace.

- The inclusion in the package of sophisticated statistical calculations routines which will do the percentage, ratio, decimal, averaging and other calculations required in the design of the various diagrams and charts at the drop of a hat!

Visual and number communication assignments

1 Imagine that you have to write a guide to visual and number communication for sales staff who sometimes need to address sales conferences. Devise a written guide in about 500 words which sets out (with illustrations) tips on the advantages and disadvantages of different types of visual and number communications.

Your guide should be clear and easy to follow, since it is intended for staff unfamiliar with this mode of communication.

2 Find out what the proportions of male to female students are in either your department at college or your year at school.

Devise a suitable form for displaying this information visually.

3 Find out the distances travelled from home to your college or school by each member of your group.

Present this information in a suitable visual form.

4 Devise a chart which would suitably record the progress made by a group of shorthand or typewriting students in increasing their speeds.

5 The following information refers to the use of A4 copy paper by the Ace Office Equipment Company. devise a suitable means of presenting this information visually at a large staff meeting:

'In the first quarter of this year, the firm used 12.4 reams of A4 copy paper, whereas last year it was 11.6 reams. In the second quarter of this year the figure rose to 14.6 reams, as against 15.3 for the same period last year. The figure for this year's third quarter was 9.3 (8.9 for the corresponding quarter last year). In this year's fourth quarter, we used 15.2 reams, compared with 13.7 for the equivalent quarter last year.'

6 The Chequered Flag Garage Limited is a busy garage which sells new and used cars, does car repairs and sells petrol and accessories. Last year, the company's sales were as follows:

new cars:	£728 000	petrol:	£542 500
used cars:	£496 300	accessories:	£54 950
repairs:	£184 250		

Last year, the company's sales of new cars were as follows: Jan £71 950; Feb £52 860; Mar £59 430; Apl £77 320; May £79 150; June £81 420; Jly £67 600; Aug £45 280; Sep £51 390; Oct £44 920; Nov £48 300; Dec £48 380.

In the same year, Chequered Flag's sales of used cars were as follows: Jan £47 250; Feb £35 120; Mar £38 790; Apl £49 620; May £53 840; June £42 370; Jly £29 840; Aug £32 180; Sep £39 530; Oct £40 810; Nov £42 320; Dec £44 630.

Last year's sales of new cars exceeded the previous year's total by £164 300, and the sale of last year's used cars was £73 200 up on the previous year.

Last year, the firm's staff totalled 27, as against 21 in the previous year, since 2 extra car salesmen had been taken on, and 4 additional mechanics. Last year's sales total for repairs was 26% up on the previous year's repairs sales.

Also last year, the company's net profit was 13% of total sales. In the previous year the net profit had been £190 480.

The managing director of The Chequered Flag Limited has supplied you with the above information. He wishes to call a meeting of all staff to present them with a briefing on the company's performance – last year as against the previous year. Using the information he has provided, he wants you to devise a set of visual/number communication charts, graphs, etc to help him convey the information simply and clearly at the staff meeting.

Devise a set of visual aids which you think will achieve the desired aim of the MD.

7 Can you think of any logical reasons which might account for the trends in new and used car sales by The Chequered Flag.

8 Assuming that the net profit of The Chequered Flag was 13% in both years, can you work out what the sales turnover must have been for the previous year?

9 Flow charts are used as a basis for designing computer programmes. Find out what a flow chart looks like, then in small groups, design a flow chart which would illustrate one of the following:
(a) making a pot of tea
(b) washing your hair
(c) finding a puncture in a bicycle inner tube

10 Next month, your college or school will be holding an Open Day, to which parents and interested members of the public will be invited. They will be able to visit the premises and grounds to view exhibitions, students at work, equipment and demonstrations, etc.

In order to help members of the public find their way about the site a suitably clear and simple map needs to be drawn, indicating the location of places of interest, etc.

Design a suitable map for the Open Day brochure.

Compare your map with those produced by other members of your group, and decide which would prove most helpful to a total stranger. **Note:** you may only use black ink on a white paper.

Briefings, factsheets and note summaries

In every type of organisation, there is a daily need to digest and absorb information and data, whether from the spoken word, in writing or as number or visual communications. Sometimes messages are passed on, as we have learned, in a mix of several communications media.

For this reason, managers and executives make frequent use of schedules which they term:

briefings
factsheets
note summaries

What each of the above three types of information digest have in common is that they are usually:

concise
schematically presented
divided into easily absorbed sections

The briefing or factsheet is usually designed to provide neutral or factual information in order to 'put someone in the picture' or to provide a simple and swift means of updating or informing organisational staff. For example, the sales representatives of a company may need to be briefed on a new company credit purchase scheme; the office staff may need to be given the principal facts about how a flexible working hours system will be introduced; clerks in a head office may need to learn quickly how to operate a new micro-fiche filing system.

In addition to the production of briefings and factsheets, sometimes it is helpful to produce a summary of a particular article or document in schematic note form. Thus, instead of writing a shortened version in continuous prose, the summariser produces a note summary with numbered and referenced sections and points which are introduced by suitably emphasised section headings. Note summaries are particularly useful if, for example, a manager wishes to refer to information during a meeting, or to make reference to a particular point in a memorandum or report.

When setting out to produce a schematic briefing, reference or note summary, the Seven Point Summarising Plan (see Unit 6) should be used in a modified form.

The first five stages in the plan remain the same:

1 Check your aims
2 Understand the original
3 Give the writing a relevant title
4 Select the main points
5 Check your list of main points against original

At this stage, with the summarising version in the notes stage, it is important to identify those ideas which will form the main headings for each of a series of sections, and to put into a logical sequence those 'sub-points' which will be listed under each section heading.

Although it is possible to express ideas in single words or phrases, there is always a danger that the point will prove incomprehensible to the reader because it has been over-compressed or abbreviated. Care must *always* be taken, therefore, to ensure that the points of note summaries are clearly and sufficiently expressed.

The following example illustrates how part of a note summary might appear:

HOW TO SUMMARISE EFFECTIVELY

1 *Using the Seven Point Plan*
In carrying out the process of summarising, there are seven main steps to follow:

1.1 Checking the main points
1.2 Understanding the original
1.3 Giving the summary a title
1.4 Selecting the main points
1.5 Checking points against original
1.6 Writing out a rough draft
1.7 Producing a final version

2 *Checking the aims*
In checking the aims of the summary, the following points should be observed:

2.1 What is the summary to be used for?

As the above example indicates, though set out in a schematic format, and employing phrases rather than full sentences, the note summary is nevertheless quite clear and easy to understand.

Contrast this first example with the following unsatisfactory alternative:

SUMMARISING

1 *Seven Point Plan*
1.1 Aims
1.2 Understanding original
1.3 Title
1.4 Main points
1.5 Check original
1.6 Rough draft
1.7 Final version

2 *Aims*
2.1 What for?
2.2 Who for?
2.3 How used?

The reader of the above version would probably puzzle out what is meant, but would not absorb the information as readily as in the first example. Its meaning suffers from over-compression; the message to be transmitted has remained largely in the mind of the writer! Note also in the fuller example, that complete sentences are sometimes included to introduce a list clearly and accurately.

Assignments

1 Devise a factsheet comprising some 250 words which outlines the subjects, learning approaches and examinations of the course you are currently following. Your factsheet is to be used by a member of staff interviewing prospective students.

2 Assume that a number of your fellow students have never used a plain paper copier before. Compose a briefing on how to use one correctly. (You may write about a particular model in your department.) Include any diagrams you consider helpful.

3 Assume that you have been detailed to help with the administration of your school or college prize-giving. You have been asked to produce a briefing in note form of what prize winners are to do.

Devise a suitable briefing detailing the information they will need in not more than 250 words. Present your briefing in a schematic format.

4 Imagine that your school or college is to be visited by a group of VIPs from overseas.

In about 300 words, compose a factsheet describing simply and clearly the main features of your school or college. The factsheet will be included in a folder to be given to each visitor.

Boost your spelling power!

Learn these words by heart

Remember, an asterisk after a word indicates that it is very commonly misspelled:

Antarctic proper noun
anxiety n   (anxious adj)
corroborate v   (corrobotation n)
convenience n   (convenient adj)
consistent adj
connoisseur n

perseverence n   (to persevere v)
pleasant adj
preliminary adj
prestige n   (prestigious adj)
professor n
pronounce v   (pronunciation n)
synonym n   (synonymous adj)
sonic adj
statutory adj   (statute n)
proprietory adj
courteous adj   (courtesy n)
criticise v   (criticism n)
cursory adj
apparent adj
appropriate adj
Arctic proper noun
argument n   (to argue v)
ascend v   (ascent n)
athletic adj   (athlete n)
audio adj
automation n   (automatic adj)
awful adj   (awe n)
coming* n, pres part   (to come v)
compatible adj

Do not forget to enter in your vocabulary book any words with which you are unfamiliar, either in terms of spelling or meaning!

Assignment

By arrangement, choose four of the above words. Compose a sentence for each, in which the word is used correctly. Compare your sentences with those devised by others in your group. This will help you to add the above list of words to your **active vocabulary.**

Here's the proof...! 7

Proof-read the following letter carefully, then write down each instance of an error or shortcoming which you detect. Then against it, write down what you consider to be the correct alteration. Finally re-write or re-type the letter as you think it should appear.

Dear Mr Simpson

Enquiry for adjustable typists chairs

I am writing to enquire whether your company stocks ajustable typists chairs which might proof suitable for use in my companys' General Office. At present som forteen audiotypists and word processing operators are employed in the office and of recent months I have received a number of complaints regarding the shortcomings of the chiars in use, some of which have been in use for over twelve years.

I have inspected the working hieghts of the desks used by the typists and find that this varies from 3.2 to 3.6 meters. The chairs would therefor need to be adjustable in a range of heights. Also, some of the ladies have criticised the suporting panels which support thier backs, and I should like to enquire if your chairs are helpfull in this regard?

The offices decor is predominately green and yellow and I wonder if you could sugest a colour which would blendin with our wall paper and carpets I should be gratefull if you would contact me with a veiw to arrangeing for one of your representatives' to call so that we could discuss the matter further.

I look forward to hearing from you.

Yours faithfully,

'Same everything!

A case study

Jennifer Saunders was 18, coming up to 19. She'd left school at 16, having followed a commercial course in the fifth form and then joined the general office staff of Wilcox Electronics Limited as a copy typist.

At the same time as Jennifer, Jim Poynter had joined Wilcox's as a junior clerk in the accounts department. They had both been at school together, and there was a strong bond of trust and friendship between them.

Looking around for somewhere to sit with his lunch tray, Jim spotted Jennifer sitting alone in a corner of the staff restaurant with her face buried in a newspaper.

'Hello, Jen, what's new in female fashions today, then?'

'Oh, hello, Jim. I wasn't reading the Women's page, actually. Between you and me I was skimming through the Situations Vacant Ads.'

'What's up? Don't tell me the delights of the Wilcox Electronics Emporium are beginning to pall? You can't have had time to savour all your fringe benefits yet!'

'There's no need to be so cheerful, Jim. I'm not in the mood. It's just that I don't seem to be getting anywhere or going anywhere. Same old typewriter, same old letters and memos, same filing, same faces – same everything!'

'My, my, you really have got the blues! Have you spoken to your boss at all? Miss Watson seems quite a sympathetic sort at heart.'

'No – well I don't really want her to think that I've switched off and don't care any more. Though I dare say it's begun to show anyway.'

'Well, what about talking to personnel? Mrs Johnson might be able to help.'

'I suppose so. I've been keeping an eye on the internal appointments noticeboard for weeks, but there's been nothing posted. It's not just me in the doldrums – the firm seems pretty well becalmed too.'

'Yes, but we're going through a recession. You can't expect every department to be expanding like mad at the moment. Maybe in a month or two things'll pick up and there will be a bit more scope. As it is, I know sales are worried about where the next order's coming from.'

'Yes, I can see that. I know I should be grateful for having a job at all right now.'

'But it doesn't really help you, if you're honest, does it, to drive those blues away?'

'I know it sounds terrible, but no, it doesn't. Not at the moment!'

'Well, if you want my advice, you'll *do* something about it! It's no good just drifting along not liking what you're doing at work. I remember once I had a holiday job packing biscuits. The pay was quite good, but the time really dragged. I used to keep looking at the clock on the wall, and every time I thought half an hour had gone by, it was about two minutes later! You know what I mean. If you've got a job you're really interested in, the time just flies past. You want to have a good hard look at yourself, what you want to do in life and then make some decisions. Then, go all out to try to make them happen!'

'It's all right for you, Jim, you've always known just where you're going, but I can't run my life on a cut and dried basis. What I'd like is a bit of excitement and adventure!'

'Look. I've got to be getting back. But think about what I said. And – keep your chin up! We in accounts need the lift from reading those dashing memos you type for Mr Green! See you around.'

As Jim left the restaurant, Jennifer opened the newspaper again. But instead of reading it, she was staring into space.

Assignments

1 In Jennifer's place, what would you do? In small groups, discuss the options which you think Jennifer has and discuss what she might best do to resolve her present state of mind.

2 What kind of approach could Wilcox's devise to cope with staff problems similar to Jennifer's? Write an outline of the sort of policies Wilcox's could introduce.

3 Is Jim right in the advice he gives to Jennifer? Of what help is it in life to follow a plan of action?

4 How far is an individual responsible for his or her own job satisfaction? Discuss this question in a general group session.

Activities and assignments

Visual and number communication

1 Explain orally to your group what a line graph is and does.

2 Write a brief note (with examples) to explain the difference between a percentage and a fraction.

3 State, in an account to your group, when you would use a table and when a line graph to record and display information.

4 Devise a suitable pair of pictograms to illustrate how they can be misleading when comparing two totals.

5 Write a clear guide for someone who has never used them before, explaining how percentages are calculated. Illustrate your piece with worked examples.

Graphics software packages

6 Find out what a 'mouse' does in the context of VDU display and then write a short explanation for your own notes.

7 First you will need access to a graphics package and some practice in 'driving' it. Then turn back to page 238 and consider the bar-chart of the Southern Shoe Company and then convert it into a pie-chart and bar-chart using the graphics package. In a group, decide which visual display is more effective and why.

8 This time turn back to page 237 and examine the line graph showing the Annual Unit Sales Of Washing Machines. Now produce the line graph using the graphics package (a) as shown, but using colour if possible, and then (b) as a stacked bar chart for the months of January, February and March. Consider which type of display is more visually appealing and easier to grasp, in your group's opinion.

Use of English: vocabulary

9 Turn each of the following infinitives or adjectives into their noun forms:

to connect	hypocritical
contagious	to install
to analyse	negotiable
to acquiesce	to omit
bureaucratic	to proceed
chaotic	to pronounce
courteous	to seize
to embarrass	to transfer
feasible	valuable
fulfilled	young

15–20: Excellent!
12–15: Well done.
 8–12: Check where you went wrong.

Spelling revision assignment

10 In pairs, test yourselves on the 15 sets of Boost your spelling power!
   One way to do this is:

The speller is given a new word to spell until he or she gets one wrong, when the tester takes over, and so on.

If you are feeling particularly confident, you may like to keep score!

11 In a general group, organise a spelling competition based on the 15 sets of words.
   The competition could be on a knock-out basis, and a Speller of the Year title awarded!

Communication: putting it together!

12 Compose a descriptive article which outlines the communication skills required of *one* of the following:

a clerical assistant
a receptionist
a typist
a secretary
a sales assistant

13 In a talk to your group, outline what you see as the major differences between using the spoken and the written word at work. When would you elect to use speech and when writing to transmit a message? You may illustrate your talk with suitable audio-visual aids.

14 You have been asked to write an article for the house magazine intended for junior staff in a large head office. The title of your article is: How to become an effective letter-writer.
   Compose an appropriate article of about 450–500 words.

15 Imagine that a new chairman has just been elected to your student association committee. You are the outgoing chairman. Either in a role played conversation, or as a personal note to him or her, summarise what you think are the important qualities a chairman should possess.

16 In a suitable report format, compose a critical assessment of your communication course, including any appropriate recommendations for future amendments or changes.

17 Imagine that you have to give a talk to students of your own age on how to be successful at a job interview. *Either* prepare and deliver a 10 minute talk (with visual aids) to your group, *or* devise a checklist of do's and don'ts which an interviewee would find useful.

18 Compose an essay entitled: The importance of developing social skills at work.